JOHN CLARE BY HIMSELF

JOHN CLARE (1793–1864) was born in Helpston, Northampton-
shire, in 1793 and spent most of his life in the countryside. His
first collection was the highly successful *Poems Descriptive of
Rural Life and Scenery* (1820). This was followed by *The Village
Minstrel* (1821), *The Shepherd's Calendar* (1827) and *The Rural
Muse* (1835). He suffered a series of severe breakdowns in later
life and spent his last twenty years in an asylum in
Northampton. *A Midsummer Cushion* was published posthu-
mously, in 1975.

ERIC ROBINSON is a world authority on John Clare and Vice
President of the John Clare Society. The many books he has
edited include John Clare's *Autobiographical Writings*, as well as
(with P.M.S. Dawson and David Powell) *A Champion for the
Poor: Political Verse & Prose, Cottage Tales* and *The Northborough
Sonnets*; and (with Richard Fitter) *John Clare's Birds*. In addition
to the books mentioned above, DAVID POWELL has also edited
The Early Poems of John Clare 1804–1822, with Eric Robinson and
Margaret Grainger.

T0170604

FyfieldBooks present poetry and prose by great as well as sometimes overlooked writers from British and Continental literatures. Clean texts at affordable prices, FyfieldBooks make available authors whose works endure within our literary tradition.

The series takes its name from the Fyfield elm mentioned in Matthew Arnold's 'The Scholar Gypsy' and in his 'Thyrsis'. The elm stood close to the building in which the Fyfield series was first conceived in 1971.

> *Roam on! The light we sought is shining still.*
> *Dost thou ask proof? Our tree yet crowns the hill,*
> *Our Scholar travels yet the loved hill-side*

from 'Thyrsis'

John Clare By Himself

Edited with an introduction by
ERIC ROBINSON and DAVID POWELL

Fyfield*Books*

CARCANET

Published in Great Britain
by Carcanet Press
4th Floor, Conavon Court
12–16 Blackfriars Street
Manchester M3 5BQ

First published by Mid Northumberland Arts Group and
Carcanet Press in 1996

This impression 2002

A CIP catalogue record for this book
is available from the British Library

ISBN 1 85754 288 6

The publisher acknowledges financial
assistance from the Arts Council of England

CONTENTS

Maps

Maps drawn by Reginald Piggott; research by Bruce Bailey

v

INTRODUCTION

From his birth in Helpston in 1793 to his death in Northampton in 1864, except for four visits to London, some months in Epping Forest and his years in the Northampton General Lunatic Asylum, John Clare never travelled more than a few miles from his native village. He lived at first under the same roof as his parents in Helpston, moved to another cottage in Northborough only a few miles away in 1832, and then from 1841 spent the remainder of his life in Northampton.

Clare's life-story is told against the background of a particular landscape with its fens, its heaths, its sheep-pastures and its villages and market-towns. (It is significant that Clare uses the word 'town' to denote any settlement, however small.) He talks of Will-o'-the-wisps (or Jenny burnt-arses), of ghosts and poachers, of spires peeping over stiles, of bird-haunted thickets, of lonely farms, and of the threshers, gleaners and weeders in his native fields. The skies of the Fens always overshadowed him, and there is no writer from whom one gets a better sense of an unbroken horizon or of the scarlet flames of sunset and sunrise. In this landscape he breathed freely: once he left it, he felt suffocated and began to lose touch with reality. He speaks constantly of the 'lordship', the area under the control of the lord of the manor, or of his 'world', the locality with which he was familiar. It is not uncommon to this day to find on the edge of English towns a pub called 'The World's End', as though when one reached the boundary of a familiar settlement one dropped over the edge of the horizon. Clare's sense of identity is intimately involved with his awareness of his birthplace and of all the living things that he remarked within his locality:

> I lovd the meadow lake with its fl[a]gs and long purples crowding the waters edge   I listend with delights to hear the wind whisper among the feather topt reeds and to see the taper bulrush nodding in gentle curves to the rippling water and

> I watchd with delight on haymaking evenings the setting sun drop behind the brigs and peep again thro the half circle of the arches as if he longs to stay[1]

The Tibbles, in their edition of Clare's prose, speak of the 'Sketches' as

> the enchanting account of a vanished English childhood and youth, far away from, while yet contemporary with, the French terror and the Napoleonic Wars...an account of a country childhood during one of the hardest periods of Enclosure, when rustic activities and customs, now swept away for ever, were still in full swing.[2]

In fact the Terror, the Napoleonic Wars, and even Enclosure are so far removed from Clare's preoccupations that they only appear on the scene as part of a local experience — in the POW camp at Norman Cross, in the strange antics of the militia, and in the inconvenience of fences. This is the world seen through the wrong end of the telescope but filled with its own strange intensity. In the London episodes, the great wander across the scene — Lamb, Coleridge, Hazlitt, Reynolds, Sir Thomas Lawrence and others — or Byron, Clare's hero, is seen through the eyes of a poor sailor, but most of the characters are purely local. Granny Bains, John Cue of Ufford, old Shepherd Newman, John Billings, George Cousins: these are people who but for Clare would have been entirely forgotten. They and their countryside become the setting for Clare's Paradise.

He tells us much about the people — of the hardships suffered by poor men, their humiliations and their sense of oppression, but also of their joys, their festivities and their songs. Sometimes, as in his 'Apology for the Poor', one hears his honest anger:

> now if the poor mans chance at these meetings is any thing better then being a sort of foot cushion for the benefit of others I shall be exceedingly happy to hear but as it is I much fear it as the poor mans lot seems to have been so long remembered as to be entirely forgotten

or when he speaks of one rude visitor:

> he then asked me some insulting libertys respecting my first acquaintance with Patty and said he understood that in this country the lower orders made their courtship in barns and pig styes and asked wether I did   I felt very vext and said that it might be the custom of high orders for aught I knew as experience made fools wise in most matters but I assured him he was very wrong respecting that custom among the lower orders here[3]

Since *Piers Plowman* there has hardly been an authoritative voice in English literature to speak for the ploughmen, the threshers, the hedgers, shepherds, woodmen and horse-keepers, until Clare began to write. Robert Bloomfield is perhaps the nearest. The farmer-journalist William Cobbett is heard loud and clear, and so, at a later date, is the gamekeeper Richard Jefferies. Joseph Ashby of Tysoe is nearer to Clare in social status, but none of these is his equal. As Edmund Blunden said, Clare's autobiographical writings contain

> fresh information on the early life and thoughts of a poet of the purest kind: originality of judgment, bold honesty; illuminating and otherwise unobtainable observations on intimate village life in England between 1793 and 1821; a good narrative — nearly as good as Bunyan — and plenty of picturesque expression. It will be a long time before a voice again speaks from a cottage window with this power over ideas and over language.[4]

The people of Clare's autobiography — Will Farrow, the cobbler; Hopkinson, one of that increasing number of clerical magistrates who posed a special problem on the bench by their mixing of law and morality; Henson the bookseller and Ranter-preacher; the servants at Milton; the head-gardener at Burghley; the boy, John Turnill — are as lively and individualized as characters from *The Canterbury Tales*, of which Clare was a great admirer. And when we move from individuals to meetings, ceremonies and occasions such as religious holidays, singing and dancing with the gypsies, drilling with the militia or walking Vauxhall Gardens in

London, there too all is light and colour, and we may well agree that 'the year was crowned with holidays'.

Clare transformed the people and the fields they roamed by suffusing them with the glow of childhood — for Clare's autobiography is as remarkable a vision of childhood as the poems of Blake and Traherne. It is a deliberate vision of Eden before the Fall and a realistic appraisal of Eden after it. The 'Sketches' are mostly representative of the former vision and the 'Autobiographical fragments' increasingly reflect the latter as Clare's disenchantment grew over the years. The 'Autobiographical fragments' are much more openly critical of the middle classes, revealing Clare's aversion to simpering misses and pompous magistrates, to pretentious militia officers and grasping farmers, to overbearing surveyors and interfering ministers.

Like other authors in the same vein, Clare's language often has a strong proverbial quality: 'I was quite in the suds'; 'Send him to Norberrey hedge corner to hear the wooden cuckoo sing'; 'I was in that mixd multitude calld the batallion which they nick namd "bum tools" for what reason I cannot tell   the light Company was calld "light bobs" and the granadeirs "bacon bolters"'; 'I was now wearing into the sunshine'; 'Another impertinent fellow of the Name of Ryde who occupys a situation which proves the old Farmers assertion that the vilest weeds are always found in the richest soil'. Indeed the same forcefulness of language runs throughout Clare's prose as one finds in the newspapers and almanacs of the day.

We ought to recognize, moreover, that Clare's autobiography belongs to that tradition of those sixpenny chapbooks hawked from door to door which shaped his childhood imagination. Clare is the hero of his own chapbook: he is his own Tom Hickathrift, Jack and the Beanstalk, or Dick Whittington making his way to London, that sink of iniquity or crucible of success. He was quite aware of the strangeness of his own rise to fame. Other tales of men and women rising from obscurity were part of folk-tradition. Even when totally fictional, they were presented as true-life stories: Swift's *Gulliver's Travels*, Defoe's *Robinson Crusoe* and

Gay's *Beggar's Opera* all belong to the tradition of marvellous lives and adventures, along with the memoirs of James Lackington, the Methodist bookseller. The newspapers were full of extracts from works such as these and they provided vigorous models for young working-men. Clare's autobiographical writings are at least partly in the tradition of the poor boy's rise from obscurity to fame, or at least to notoriety: the boy practising his writing on a slate, or having his poems — written on grocer's paper — used by his mother to light the stove. Clare was even more deeply entrenched in the idiom than Defoe, Gay and Swift because for many years the chapbooks were almost his sole literary diet. His imagination was nourished by the popular songs and stories that have always fed the minds of the poor and compensated them for their deprivations with a rich world of fantasy. Clare's dreams were made from tales of knight-errantry, the adventures of Robin Hood, the story of Joseph and even the true stories of Chatterton, Kirke White and Bloomfield.

At all times of his life, sane or insane, Clare identified himself with some hero. In his insane years he seems to have been unable to keep fact and fiction apart: was he Clare or was he Byron, or Burns, or Shakespeare? Was he Nelson or was he Ben Caunt, the prize-fighter? His life always had its elements of fantasy: did he really drub a bullying corporal in the army, or was it merely that he would have liked to do so? Is he not a bit like the farm-boy in his verse-tale, 'The Lodge House'? Were the amorous advances he thought were made to him by the governess at Birch Reynard-son's house any more real than the mind-games he played with Eliza Emmerson or Mary Howitt? What conflicts arose within him when he saw that his fantasies of fame and fortune were never to be realized? If our disappointments as editors in our struggles to obtain full recognition for him are bitter, how much greater his own must have been!

Clare wanted to believe in his own special destiny, to feel that he had been marked out by fate. Was not his providential birth and survival to be contrasted with the death of his twin sister, who had seemed to be more robust? Was it not for some great reason that he was twice saved from drowning and preserved from a dangerous fall when he was birds-nesting? Why was it that he was not buried in the collapse of a barn in which he and his fellows, only a few hours before, had been carousing? The resemblances to other providential escapes related in religious biographies are very clear.

During his visits to London, Clare is fascinated by kidnappers, cheats and ladies of the town. He enjoys the *frisson* of the tale of Sweeney Todd. Later, as he sets out on his walk from Essex, he presents himself as a general marshalling his forces. At Northampton he sees himself as Burns or as Byron. Fantasy was a deeply imbedded aspect of his nature. It is not that he tells lies, but that he views the truth in a peculiar light. He chops and changes throughout his life in his attitude to public affairs and it is often impossible to nail him down.

In the 'Sketches', Clare is presenting his life-story to his publisher, John Taylor, and to his patrons, all of whom were imbued to a greater or lesser degree with the evangelicalism of the time. They wanted to assist a talented member of the deserving poor, someone honest, sober and hardworking; Christian — preferably Anglican — and critical of popular superstition; patriotic and law-abiding; a decent family man with acceptable sexual habits; respectful and grateful. Clare therefore presents himself as a model for Hogarth's industrious Apprentice:

> I resignd myself willingly to the hardest toils and tho one of the weakest was stubbor[n] and stomachful and never flinched from the roughest labour   by that means I always secured the favour of my masters and escaped the ignominy that brands the name of idleness...[5]

He spends all his free time improving his handwriting and working out problems in 'Pounds, Shillings and Pence'. All his efforts are directed towards the repayment of his parents. He says little about his unreadiness for starting work. (More of that story is to be found in the 'Autobiographical fragments'.) He admits to escaping from church on Sundays but has suggestions to make about the way in which the Scriptures should be taught to children. In general, he is a much more conforming character in the 'Sketches' than he was in real life. In the 'Sketches' he defends himself from the suggestion that the Billings brothers were poachers, whereas in the 'Autobiographical fragments' he tells a story of a miraculous escape from the explosion of a flintlock on a poaching expedition.

There is no question that Clare is trying to present himself in a good light while revealing as much about himself as he safely can. He does confess to drinking too much and having too many flirtations, however he ends by saying that 'mercy spared me to be schoold by experience who learnd me better'.[6] It is doubtful whether Clare often spoke that way to his cronies. In his letters, even those to Taylor, he is often more open. All this adds to, rather than detracts from, the interest of his memoirs. We see that we are dealing with a complex character.

II

There have been several biographies of John Clare, but none that is entirely satisfactory. The problem with most is that their writers were not deeply enough read in Clare's own manuscripts. The Oxford English Text edition of his collected poetry is nearing completion, in nine volumes. There is no collected edition of Clare's prose, and the Tibble selections are unreliable, but Margaret Grainger's *The Natural History Prose Writings of John Clare* (Oxford: Clarendon Press, 1983) is a first-rate edition of those pieces she has included. Mark Storey's *The Letters of John Clare* (Oxford: Clarendon Press, 1985) is the standard edition of Clare's outgoing letters. No one has tackled the mass of incoming correspondence. It is not surprising, therefore, that biographers have been handicapped by the lack of printed sources.

The first biography of Clare was Frederick Martin's *The Life of John Clare* (London and Cambridge, 1865; second edition, eds E. Robinson and G. Summerfield, 1964), a lively, emotional but unreliable account, which nevertheless used original sources. There is evidence in J.L. Cherry's *Life and Remains of John Clare the 'Northamptonshire Peasant Poet'* (London and Northampton, 1873) that the author had access to original Clare manuscripts. He refers on page 9 to 'a few undecipherable lines commencing "Good morning to ye, ballad-singing thrush"' written in an arithmetical and geometrical exercise-book which is now Northampton MS 11. Cherry also quotes extensively from Clare's 'Journal' and letters to and from him. But the best biography is still J.W. and Anne Tibble's *John Clare: A Life* (1932), which deserves to be reissued. A subsequent volume by the same authors, *John Clare: His Life and Poetry* (1956), adds new information but is less successful as a whole and is, in general, a rather strange mixture of biography and criticism.[7] What always brings these biographies to life is the quotations from Clare's own autobiographical statements, reflective or satirical, nostalgic or ironic, contemplative or indignant.

III

Clare had the idea of collecting facts for his life-story very early on. He wrote to J.A. Hessey (John Taylor's publishing partner) on 29 June 1820:

> — I mean to leave Taylor the trouble of writing my Life merely to stop the mouths of others — & for that purpose shall collect a great many facts which I shall send when death brings in his bill —[8]

At the time, he was composing his will. Keats, as Clare learned from Taylor, was seriously ill. Some of Clare's Helpston friends were dying off. He never thought that he himself would make old bones. Yet at the same time he was getting his first experience of fame — his first volume, *Poems Descriptive of Rural life and Scenery*, had been published in January 1820. Lord Radstock had become his patron, the local gentry were making him 'the stranger's poppet Show', and he was enquiring from Captain Sherwill

xiv

whether he knew Wordsworth and Coleridge personally,[9] asking Taylor to give his regards to Keats,[10] and reporting to Taylor that his fellow regional poets, Robert Bloomfield and James Montgomery, were recognizing him, and had 'written me & praisd me sky high & added not a little to my vanity I assure ye'.[11] Local rivals such as Ann Adcock, S. Messing and Edward Preston were springing up.[12] How long would he stay ahead of them? The newspapers were stuffed with the poems of unknown writers, some of them awful, others not half-bad. Meanwhile his publishers, Edward Drury of Stamford and John Taylor, were bickering about their rights in him; Lord Radstock and Mrs Emmerson, his evangelical patrons, were trying to censor him; and his village friends were beginning to regard him with suspicion. He was anxious to have his true story set down on paper, even if he intended to leave it to Taylor to write the finished biography after his death. Several of his patrons seemed anxious to build their own fame on his pitiful scaffolding.

Clare was not the shrinking violet he has sometimes been thought to be. As many of his early poems reveal, he was preoccupied with fame in general and his own in particular. It may be local fame — that of the young soldier who goes off to the wars, or of the boxer or wrestler who wins a bout at the local fair, or of a village schoolmaster or schoolmistress — or the fame of Shakespeare, Byron or Keats. It may be the fame of a place or monument — the River Welland, Burthorp Oak or St Guthlac's Stone; even the false fame of the Revd Mr Twopenny or of a quack doctor.[13] Clare's greatest fear was obscurity, and it was to 'Obscurity' that, 'in a fit of Despondency', he wrote one of his earliest sonnets.[14] He did not wish to vanish from the records like old Shepherd Newman or the Ruins of Pickworth. His own aspirations are wittily expressed in 'The Authors Address to his Book', in which he sees himself and his book, like fellow vagrants and beggars, tramping towards their destiny:

> No never be asham'd to own it
> For better folks than I have known it

But tell em how thou left him moping
Thro oblivions darkness grouping
Still in its dark corner ryhmeing
& as usual ballad chyming
Wi' few ha'pence left to speed wi'
Poor & rag'd as beggars need be
— Money would be useful stuff
To the wise a hints enough
Then might we face every weather
Gogging hand in hand together
Tow'rds our Journeys end & aim
That fine place ycleped fame . . .[15]

Is there a reference here to Chaucer's *House of Fame*? The poem is typical of Clare: though he apologizes for his rough upbringing and lack of education, he has confidence in his own genius and in the fame it will eventually bring him. Whether his fame is in the local pub or on the national scene, he always has his eyes on greater things. In poems such as 'Dawning of Genius', 'Some Account of my Kin, my Tallents and Myself', 'In shades obscure & gloomy warmd to sing'[16] and many more, Clare returns to the theme of the rise from obscurity to fame. Much of his autobiographical writing in prose is occupied with the same matters.

IV

By January 1821, Clare was trying his hand at prose. 'Charicteristic Descriptive Pastorals in prose on rural life & manners', in the hope of eventually publishing a volume entitled 'Pastorals in Prose'.[17] He was also assembling facts for Taylor to go into the introduction to *The Village Minstrel*:

I will fill your last ruled Quarto with as much of my little life as I can & get it done doubtless to bring up with me in summer as I then intend to storm the hospitality of Fleet St —[18]

It is not the hospitality of Fleet Street that he intends to storm but the bastions of literary fame. On 8 February 1821 he told Taylor, '— I have been getting on with my "Memoirs" & shall have it for your inspection by summer'.[19] By 7 March he could promise 'the "Sketches of my Life" ready for sending you in a fortnight at most',[20] and they were actually sent off on 3 April 1821.[21] He promised Taylor sole ownership of the manuscript and that no copies would be provided to anyone else.[22]

It seems probable, however, that Edward Drury had already seen part of it. Mark Storey has brought to our attention a 'Memoir' of Clare in the Bodleian Library (MS Don. d.36), attributed to Hessey but actually by Drury. It is dated 'May 6. 1819' and is based on information that clearly formed part of the 'Sketches': Clare's early admiration for Pomfret's poems, especially the woodcuts; the borrowing of *Robinson Crusoe*; and the purchase of Thomson's Seasons.[23] The poet's name is even misspelt 'Thompson', as in the 'Sketches', suggesting that the information was transmitted in a document rather than orally.

When Taylor received the 'Sketches', he thought them the best things he had ever seen from Clare in the prose line,[24] and he did use parts of them for his introduction to *The Village Minstrel* (published in September 1821). The subsequent history of the 'Sketches' is a little obscure until they become MS 14 in the Clare collection at the Northampton Central Public Library. Frederick Martin, in the preface to his *Life of John Clare*, refers to 'some very curious autobiographical sketches',[25] and it was from his daughter, Miss Louisa Martin, that Edmund Blunden received permission to publish his edition of the 'Sketches' in 1931.[26] Did Martin also have access to the 'Autobiographical fragments'? Very probably so, since he speaks of Granny Bains, the 'old Mary Bains the cow keeper famous for the memory of old customs', whose existence was later wrongly questioned by the Tibbles.[27]

It is clear that Clare did not abandon his autobiography after sending off the 'Sketches', because he wrote to Taylor on 11 August 1821, 'I have ideas of writing my Literary Life & continuing it on till I live'.[28] In several Clare manuscripts there appear

'Autobiograhical fragments' that supplement the 'Sketches' in important ways. First of all they continue Clare's story fragmentarily down to the year 1828. Secondly, they provide pen-portraits of his literary acquaintances in London and describe his visits to the metropolis. They also include much additional material.

Clare wrote to H.F. Cary, the translator of Dante and biographer of Chatterton (one of Clare's heroes), on 30 December 1824 asking him to read his memoirs and to give his opinion of them.[29] Cary replied on 19 February 1825, saying that he would 'read the memoirs of yourself which you propose sending me; & not fail to tell you, if I think you have spoken of others with more acrimony than you ought.'[30] Clare, who was becoming increasingly disenchanted with John Taylor at this time, may have written some critical comments about him, but as *The Shepherd's Calendar* was in progress, Clare would not have wanted to imperil its publication. What were these memoirs: a more or less finished version drawn from the 'Autobiographic fragments', or the fragments themselves? If Clare were going to submit them to Cary, they would have had to be in a more finished form than they are in now, in the surviving manuscripts. The Tibbles suggest that Clare never sent anything to Cary,[31] and certainly we hear no more about them in Cary's surviving correspondence. Yet even if they were never sent, the fact that many of them are crossed through or marked 'done for' suggests that Clare was following his usual practice of writing up a fair copy from his scattered notes.

When Clare wrote to Cary, he spoke of having 'gotten 8 chapters done' and having 'carried it [the Memoirs] up to the publication of the "Poems on rural life &c."'[32] This is clearly a reference to *Poems Descriptive of Rural Life and Scenery*. Northampton MS 14, on which Blunden's edition of the 'Sketches' is based, shows no chapter divisions. Is Clare therefore referring to an expanded memoir – already planned when he wrote to Taylor back in 1821 – divided by December 1824 into eight chapters? Clare's Journal shows him at work on the life on 12 and 28 September 1824, and 20 November has the entry: 'finishd the 8th Chapter of my life'.[33]

He was finding the task more difficult than he had expected, and he adds:

> in the last sketch which I wrote for Taylor I had little vanitys about me to gloss over failing[s] which I shall now take care to lay bare & readers if they ever are published [may] comment upon [them] as they please   in my last 4 years I shall give my likes and dis likes of friends & acquaintance as free as I do of my self.

Clare told E.V. Rippingille on 14 May 1826, 'I have nearly finished my life having brought it down as far as our last visit to London & as soon as its done I think of offering it for sale.'[34] We find it difficult to believe that Clare could have contemplated offering for sale anything so fragmentary as the paragraphs we have printed here as 'Autobiographical fragments', and it also seems clear that he had improved on the material he had earlier sent to Taylor. It should be noticed, too, that he is proposing to *sell* this material while he had promised the 'Sketches' exclusively to Taylor.

By 1825, as is revealed by partially deleted passages in the Journal, Clare had grown disillusioned with Taylor.[35] In the entry for 17 April 1825 he has heavily deleted a reference to 'the pretending and hypocritical friendship of booksellers', and there are other entries to similar effect. By the time *The Shepherd's Calendar* was published, perhaps he felt that he could not afford to reveal his true feelings about Taylor, and suppressed the new version of his life. We cannot agree with the Tibbles' suggestion that the 'Autobiographical fragments' represent the totality of his autobiographical writings in these years, though they may well be correct in suggesting that he changed his mind about submitting anything to Cary. We therefore agree with Blunden in thinking that Clare probably wrote an extended version of his life, for which the 'Autobiographical fragments' are first drafts, but we consider it a possibility that Clare deliberately destroyed the new version.

V

We welcome the opportunity to bring together in one volume some of Clare's most important autobiographical records, chiefly the Journal, his 'Sketches' and the 'Autobiographical fragments'.

In their *Prose of John Clare*, the Tibbles reconstructed chapters for Clare's 'Autobiography', and it is certainly true that there are chapter numbers and chapter headings here and there in the manuscripts. Thus there are chapter numbers 3, 4, 5, 6 and 7. Chapter 4 has the heading 'My first feelings and attempts at poetry', and chapter 5 is headed 'My first attempts at poetry', so that the subject-matter of these two chapters is not clearly differentiated. Chapter 10 is headed 'My visit to London (I)' and chapter 11 'My visit to London (II)'. It is not clear to us where these chapters begin or end, so we have grouped the 'autobiographical fragments' in what appears to us to be the most logical order. To print the fragments in the order in which they appear in the manuscripts, as catalogued by David Powell and Margaret Grainger, would have been confusing. We always indicate in square brackets the location of a passage in the manuscripts. If the MS is from the Peterborough Museum collection, it is preceded by a capital letter, according to the numbering in Dr Grainger's catalogue. The number after the comma is the page number: [A32, R12], for example, indicates that the material appears upside down on page 12 of Peterborough MS A32. A MS preceded by the letter N denotes that it is to be found in the Northampton collection. BL and Pfz are the abbreviations used for the occasional passage taken from the British Library and the Pforzheimer collection in New York.

We have been able to include Clare's Journal in this volume, very occasionally improving on Margaret Grainger's readings, although we do not have the space to match her wonderful annotations on natural history. Unlike Dr Grainger, however, we have not regularized Clare's dating. The Journal is an essential part of Clare's general autobiographical record, providing evidence of his correspondence, his reading, his relationship with his publishers, and his family affairs. It reveals how much almanacs and newspapers formed part of his daily reading and how he became increasingly interested in archaeology. Natural history was of course a critical part of his life — the Journal shows how deeply he was interested in the history of old trees, for instance — but so also was a serious study of religious writings. The Journal is a true record of Clare's intellectual diversity.

The autobiographical writings so far mentioned only take us up to 1828, thirty-six years before Clare's death. We have therefore thought it desirable to add one or two pieces dealing with Clare's later years. We print here his 'Journey out of Essex', describing his journey on foot from Dr Allen's asylum in Epping Forest to Northborough. We also include a few of Clare's asylum letters from Northampton because they show how closely he retained in memory his friends and neighbours in Helpston. Many more are to be found, of course, in Storey's edition of Clare's letters. Our readings of all documents have been made independently, though we have benefited from the opportunity of making comparisons with other editors' readings.

All Clare's work needs, ideally, to be read aloud, for the sound of the local Helpston voice vibrates throughout it. Clare grew to be critical of punctuation and increasingly dispensed with it. This means that the reader has to allow the meanings of the prose to dictate the rhythm and movement: one has to feel one's way carefully as if looking for a nest in a thicket. We have tried to help by leaving spaces between sentences, for sentences and natural breaks there are, if seldom pointed. But in the 'Sketches' Clare sprinkled commas and semi-colons all over the place. We have chosen to remove much of that punctuation to bring the work into closer alignment with his maturer method of composition. As he himself wrote: 'do I write intelligible   I am gennerally understood tho I do not use that awkard squad of pointings called commas colons semicolons etc...'[36]

We have not changed spellings — except that ampersands have been translated to 'and' — nor standardized grammar because Clare's practice in such matters was highly personal, and he came to object ever more strongly to such interference with his work.

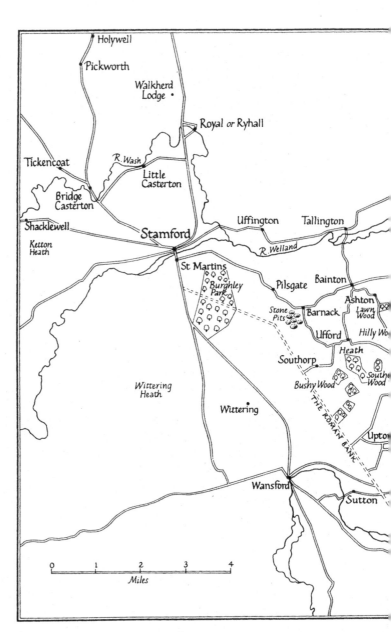

CLARE'S COUNTRYSIDE

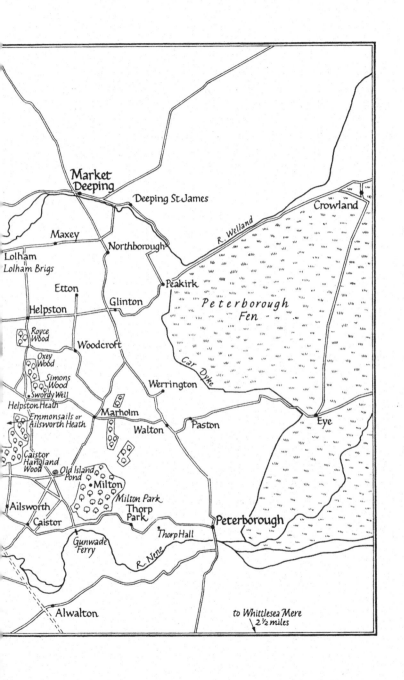

Market
Deeping

Deeping St James

Crowland

Maxey

Northborough

R. Welland

Lolham
Lolham Brigs

Peakirk

Etton

Glinton

*Peterborough
Fen*

Helpston

Royce
Wood

Woodcroft

Oxey
Wood

Car Dyke

Simons
Wood

Swordy Well

Werrington

Helpston Heath

Emmonsails or
Ailsworth Heath

Marholm

Eye

Walton

Paston

Caistor
Hangland
Wood

Old Island
Pond

Milton

Ailsworth

Milton Park
Thorp
Park

Caistor

Peterborough

Gunwade
Ferry

Thorp Hall

R. Nene

Alwalton

to Whittlesea Mere
2½ miles

Some previous editors have substituted standardized words such as 'shrill' and 'porch' for the dialect forms 'shill' and 'poach'. We do not intend to cramp Clare's writings into a conformity entirely foreign to them. All editors of Clare tread a fine line in such matters. We do not believe that we are justified in making verbs and subjects agree in number, or in removing double negatives when it is certain that such practices were part of Clare's speech and grammatical habits. The reader will soon find it easy to come to terms with Clare's language: again, the best test for the reader to adopt is to read a puzzling word aloud. We have included a glossary for all difficult words just as Clare's first publisher, Taylor, did.

A space between square brackets in the text means that Clare has left a space in which he intended later to fill in a word or words but has failed to do so. Words or letters between square brackets are supplied by the editors and are not in the text. Clare may have omitted them inadvertently. In other cases, the paper has deteriorated since Clare wrote. In this text, intended for the general reader, we have not shown minor deletions and alterations but have mentioned those which seem to us to be of importance to the meaning or to illustrate Clare's intentions in some significant way.

No edition of Clare will ever be final, but a generation has passed since the publication of *The Autobiographical Writings of John Clare*. This volume is undoubtedly more accurate and we hope that it will replace that edition as a reference source. Here is the best we can now contrive; in another twenty years, if more autobiographical material comes to light, the work may have to be done again. But that is the nature of editorial work: it is never finished.

SKETCHES IN THE LIFE OF JOHN CLARE

WRITTEN BY HIMSELF
AND ADDRESSED TO HIS FRIEND
JOHN TAYLOR ESQR
MARCH 1821

There is a pleasure in recalling ones past years to reccollection; in this I believe every bosoms agrees and returns a ready echo of approbation and I think a double gratifycation is witness'd as we turn to a repetition of our early days by writing them down on paper   on this head my own approbation must shelter its vanity while thus employ'd, by consieting self-satisfaction a sufficient appology. But I am carless of praise and fearless of censure in the business, my only wish being to give a friend pleasure in its perusal for whom and by whose request it is written and as I have little doubt of being able to accomplish that matter those who (strangers to the writer) that it displeases need not be startled at the dissapointment[1]

I was born July 13, 1793 at Helpstone, a gloomy village in Northamptonshire, on the brink of the Lincolnshire fens; my mothers maiden name was Stimson, a native of Caistor, a neighboring village, whose father was a town shepherd as they are calld, who has the care of all the flocks of the village   my father was one of fates chance-lings who drop into the world without the honour of matrimony   he took the surname of his mother, who to commemorate the memory of a worthless father with more tenderness of love lorn feeling than he doubtless deservd, gave him his sirname at his christening, who was a Scotchman by birth and a schoolmaster by profession and in his stay at this and the neighboring villages went by the Name of John Donald Parker   this I had from John Cue of Ufford,[2] an old man who in his young days was a companion and confidential to my run-a-gate of a grandfather, for he left the village and my grandmother soon after the deplorable accident of misplaced love was revealed to him, but her love was not that frenzy which shortens the days of the victim of seduction, for she liv'd to the age of 86 and left this world of troubles Jan. 1. 1820.   Both my parents was illiterate to the last degree   my mother knew not a single letter and superstition went so far with her that she beleved the higher parts of learing was the blackest arts of witchcraft and that no other means coud attain them   my father coud read a little in a bible or testament and was very fond of the supersti[ti]ous tales that are hawked about a sheet for a penny, such as old Nixons Prophesies, Mother Bunches Fairey Tales, and Mother Shiptons Legacy[3] etc etc   he was likewise fond of Ballads and I have heard him make a boast of it over his horn of ale with his merry companions at the Blue bell public house which was next door[4] that he coud sing or recite above a hundred   he had a tollerable good voice and was often calld upon to sing at those convivials of bacchanalian merry makings in my early years I was of a waukly constitution, so much so that my mother often told me she never coud have dreamd I shoud

2

live to make a man, while the sister that was born with me[5] being a twin was as much to the contrary a fine livley bonny wench whose turn it was to die first for she livd but a few weeks, proving the old saying for once mistaken 'that the weakest always goeth to the wall.' As my parents had the good fate to have but a small family, I being the eldest of 4, two of whom dyed in their Infancy my mothers hopfull ambition ran high of being able to make me a good scholar, as she said she expirenced enough in her own case to avoid bringing up her childern in ignorance, but god help her, her hopful and tender kindness was

often crossd with difficultys, for there was often enough to do to keep cart upon wheels, as the saying is, without incuring an extra expence of putting me to school, though she never lost the oppertunity when she was able to send me, nor woud my father interfere till downright nessesity from poverty forced him to check her kind intentions; for he was a tender father to his childern, and I have every reason to turn to their memorys with the warmest feelings of gratitude and satisfaction, and if doing well to their childern be an addition to rightousness I am certain god cannot forget to bless them with a portion of felicity in the other world, when souls are called to judgment and receive the reward due to their actions commited below. In cases of extreeme poverty my father took me to labour with him and made me a light flail for threshing, learing me betimes the hardship which adam and Eve[6] inflicted on their childern by their inexperienced misdeeds, incuring the perpetual curse from god of labouring for a livlihood, which the teeming earth is said to have produced of itself before, but use is second nature, at least it learns us patience   I

3

resignd myself willingly to the hardest toils and tho one of the weakest was stubbor[n] and stomachful and never flinched from the roughest labour   by that means I always secured the favour of my masters and escaped the ignominy that brands the name of idleness   my character was always 'weak but willing'.   I believe I was not older then 10 when my father took me to seek the scanty rewards of industry   Winter was generally my season of imprisonment in the dusty barn   Spring and Summer my assistance was wanted elswere in tending sheep or horses in the fields or scaring birds from the grain or weeding it, which was a delightfull employment, as the old womens memorys never faild of tales to smoothen our labour, for as every day came new Jiants, Hobgobblins, and faireys was ready to pass it away   as to my schooling, I think never a year passd me till I was 11 or 12 but 3 months or more at the worst of times was luckily spared for my improvment, first with an old woman in the village and latterly with a master at a distance[7] from it   here soon as I began to learn to write, the readiness of the Boys always practising urgd and prompted my ambition to make the best use of my abscence from school, as well as at it, and my master was always supprisd to find me improved every fresh visit, instead of having lost what I had learned before for which to my benefit he never faild to give me tokens of encouragment   never a leisure hour pass'd me with out making use of it   every winter night our once unletterd hut was wonderfully changd in its appearence to a school room   the old table, which old as it was doubtless never was honourd with higher employment all its days then the convenience of bearing at meal times the luxury of a barley loaf or dish of potatoes, was now coverd with the rude begg[in]ings of scientifical requ[i]sitions, pens, ink, and paper one hour, jobbling the pen at sheep hooks and tarbottles, and another trying on a slate a knotty question in Numeration, or Pounds, Shillings, and Pence, at which times my parents triumphant anxiety was pleasingly experiencd, for my mother woud often stop her wheel or look off from her work to urge with a smile of the warmest rapture in my fathers face her prophesy of my success, saying

4

'shed be bound, I shoud one day be able to reward them with my pen, for the trouble they had taken in giveing me schooling', and I have to return hearty thanks to a kind providence in bringing her prophesy to pass and giving me the pleasure of being able to stay the storm of poverty and smoothen their latter days; and as a recompense for the rough beginnings of life bid their tottering steps decline in peacful tranquility to their long home, the grave. here my highest ambition was gratifyd for my greatest wish was to let my parents see a printed copy of my poems   that pleasure I have witness'd and they have moreover livd to see with astonishment and joy their humble offspring noticed by thousands of friends and among them names of the greatest distinction, the flower and honour of his native country[8]   surely it is a thrilling pleasure to hear a crippled father seated in his easy arm chair comparing the past with the present, saying 'Boy who coud have thought, when we was threshing together some years back, thou woudst be thus noticed and be enabled to make us all thus happy.' About this time, which my fathers bursts of feeling aludes too, I began to wean off from my companions and sholl about the woods and fields on Sundays alone   conjectures filld the village about my future destinations on the stage of life, some fanc[y]ing it symtoms of lunacy and that my mothers prophecys woud be verified to her sorrow and that my reading of books (they woud jeeringly say) was for no other improvment then quallyfiing an idiot for a workhouse, for at this time my taste and pasion for reading began to be furious and I never sholld out on a Sabbath day but some scrap or other was pocketed for my amusment   I deeply regret usefull books was out of my reach, for as I was always shy and reserved I never woud own to my more learned neighbours that I was fond of books, otherwise then the bible[9] and Prayer Book, the prophetical parts of the former, with the fine hebrew Poem of Job, and the prayers and simple translation of the Psalms   in the latter was such favourite readings with me that I coud recite abundance of passages by heart   I am sorry to find the knowledge of other books shoud diminish the delight ones childhood experiences in our first perusal of those divine writings. I must digress to say that I think the manner of learing childern in village schools very erronious, that is soon as they learn their letters to task them with lessons from the bible and testament and keeping them dinging at them, without any change, till they leave it   A dull boy never turns with pleasures to his school days when he has often been beat 4 times for bad readings in 5 verses of Scripture, no more then a Man in renewd prosperity to the time when he was a debtor in a Jail Other books as they grow up become a novelty and their task book at school, the Bible, looses its relish   the painful task of learning wearied the memory   irksome inconvenience never prompts reccolection   the bible is laid by on its peacful shelf and by 9 Cottages out of 10 never disturb'd or turnd too further then the minutes referance for reciting the text on a Sunday, a task which most christians nowadays think a sufficient duty at least in the lower orders   I cannot speak with assurance only where expirience informs me   so much for village schools About now all my stock of learning was gleaned from the Sixpenny Romances of 'Cinderella', 'Little Red Riding hood', 'Jack and the bean Stalk', 'Zig Zag', 'Prince Cherry',[10] etc etc etc and great was the pleasure, pain, or surprise increased by allowing them authenticity, for I firmly believed every page I read and considerd I possesd in these the chief learning and literature of the country   But as it is common in villages to pass judgment on a lover of books as a sure indication of laziness, I was drove to the narrow nessesity of stinted oppertunitys to hide in woods and dingles of thorns in the fields on Sundays to read these things, which every sixpence thro the indefatigible savings of a penny and halfpenny when collected was willingly thrown away for them, as oppertunity offered when hawkers offerd them for sale at the door   to read such things on sundays was not right while nessesity is a good apology for iniquity and ignorance is more so I knew no better and it may be said that ignorance is one of the sweetest hopes that a poor man carries to the grave, when his manhood muses oer the exclamation of his dying Saviour, asking and offering the same plea for the worst of Sinners 'Father

forgive them, they know not what they do'[11]   Clergymen may
say tis an enlightend age and when a man can have oppertunitys
to hear good from bad every Sunday he has no longer the cloak of
ignorance to skulk from iniquity as the west indian and the
Cherokee   digressions may become tiresome and ill grounded
opinions may be reckoned consciets but, while it is pleasant to
turn out of the way for a b[e]autiful blossom, tis nothing short of
humanity to release the plund[er]ing fox from the snare — hopes
unrealized are hopes in reality   blessings possesd are hopes
no longer   tis the weakness and not the fault of nature to
throw a cloak over its imperfections when it seeks for heaven as
a better place then it posseses   A staff to the maimed and a
couch to the weary traveller are desirable blessings and usful to
wish for as blessings thats wanted.

I have often absentet my self the whole Sunday at this time nor
coud the chiming bells draw me from my hiding place to go to
church, tho at night I was sure to pay for my abscence from it by
a strong snubbing   I at length got an higher notion of learning
by going to school and every leisure minute was employ'd in draw-
ing squares and triangles upon the dusty walls of the barn   this
was also my practice in learning to write   I also devourd for
these purposes every morsel of brown or blue paper (it matterd
not which) that my mother had her tea and sugar lapt in from the
shop   but this was in cases of poverty when I coud not muster
three farthings for a sheet of writing paper   the saying of 'a
little learning is a dangerous thing'[12] is not far from fact   after
I left school for good (nearly as wise as I went save reading and
writing) I felt an itching after every thing   I now began to pro-
vide my self with books of many puzzling systems Bonny-
castles Mensuration,[13] Fennings Arithmetic, and Algebra was
now my constant teachers and as I read the rules of each Problem
with great care I preseverd so far as to solve many of the questions
in those books   my pride fancyd it self climbing the ladder of
learning very rapidly, on the top of which harvests of unbounded
wonders was concieved to be bursting upon me and was sufficient
fire to promt my ambition, but in becoming acquainted with a

neighbour, one John Turnill,[14] who was a good mathematical scholar, I found I was not sufficient to become master of these things without better assistance as a superficial knowledge of them was next to nothing and I had no more   he kindly enough put me in a plan but cirscumstances soon calld him from me and I luckily abandond the project, not without great reluctance — I was now thought fit for some other employment then th[r]eshing with my father which the neighbours said was far too hard for my weak constitution and the first step taken for my releasment from it was an application to put me apprentice to a shoemaker[15] to a neighbour in the town, but this, on my being apprisd of it, I dislikd, for at that time I hardly knew what I liked   I was such a silly, shanny boy that I dreaded leaving home were I had been coddled up so tenderly and so long and my mother was determind if I was [i.e. bound to] a trade that I shoud have my choice, far as cirscumstances woud let me, for they coud give not a sixpence with me — however my lot was not for shoe making nor did I ever repent missing it — a next door neighbour, who kept the Blue Bell public house, got me a week or two to drive plough for him, having a small cottage of 6 or 8 acres, and knowing me and my parents he usd me uncommon well   his name was Francis Gregory[16]   he was a single man and lived with his Mother   they both used me as well as if I was their own and after I had been there awhile I got used to them   they hired me for a year, the only year I livd in hired service in my life   my master was of very bad health and dyd a year or two after I left   I have reason to drop a good word to his memory   my friend John Turnill wrote his epitaph on his grave stone, such as it is; for he used to dabble in poetry tho I saw very little of it — Here I got into a habit of musing and muttering to ones self as pastime to divert melancholly, singing over things which I calld songs and attempting to describe scenes that struck me   tis irksome to a boy to be alone and he is ready in such situations to snatch hold of any trifle to divert his loss of company and make up for pleasenter amusments, for as my master was weak and unwell he seldom went to work with me unless necessary as ploughing etc   I

8

always went by my self to weeding the grain, tending horses and such like.   Once every week I had to go for a bag of flower to Maxey, a village distant about 2 Miles, as it was sold cheaper then at home and as my mistress was an economist she never lost sight of cheap pennyworths   in the short days of winter its often been dark ere I got home and even by times dusk before I started

I was of a very timid disposition   the traditional Registers of the Village was uncommonly superstitious (Gossips and Granneys) and I had two or three haunted Spots to pass for it was

impossible to go half a mile any were about the Lordship were there had nothing been said to be seen by these old women or some one else in their younger days.   therefore I must in such extremitys seize the best remedy to keep such things out of my head as well as I coud, so on these journeys I mutterd over tales of my own fancy and contriving them into ryhmes as well as my abilities was able; they was always romantic wanderings of Sailors, Soldiers etc following them step by step from their starting out to their return, for I always lovd to see a tale end happy and as I had only my self to please I always contrivd that my taste shoud be suited in such matters   Sometimes I was tracking my own adventures as I wishd they might be going on from the plough and flail to the easy arm chair of old age reciting armours, intrigues of meeting always good fortune and marrying Ladies etc   Hope was now budding and its summer skye warmd me with thrilling extacy and tho however romantic my story might be I had always cautions, fearful enough no doubt, to keep ghosts and hobgoblings out of the question   what I did was to erase them and not bring them to remembrance, tho twas impossible,

9

for as I passd those awful places, tho I dare not look boldly up, my eye was warily on the watch, glegging under my hat at every stir of a leaf or murmur of the wind and a quaking thistle was able to make me swoon with terror

I generaly kept looking on the ground and I have been so taken with my story that I have gone muttering it over into the town before I knew I got there   this has often embarrasd me by being overheard by some one who has asked me who I was talking too?   I think I was 13 years of age now but trifling things are never pun[c]tually rememberd as their occurence is never strikingly impressd on the memory, so I cannot say with assurance   none of these things was committed to paper   this summer I met with a fragment of Thompsons Seasons[17]   a young man, by trade a weaver, much older then myself, then in the village, show'd it me   I knew nothing of blank verse nor ryhme either otherwise than by the trash of Ballad Singers, but I still remember my sensations in reading the opening of Spring   I cant say the reason, but the following lines made my heart twitter with joy.

> Come gentle Spring, ethereal mildness come
> And from the bosom of yon dropping cloud,
> While music wakes around, veild in a shower
> Of shadowing roses, on our plains desend.[18]

I greedily read over all I coud before I returnd it and resolvd to posses one my self, the price of it being only 1s/6d   I expressd my supprise at seeing such a fine poem so carlessly handld, most part of Winter being gone, but the owner only laughd at me and said 'twas reckoned nothing of by himself or friends'   he and his friends were methodists and he presented Wesleys hymns as a rival of exellence   I said nothing but thought (whatever his religion might be) the taste of him and his friends was worth little notice   I have since seen plenty of these fanatics to strengthen my first opinion, as some of them will not read a book that has not the words Lord and God[19] in it   this I assert as a fact to my knowledge and I have always lookd on their concieted affectations

10

with disgust   their founder was rather credolous but I believe
him a good man and reverence his Memory   his followers,
both in preaching and practice, have brought his principles into
disgrace   I have seen plenty to justify the remark.   On the
next Sunday I started to stamford to buy Thompson, for I teazd
my father out of the 1^s/6^d and woud not let him have any peace till
he consented to give it me, but when I got there I was told by a
young shop boy in the street who had a book in his hand which I
found to be 'Collins Odes and poems' that the booksellers woud
not open the shop on a Sunday   this was a dissapointment
most strongly felt and I returned home in very low spirits, but
haveing to tend horses the next week in company with other boys
I plannd a scheme in secret to obtain my wishes by stelth, giving
one of the boys a penny to keep my horses in my absence, with
an additional penny to keep the Secret   I started off and as we
was generally soon with getteing out our horses that they might
fill themselves before the flyes was out I got to Stamford I dare say
before a door had been opend and I loiterd about the town for
hours ere I coud obtain my wishes   I at length got it with an
agreeable dissapointment in return for my first, buying it for 6^d
less then I had propos'd and never was I more pleasd with a bar-
gain then I was with this shilling purchase   On my return the
Sun got up and it was a beautiful morning   I coud not wait till
I got back without reading it and as I did not like to let any body
see me reading on the road of a working day I clumb over the wall
into Burghly Park[20] and nestled in a lawn at the wall side   the
Scenery around me was uncommonly beautiful at that time of the
year and what with reading the book and beholding the beautys
of artful nature in the park I got into a strain of descriptive ryhm-
ing on my journey home   this was 'the morning walk'[21] the
first thing I commited to paper   I afterwards wrote the even-
ing walk[22] and several descriptions of Local Spots in the fields
which I had frequented for Pootys, flowers, or Nests in my early
child hood   I burned most of these after I got to consiet I knew
better how to make poetry   others I corrected perhaps 20
times over till their origional form was entirley lost such as the

11

Morning walk now extant   I always turn to this years service with F. Gregory as one of the pleasentest occurrences in my existance   I was never hurried in my toils for he was no task master or swore at for commiting a fault   a gentle chiding he always deemd sufficient for any thing that I might do wrong   I believe this usuage and this place to have been the Nursery for fostering my rustic Song   after leaving here awhile somthing came into my head that I woud be a gardiner and for this purpose I went with my father to Burg[h]ley, the Seat of one of my kindest benefactors and Patrons, the Marquis of Exeter, to whom at that time and till the publication of my first Vol of poems I was a stranger.   we went to the Master of the Kitchen Garden[23] as most suitable for my destination of working in future in the village were flower gardens are but little store set bye, as the taste of Farmers turns entirely on profit   it may suffice to say we succeeded in getting the wishd for situation.   one circscumstance in appearing before the Master of the garden will show the mistaken notions of grandeur and distinction in a clown that has not seen the world   my father as well as my self thought that as he appeard with white stockings and neck cloth and as he was under such a great man as a Marquis he must certainly be homaged as a gentleman of great consequence himself so with all humilitation to his greatness we met him with our hats in our hands and made a profound Bow even to our knees ere we proceeded in the enquirey   I accordingly went the next week as a temporary apprentice for 3 years for I was not bound   I did not like his looks from the first and to my inconveneonce provd a good phisigionomist in the end, so after I had been here nearly a twelve month I fled from him, for I coud stand him no longer   I was very timid and fearful and he was always for sending me to Stamford in the night and swearing at me in his passions for things which were two trifling to be calld faults, tho to give him[24] his due he used me better then he had done others before and even after I left him gave me a good word as a still and willing boy   on this ramble[25] I visited Grantham, Newark etc, and then returnd to my parents, were I commenced Gardiner, but my employment

in that character was short, for I liked to work in the fields best
the continued sameness of a garden cloyed me and I resumed my
old employments with pleasure were I coud look on the wild
heath, the wide spreading variety of cultured and fallow fields,
green meadows, and crooking brooks, and the dark woods,
waving to the murmering winds   these were my delights and
here I coud mutter to myself as usual, unheard and unoticd by
the sneering clown and conscieted cox comb, and here my old
habits and feelings returnd with redoubled ardour, for they
left me while I was a gardiner   I now venturd to commit my
musings readily to paper but with all secresey possible, hiding
them when written in an old unused cubbard in the chamber,
which when taken for other purposes drove me to the nessesity
of seeking another safety in a hole under it in the wall   here
my mother when clearing the chamber found me out and secretly
took my papers for her own use as occassion calld for them and
as I had no other desire in me but to keep them from being read
when laid in this fancied safe repository, that desire seemd com-
pleated and I rarely turnd to a reperusal of them   consequently
my stolen fugitives went a long time ere they was miss'd   my
mother thought they was nothing more then Copies as attempts
of improving my self in writing   she knew nothing of poetry,
at least little dreamed her son was employd in that business, and
as I was ashamed of being found out as an attempter in that way,
when I discoverd her thefts I humourd her mistake a long time
and said they was nothing more then what she supposed them to
be so she might take them.   but when I did things that I liked
better then others I provided safer lodgings for them — at length
I begun to shake of[f] this reserve with my parents and half con-
fess what I was doing   my father woud sometimes be huming
over a song, a wretched composition of those halfpenny ball[a]ds,
and my boast was that I thought I coud beat it   in a few days
afterwards I used to read my composition for his judgment to
decide, but their frequent critisisms and laughable remarks drove
me to use a process of cunning in the business some time after,
for they damp'd me a long time from proceeding.   My method

13

on resuming the matter again was to say I had written it out of a borrowd book and that it was not my own   the love of rhyming which I was loath to quit, growing fonder of it every day, drove me to the nessesity of a lie to try the value of their critisisms and by this way I got their remarks unadulterated with prejudice — in this case their expressions woud be, 'Aye, boy, if you coud write so, you woud do.'   this got me into the secret at once and without divulging mine   I scribbld on unceasing for 2 or 3 years, reciting them every night as I wrote them when my father returnd home from labour and we was all seated by the fire side   their remarks was very useful to me   at somethings they woud laugh   here I distinguishd Affectation and consiet from nature   some verses they woud desire me to repeat again as they said they coud not understand them   here I discoverd obscurity from common sense and always benefited by making it as much like the latter as I coud, for I thought if they coud not understand me my taste shoud be wrong founded and not agreeable to nature, so I always strove to shun it for the future and wrote my pieces according to their critisisms, little thinking when they heard me read them that I was the author   My own Judgment began to expand and improve, at least I consieted so, and thinking my critisisms better then theirs I selected my pieces approvd of by them and even found most of em fit for nothing but my mothers old purposes, for as I kept sorting them over and over there was few that escaped that destiny in the end.   what first induced me to ryhme I cannot hardly say   the first thing that I heard of poetry that may be called poetry was a romantic story, which I have since found to be Pomfrets 'Love triumphant over reason'[26] by reading of it over since to my father who rememberd the Story, but I coud benefit little by this as I used to hear it before I coud read and my father was but a sorry reader of poetry to improve his hearers by reciting it   the relating any thing under the character of a dream is a captivating way of drawing the attention of the vulgar and to my knowledge this tale or vision as it is called of Pomfrets is more known among the lower orders then any thing else of poetry at least with us   the Romance of

14

'Robinson Crusoe' was the first book of any merit I got hold of after I coud read   twas in the winter and I borrowd it of a boy at s[c]hool, who said it was his uncles and seemed very loath to lend it me, but pressing him with anxious persuasions and asuring him of its saftey while in my hands he lent it me that day to be returnd in the morning when I came to school, but in the night a great snow fell which made it impossible to keep my promise as I coud not get, Glinton being 2 miles from our village were I went to school, so I had the pleasure of this delightful companion for a week   new ideas from the perusal of this book was now up in arms   new Crusoes and new Islands of Solitude was continually mutterd over in my Journeys to and from school but as I had not the chance of reading it well I coud not come at the spirit of the thing to graft a lasting impression on the memory, which if I had woud perhaps have been little benefit to my future attempts   I also got an early perusal of The Pilgrims Progress which pleased me mightily — All I can reccole[c]t of the old book of Pomfrets, which my father used to read to me, was that it was full of wooden cuts and one at the beginning of every poem, the first of which was two childern holding up a great Letter   these pictures lured me to make an end of the book for one day I made use of an oppertunity to cut them out and burnt the rest to avoid detection — But to return to the narritive, having made use of my parents critisisms till (as I said before) my consiet fancyd I coud do without em, I ryhmd and read them in secret and my mother giving me a small box to put my books, clothes, etc in, with a lock and key   as she said I was now getting a big boy and to learn me how to be saving, she first learned me how to take care of my own things by resigning them to my care with this prudent admonition and advice, 'You must now, my boy, think of somthing to do you good   you must go to service after all if you wish to get on and as you dont like farmers service I will seek a friend that shall get you somthing better   so leave off writing and buy no more books, tho I own its better then spending your money in beer, but you want cloths and ought to save every farthing for that purpose   I give you this box and you will find it useful when you get from me to keep your few things together   when you once get from me you will think nothing of it and you'll find it far better then drudging at home year after year in the barn and the field for little or nothing.'   this advice however good it might be was but little attended too   the box when in my possesion made me an exelent receptacle for my writings and books were they lay snug and safe from all dangers and I continued as hot as ever at reading and scribbling and, as I always looked sullen when my mother talkd of Service, she at length gave up teazing me, tho I have often heard discourse with my father that her hopes were lost and that I shoud never be anything   this when heard dampd me a little but I preseverd with my avocations and as they both began to dislike my love of books and writing, thinking it of no longer use since I had determind to stick at hard labour, I pursued it with all secresey possible and every shilling I coud save unknown to them I bought books and paper with   my Library about now consisted of the following: 'Abercrombies Gardiners Journal,' 'Thompsons Seasons,' A Shatterd Copy of 'Miltons Paradise lost,' 'Wards Mathematics,' Fishers 'Young mans companion,' 'Robin Hoods Garland', 'Bonnycastles Mensuration,' and 'Algebra,' 'Fennings Arithmetic,' 'Death of Abel,' 'Joe Millers Jests,' A 'Collection of Hymns,'[27] with some odd Pamphlets of Sermons by the Bishop of Peterborough. — I now began to value my abilitys as superiour to my companions and exulted over it in secret, tho by learing them at school they had the boast of reading and writing better and coud use their compasses at ovals, triangles, Squares etc and talk about plotting grounds etc and many things which, tho I knew a superficial knowledge of, the groundworks was greek to me, but I cared little for these things for I considerd walking in the track of others and copying and dinging at things that had been found out some hundreds of years ago had as little merit in it as a child walking in leading strings ere it can walk by itself   when I happend with them in my sunday Walks I often try'd their taste by pointing out some striking beauty in a wild flower or object in the surrounding senery to which they woud seldom make an answer, and if they did twas

16

such as 'they coud see nothing worth looking at' turning carless to reasume their old discourse and laughing at my 'droll fancies' as they woud call them   I often wondered that, while I was peeping about and finding such quantitys of pleasing things to stop and pause over, another shoud pass me as carless as if he was blind   I thought somtimes that I surely had a taste peculialy by myself and that nobody else thought or saw things as I did   still as my highest ambition at that time was nothing else but the trifle of pleasing ones self, these fancys coud dishearten me very little while that gratification was always at hand, but a cirscumstance occurd which nearly stopd me from writing even for my own amusment   borrowing a school book of a companion, having some entertaining things in it both in prose and Verse with an introduction by the compiler, who doubtless like my self knew little about either (for such like affect to give advice to others while they want it themselves), in this introduction was rules both for writing as well as reading Compositions in prose and verse, were, stumbling on a remark that a person who knew nothing of grammer[28] was not capable of writing a letter nor even a bill of parcels, I was quite in the suds, seeing that I had gone on thus far without learing the first rudiments of doing it properly for I had hardly h[e]ard the name of grammer while at school — but as I had an itch for trying at every thing I got hold of I determ[i]ned to try grammer, and for that purpose, by the advice of a friend, bought the 'Universal Spelling Book'[29] as the most easy assistant for my starting out, but finding a jumble of words classd under this name and that name and this such a figure of speech and that another hard worded figure I turned from further notice of it in instant disgust for as I knew I coud talk to be understood I thought by the same method my writing might be made out as easy and as proper, so in the teeth of grammer I pursued my literary journey as warm as usual, working hard all day and scribbling at night or any leisure hour in any convenient hole or corner I could shove in unseen, for I always carried a pencil in my pocket having once bought at Stamford fair a dozen of a Jew for a Shilling which lasted me for

17

years   while nessesity as I got up towards manhood urgd
me to look for somthing more then pleasing ones self, my poems
had been kept with the greatest industry under wishd consceal-
ment, having no choice to gratify by their disclosure but on the
contrary chilling damp with fear whenever I thought of it, the
laughs and jeers of those around me when they found out I was
a poet was present death to my ambitious apprehensions for in
our unletterd villages the best of the inhabitents have little more
knowledge in reading then what can be gleaned from a weekly
News paper, Old Moors Almanack, and a Prayer Book on Sun-
days at Church, while the labouring classes remain as blind in
such matters as the Slaves in Africa — but in spite of what they
might say and do, Nessesity as I said before urgd me to think of
Somthing   my father, who had been often crippled for months
together with the rumatics for 10 or 12 years past, was now tottaly
drove from hard labour by them and forced to the last shifts of
standing out against poverty — My fathers Spirit was strongly
knitted with independence and the thoughts of being forced to
bend before the frowns of a Parish to him was the greatest despair,
so he stubbornly strove with his infirmitys and potterd about
the roads putting stones in the ruts for his 5 shillings a week,
fancying he was not so much beholden to their forced generosity
as if he had taken it for nothing   I my self was of a week
const[i]tution and a severe indisposition keeping me from work
for a twelvemonthe ran us in debt   we had back rents to make
up, shoe bills, and Bakers etc etc   my fathers asistance was now
disabled and the whole weight fell upon myself, who at the best
of times was little capable to bear it, with the hopes of clearing
it off — my indisposition, (for I cannot call it illness) origionated
in fainting fits, the cause of which I always imagined came from
seeing when I was younger a man name Thomas Drake after he
had fell off a load of hay and broke his neck   the gastly palness
of death struck such a terror on me that I coud not forget it for
years and my dreams was constantly wanderings in church
yards, digging graves, seeing spirits in charnel houses etc etc
in my fits I swooned away without a struggle and felt nothing

more then if I'd been in a dreamless sleep after I came to my self but I was always warnd of their coming by a chillness and dithering that seemd to creep from ones toe ends till it got up to ones head, when I turnd sensless and fell; sparks as if fire often flashd from my eyes or seemd to do so when I dropt, which I layd to the fall — these fits was stopt by a Mr Arnold M.D.[30] of Stamford, of some notoirety as a medical gentleman and one whom I respect with gratful remembrances for he certainly did me great benefit, tho every spring and autum since the accident happend my fears are agitated to an extreem degree and the dread of death involves me in a stupor of chilling indisposition as usual, tho I have had but one or two swoonings since they first left me

In this dilemma of Embaresment which my fathers misfortune with the addition of my own above mentioned involvd us, I began to consider about the method of revealing the Secret of my poetry   I had a confidential friend, one Thomas Porter of Ashton-Green,[31] a lone cottage about a mile from helpstone, who being a lover of books was a pleasant companion and to whose house I went almost every sunday for several years

our tastes was parrarel excepting poetry   he lovd to walk the wood for wild flowers and to pore over old book stalls at a fair   such like pastimes to him as myself was the greatest entertainments we coud meet with   to him I showd the first Specimen of my talent at poetry but being a bad Judge of it and considering the scirscumstance of its coming from me he said little of it but kept the Secret inviolate   I cared little about his reserve in stating his opinion as I knew he understood little to give a just one   I askd him if he understood it and he merely said 'yes', for he was a strict observer of nature and acquainted with most of her various pictures thro the changes of Seasons

this reccomendation was plenty for me as I found his eyes viewd things as mine did and his notice observed them as I expressd them and wether prose or poetry he knew of its merits no further   from this time I began to select my pieces and copy them off, for the inspection of sombody that might be a judge but who I knew not or where to apply   I a year or two after

19

went to Deeping Fair and applyd to a Bookseller[32] there for a book of blank Paper but having none that I wanted he promised to bind me one up and send it, in the mean time seeming half inclined to enquire what use I was going to put it to and I on my part as willing to inform him and being at that time releasd from my timid embarasment of reserve from a free application of Ale in the fair, I bluntly told him my intentions and as he was a printer of that extent of business in having types sufficient to enable him to print a pamphlet or small book now and then when he coud happen of employment he doubtless fancyd I was a bargain, so he wishd to see some of my poems and a while after I took him 'The setting Sun' 'To a primrose'[33] etc etc which with doubtless little credit to his taste he seemed to highly approve and we enterd into proposals about the manner most beneficial to get them out and as a specimen of his abilities in printing he shewed me the 'Life of Joseph', then in the press printing for if I reccolect right 'W. Baines Paternoster row London', which, tho I little understood the elegance of printing, thought it deservd small praise as to that matter but the manner of printing my poems was to me of little consequence   to get them printed at all was sufficient so I readily agreed that he was capable of publishing my trifles and the best way for so doing he said was by subscription   force puts us to no choice or else I detested the thoughts of Subscription as being little better then begging money from people that knew nothing of their purchase, who when they had got it woud laugh and jeer the writer for jeerings sake, for theres nothing more common then consiet atributing the word foolish to and laughing at what it dont understand, reckoning all vanity thats above the comprehension of its own little knowledge and such was most of the individuals around me which made me decline coming to an imediate agreement, tho want of money was another obstacle that coud not be surmounted just then as he said people must be informed of it before they coud subscribe and that a prospectus of the plan with a Specimen of the poetry etc was quite nessesary, 300 of which he said when I had drawn one up he woud print on a double leaf of

foolscap 8vo for £1 for he seemed timid to write one himself, as
I proposed, which made me consider him incapable of publishing
a selection with any credit to me as my judgment of what woud
do etc was worth nothing, but this he woud do at any time wether
I saw him again or not if I woud but inform him by letter and
send an 'Address to the Public' which I knew little about addres-
sing   soon after this I left Helpstone in company with an out
o town labourer who followed the employment of burning lime,
name Stephen Gordon,[34] who came from Kingsthorp near North-
ampton, who got me from home with the promise of many
advantages from working with him which he never intended
or at least never was able to perform   we at first worked for
Mr Wilders[35] at Bridge Casterton in Rutland   the whole addi-
tion to my fortunes accumulated here was the acquaintance with
a young girl who was destined for my future companion thro this
life and a poor mans meeting with a wife is reckoned but little
improvment to his condition and particular with the embares-
ments labourd under at that time   we staid at this place till
the latter end of the year and then went to Pickworth,[36] a hamlet
which seems by its large stretch of old foundations and ruins to
have been a town of some magnitude in past times tho it is now
nothing more then a half solitude of huts and odd farm houses
scatterd about some furlongs asunder   the marks of the ruins
may be traced 2 miles or further from beginning to end   here
by hard wo[r]king nearly day and night I at last got my £1 saved
for the printing the proposals, which I never lost sight of, and
getting a many more poems written as ex[c]ited by change of
Scenery, and from being for the first time[37] over head and ears
in love, above all the most urgent propensity to scribbling, I
fancyd myself more quallified for the undertaking, considering
the latter materials much better then what I had done, which no
doubt was the case, so I wrote a letter from this place imediatly
to Henson of M. Deeping, wishing him to begin the proposals
and address the public himself, urging he coud do it far better
then myself but his Answer was that I must do it, after which
I made some attempts but having not a fit place for doing any

thing of that kind, lodging at a public house and pesterd with many other inconviniences, I coud not suit myself with doing it in a hurry, so it kept passing from time to time till at last I determined good or bad to produce somthing and as we had another lime kiln at Ryhall about 3 miles from Pickworth I often went there to work by myself were I had leisure to study over such things on my journeys of going and returning to and fro; and on these walks morning and night I have dropd down 5 or 6 times, to plan this troublsome task of An address etc   in one of these musings my prosing thoughts lost them selves in rhyme, in taking a view as I sat neath the shelter of a woodland hedge

of my parents distresses at home and of my laboring so hard and so vainly to get out of debt and of my still added perplexitys of ill timed love — striving to remedy all and all to no purpose I burst out in an exclamation of distress, 'What is Life',[38] and instantly reccolecting such a subject woud be a good one for a poem I hastily scratted down the 2 first Verses of it as it stands as the begining of the plan which I intended to adopt and continued my jorney to work, but when at the kiln I coud not work for thinking about what I had so long been trying at; so I set me down on a lime skuttle and out with my pencil for an address of some sort, which good or bad I determind to send off that day and for that purpose when finished I accordingly started to Stamford about 3 miles from me   still along the road I was in a hundred minds wether I shoud throw all thoughts up about the matter or stay while a fitter oppertunity to have the advice of some friend or other but on turning it over in ones mind agen a second thought informd me that I had none   I was turnd

adrift on the broad ocean of life and must either sink or swim:
so I weighd matters on both sides and fancied let what bad woud
come they coud but ballance with the former   if my hopes
of the Poems failed I shoud be not a pin worse then usual — I
coud but work then as I did already — nay I considerd I shoud
reap benefit from disapointment   their downfall woud free
my mind from all foolish hopes and let me know that I had
nothing to trust to but work, so with this favourable idea I pur-
sued my intention, dropping down on a stone heap before I got
in the town to give it a second reading and correct what I thought
amiss   as I found my printer had little abilitys that way, I was
feign to do my best at it to escape being laughd at   When I got
to the Post Office they wanted a Penny as I was past the hour,
but as I had none and hating to look so little as to make the con-
fession I said with a little petteshness that it was not mine and
that I shoud not pay for other peoples letters   the man lookd
a little supprisd at the unusual garb of the letter which I was half
ashamd of — directed with a pencil, written on a sheet of paper
that was crumpled and grizzld with lying in ones pocket so long
and to add to its novelty sealed with shoemakers wax.   I saw
his smile and retreated as fast as I coud from the town   in the
course of another week 100 of printed proposals came, directed
to pickworth, accompanyd with a letter wishing me to meet him
at a public house in Stamford on a set day to discuss on further
particulars, which turnd out to be nothing more particular then
paying him for his printing and when he presented his bill I
found he had added 5ˢ /- more to the £1 agreement   this led
me into his principles of overreaching and encroaching and from
that time I considerd him in his true light as being no friend of
mine further then interest directed him, which turnd out exactly
the case   I distributed my papers accordingly but as I coud
get at no way of pushing them into higher circles then those
with whom I was accquainted they consequently passd off as
qu[i]etly as if they had still been in my possesion unprinted and
unseen   as soon as he got one 100 Subscribers he said he
woud begin to print, which after awhile he pretended he had

23

got, so I lost aweeks work to go home and arange matters but when I got there to him he said he coud not begin the book unless I advanced him £15,   this was plenty for me   I now found the man what I considerd him and determind in my mind he shoud not print it at all tho I said nothing then — I had not 15 pence nor 15 Farthings to call my own then — so I gave up all thoughts of his doing it   At this season of difficulty when I was embaras'd over head and ears in debt from down right nessesity I was still playing the fool with myself and coud not help running unnessary expences even then   I had been taking the 'Enquirer'[39] by Nos and had consequently ran in debt with a Bookseller to make up the matter   this was a M[r] Thompson,[40] who kept the 'New public Library' in the high street, Stamford   how to get straight with him I did not know but to let him see I had some prospect in the wind and hoping he woud befriend me in the matter a little by thinking he woud get his money in so doing I sent him 3 or 4 prospectuses with a short note and the names of 3 or 4 Subscribers, but he treated my humble vanity with contempt and told the bearer (Thomas Porter of Ashton) that the money was what he wanted and the money he woud have   M[r] Drury[41] had taken the Shop and seeing the prospectuses, thinking no doubt he might do it with benefit, paid the money immediatly without knowing further of me then what my friend related nor of my abilities then the prospectus specified, for his account of first meeting with the Sonnet to the Setting Sun in MSS is all a hoax and of no other foundation then his own fancy: but wether a mistake or intended falsity I cant justly assert, but I am apt to imagine what I am loth to discover   we have all foibles, and be it as it may, I respect him.   accordingly from the accidental cirscumstance of seeing the prospectus, he hunted me up on the following Sunday in company with a friend   I was not at home then, being at a neighbou[r]s house in the village known as a harmless resort of young men by the appelation of 'Bachellors Hall'[42] the possesors of which being two bachellors, John and James Billings,[43] whom I am still fond of visiting as companions tho much older then my self in spite of snarling mischief-makers who woud feignly belye me into discredit for so doing, by pretending nightly depredations are misterously and frequently going forward, such as stealing Game etc etc   I never in my life saw any such thing commited there, or any were else, and I woud give it on oath, not only for myself but on the credit of these men, that such calumniators are liars of the vilest and most dangerous class, and that I should always feel myself more safer in the company of my old neighbours then in those of that description   But again to our narrative   on being fetchd home with the news that gentlemen[44] was waiting to see me, I felt very awkard and had a good mind to keep away   I always felt and still feel very irksome among superiours so that its nothing now but down right force that hauls me into it   however I made my appearence and they both said they had came to become subscribers   I thankd them   they moreover wishd to see some of my MSS   what I had I showd them and they was seemlingly pleasd with them   they also askd me on what terms I stood with Henson of Deeping   I told them and hinted my intention of leaving him   they said little either for it or against it, but to their credit perhaps it may be justice to remark that they observed if I had pledgd my word of honour to him not to break it by any means — I said nothing further about it but thought that as he had broke his word and seemd by his actions to set very little store by honour in the matter that I had little cause to be sticking at that point and shoud be guilty of very small faults if I set as little store by mine on the occasion, for an agreement once found unjustifiable or broken in any part is no longer honourable, while receeding from it is nothing more then Justifying ones self from an error — they said before they left me, at least Mr Drury did, that if I got the MSS from Henson he shoud like to see them and woud then arange matters with me if I pleased and print them without any advancment of money on my part   this was what I wanted and just suited me so I promised him he shoud   they made ready for starting and Mr Drurys friend invited me to come over and dine with him in the

ensuing week but doubtless repenting of his free spoken kind-
ness and thinking if he 'gave me an inch I shoud take an ell' by
making unasked additional visits and by that means become
troublesome, for theres nothing more common here now adays,
so he opened the door agen and said 'If you get the MSS from
deeping Mr Clare, we shall be glad to see you if not we can say
nothing further about the matter.'   thus ended the exibition
of my two proffers of subscription like a showmans touchstone
of 'presto, quick, change, and be gone, soon as the words spoke,
the tricks done.'   I was hipt most cursedly at what ended their
visit and wishd I had not came home   what ever his reasons
was for chewing his kindness over again I know not   if he by
second thoughts fancyied I might be an intruder he afterwards
found himself mistaken, for I never paid it even according to
his alterd conditions.   Drury may make what he pleases of
his meeting with me at first if I shoud ever become of that con-
sequence in his opinion to require that notice — he may con-
tradict, add, alter, or shuffle it about in what shape he pleases —
here is the plain truth without the least desire to offend or wish
to please any of the parties conserned — I respect them on the
list of my other friends as far as they are respectable and thats
all I can say in this part of the Story or all I care about the con-
sequence.   I have one fault which had ought to be noticed, a
heated spirit that instantly kindles in too hasty bursts of praise
or censure   this will be found in my corespondence   when
I fancy my self injured I cannot brook it, no more then stifle my
gratitude when I am under obligations: one flowes as freely as
the other   nor do I repent it   when I am under misconscep-
tions and accuse wrongfully I shall meet forgiveness; when I do
not I neither need it nor require it   my spirit of independence
I set store by myself and I rest alike careless of succeeding callum-
niatures who by adducing their consiets as examples may abuse
me either for wanting or possesing it just as they please to decide
— so be it — tryed friendship shall never find me ungratfull in
the end or shifting after benefits — I wish others to see me as
freely as I will them, which no doubt plenty of them does, tho

26

under the mistery of false colours — what I have and shall say in this sketch is matured by reflection, so I wish every thing at least the substance to remain as it is written. I shall recant nothing. The same week my mother went over to Deeping and fetched the MSS home again and as soon as I got them in my possesion I started off to Drurys   To get the book printed for no expence on my part and a certain sum gaind by it in the bargain was a temptation I coud not let slip   when I appeared with them he gave me a Guinea as an ansel or ernest to the bargain and I readily left them and proceeded as he wishd in sending others as I copied them out, with no other agreement then word-of-mouth at that time   he praised some gentlemen into whose hands he intended to entrust the MSS uncommonly and I felt very anxious of knowing who the gentlman shoud be but he kept it as a secret a long time and at length told me twas John Taylor[45] of London a cousin of his   moreover he read me extracts from some of the above gentlemans letters to convince me of his abilities and I deemd it very lucky that such a man shoud fall in the way to correct and supperintend the publication and I have still the happiness to remember that when the thing came to be realized I met with no dissapointment but found the good character of the gentlemen given by Drury was not exaggerated in the least, but on the contrary, many things before unknown to me served to heighten my expectations rather then deminish them — Drury by some jealous advisers, or one how or other, wanted an agreement after a time had expired and wishing to please every body as far as I was able, I with some reluctance signed one with out considering in the least what it might contain for tho it was read over to me I took no heed of it as I knew nothing about such things — but reccolecting afterwards of hearing somthing about not only the present publication then in hand but what ever publications I might be encouraged to publish was all bound and apprenticed to this agreement — this I coud not stand, so I determined to break all such bondages and acted accordingly, and now leaving this long digression of trifleing I shall resume the story of my occupations and labours

I continued to work at Pickworth till the winter and then went to Casterton were I stopt a little while again with Mr Wilders till the frost set in that he coud not employ me longer
I then returnd home and had a good winters work of Scribbling etc for the forthcoming book   after the Spring came on I was sent for again to work for Mr Wilders were I continued all summer till the latter end of the year when a drop of wages against our first agreement made me leave the place   My amourous intrigues and connections with Patty,[46] the girl before mentioned, now began to disclose dangers which marriage alone coud remedy   I was little fit or inclined for marrying but my thoughtless and ram headed proceedings, as I was never all my life any thing else but a fool, commiting rashly and repenting too late having injured her character as well as my own   as for mine, I cared not a farthing about it   twas bad enough I knew and made ten times worse by meddling lyars but the ruination of one whom I almost adored was a wickedness my heart, however callous it might be to its own deceptions, coud not act
the wide mouth of the world was open against her, swallowing every thing that started to discredit her and sounding their ecchos in my ears to torment me and set me against her   hurt and vex me it did, but I felt more affection for her then ever and I determind to support her   I had that satisfaction on my consience that she was the only one I ever had injured and I had that oppertunity of easing my present trouble by making her amends
      I therefore made use of it and married her March 16 1820 and my only repentance was that I had not became acquainted with her sooner then I did.   I shoud have been as rich had I married 5 or 6 years sooner as I had been while single, for after I grew up I got into many scrapes I shoud other wise have shunned in the company of one I esteemed, for till my arrival at Casterton my dealings with love was but temporary   when a face pleased me I scribbled a Song or so in her praise, tryd to get in her company for the sake of pastime meerely as its calld on a Sunday eve a time or two and then left off for new alurements in fresh faces that took my fancy as supperiors — but these trifles, were as

28

innosent and harmless as trifling had I kept free from all others.

temptations were things that I rarely resisted   when the partiallity of the moment gave no time for reflection I was sure to seize it what ever might be the consequence.   still I have been no ones enemmy but my own   my easy nature, either in drinking or any thing else, was always ready to submit to persuasions of profligate companions who often led me into snares and laughd at me in the bargain when they had done so.   such times as at fairs, coaxed about to bad houses, those painted pills of poison, by whom many ungarded youths are hurried to destruction, like the ox to the slaughter house without knowing the danger that awaits them in the end — here not only my health but my life has often been on the eve of its sacrafice by an illness too well known, and to[o] disgusting to mention.

but mercey spared me to be schoold by experience who learnd me better.   perhaps its not improper or too insignificant to mention that my first feelings of love was created at school even while a boy   a young girl, I may say a child, won my affections not only by her face which I still think very handsome but by her meek modest and quiet disposition, the stillest and most good natured girl in the school   her name was Mary[47] and my regard for her lasted a long time after school days was over but it was platonic affection, nothing else but love in idea for she knew nothing of my fondness for her, no more then I did of her inclinations, to forbid or encourage me, had I disclosed after wards — but other Marys etc excited my admiration and the first creator of my warm passions was lost in a perplexd multitude of names that woud fill a vol to Callender them down ere a bearded chin coud make the lawfull appology for my entering the lists of Cupid.   Thus began and ended my amourous career.   My faults I believe to be faults of most people — nature like a bird in its shell came into the world with errors and propensitys to do wrong mantled round her as garments and tho not belonging to her substance are so fastned round her person by the intricate puzzles of temptation that wisdom has not the power or the skill to unloose her nott that fastens them — virtue, or innosence,

29

pretending perfection in this world is to common sense a painted Sepulchre.   the mercey of perfection must look on all with many indulgences or the best will fall short of their wishd reward.

In matters of religion I never was and I doubt never shall be so good as I ought to be — tho I am at heart a protestant, perhaps like many more I have been to church [more] often then I have been seriously inclined to recieve benefit or put its wholsome and reasonable admonitions to practice — still I reverence the church and do from my soul as much as any one curse the hand thats lifted to undermine its constitution — I never did like the runnings and racings after novelty in any thing, keeping in mind the proverb 'When the old ones gone there seldom comes a better.'   The 'free will' of ranters,[48] 'new light' of methodists, and 'Election Lottery' of Calvanism I always heard with disgust and considered their enthusiastic ravings little more intelligable or sensible then the belowings of Bedlam.   In politics I never dabbled to understand them thoroughly with the old dish that was served to my forefathers I am content.
    but I believe the reading a small pamphlet on the Murder of the french King many years ago with other inhuman butcheries cured me very early from thinking favourably of radicalism the words 'revolution and reform' so much in fashion with sneering arch infidels thrills me with terror when ever I see them — there was a Robspiere,[49] or somthing like that name, a most indefatigable butcher in the cause of the french levellers, and if the account of him be true, hell has never reeked juster revenge on a villian since it was first opened for their torture — may the foes of my country ever find their hopes blasted by dissappointments and the silent prayers of the honest man to a power that governs with justice for their destruction meet always with success.   thats the creed of my consience — and I care for nobody else's — all have liberty to think as they please and he is a knave that cheats his heart with false appearences, be his opinions as they may — here is as faithful account of myself as I can possibly

give   I have been as free to disclose my own faults as a meddler is those of his neighbours — and by so doing have doubtless baffled the aims of skulking assasins from throwing weapons in the dark with the force they woud have done had I made myself better then I am.   'Tell the truth and shame the devil'[50]

I am
ever faithfully
yours etc
John Clare

To John Taylor Esq[r]
London.   [N14]

MORE HINTS IN THE LIFE ETC

I have dipt into several sorts of Studies at several times in my boyish days   my vanity was such that what ever Book on art or Science I could come at I fancied I could learn it and Instantly with as much ardour and Enthuiseism (perhaps) as the author that wrote it.   I have sat down studying it page by page with an anxious delight not to be describd but where any thing happened to come above my Comprehension it was a Painfull task   I have had repeated t[o]uches at a Mathematics Question for a month together and while it remaind a Secret I have had with out knowing the cause such a longing Sickness on me that I could eat (in the time) little or nothing   In this manner I eagerly dipt into Most arts and Sciences that came in my way

These where Mathematics Particulary Navigation and Algebra Dialling Use of the Globes Botany Natural History Short Hand with History of all Kinds Drawing Music etc etc   I had once a very great desire to learn the Latin Language but the happy fate of not meeting with proper Books in that age of Vanity saved me the trouble of Expeirencing many an aching head (Study always left a sinking sickening pain in my head otherways unaccount-able) and many an Envious Staring throbbing thro my bosom which always was the case when I found my attempts in vain — etc etc

On Sundays I Generally stole from my Companions whose Manners and Play was no ways Agreable to me and sholld into the Woods Where I was most happy as I always lovd to be by my self   I have spent whole days (Sundays) in Searching Curious wild Flowers of which I was very fond and I often won-dered when in Company with others that they never noticed them and that they never in the least noticed my remarks on such and such beauties when I have stooped down and cropped the flower to explain my Ideas in vain   I was very fond of 'birds Nesting' as we us'd to call it when I was a Child but this hard hearted practise of Robbing Poor birds was soon laid aside as

I grew up   Searching of Snail shells we call 'Pooties' was a Favou[r]ite Amusement — I must remark too the Aspiring Pride of being first Scholar in the school (as I always was)   If I had the least fear of a Superior I labourd night and day at my Question till the Masters praises put me out of doubt — This Vanity had its Origin at the first (or nearly so) school I went to   A Mr Seaton once Schoolmaster at Glinton us'd to give his best scholars premiums that is such as Got Tasks and spelling the best and the most of either   he always took a great delight (as I could percieve) in Questioning and rewarding me even som times when I did not deserve it but his reasons for so doing I cannot tell as I was quite a stranger to him   he once set me the task of getting a Chap[ter] of Job   I think the 3rd   this suprisd me but he told me not to fear for he was sure I could do it   I accordingly compleated the task in the Christmas week   I was rewarded exellently for my abilities with 6^d and praises of the Master ever after the boys where so dampt that they would not try in things in which I was concernd so that I got the prizes without trouble and have come in for some time as much as threepence in a Week   this I savd unknown to my parents to buy books etc etc etc etc

I forgot to mention that I was while at school very much delighted with the perusal of 'Robinson Crusoe' as lent me by a school fellow   it is an entertaining book and the effect of its perusal was such that I still remember it with pleasure

Grammer I never read a page of in my Life nor do I believe my master knew any more then I did about the matter

I have a Superficial Knowledge of the Mathematics which I gaind partly by self Tuition (as I was very fond of them once) and partly by the assistance of a Friend whom I shall ever remember with Gratitude*

I never went to meals with out employing every leisure minute in the perusal of a book   practiseing thus I began to Read and comprehend the meaneing of what I read well   [N22, 3]

* Mr John Turnill Late of Helpstone now in the Excise [Clare's footnote]

AUTOBIOGRAPHICAL FRAGMENTS

I cannot trace my name to any remote period a century and a half is the utmost and in this I have found no great ancestors to boast in the breed — all I can make out is that they were Gardeners Parish Clerks and fiddlers and from these has sprung a large family of the name still increasing were kindred has forgotten its claims and 2nd and 3rd cousins are worn out   [A32, 7]

[*Holidays*]

What ups and downs have I met with since I was a boy   how barren the world looking about me   now years come and go like messengers without errands and are not noticd for the tales which they tell are not worth stopping them to hear   nothing but cares and dissa[point]ments   when I was[1] a boy a week

34

scarcly came without a promise of some fresh delight   Hopes
were always awake with expectations   the year was crowned
with holidays   [B5, 46]

and then the year usd to be crownd with its holidays as thick as
the boughs on a harvest home   there was the long wishd for
christmass day the celebrated week with two sundays when we
usd to watch the clerk return with his bundle of ever greens and
run for our bunch to stick the windows and empty candlesticks
hanging in the corner or hasten to the woods to gett ivy branches
with its joccolate berrys which our parents usd to color with
whitening and the blu[e]bag sticking the branches behind the
pictures on the walls
then came valentine   tho young we was not without loves
    we had our favourites in the village and we listend the
expected noises of creeping feet and the tinkling latch as eagerly
as upgrown loves   wether they came or not it made no matter
    dissapointments was nothing in those matters then   the
pleasures of anticipation was all — then came the first of april
o how we talkd and harpd of it ere it came of how we woud make
april fools of others and take care not to be catchd our selves
when as soon as the day came we were the first to be taken in by
running unconsiously on errands for Piegons milk glass eyd
needles or some such april fool errands   when we were un-
decievd we blushd for shame and took care not to be taken in till
the day returnd again — when the old deceptions were so far for-
gotten as to decieve us again   then there was the first of may
    we were too young to be claimants in the upgrown sports but
we joind our little interferances with them and run under the
extended hankerchiefs at duck under water with the rest un-
molested   then came the feast when the cross was throngd
round with stalls of toys and sweets horses on w[h]eels with their
flowing manes and lambs with their red necklaces box cuckoos
and we lookd on these finerys till the imaganation almost coaxd
our itching fingers to steal and seemd to upbraid our fears for not
daring to do it   then the sweet meats was unbounded

their was barly sugar candied lemon candied hore[h]ound and .
candied peppermint with swarms of colord sugar plumbs and
tins of lollipop   our mouths waterd at such luxurys   we
had our penny but we knew not how to lay it out   there was
ginger bread coaches and ginger bread milk maids and to gratifye
two propensitys the taste and the fancy together we bought one
of these gilded toys and thought we had husbanded our pennys
well till they was gone and then we went runing and coaxing our
parents for more thinking of making better bargains when we got
money agen   then there was eastwell spring[2] famous in those
days for its spaws and its trough at the fountain were we usd to
meet of a sunday and have sugard drink   then came the she[e]p-
[s]heerings were we was sure of frumity from the old shepherds
if we sought the clipping pens and lastly came the harvest home[3]
and its cross shittles   ah what a paradise begins with the
ignorance of life and what a wilderness the knowledge of the
world discloses   surely the garden of eden was nothing more
then our first parents entrance upon life and the loss of it their
knowledge of the world   [B8, R127-R126]

surely our play prolonging moon on spring evenings shed a
richer lustre then the mid day sun that surrounds us now in man-
hood for its poetical sunshine hath left us   it is the same iden-
tical sun and we have learned to know that — for when boys
every new day brought a new sun   we knew no better and we
was happy in our ignorance — there is nothing of that new and
refreshing sunshine upon the picture now   it shines from the
heavens upon real matter of fact existances and weary occupa-
tions   [A46, 106]

The spring of our life — our youth — is the midsumer of our
happiness — our pleasures are then real and heart stiring — they
are but assosiations afterwards — where we laughed in child
hood at the reality of the enjoyment felt we only smile in man
hood[4] at the reccolections of those enjoyments — they are then
but the reflections of past happiness and have no more to do with

36

happiness in the reality then the image of a beautiful girl seen in a looking glass has in comparison with the origional — our minds only retain the resemblance   the glass is a blank after her departure — we only feel the joy we possesed — we see the daisey and love it because it was our first favourite in child hood
       we hear the nightingale and are delighted because it was such a favourite in youth and the haunts of its annual visits being the paradise of boyhood — green thickets where the leaves hid him from all but joys   [D10, 7r]

There is nothing but poetry about the existance of childhood real simple soul moving poetry the laughter and joy of poetry and not its philosophy and there is nothing of poetry about manhood but the reflection and the remembrance of what has been   nothing more   [A46, 106]

[Leisure]

I lovd to employ leisure when a boy in wandering about the fields watching the habits of birds to see the wood pecker s[w]eeing away in its ups and downs and the jay bird chattering by the wood side its restless warnings of passing clowns the travels of insects were the black beetle nimbld along and the opening of field flowers   such amusments gave me the greatest of pleasures but I coud not acco[u]nt for the reason why they did so
       a lonly nook a rude bridge or woodland style with ivy grow-ing around the posts delighted me and made lasting impressions on my feelings but I knew nothing of poetry then   yet I noticd every thing as anxious as I do now and every thing pleasd me as much   I thought the gipseys camp by the green wood side a picturesque and an adorning object to nature and I lovd the gipseys for the beautys which they added to the landscape   I heard the cuckoos 'wandering voise' and the restless song of the Nightingale and was delighted while I pausd and mutterd its

37

sweet jug jug as I passd its black thorn bower   I often pulld my
hat over my eyes to watch the rising of the lark or to see the hawk
hang in the summer sky and the kite take its circles round the
wood   I have often lingerd a minute on the woodland stile to
hear the wood pigions clapping their wings among the dark oaks
      I hunted curious flowers in raptures and mutterd thoughts
in their praise   I lovd the pasture with its rushes and thistles
and sheep tracks   I adord the wild marshy fen with its solitary
hernshaw sweeing along in its mellan[c]holy sky   I wandered
the heath in raptures among the rabbit burrows and golden
blossomd furze   I dropt down on a thymy mole hill or mossy
eminence to survey the summer landscape as full of raptures
as now   I markd the varied colors in flat spreading fields
checkerd with closes of different tinted grain like the colors in a
map the copper tinted colors of clover in blossom the sun tand
green of the ripening hay the lighter hues of wheat and barley
intermixd with the sunny glare of the yellow c[h]arlock and the
sunset imitation of the scarlet head aches with the blue corn
bottles crowding thier splendid colors in large sheets over the
lands and 'troubling the corn fields' with destroying beauty the
different greens of the woodland trees the dark oak the paler ash
the mellow Lime the white poplar peeping above the rest like
leafy steeples the grey willow shining chilly in the sun as if the
morning mist still lingerd in its cool green   I felt the beauty of
these with eager delight   the gad flyes noon day hum the
fainter murmer of the bee flye 'spiring in the evening ray' the
dragon flyes in their spangld coats darting like 'winged arrows
down the stream' the swallow darting through its one arched brig
the shepherd hiding from a thunder shower in an hollow dotterel
the wild geese scudding along and making all the letters of the
Alphabet as they flew the motley clouds the whispering wind
that mutterd to the leaves and summer grass as it flutterd among
them like things at play   I observd all this with the same
raptures as I have done since but I knew nothing of poetry   it
was felt and not utterd   most of my sundays was spent in this
manner about the fields with such merry company   I heard

the black and the brown beetle sing their evening songs with rapture and lovd to see the black snail steal out upon its dewy baulks   I saw the humble horse bee at noon 'spiring' on wanton wing   I lovd to meet the woodman whistling away to his toils and to see the shepherd bending oer his hook on the thistly green chatting love storys to the listening maiden while she milkd her brindld cow   the first primrose in spring was as delightful as it is now   the copper colord clouds of the morning was watchd and the little ups and downs and roly poly child mountains of the broken heath with their brown mossy crowns and little green bottoms were the sheep feed and hide from the sun   the stone quarry with its magnified precipic[e]s   the wind mills sweeing idly to the sum[m]er wind   the steeples peeping among the trees round the orisons circle

I noticd the cracking of the stubbs to the increasing sun while I gleand among them   I lovd to see the heavey grassopper in his coat of delicate green bounce from stub to stub   I listend the hedge cricket with raptures

the evening call of the patridge   the misterious spring sound of the land rail that cometh with the green corn

I lovd the meadow lake with its fl[a]gs and long purples crowding the waters edge   I listend with delights to hear the wind whisper among the feather topt reeds and to see the taper bulrush nodding in gentle curves to the rippling water and I watchd with delight on haymaking evenings the setting sun drop behind the brigs and peep again thro the half circle of the arches as if he longs to stay   [A34, R16-R14]

I had plenty of leisure but it was the leisure of solitude for my Sundays was demanded to be spent in the fields at horse or cow tending   my whole summer was one days employment as it were in the fields   I grew so much into the qu[i]et love of nature[s] presence that I was never easy but when I was in the fields passing my sabbaths and leisures with the shepherds and herd boys[5] as fancys prompted somtimes playing at marbles on the smooth beaten sheep tracks or leap frog among the thimey

39

molehills somtimes ranging among the corn to get the red and
blue flowers for cockades to play at soldiers or runing into the
woods to hunt strawberrys or stealing peas in church time when
the owners was safe to boil at the gipseys fire who went half
shares at our stolen luxury   we heard the bells chime but the
fields was our church and we seemd to feel a religious feeling in
our haunts on the sabbath while some old shepherd sat on a mole
hill reading aloud some favour[i]te chapter from an old fragment
of a Bible which he carried in his pocket for the day a family relic
which possesd on its covers and title pages in rude scrawls
geneoligys of the third and fourth Generations when aunts
uncles and grandmothers dyd and when cousins etc were
marri[e]d and brothers and sisters born occupying all the blank
leaves in the book and the title pages bhorders which leaves were
prese[r]ved with a sacred veneration tho half the contents had
been sufferd to drop out and be lost

I lovd this solitary disposition from a boy and felt a curosity
to wander about the spots were I had never been before   I
remember one incident of this feeling when I was very young
it cost my parents some anxiety   it was in summer and I
started off in the morning to get rotten sticks from the woods but
I had a feeling to wander about the fields and I indulgd it   I
had often seen the large heath calld Emmonsales[6] stretching its
yellow furze from my eye into unknown solitudes when I went
with the mere openers and my curosity urgd me to steal an opper-
tunity to explore it that morning   I had imagind that the
worlds end was at the edge of the orison and that a days journey
was able to find it   so I went on with my heart full of hopes
pleasures and discoverys expecting when I got to the brink of the
world that I coud look down like looking into a large pit and see
into its secrets the same as I believd I coud see heaven by looking
into the water   so I eagerly wanderd on and rambled among
the furze the whole day till I got out of my knowledge when the
very wild flowers and birds seemd to forget me and I imagind
they were the inhabitants of new countrys   the very sun
seemd to be a new one and shining in a different quarter of the

sky   still I felt no fear   my wonder seeking happiness had
no room for it   I was finding new wonders every minute and
was walking in a new world[7] often wondering to my self that I
had not found the end of the old one   the sky still touchd the
ground in the distance as usual and my childish wisdoms was
puzzld in perplexitys   night crept on before I had time to fancy
the morning was bye when the white moth had begun to flutter
beneath the bushes the black snail was out upon the grass and
the frog was leaping across the rabbit tracks on his evening jour-
neys and the little mice was nimbling about and twittering their
little earpiercing song with the hedge cricket whispering the hour
of waking spirits was at hand which made me hasten to seek
home   I knew not which way to turn but chance put me in the
right track and when I got into my own fields I did not know them
      every thing seemd so different   the church peeping over
the woods coud hardly reconcile me   when I got home I found
my parents in the greatest distress and half the vill[a]ge about
hunting me   one of the wood men in the woods had been killd
by the fall of a tree and it servd to strengthen their terrors that
some similar accident had befallen myself as they often leave the
oaks half cut down till the bark men can come up to pill them
which if a wind happens to rise fall down unexpected
[A34, R8, R6]

I usd to be fondly attachd to spots about the fields and there were
3 or 4 were I used to go to visit on sundays   one of these was
under an old Ivied Oak in Oxey wood were I twisted a sallow
stoven into an harbour which grew into the crampd way in which
I had made it   two others were under a broad oak in a field
calld the Barrows and Langley Bush[8] and all my favourite places
have met with misfortunes   the old ivied tree was cut down
when the wood was cut down and my bower was destroyd
the woodmen fancied it a resort for robbers and some thought the
crampd way in which the things grew were witch knotts and that
the spot was a haunt were witches met   I never unriddeld the
mystery and it is believd so still for I got there often to hide myself

41

and was ashamd to acknowledge it — Lee Close Oak was cut down in the inclosure and Langley bush was broken up by some wanton fellows while kidding furze on the heath — the Carpenter that bought Lee Close oak hearing it was a favourite tree of mine made me two rules and sent me and I prese[r]ved a piece of the old Ivy the thickest I have ever seen   [A33, 7]

What a many such escapes from death doth a boys heedless life meet with   I met with many in mine   once when wading in the meadow pits a lot of cow tending boys we tryd to to[p] each others tasks   we had gone several times and it was my turn to attempt again when I unconscously got beside a gravel ledge into deep water when my heels slipt up and I siled down to the bottom

I felt the water choke me and thunder in my ears and I thought all was past but some of the boys coud swim and so I escapd   another time we were swiming on bundles of bull rushes when mine getting to one end suddenly bouncd from under me like a cork and I made shift to struggle to a sallow bush and catching hold of the branches I got out but how I did it I know not for the water was very deep and yet we had dabbld there sunday after sunday without the least fear of danger

once when birds nesting in the woods of which I was very fond we found a large tree on which was a buzzards nest   it was a very hard tree to climb   there were no twigs to take hold of and it was two thick to swarm so we consulted for awhile some proposing one thing and some another till it was decided that a hook tyd to the end of a long pole that woud reach to the collar of the tree woud be the best to get up by   in taking hold of it and swarming several attempted to no purpose and at last I tryd tho I was rather loath to try the experiment   I succeeded at getting up to the collar which swelld in such a projection from the tree that I coud not make a landing without hazarding the dangerous attempt of clinging with my hands to the grain and flinging my feet over it   I attempted it and faild so there I hung with my hands and my feet dangling in the air   I expected every moment to drop and be pashd to pieces for I was a great height but some of my companions below while some ran away had the shrewdness to put the pole under me and by that means I got on the grain just in time before I was quite exausted and savd my life   another time when I was grown up I went to the woods to gather acorns and getting on a tree which was very full I sat on a large grain dashing them which broke and I fell to the ground about 14 or 15 foot were I lay for a long time and knew nothing   on coming to my self I crawld up and saw that the large grain just lodgd above me   I was agonized   I coud not catch my breath unless by deep groans and I got over that

[B7, R92-R91]

I thought I was up sooner then usual and before morning was on the stir out of doors but I am pleasantly dissapointed by the whistle of the ploughboy past the window making himself merry and trying to make the dull weather dance to a very pleasant tune which I know well and yet cannot reccollect the song   but there are hundreds of these pleasant tunes familiar to the plough and the splashing steam[9] and the little fields of spring that have lain out the brown rest of winter and green into mirth with the sprouting grain the songs of the sky lark and the old songs and ballads that ever accompany field happiness in following the plough — but[10] neither heard known or noticed by all the world beside   [B6, 99]

In spring the leafing hedges brings to my memory the times when I anxiously rambld about them at leisure hours hunting the birds nest[s] and pootys and I cannot help peeping among

43

them still tho I feel almost ashamed of my childish propensitys and cannot help blushing if I am observed by a passing neighbour

Thus the same thing of every thing   flowers have happy assosiations of youth   they are its sweetest chronicles   the herds man cannot neglect the wild thyme on the hill that made him seats when a boy or the blue caps in the wheat [with] which he trim[m]ed his cockade to play at soldiers   to the old woman[11] the little blue flower aside the brook called in botany water mouse ear brings the lovers reccolections when she was young   she still stoops down and fancys that it smile[s] upward in her eye forget me not

[B3, 60]

At the end of a little common when I was a boy called Tankers Moor there was a little spring of beautiful soft water which was never dry   it used to flow from under an edding at the end of a land out of a little hole about as deep and round as a cuttin[g] — it used then to dribble its way thro the grass in a little ripple of its own making no bigger than a grip or cart rut — and in this little spring head there used to be hundreds of the little fish called a minnow not so big as the struttle and these used to be found in that hole every year but how they came there I could not tell some years a quantity of struttle was found and often a few gudgeons — when a boy we used to go on a sunday in harvest and leck it out with a dish and string the fish on rushes — and therebye thinking ourselves great fishers from the number we had caught not heeding the size

[A49, 73]

44

the Marquis[12] was then a boy   I have him in my minds eye in
his clean jerkin and trowsers shooting in the park or fishing on
the river   [A34, R13]

tho I always felt in company a disbelief of ghost witches etc yet
when I was a lone in the night my fancys created thousands and
my fears was always on the look out every now and then turning
around to see if aught was behind me   I was terribly frighted
on seeing a will owisp for the first time and tho my fears grew less
by custom for there are crowds about our fenny flats yet I never
coud take them on the credit of philos[oph]y as natural phenome-
nons at night time but always had a suspicion of somthing super-
natural belonging to them — I have had a many 'night fears' and
usd to be terribly anoyd when a boy in takeing the horses away at
the evening to heath in spring time when the badgers made a
horrible squeeling noise in the woods resembling the screams of
a woman and the crooning of the [wood pigeons] but the worst
fright I ever met with was on a harvest night when I workd at
Bassets of Ashton   we was always late ere we gave over work
as harvesters generally are and ere we finishd our suppers it was
nigh midnight by the time I started home which was but the dis-
tance of a short mile but I had a terror haunting spot to cross calld
Baron parks in which was several ruins of roman camps and
saxon castles and of course was people[d] with many mysterys of
spirits   the tales were numberless of ghosts and goblings that
were seen there and I never passd it without my memory keeping
a strict eye to look for them and one night rather late I fan[c]yd
I saw somthing stand wavering in the path way but my hopes
put it off as a shadow till on coming nearer I found that it was
somthing but wether of flesh and blood was a question   my
astonishd terrors magnified it into a horrible figure   it appeard
to have ears of a vas[t] length and the hair seemd to hang about
it like [   ]   I trembld and almost wishd the earth woud open
to hide me   I woud have spoke but I coud not and on attempt-
ing to pass it I gave it the road and ran off as fast as I coud and on
stopping at the stile to look were it was my increasd terror found

45

it close at my heels   I thought it was nothing but infernal now
and scarce [know]ing what I did I took to my heels and when I got
home I felt nearly fit to dye   I felt assurd that ghosts did exist
and I dare not pass the close the next day till quite late in the day
when every body was abroad when to my supprise I found it was
nothing but a poor cade foal[13] that had lost its mother and had
been raisd with milk till it was grown up and had been turnd
ther[e] to wean it the day before   it followd me again and my
disbelief in ghosts was more hardend then ever   [D2, 5-6]

'Will with a whisp' 'Jimmy Whisk' 'Jack with a lanthorn   in
this november month they are often out in the dark misty nights
— on 'Rotten Moor' 'Dead Moor' Eastwell moor — Banton green
end Lolham Briggs Rine dyke furlong and many other places in
the lordship[14]   I have my self seen them on most of these spots
— one dark night I was coming accross the new parks when a
sudden light wild and pale appeared all round me on my left
hand for a hundred yards or more accompan[i]ed by a crackling
noise like that of peas straw burning   I stood looking for
a minute or so and felt rather alarmed when darkness came round
me again and one of the dancing jack a la[n]thens was whisking
away in the distance which caused the odd luminous light
around me — crossing the meadow one dark sunday night I saw
when coming over the Nunton bridge a light like a lanthorn
standing on the wall of the other bridge   I kept my eyes on it
for awhile and hastened to come up to it — but ere I got half over
the meadow it suddenly fell and tumbled into the stream — but
when I got on the bridge I looked down it and saw the will o
whi[s]p vapour like a light in a bladder whisking along close to
the water as if swimming along its surface but what supprised me
was that it was going contrary to the stream   [A49, 49]

[15]how many days hath passd since we usd to hunt the stag or hunt
the slipper but there usd to be one crook horn etc in those days
and duck under water on May eve and tossing the cowslip balls
over the garland that hung from chimney to chimney across the

street and then there was going to east well on a sunday to drink sugar and water at the spring head but inclosure came and drove these from the village — I usd to be very fond of fishing and of a sunday morning I have been out before the sun delving for worms in some old weed blanketed dunghill and steering off across the wet grain that over hung the narrow path and then I usd to stoop to w[r]ing my wet trowser bottoms now and then and off agen beating the heavy drops off the grain with my pole end till I came to the flood washd meadow stream and then my tackle was eagerly fastend on and my heart woud thrill with hopes of success as I saw a sizable gudgeon twinkle round the glossy pebbles or a fish lap after a flye or a floating somthing on the deeper water   were is the angler that hath not felt these delights in his young days and were is a angler that doth not feel taken with their memory when he is old   I usd also to be very fond of poking about the hedges in spring to hunt pootys and I was no less fond of robing the poor birds nests or searching among the prickly furze on the heath poking a stick into the rabbit holes and carefully observing when I took it out if there was down at the end which was a sign of a nest with young   then in went the arm up to the shoulder and then fear came upon us that a snake might be conseald in the hole and then our bloods ran cold within us and startld us off to other sports and then we usd to chase the squirrels in the woods from grain to grain that woud sit washing their faces on the other side and then peep at us again and then we usd to get boughs from the trees to beat a whasps nest till some of us were stung and then we ran away to other amusments   [B8, R128-R127]

[Northborough]

There is a saying or rather an old superstition connected with this place as well known all round the neighbourhood as some of the sayings of Gotham are — when any one who was awkard at his

work and would not be shown his companions would say —
'Send him to Norborrey (Northborough) hedge corner to hear the
wooden cuckoo sing'[16] and this spot was one of the curiositys that
my imagination when a boy yearnd to see — from the frequency
of the above saying it grew a natural curiosity and a sort of classic
spot for the travels of my fancys — but I never learnt from where
it sprung — I apprehend it was some foolish charter of some
feudal occupier of the old castle in the days of chivalry — for in a
neighbourhood a little distant an old man told me there was a
little spot about as large as a pin fold enclosed with quick which
fence the parish was obliged to mend and repair every year on
a particular day under the foolish appelation of 'hedging the
cuckoo in' — in our fields there was a similar enclosure called the
'Cow pen' but the custome if customes there were of repairing etc
were all lost and forgotten long before I was born — yet the ghost
stories conected with its lonely situation was as fresh as a dew
fall   they are forgetting the old memories now and the young
ones are too [un]caring to heed them — but I do assure you I
would not pass such spots now at nightfal if I could help and to
pass them at midnight between the twelve and one if wager was
offered that [would] make me a gentleman I dare not win it
                                                              [A46, 154]

Mr T[aylor] seems to fancy it a gift but I cannot feel any thing to
expect or deserve such a distinction from a family who have been
kind to me even to an extream   I therefore enter upon it with
no other expectation then that of my neighbours and then it will
be a home that I have long wished for and never had the luck to
come at till now — for to have such men for Landlords is a satis-
factory happiness — for so long as the Miltons and the Exeters have
been a name in this neighbourhood — there is not one instance
that I know of where they have treated success in his willing
industry with unkindness in either insulting dependants with
oppression or treating poverty with cruelty — not one — and this
is a proof to me that nobility is the chief support to industry and
that their power is its strongest protection   [Pfz 198, 40]

Chusing Friends Chapter 6th

Among all the friendships I have made in life those of school
friendship and childish acquaintance are the sweetest to remem-
ber   there is no deseption among them   their is nothing of
regret in them but the loss   they are the fairest and sunniest
pages memory ever doubles down in the checkerd volume of life
to refer to   there is no blotches upon them — they are not
found like bargains on matters of interest nor broken for selfish
ends — I made but few close friendships for I found few with the
like tastes inclinations and feelings

one of my first friendships was with Richard the brother of
John Turnill   it began with infancy from playing at feasts by
the cottage wall with broken pots and gathering the crumpled
seeds of the mallow for cheeses making houses and fires of sticks
stones and clay to the second stage of hunting birds nests and
painted pooty shells among the dewy boughs and busy growing
grass in the spring and the partnerships of labours toils and sun-
day leisures but death came while we were growing up into each
others pleasures like twin flowers and took him away before our
budding friendships coud blossom — yet it was [an] image of
happiness — what numberless hopes of successes did we chatter
over as we hunted among the short snubby bushes of the heath
or on hedge rows and crept among the black thorn spreys after
the nest of the nightingales and what happy discourses of plan-
ning pleasures did we talk over as we lay on the soft summer
grass gazing on the blue sky shaping the passing clouds to things
familiar with our memorys and dreaming of the days to come
when we shoud mix with the world and be men little thinking
that we shoud chew the cud of sweet and bitter fancys when we
met it   but he never did   I have mentiond were he dyd and
was buried a while back   his brother Johns acquaintance
began with learning me on the winter nights to write and sum

he was of a studious musing turn of mind and fond of books
always carr[y]ing one of some sort or other in his pocket to read
between toils at leisure hours   they were somtimes sixpenny

49

books of storys and at other times the books which he usd at
school for he had been [at] boarding school and read in books
there that are unknown in a village school   I remember being
often delighted with one which he repeated by heart in ryhme a
story of a young lady being killd in battle by a shield ball[17] while
seeking her lover and another tale in prose of the old man and his
ass[18] which was a favour[i]te and he always contrivd to bring the
News paper in his pocket in weeding time which I was always
very anxious to read   his father was a farmer and I usd to work
for them in the weeding and haymaking seasons   his mind
was always anxious after knowledge and too restless to stick to
any thing long so he had a superficial knowledge of many things
and a solid information with none   one season he woud be
learned and occupied with Mathematics working problems of
algebra or Geometry   he was also ambitious of shining in the
almanack diarys and attempted to unriddle the puzzles for the
prizes and to ryhme new charad[e]s reddles and rebuses on a
slate which he fitted to his pocket and making dials on a board
and fixing them on the top of his weed hook shaft to enquire the
hour of the day   then before he had formd half an acquain-
tance with them he woud be making his telescopes of paste board
and studying the stars with the assistance of a book which he had
purchasd a cheap penny worth at some second hand book stall
      somtimes he woud be after drawing by perspective and he
made an instrument from a shilling art of painting which he had
purchasd that was to take landscapes almost by itself   it was of
a long square shape with a hole at one end to look thro and a
number of diferent colord threads crossd into little squares at the
other   from each of these squares different portions of the
Landscape was to be taken one after the other and put down in a
facsimile of these squares done with a pencil on the paper   but
his attempts made but poor reflelctions of the objects and when
they were finishd in his best colors they were far from being even
poor shadows of the origional and the sun with its instantaneous
sketches made better figures of the objects in their shadows
once he happend in with Lilys astrology[19] at Deeping fair and then

his head was forever after Nativitys and fortune telling by the stars
his mother was skilld in huswife phisic and Culpeppers
Herbal[20] and he usd to be up after gathering herbs at the proper
time of the planets that was said to rule them expecting they
woud perform Miracles — I remember the last thing which he
was busy after were studying a book on bees and a restless desire
after glass hives   once he got a book on the mysterys of nature
which told him how to turn metals into gold to find jewels in a
toads head and gather brake seed on midsummer eve for my[s]ti-
cal purposes which I have now forgotten   but in the midst of
all his inventions and thirst for knowledge a couzin came down
from London who had a power of getting him a place in the excise
his present occupation so his parents hopes were ripend and he
was sent to school and then to the excise and   his hopes anxietys
crowds of schemes and happy memorys were left unfinishd
behind him to make room for new ones   [A25, R34-R32]

I found another boy acquantance which grew up with a few
breaks in it to manhood with Tom Porter who lives in a lone
cottage on Ashton green   he had a fondness for flowers and
gardening and possesd a few old Books which were old 'heir
longs' in the family once belonging to his great grand father who
had been steward to the Noells at Walcott Hall[21]   two which I
usd to be most pleasd with were Sandys travels and Parkinsons
Herbal[22] and I usd often to make sunday visits to read them[23]
his[24] fondness for books were those of gardening and he bought
and buys still all the second hand one[s] that treat upon that subject
which chance lays his hands on   we usd to go out on sundays
in the fields to hunt curious wild flowers to plant in the garden
such as the orchises   From these friendships I gatherd more
acquantance with books which like chances oppertunitys were
but sparing   [A25, R32]

I usd to spend many of my winter nights and sabbath leisures
when I grew up in the world at a neighbours house of the name
of Billings   it was a sort of meeting house for the young fellows

of the town were the[y] usd to join for ale and tobacco and sing
and drink the night away   the occupiers were two Bachelors
and their cottage was calld bachelors hall   it is an old ruinous
hut and hath needed repairs ever since I knew it for they neither
mend up the walls nor thatch the roof being negligent men but
quiet and innofensive neighbours   I still frequent their house

it has more the appearence of a deserted hermitage then an
inhabited dwelling   I have sat ta[l]king of witch and ghost
storys over our cups on winter nights till I felt fearful of going
home   John Billings the elder had a very haunted mind for
such things and had scarce been out on a journey with the night
without seeing a gost a will o whisp or some such shadowy mys-
terys and such reccolections of midnight wanderings furnishd
him with storys for a whole winters fire side   we usd to go
often to the wood to pill oaks²⁵ in the winters evening or in fact
any thing chance started and once we went on a sabbath day
there was three of us and James Billings was the gunner for I had
no eye to kill any thing even if I was close to it tho my will perhaps
was as good as the rest and on rustling about among the bushes
we started a hare which hopd on a little way and stood to listen
when my companion lifted his old gun to take a aim and a sudden
shock tingld in my ears like the momentary sound of broken
glasses   we was astounded and lookd on each others faces
with vacancy — the gun had bursted and all the barrel was
carr[i]ed aw[a]y to the lock and part of the lock likwise   we
saw danger in each others faces and dare not make enquirey what
was the matter as all of us expected we were wounded but as
soon as the fright was over we found none of us was hurt
what became of the gun we coud not tell for we coud not find a
fragment but that which he held in his hand — was not this an
alarm to tell our conscence that we were doing wrong and wether
it was chance or providence that interferd it was a narrow escape

I felt the warning for once and never was caught on the same
errand again

[A25, R31-R30]

John Billings was an inofensive man   he believes every thing
that he sees in print as true and has a cupboard full of penny
books the king and the cobler Seven Sleepers[26] acounts of People
being buried so many days and then dug up alive Of bells in
churches ringing in the middle of the night Of spirits warning
men when they was to dye etc each of the relations attested by
the overseers churchwardens etc of the parish were the strange
relations happend always a century back were none lives to con-
tradict it   such things as these have had personal existances
with his memory on as firm footings as the bible history it self
      he is fond of getting cuckoos blue bells Primroses and any
favou[ri]te flowers from the fields and woods to set in his garden
and his sundays best lesures is when the weather and seasons
permits him to ramble by the river sides a fishing and we have
spent many sundays together in that diversion   [A25, R30]

these are universal feelings and the stuff which true poesy is
made of is little else   it is the eccho [of] what has been or may
be   when the reader peruses real poesy he often whispers to
[himself] 'bless me Ive felt this myself and often had such thoughts
in my memory' tho he was ignorant of poetry   nature is the
same every were   the little daisey wears the self same golden
eye and silver rim with its delicate blushing stains underneath in
our fenny flats as it does on the mountains of switzerland if it
grows there — my companion had no knowledge of poesy by
books   he had never read Thompson or Cowper or Words-
worth or perhaps heard of their names yet nature gives every one
a natural simplicity of heart to read her language tho the grosser
interferences of the world adulterate them like the bee by the
flower and deaden the heart with ignorance — he usd often to
carry a curious old book in his pocket very often a sort of jest
book calld the Pleasant art of money catching[27] and another of
Tales whose title was 'Laugh and be fat' and he felt as happy over
these while we wild away the impatience of a bad fishing day
under a green willow or an odd thorn as I did over Thompson
Cowper and Walton which I often took in my pocket to read

53

my companions books were very old and curious   the one on 'Money catching' there was a tale in it of Jougler Percy and the Butchers dog and several rules and reciepts for savings and cheap living and a colection of proverbs and a long poem of 40 or 50 verses the middle of which was gone   I fancyd some of the verses good and I think they are written by a poet perhaps Randolph[28] for there was some of his poems in the Vol particulary a satirical one on 'Importunate duns'   the verses I aluded to above are entitled lessons of Thrift some jests by Tarlton[29]   I copyd some of them out some years back and I will insert them here[30]   [A25, 9]

Lord Radstock[31] was my best friend   it was owing to him that the first Poems succeeded   he introduced them into all places were he had connections got them noticed in news papers and other [places] and if it did nothing more it made them known — he kindly undertook to settle my affairs with my Publishers which they kindly enough on their parts deffered and its not settled yet — he wrote Taylor a letter wishing him to draw up an agreement in 'black and white' as his Lordship expressd it as faiths in men was not to be trusted   Taylor pretended to be insulted at this and wrote his Lordship a genteel saucey one that setteld the affair in the present confusion of no settlings at all nay they will neither publish my poems or give them up

Lord Radstock at first sight appears to be of a stern and haughty character but the moment he speaks his countenance kindles up into a free blunt good hearted man one whom you expect to hear speak exactly as he thinks   he has no notion of either offending or pleasing by his talk and care[s] as little for the consequences of either   there is a good deal of the bluntness and openheartedness about him and there is nothing of pride or fashion   he is as plain in manner and dress as the old country squire   a stranger woud never guess that he was speaking to a Lord and tho he is one of the nobiest familys in England he seems to think nothing [of his position]   I have often observed this in real Titles   while a consieted bastard squire expects Sir at the end

54

of every word a Lord seems to take no notice how he is talkd too
— the first is jealous of his gentility and knows that his title is
nothing but the breath of words the latter knows that his was
born with him and it is a familiar [title] that sits easy on his name
— his Lordship is a large man of a commanding figure   the
bust by Behnes[32] is very like but wants expression as does the
engraving   his Lordship has only one fault and that is a faith
that takes every man [at his face value]   he and Lord fitz-
william[33] are the two [best patrons I have had]   [B6, R84]

[The Revd Isaiah Holland[34] was another friend] and [one] who
had given his undisguised opinion of them [i.e. Clare's poems]
when praise was of most value and when nobody else had even
ventured an opinion except a doubt of their merits and whom I
aught to have mentiond first on my list of friends   he came
over as soon as the book was publis[h]ed and before I was aware
of its fate but I instantly read my success in his countenance for he
opend the door eagerly and laughd as he shook me by the hand
saying 'Well am not I a good prophet'   I told him that I had
not heard the fate of the book as yet and he said then I am more
happy in being the herald of good News for I can assure you that
your utmost hopes has succeeded as I recieved a letter this morn-
ing from a literary friend who spoke it as a certainty that your
poems woud take and he has given them hearty praise   this
enlivend me and we chatterd over the results of the future all the
afternoon — when he first came to see me I was copying out the
'Village funeral'[35] to send to Drury and as he leand over my shoul-
der to read it he said 'these are the things that will do and if they
do not succeed the world deserves a worse opinion then I am
inclined to give it but go on and be not cast down by the doubts
or surmises of any one'   this was the prophecy to which he
aluded when he came to tell me of my success — I dedicated the
poem of the Woodman[36] to him as a trifling return for his kind-
ness   the chance that led me to his acquantance was his meet-
ing with one of the papers printed by Henson of Deeping and he
made further enquireys at a farmers house were he used to visit

who was well acquanted with me and my family and as they gave
a favourable account of my character as a quiet inoffensive fellow
he expressd a desire to see me and sent for me but I did not like
to show my head any were at that time so my mother went over
in my stead when as he asked her several enquireys and desired
her to caution me against Hensons printing the poems as he
thought it woud go a great way to ruin the success they might
meet with else were and said he woud come over to see me as he
accordingly did   he was excessively fond of Kirk White[37]
such a friendship as this is worth the remembrance   he had no
other interest then that of wishing me well and did it heartily
he now lives at St Ives and if the Newspapers tell the truth he is
married   [A25, 21-2]

[Books]

My acquantance of books is not so good as later oppertunitys
might have made it for I cannot and never coud plod thro every a
book in a regular mecanical way   as I meet with [it] I dip in to
it here and there and if it does not suit I lay it down and seldom
take it up again but in the same manner I read Thompsons Sea-
sons and Miltons Paradise Lost thro when I was a boy and they
are the only books of Poetry that I have reguraly read thro yet
as to history I never met with the chance of getting at [it] yet and
in novels my taste is very limited   Tom Jones Robinson Crusoe
and the Vicar of Wakefield are all that I am acquainted with
they are old acquantan[ces] and I care not to make new ones
tho I have often been offerd the perusal of the Waverly Novels I
declind it and [though] the readily remaining in ignorance of
them is no trouble yet my taste may be doubted for I hear much
in their praise and believe them good — I read the vicar of Wake-
field over every Winter and am delighted tho I always feel dissap-
pointed at the end[ing] of it happily with the partings   my
mind cannot feel that it ends happily with [the] reader   I usd

56

to be uncommonly fond of looking over catalogues of books and am so still they [are] some of the earliest readings that oppertunitys alowd me to come at if ever I bought a penny worth of slate pencils or[38] Wafers or a few sheets of Paper at Drakards[39] they were sure to be lapt in a catalogue and I considerd them as the most va[l]uable parts of my purchase and greedily lookd over their contents and now in cutting open a new book or Magazine I always naturaly turn to the end first to read the book list and take the rest as a secondary pleasure

Anticipation is the sweetest of earthly pleasures it is smiling hope standing on tiptoes to look for pleasure — the cutting open a new book the watching the opening of a new planted flower at spring etc   [A34,1][40]

The first books I got hold of beside the bible and prayer book was an old book of Essays with no title and then a large one on Farming Robin hoods Garland and the Scotch Rogue[41] — The old book of Farming and Essays belongd to an old Mr Gee[42] who had been a farmer and who lived in a part of our house which once was his own — he had had a good bringing up and was a desent scholar and he was always pleasd to lend me them even before I coud read them without so much spelling and guesses at words so as to be able to make much of them or understand them
                                                                            [A31, 216]

I became acquainted with Robinson Crusoe very early in life having borrowd it of a boy at Glinton school of the name of Stimson who only dare lend it me for a few days for fear of his uncles knowing of it to whom it belongd yet I had it a sufficient time to fill my fancys with new Crusoes and adventures

From these friendships I gatherd more acquaintance with books which like chances oppertunitys were but sparing
                                                                            [A25, R32]

the common people know the name of Chatterton as an unfortunate poet and the name of Shakspear as a great play writer but the ballad monger whose productions supplies hawkers with their ware are poets with them and they imagine one as great as the other   so much for that envied eminence of common fame — on the other hand there is somthing in it to wish for because there are things as old as England that has out lived centurys of popularitys nay left half its historys in darkness and lives on as common on every memory as the seasons and as familiar to childern even as the rain and spring flowers — I alude to the old superstitions fragments of l[e]gends and storys in ryhme that are said to be norman and saxon etc   there is a many desires too to meet this common fame and it is mostly met with in a manner where it is the least expected — while some affectations are striveing for a life time to hit all tastes by writing as they *fancy* and as they falsely believe all feel and misses the mark by a wide throw — an unconsious poet of little name [f]or fame writes a trifle as he feels without thinking of others [nor] *fancying* he feels it and becomes a common name unaffected simpley [in] the truth of nature and her every day picture — thus [the] little childerns favourites of Cock robin little red riding hood [and] babes in the wood etc etc have impressions at the core that grow [up] with manhood and are beloved on a poet anxious after common fame as some of the 'naturals' seem to be imitate[ing] these things by affected simplicity and become unnatural — these things have found fames were the greatest names are still oblivions   a literary man might enquire after the names of Spencer and Milton etc in vain thro half the villages in england even among what are call[d] its gentry but I believe it woud be hard to find a corner in any county were the others were not known — I[n] my days some of the pieces of the modern poets have gaind this common popularity which must be distinguished [from] fame as it may only live for a season — Wordsworths beautiful simple ballad 'We are seven' I have seen hawkd about in penny ballads and Tannahill song of Jessey[43] has met with more popularity then all the songs English and Scottish put together

[B3, 79]

If common fame was the highest species of fame — I woud rather
chuse to be the Author of cock robin the babes in the wood etc
then Paradise lost or the fairey queen for you cannot find a village
in england that owns an old woman to be a stranger to cock robin
or the babes in the wood   you may find a thousand were even
the highest people in it know nothing of Spencer or Milton
further then the name and very often not that   [B3, 80]

[*Learning*]

As to my learning I am not wonderfully deep in s[c]i[e]nce or
[   ] nor so wonderfully ignorant as many may have fancied
from reading the accounts which my friends gave of me   if I
was to brag of it I might like the village schoolmaster boast of
knowing a little of every thing a jack of all trades and master of
none   I puzzled over every thing in my hours of leisure that
came in my way Mathematics Astronomy Botany and other
things with a restless curiosity that was ever on the enquirey and
never satisfied and when I got set fast with one thing I did not tire
but tryed at another tho with the same success in the end   yet
it never sickened me   I still pursued Knowledge in a new path
and tho I never came off victor I was never conqured[44]

[B3, 81]

Common sense would never covet the property that belongs to
another   I could not feel happy with the wealth that I had
no right to and therefore feel a greater happiness in peace and
poverty then I should do in the riches of lawless force and un-
checked rebellion — I do not know from what cause I inherit this
feeling unless the little wisdom I have gotten imbued me with it
— but this I do think   if I had not been taught to read and write
I should not have indulged in such scruples   tho I might not
have joined the violence of mobs I should not have seen the
unlawful cupidity of their notions of right and freedom as I do

59

now and therefore I feel happy with the little learning that my
parents gave me as the best legacy fortune could ever bestow

[B5, 74]

The neighbours believing my learning to be great thought it a folly
in me to continue at hard work when they fancyd I might easily
better my self by my learning and as Lord Milton[45] was a great
friend to my father they persuaded me to go to Milton[46] to see what
he woud do for me and the parish clerk a man of busy merits who
taught the sunday school offerd to go with me as he knew his
Lordship better then I did by seeing him at the Sunday school
often   I accepted the proposal and started once more upon
ambitious and hithertoo fruitless errands   I remember the
morning   we saw two crows as soon as we got into the fields
and harpd on good luck and success[47] and my companion gave
me advice with the authority of a patron as well as a frend   as
soon as we got there on making the nessesary enquiries we was
told that his Lordship woud see us bye and bye and hour passd
after hour till night came and told us we was dissapointed and the
porter conforted us by saying we shoud call again tomorning but
my friend the Clerk had more wits in the way and we met his
Lordship the next day at the heath farm near home which he was
in the habit of visiting often   as soon as we came up to his
Lordship my companion began to descant on my merrits in a way
that made me hang my head but I found he had a double errand
for before he finishd his tale of my [talents] he pulld an antique
box out of his pocket which he had found in leveling some head-
lands near eastwell spring a spot famous for summer sunday
revels   it was in the for[m] of an apple pye and containd
several farthings of king charles the firsts or second[s] reign and
begd his lordship to do somthing for me and upon hearing to
whom I belongd he promisd he woud   his Lordship smild and
took it and gave him a good exchange for his curosity which raisd
the clerks voice in the conclusion of his story of me and when his
Lordship heard to whom I belongd he promisd to do somthing
for me but such trifling things are soon shovd out of the memorys

of such people who have plenty of other things to think of   I
heard no more of it and workd on at my old employments as usual
     I had now many schemes and plans in my mind of what I coud
or might do   I had improvd by frequent trials in ryhming and
often felt that I might gain some notice in times to come   I fancyd
too that I was book learnd for I had gotten together by savings a
quantity of old books of motly merits all of which Drury got for a
little or nothing   I will reccolect some of them   there was
the yong mans best companion Dilworths Wingates Hodders
Vyses and Cockers Arithmetic   the last was a favourite with
me and I kept it   Bonnycastles and Horners Mensuration and
Wards Mathematics Leybourns and Morgans Dialling Female
Shipwright Robinson Crusoe Pilgrims Progress Martindales Land
surveying and Cockers Land surveying Hills Herbal Balls Astrol-
ogy Culpeppers Herbal Rays History of the Rebellion Hudibras
some Numbers of Josephus Parnells Poems Miltons Paradise Lost
Thompsons Seasons Sam Westleys Poems Hemmings Algebra
Sturms Reflections Harveys Meditations Wallers Poems Westleys
Philosophy Thompsons Travels Lestranges Fables of Esop A book
on Commets Life of Barnfield more Carew The Art of Gauging
Duty of Man Watts Hymns Lees Botany Waltons Angler Kings
Tricks of London laid open The Fathers Legacy or seven stages of
Life[48] Bloomfields Poems   some of these books were great
favourites particularly Waltons Angler tho I never caught any
more fish then usual by its instructions   I bought it at a book
stall kept by a shoe k[n]acker of the name of Adams at Stamford
for 2 shillings and I gave it to my friend O. Gilchrist[49]   the
Female Shipwright was a winter evening favourite in my first book
days   it b[e]llongd to my uncle and was a true story printed by
subscription for the woman whose history it related   Bloom-
fields Poems was great favourites and Hills Herbal gave me a taste
for wild flowers which I lovd to hunt after and collect to plant in
my garden which my father let me have in one corner of the garden
and on happening to meet with Lees Botany second hand I fell to
collecting them into familys and tribes but it was a dark system
and I abandond it with a dissatisfaction   (A25, 2-4]

I have puzzled wasted hours over Lees Botany to understand a shadow of the system so as to be able to class the wild flowers peculiar to my own neighbourhood for I find it woud require a second Adam to find names for them in my way and a second Solomon to understand them in Lennsis system — moder[n] works are so mystified by systematic symbols that one cannot understand them till the wrong end of ones lifetime and when one turns to the works of Ray Parkinson and Gerrard[51] were there is more of nature and less of Art it is like meeting the fresh air and balmy summer of a dewey morning after the troubled dreams of a nightmare   [B3, 73]

to look at nature with a poetic feeling magnifyes the pleasure yet Naturalists and Botanists seem to have little or no taste for this sort of feeling   they merely make a collection of dryd specimens classing[52] them after Lienneus into tribes and familys as a sort of curiosity and fame   I have nothing of this curosity about me tho I feel as happy as they can in finding a new spiecies of field flower or butterflye which I have not before seen   yet I have no desire further to dry the plant or torture the Butterflye by sticking it on a cork board with a pin   I have no wish to do this if my feelings woud let me   I only wish them to settle on a flower till I can come up with them to examine the powderd colours on their wings and then they may flutter off from fancyd danger and welcom   I feel gratified   [B5, 46]

I also was fond of gather[ing] fossil stones   tho I never knew these was the subject of books yet I was pleasd to find and collect them which I did many years tho my mother threw them out of doors when they was in her way   a D[r] Dupere of Crowland collected such things and my friend John Turnill got some for him   this gave me the taste for fossil hunting   my friend Artis[53] had what was left when I became acquainted with him   my habits of Study grew anxious and restless and increasd into a multiplicity of things poetry natural history Mathematics etc but I had little ambition to write down any thing but my ryhmes   these were on local circumstances mostly and on spots and things which I felt a fondness for   two or three of a Satirical nature I will insert here   the 'Elegy on the Death of a quack' was written on a quack Docter who came to Deeping and whom the dupd people calld Docter Touch[54] as it was rumourd about on his first appear[en]ce there that he curd all diseases by touching the patient with his hand which made the Villages round all anxious to know the truth of it   lame and blind and such felt a vain hope that he might be inspird and sent on purpose for their relief and Deeping was threatend to be as crowded with cripples as the Pool of Bethsheba[55]   my Father and Will Farrow the shoemaker mentiond awhile back[56] went over to Deeping directly on his arival there to assertain the truth and leave their infirmitys behind them if possible but experience put a new face on the story   the fellow did not cure them by touch but by blisters which he laid on in unmercifull sizes at half a guinea a blister and the money was to be paid down before he did his work

this last demand compleatly shook my fathers faith as to his mission for he understood that [the] prophets of old curd for nothing and he expected to see modern miracles performd in the same manner but when he found it was no such thing he and his companion refusd to have any thing to do with the medical prophet who was very importunate and even abusive at their credulity   when they returnd home and told their tale I sat down and wrote the following Epitaph[57]   the fellow stopt at Deeping a good while for he found plenty of believers to mentain his hoaxing pretensions   in his bills he made a great parade against all knowledge and the faculty and made a boast of his ignorance by starting what he thought a better plea in making his patients believe he was born a docter by being the seventh son of a parent who was himself a seventh son and the seventh son of a seventh son is reckond among the lower orders of people as [a] prodigy in medicine who is born to perform miracles so he readily got into fame amongst them till 2 or 3 of his patients dyd under his hands and then on the turning of the tide he decampd in the night   I wrote another long tale on the Docter and the shoe-

63

maker but it is not worth inserting[58]   the following was writ-
ten on an old woman with a terrible share of tongue who was
actually married to a sixth husband and survivd them[59]   I only
regret the loss of one of my early poems a sort of Pastoral   the
title was 'labour and luxury'   the plan was a labourers going to
his work one morning overheard a lean figure [accosted] in a
taunting manner by a bloated stranger the phantom of luxury
whence the dialogue ensues   labour makes its complaints and
the other taunts and jeers him till the lean figure turns away in
dispair[60]   [A25, 2-6]

Beginnings with the World

I never had much relish for the pastimes of youth   instead of
going out on the green at the town end on Winter sundays to play
foot ball I stuck to my corner stool poreing over a book   in fact
I grew so fond of being alone at last that my mother was feign to
force me into company for the neighbours had assured her mind
into the fact that I was no better then crazy   at length my
school days was to be at an end as I was thought learned enough
for my intended trade which was to be a shoe maker
                                                      [B8, R128]

My scholarship was to extend no farther than to qualify me for
the business of a shoemaker or Stone Mason so I learnd cross
multiplication for the one and bills of accounts for the other but I
was not to be either   at last a man of the Name of Mowbray of
Glinton woud have taken me for a trifle and another at home
namd Farrow a little deformd fellow was desirious of taking me
merely out of kindness to my father but the trifle they wanted
coud not be found and I did not much relish the confinment of
apprentiship   this Will Farrow was a village wit a very droll
fellow a sort of Easop   his shop usd to be a place of amusment
for the young ploughmen and labour[er]s on winter evenings

64

he was famous for a joke and a droll story and had a peculiar knack at making up laughable anecdotes on any circumstance which happend in the village — and a satirical turn for applying nicknames to people who was almost sure to be call[d] by the one given till the day they dyd and remem[b]erd by it afterwards when their own was forgotten   many of his names are now afloat in the village — he has a brother living now who was a sailor 21 years and who kept a Journal of his life which he got me to copy out in part   there was nothing particular in it but a mention of Lord Byron who saild in the same ship and was known among the sailors as a Traveller and not as a poet and I myself was ignorant of him alltogether when I copied out his account of him

I cannot ascertain what time it was when he saild with him but doubtless child Harrold had no existance with the world then

I have since reflected on this interesting circumstance and often tryd to remember it   he describd him as a odd young man lame of one foot on which he wore a cloth shoe who was of a resolute temper fond of bathing in the sea and going ashore to see ruins in a rough sea when it required 6 hands to manage the boat   such additional trouble teazd the sailors and teazd them so much that his name became a bye word in the ship for unessesary trouble   Tom Farrow I believe was then an ableseaman in the Fox Cutter   he now lives at Deeping St James and follows his trade of a Mason and bricklayer   [B8, 103-2]

After I had done with going to school it was proposd that I shoud be bound apprentice to a shoe maker[61] but I rather dislikd this bondage   I whimperd and turned a sullen eye upon every persuasion till they gave me my will   A neighbour then offerd to learn me his trade to be a stone mason but I dislikd this too and shoyd off with the excuse of not liking to climb tho I had clumb trees in raptures after the nests of Kites and magpies   my parents not liking to force me to any thing against my inclination their hopes was once more at a stand   I was then sent for to drive plough at woodcroft castle of Oliver Cromwell memory tho Mrs Bellairs[62] the mistress was a kind good woman and

65

tho the place was a very good one for living my mind was set against it from the first and I was uneasily at rest   one of the disagreeable things was getting up so soon in the morning as they are much earlier in some places then in others and another was getting wetshod in my feet every morning and night for in wet weather the moat usd to flow over the causway that led to the porch and as there was but one way to the house we was obligd to wade up to the knees to go in and out excepting when the head man carried the boys over on his back as he somtimes woud   I staid here one month and then on coming home to see my parents they coud not persuade me to return   they now gave up all hopes of doing any good with me and fancied that I shoud make nothing but a soldier but luckily in this dilemma a next door neighbour at the Blue Bell Francis Gregory wanted me to drive plough and as I suited him he made proposals to hire me for a year which as it had my consent my parents readily agreed to it was a good place   they treated me more like a son then a servant   I believe I may say that this place was the nursery for my ryhmes   [B8, 101]

F Gregory

He was fond of amusment and a singer tho his notes was not more varied then those of the cuckoo as he had but 2 Songs for all companys one called 'the milking pail' and the other 'Jack with his broom'[63]   his jokes too were like a pack of cards   they were always the same but told in a different turn[64]

[D2, 2]

I livd at this place a year and left with the restless hope of being somthing better than a plough boy   my little ambitions kept burning about me every now and then[65] to make a better figure in the world and I knew not what to be at — A bragging fellow name Manton from Market Deeping usd to frequent the public house

when I livd there   he was a stone cutter and sign painter
    he usd to pretend to discover somthing in me as deserving
encouragment and wanted to take me apprentice to learn the mis-
terys of his art but then he wanted the trifle with me that had dis-
sapointed my former prosperitys   he usd to talk of his abilitys
in sculpture and painting over his beer till I was almost mad with
anxiety to be a sign painter and stone cutter but it was usless[66]
    such things made my mind restless and on hearing from a
friend Tom Porter of Ashton Green that the Kitchen Gardiner at
Burghley wanted an apprent[ice][67]   [B3, 83]

I was with them without a salary   I thought it was a chance of
being somthing so I got my father to go with me to see if I might
be excepted   [A34, R7]

[*Clare considered various opportunities of employment before he entered
the kitchen-garden at Burghley: as a shoemaker's apprentice with Will
Farrow, as a stonemason's apprentice with George Shelton, as a sign-
painter (this possibly with Mowbray of Glinton), and as a clerk to his
uncle's employer at Wisbech. Before the last of these opportunities arose
he also worked as a ploughboy for Mrs Bellairs at Woodcroft Castle. Upon
his rejection at Wisbech he entered the service of Francis Gregory at the
Blue Bell. It was from Gregory's service that he moved to Burghley. It is
impossible to preserve the order of these events in Clare's autobiographi-
cal fragments and so we must now retrace our steps a little and hear what
Clare has to say about George Shelton, Woodcroft Castle, and Wisbech
before once again taking up the narrative at the point where he left Greg-
ory's and started work at Burghley. Eds.*]

George Shelton too a Stone Mason woud have taken me but I got
off by urging a dislike to climbing tho my fondness for climbing
trees after birds nests went against me and my parents hopes
were almost gone as they thought I sham[me]d abraham with a
dislike to work and a view to have my liberty and to remain idle
but the fact was I felt timid and fearful of undertaking the first trial
in every thing   they woud not urge me to any thing against

my will so I livd on at home taking Work as it fell   I went weed-
ing wheat in the Spring with old women listening to their songs
and storys which shortend the day and in summer I joind the
haymakers in the meadow or helpd upon the stacks   when I
was out of work I went to the woods gathering rotten sticks or
picking up the dryd cow dung on the pasture which we calld
cazons for fireing[68]   thus I livd a season spending the intervals
at play along with she[e]ptenders or herd boys in lone spots out
of sight for I had grown big enough to feel ashamd of it and I felt a
sort of hopless prospect around me of not being able to meet man-
hood as I coud wish for I had always that feeling of ambition
about me that wishes to do somthing to gain notice or to rise
above its fellows   my ambition then was to be a good writer
and I took great pains in winter nights to learn my Friend John
Turnill setting me copies who by the bye was far from a good
writer himself   I was fond of books before I began to write
poetry   these were such that chance came at — 6py Pamphlets
that are in the possession of every door calling hawker and found
on every book stall at fairs and markets whose titles are as familiar
with every one as his own name   shall I repeat some of them
    'Little red riding hood'[69] 'Valentine and Orson' 'Jack and the
Jiant' 'Tom Long the carrier' 'The king and the cobler' 'Sawney
Bean' 'The seven Sleepers' 'Tom Hickathrift' 'Johnny Armstrong'
'Idle Laurence' who carried that power spell about him that laid
every body to sleep — 'old mother Bunch' 'Robin Hoods garland'
'old mother Shipton and old Nixons Prophecys' 'History of
Gotham' and many others   shall I go on   no these have
memorys as common as Prayer books and Psalters with the
peasentry   such were the books that delighted me and I savd
all the pence I got to buy them for they were the whole world of
literature to me and I knew of no other   I carried them in my
pocket and read them at my leisure and they was the never weary
food of winter evenings ere milton Shakspear and thompson had
an existe[nce] in my memory and I even feel a love for them still
    nay I cannot help fancying now that cock robin babes in the
wood mother hubbard and her cat etc etc are real poetry in all its

68

native simplicity and as it shoud be   I know I am foolish enough to have fancys different from others and childhood is a strong spell over my feelings but I think so on and cannot help it

after I had been left to my idle leisures while doing jobs as I coud catch them I was sent for to drive plough at Woodcroft Castle of Oliver Cromwell memory[70]. . . it is a curious old place and was made rather famous in the rebellion of Oliver Cromwell — some years back there was a curious old bow found in one of the chimneys and the vulgar notion was that it was the identical bow that belongd to robin hood so readily does that name assosiate it self in the imagination with such things and places   I had a coin of Cromwells brought me last year by a neighbour pickd up in the neighboring field as large as a crown piece which I gave to my friend Artis   I stopt at this first place about a month and then on coming home to see my parents they coud not persuade me to return   they now gave up all hopes of doing any thing with me and fancyd that I shoud make nothing but a soldier

it was but a bad start to be sure and I felt ashamd of myself almost but my mind woud be master and I coud not act other wise

in this dilemma my Uncle who livd as footman with a counselor at Wisbeach came over to see us and said there was a vacancy in his masters office and he woud try and get me the place as he was certain I was scholar good enough for it and tho my father and mother was full as certain of it I doubted my abilitys very strongly but was glad to accept the proposal of going over to try[71]

[B8, 104-5]

Wisbeach

My uncle morris came over to see us and said he woud ask his master to take me as a writer

My hopes of bettering my station with the world was again revised and I started for Wisbeach with a timid sort of pleasure and when I got to Glinton turnpike I turnd back to look on the old church as if I was going in to another co[u]ntry   Wisbeach was a foreign land to me for I had never been above 8 miles from home in my life and I coud not fancy england much larger then the part I knew   at Peterboro Brig I got into the boat that carrys passengers to wisbeach once a week and returns the third day a distance of 21 miles for eighteenpence   I kept thinking all the way in the boat what answers I shoud make to the questions askd and then I put questions to myself and shapd proper replies as I thought woud succeed and then my heart burnt within me at the hopes of success and thoughts of the figure I shoud make afterwards when I went home to see my friends dressd up as a writer in a law[y]ers office   I coud scarcely contain my self at times and even broke out into a tittering laugh but I was dampd quickly when I thought of the impossibilitys of success for I had no prepossesing appearance to win favours for such a place   my mother had turnd me up as smart as she coud   she had pressd me a white neckcloth and got me a pair of gloves to hide my coarse hands but I had out grown my coat and almost left the sleeves at the elbows and all my other garments betrayd too old an acquantance with me to make me as genteel as coud have been wishd but I had got my fathers and mothers blessings and encouragments and my own hopes in the bargain made me alltogether stout in the dreams of success   at length the end of my journey approachd when the passengers lookd out to see wisbeach brig that stretches over the river in one arch   my heart swoond within me at [the] near approach of my destiny 'to be or not to be'   I kept working my wits up how to make the best use of my tongue while the boatmen was steering for the shore and when I was landed my thoughts was so busy that I had almost forgot the method of finding out the house by enquiring for Counseler Bellamys   people star[e]d at me and pausd before they pointed down the street as if they thought me mistaken in the name   'And are you sure it is Counseller Bellamys you want' said another — 'I am sure of it' I said and they showed me the house in a reluctanty way   when I got up to the house I was puzzld as I often have been in finding but one entrance were a

fine garden gate with a 'ring the bell' seemd to frown upon me as
upon one too mean to be admitted   I pausd and felt fearful to
ring   [B3, 78]

I was puzzld what to do and wish[d] my self a thousand times
over in my old corner at home   at length my hand trembld and
pulld the bell   it wrang and to my great satisfaction my uncle
came being the only man servant and bade me welcome — I have
told master about your coming said he   you must not hang
your head but look up boldly and tell him what you can do — so
I went into the kitchen as bold as I coud and sat down to tea but
ate nothing   I had filld my stomach with thoughts by the way
      at length the counsellor appeard and I held up my head as
well as I coud but it was like my hat almost under my arm
'Aye aye so this is your Nephew Morris is he' said the couns[e]llor
      'yes Sir' said my uncle   'Aye aye so this is your Nephew'
repeated the counsellor rubbing his hands as he left the room
'well I shall see him agen' — but he never saw me agen to this day
— I felt happily mortified for the trial was over   I was not
much dissapointed for I thought all the way that I cut but a poor
figure for a law[y]ers clerk   so far it seems I was right   the
next morning my uncle said that his mistress had bade him to
make me welcome and to keep me till sunday morning when the
boat returnd to Peterbro so I spent Saturday a[72] looking about the
town after amusment   I was fond of peeping into booksellers
windows and I found one full of paintings as specimens of a
painter who was taking portraits and teaching drawing in the
town   they was the early travels after fame of a name well
known with the World now — Rippingille[73] — I remember one of
them was the 'Village ale house' another was a pencil sketch of
the Letter carrier in the town whose face seemd to be familiar
with every one that passd by   the rest I have forgotten — I
little thought when I was looking at these things that I shoud be
a poet and become a familiar accquantance with that painter who
had blinded the windows with his attempts for fame — Poets and
painters grow ashamd of their early productions and perhaps

71

my friend Rippengill will not thank me for bringing up this assosiation of his early days   yet I dont see what occasion they have to feel so for all things have a begining and surely it is a pleasure in happiness to review the rough road of anxietys and trouble in gaining it — on Sunday morning my uncle saw me to the boat and I left Wisbeach and my disapointment behind me with an ernest tho melancholy feeling of satisfaction and I made up for my lost ambition by the thoughts of once more seeing home and its snug fireside   my parents welcomd me home with a mellancholy smile that bespoke their feelings of dissapointment as I sat upon my corner stool and related my adventures but good luck was at my elbow with a more humble and more suitable occupation   Francis Gregory our neighbour at the blue bell wanted a servant and hir[e]d me for a year   I was glad and readily agreed   it was a good place and they treated me more like a son then a servant and I believe this place was the nursery for that lonly and solitary musing which ended in rhyme

I usd to be generaly left alone to my toils for the master was a very weak man and always ailing and my labours were not very burthensome being horse or cow tending weeding etc when I made up for the loss of company by talking to myself and enga[gi]ng my thoughts with any subject that came uppermost in my mind   one of my worst labours was a journey to a distant village name Maxey in winter afternoons to fetch flour once and somtimes twice every week   in these journeys I had hanted spots to pass   as the often heard tales of ghosts and hobgobblings had made me very fearful to pass such places at night it being often nearly dark ere I got there I usd to employ my mind as well as I was able to put them out of my head so I usd to imagine tales and mutter them over as I went on making my self the hero somtimes making my self a soldier and tracing the valours [of] history onwards thro varius successes till I became a great man   somtimes it was a love story not fraught with many incidents of knight errant[r]y but full of successes as uncommon and out of the way as a romance travelling about in foreign lands and under going a variety of adventures till at

length a fine lady was found with a great fortune that made me a
gentleman and my mind woud be so bent on the reveries som-
times that I have often got to the town unawares and felt a sort of
dissapointment in not being able to finish my story tho I was glad
of the escape from the haunted places   I know not what made
me write poetry but these journeys and my toiling in the fields by
myself gave me such a habit for thinking that I never forgot it and
I always mutterd and talkd to myself afterwards and have often
felt ashamd at being overheard by people that overtook me   it
made my thoughts so active that they become troublesome to me
in company and I felt the most happy to be alone   On sundays
I usd to feel a pleasure to hide in the woods instead of going to
church to nestle among the leaves and lye upon a mossy bank
were the fir like fern its under forest keeps

'In a strange stillness'

watching for hours the little insects climb up and down the tall
stems of the woodgrass and broad leaves

'Oer the smooth plantain leaf a spacious plain'[74]

or reading the often thumbd books which I possesd till fancy
'made them living things'   I lovd the lonly nooks in the fields
and woods and many favourite spots had lasting places in my
Memory   'the boughs that when a school boy screend my
head' before inclosure destroyd them[75]   [A43, R18-R16]

Gardener Boy at Burghley

It was thought that I shoud never be able for hard work and I
chusd the trade of a Gardener when A companion of mine
Thomas Porter of Ashton told me that the master of the kitchen
gardens at burghley wanted an apprentice so off my father took
me   it was a fine sabbath morning and when we arrivd he mis-
taking every body for gentlemen that wore white stockings pulld

off his hat to the gardiner as if it had been the Marquis himself
    I often thought after wards how the fellow felt his consequ-
ence at the sight for he was an ignorant proud fellow   he took
me and I was to stop three years   my work for the time I staid
was taking vegetables and fruit down to the hall once or twice a
day and go on errand to Stamford as requird...[76]

[A34, R12]

and I was often sent to Stamford at all hours in the night for one
thing or other somtimes for liquors and somtimes to seek him by
the mistresses orders and as I was of a timid disposition I [was]
very often fearful of going and instead of seeking him I usd to lye
down under a tree in the Park and fall a sleep and in the Autumn
nights the ryhme usd to fall and cover me on one side like a sheet
which affected my side with a numbness and I have felt it ever
since at spring and fall and I often times think that the illness
which oppresses me now while I write this narative proceeds
from the like cause tho I have often made the fields a bed since
then when I have been at merry makings and stopt out when all
were abed and at other times when I had taken too much of Sir
John Barleycorn and coud get no further   after I had been there
a few weeks I savd my money to purchase Abercrombies Garden-
ing which became my chief study   the gardens was very large
but when I was there[77]   and I remember finding some curious
flowers which I had never seen before growing wild among the
vegetables   one was a yellow head ache perrenial and another
was a blue one   anual   I never saw none like them before
or since   [A34, R4]

I learnt irregular habbits at this place which I had been a stranger
too had I kept at home   tho we was far from a town yet con-
finement sweetens liberty and we stole every oppertunity to get
over to Stamford on summer evenings   when I had no money
to spend my elder companions woud offer to treat me for the
sake of my company there and back agen and to keep me from
divulging the secret to my master by making me a partner in their

74

midnight revels   we usd to get out of the window and climb
over the high wall of the extensive gardens for we slept in the
garden house and was locked in every night to keep us from rob-
bing the fruit I expect — Our place of rendevouse was a public
house calld 'the Hole in the wall' famous for strong ale and mid-
night merriment kept by a hearty sort of fellow calld Tant Baker
(I suppose the short name for Antony)[78]   he had formerly been
a servant at Burghley and his house in consequence was a favour-
ite place with the burghley servants always   he dyd last year
1822 very rich — I wrote a long poem in praise of his ale in the
favourit scotch metre of Ramsay and Burns[79]   it was not good
but there are parts of it worthy as I think of a better fate then being
utterly lost   it has long been out of my possesion   My
friend Gilchrist told me after I had shown it to him that the house
had been long celebrated by drunken Barnaby and that he him-
self had gaind a nich[e] of [im]mortality for Tant Baker in a new
Edition of that work   [A34, R13]

G. Cousins

I workd with a man here of a very singular character who knew
more ghost storys and marvelous adventures then I had ever met
with before and he was one of the most s[i]mple mind   he
even believd any thing that was imposd on him for truth in a seri-
ous manner and nothing but a laugh at his credulity woud shake
his faith   he was of a good memory and the only books he read
was Abercrombies gardening and the Bible and he woud repeat
a whole chapter by heart and remember the texts which he heard
at church years bye   he believd in witches and often whisperd
his suspicions of suspected neighbours in the Village   he had
a great taste for looking about churches and church yards and
woud go ten miles on a sunday to visit one which he had not seen
before to read the epitaphs and get those he liked best by heart
     he had an odd taste for gentlemans coats of arms and collected

75

all the livery buttons he coud meet with   he had workd in the garden 33 years   his name was George Cousins[80]   he was one of the most singular inofensive men I ever met with

[A34, R11]

...the man [master of the kitchen gardens] was of so harsh a temper that none likd him and the foreman being weary of the place as well as myself he persuaded me to go with him so we got up early one morning in the autumn and started for Grantham[81] which we reachd the first night a distance of 21 miles and I thought to be sure I was out of the world   we slept at an alehouse calld the crown and anchor and I wishd my self at home often enough before morning but it was too late then   our enquireys not meeting work there we travelld on to Newark on trent[82] and there we got Work at a Nurserymans of the name of Withers and lodgd at a lame mans house of the Name of Brown whose son was a carpenter and celebrated for making fiddles I felt quite lost while I was here tho it was a very livly town but I had never been from hom[e] before scarc[e]ly farther then out of the sight of the steeple   I became so ignorant in this far land that I coud not tell what quarter the wind blew from and I even was foolish enough to think the suns course was alterd and that it rose in the west and sat in the east   I often puzzld at it to set my self right but I still thought so   I rem[em]ber the fine old castle that stands bye the river and I stood upon the bridge one night to look at it by moonlight and if I remember rightly there is a brick mansion raisd up in its ruins which are inhabited and the light from the windows gleaming thro the ruins gave it an awful appearance at night somthing akin to the old ruined castles inhabited by banditti in roman[c]es   we did not stay here long for the master did not give us wages sufficient paying us one part and promising us the rest if we suited him by a further trial so we[83] got up earlier then usual one morning to start and as we was not much burthend with luggage we easily stole away undetected and left our credit with our host ninepence half penny in debt we got to Stamford the same night but dare not show ourselves in a

76

public house so we went thro and lay under a tree in the park
the ryhme fell thick in the night and we was coverd as white as a
sheet when we got up   [A34, R12-R11]

We workd awhile in the nursery at hoeing the weeds up between
the young trees and as the ground was baked very hard in the sun
it was much too heavy for my strength for I was but a boy   the
wages we got was small tho the master promisd us more if we
suited him by a further trial but neither the wages or work suited
me for my mind was ill at rest   the strength of my companion
was stubborn enough for any toil but mine was young and feeble
and like my mind strange and unfit with the world[84]   the
Nottinghamshire Milit[i]a was then recruiting at Newark[85] and
I fled my toils and listed tho I was of a timid disposition but
Milit[i]a had not the terror hanting name of a regular soldier   I
went to Nottingham to be sworn in but was found too short and
felt very glad of the escape afterwards — (the road parts at the
foot of Newark bridge into a Y and that towards the left was the
road for [Nottingham]   I had often heard of Nott[ing]ham in
Robin Hoods Songs and thought it was [incomplete]
                                        [A34, R11-R10]

Chapter 5   My first attempts at Poetry etc etc

I now followd gardening for a while in the Farmers Gardens
about the village and workd in the fields when I had no other
employment to go too   poetry was a troublsome but pleasant
companion anoying and cheering me at my toils   I coud not
stop my thoughts and often faild to keep them till night so when
I fancyd I had hit upon a good image or natural description I usd
to steal into a corner of the garden and clap it down but the
appearance of my employers often put my fancys to flight and
made me loose the thought and the muse together for I always
felt anx[i]ous to consceal my scribbling and woud as leave have

confessd to be a robber as a ryhmer   when I workd in the fields
I had more oppertunitys to set down my thoughts and for this
reason I liked to work in the fields and bye and bye forsook gar-
dening all together till I resumd at Casterton   I usd to drop
down behind a hedge bush or dyke and write down my things
upon the crown of my hat and when I was more in a hip for think-
ing then usual I usd to stop later at nights to make up my lost time
in the day[86]   thus I went on writing my thoughts down and
correcting them at leisure spending my sundays in the woods or
heaths to be alone for that purpose and I got a bad name among
the weekly church goers forsaking the 'church going bell' and
seeking the religion of the fields tho I did it for no dislike to church
for I felt uncomfortable very often but my heart burnt over the
pleasures of solitude and the restless revels of ryhme that was
eternaly sapping my memorys like the summer sun over the tink-
ling brook till it one day shoud leave them dry and unconsous of
the thrilling joys brin[g]ing anxiety and restless cares which it
had created and the praises and censures which I shall leave
behind me   I knew nothing of the poets experience then or I
shoud have remaind a labourer on and not livd to envy the ignor-
ance of my old companions and fellow clowns   I wish I had
never known any other   tho I was not known as a poet my odd
habits did not escape notice   they fancied I kept aloof from
company for some sort of study   others believd me crazd and
some put more criminal interpretations to my rambles and said I
was night walking assosiate with the gipseys robbing the woods
ot the hares and pheasants because I was often in their company
and I must confess I found them far more honest then their callum-
niators whom I knew to be of that description   Scandal and
Fame are cheaply purchasd in a Village   the first is a nimble
tongud gossip and the latter a credoulous and ready believer who
woud not hesitate but believd any thing   I had got the fame of
being a good scholar and in fact I had vanity enough to fancy I
was far from a bad one my self while I coud puzzle the village
schoolmasters over my quart for I had no tongue to brag with till
I was inspird with ale with solving algebrai[c] questions   for

I had once struggld hard to get fame in that crabbed wilderness but my brains was not made for it and woud not reach it   tho it was a mystery scarcly half unveild to my capacity yet I made enough of it to astonish their ignorance for a village schoolmaster is one of the most pretending and most ignorant of men — and their fame is often of the sort which that droll genius Peter Pindar[87] describes — Whats christend merit often wants a auth[or]

[A25, 1-2]

I kept up gardening and workd with a lime burner name Gordon who came from kings[t]ho[r]p near northampton   [A25, 29]

I now left home and went with a brother of Gordons to burn lime for Wilders of Bridge Casterton were we workd at first from light to dark (and in some emergencys all night) to get some money to appear a little descent in a strange place having arivd pennyless with but a shabby appearence   in the bargain we got lodgings at a house of scant fame a professd lodging house kept by a man and his wife of the name of Cole and we was troubld at night with threble fares in each bed an inconvinence which I had never been usd too   they took in men of all descriptions the more the merrier for their profits and when they all assembled round the evening fire the motly co[u]ntenances of many characters lookd like an assembledge of robbers in the rude hut dimly and my[s]teriously lighted by the domestic savings of a farthing taper and I remember a droll mistake in a stranger on my first coming there which created a deal of merriment among the lodgers tho too serious in the strangers feelings to be laughd at — at an Election some were in Lincolnshire or Yorkshire one of the contending MPs decoyd a great many of his canvassers from London who was brought down at their decoyers expence and left to go home at their own   one of these unfortunates a delicate looking man with manners and habits bordering on genteelity wanderd back with the pass of providence for his only friend somtimes walking and some times riding as chances fell out by the way and he arrived in the evening at the new Inn just soon enough to learn that all the beds were occupied by more successfull travellers and just late enough to make his dissapointment a nessesity to keep it or do worse so he was reccomended to our lodging house and being a thorough bred Londoner his simple wonderings at every thing he saw started the titter among the other lodgers who fanc[i]ed that such simple enquireys bespoke the man a runaway from bedlam   he on the contrary not thinking it possible that his serious enqu[i]reys coud be construed into any thing laughable fancyd as the fears in his co[u]ntenance easily dechypherd that we had mystical designs about us and felt for his safty no doubt enough to wish him self at home   one of his mistakes was a startling one to be sure   on walking in the garden in the evening he pulld up a flower of the white nettle by the wall and admird it as one of the finest flowers he had ever[88] seen in a count[r]y garden   there might be some affectation of cockney ignorance mixd up with it but I never forgot it and fancyd that the man had been bro[u]ght up out of the world and the laugh and whisper went round the cottage fire and made him dream of danger so instead of going to bed he begd leave to sit up in his chair till morning when he gladly started and told the people at the Inn that he were in great danger of loosing his life among a gang of robbers over the way and that in the middle of the night he verily believd some one had been murderd in the chamber above his head so he took care to keep awake till morning   the noise he mistook for murder was the groans and noise of a man that was troubled with the nightmare — When we first went we workd hard to save money and tryd to be saving[89]   in which we succeeded for a time as I got a about 50 shillings in about 6 weeks with which I intended to purchase a new olive green coat a color which I had long aimd at and for which I was measured already ere I left home expecting to be able to pay for it in a short time but a accident happend in the way which prevented me the gipseys etc etc [*incomplete*]   [B7, 79-80]

It was a pleasant liv[e]ly town co[n]sisting of a row of houses on each side the turnpike about a furlong long   the river gwash ran its crooked course at the back of them on the south side and washd the foot of the gardens till it crossd the turnpike under a modern looking bridge and wound along a sloping meadow northward loosing its name and its waters into strangers streams

there is some beautiful spots on its banks particularly towards the little village of Tikencoat southward were the bank on the field side rises very stunt in some places from the edge of the river and may by a fancy usd to a flat country be easily imagind into mountains   the whole prospect is diversified by gently swelling slopes and easy sunny vallys

at the back of Wilders house is a beautiful encampment or trench very perfect in the shape of a half moon   the common name for it is 'the dykes'   wether it be roman or Saxon I know not   one corner comes in the yard at the back of a stable and the other curves away to the edge of the river near the bridge it is the widest in the middle of the curve and the highest the bank is throw up on the south east side which commands the sight of another hill about a short mile distant on which there is said to be a similar encampment   [A32, 12]

the[re] was some literary assosiations too belonging to this spot
     it was the place were Tycho Wing[90] the celebrated astrono-
mer was born and lived and the hall of his Ancestors is still tracd
by a heap of ruins and moats and fish ponds of black melancholy
looking water partly in a close and partly in a wood calld 'wood
head'   the moat and fish ponds are open and the water looks
black and deep[91]   the ruins of the hall appear to be large and
part of them is overgrown by bushwood among which a great
many wild goosbery bushes lingers yet and wears the memorys
of its former domestic assosiations   In a large farm house were
Tycho Wing once resided it is said that his study is still to be seen
in the form he left [it] were the walls are stuck round with the old
almanacks he made but I have not seen it and can say no further
for its correctness   [A32, 13]

As soon as I got here the Smiths[92] gang of gipseys came and
encam[p]d near the town and as I began to be a desent scraper we
had a desent round of merriment for a fortnight some times going
to dance or drink at the camp and at other times at the publick
house   [B7, R88]

Once in these midnight revels we escapd a great danger very
narrowly   on going for ale at the dancing a quarrel ensued
when one party determind on cheating the other by running off
with the beer   I was one and we got into an old barn to hide
ourselves while we drank it taking a lanthorn from the public
house which had been open to the weather for years and had
been falling a long time   we saw no danger and hugd our-
selves over our bottle till we had finishd it when we started and
the next day when I passd the place the gable end we had sat
under was down and a heap of rubbish
                                                                          [B7, 91]

[*Gipseys*]

at these feasts and merry makings I got acquainted with the
gipseys and often assos[i]ated with them at their camps to learn
the fiddle of which I was very fond   the first acquantance I
made was with the Boswells Crew[93] as they were calld a popular
tribe well known about here and famous for fidd[l]ers and for-
tunetellers   the old Father who was calld king Boswell dyd at
a great age be[in]g above a 100 this year and was buried at [Witter-
ing] in singular pomp 30 childern and grandchildern all grown
up following him to the grave[94]   (I had often heard of the
mistic language and black arts which the gipseys possesd but on
familiar acquantance with them I found that their mystic lan-
guage was nothing more then things calld by slang names like
village provincialisms and that no two tribes spoke the same
dilacet exactly   their black arts was nothing more of witchcraft
then the knowledge of village gossips and petty deceptions playd
off on believing ignorance but every thing that is bad is thrown
upon the gipseys   their name has grown into an ill omen and
when any of the tribe are guilty of a petty theft the odium is
thrown upon the whole tribe

An ignorant iron hearted Justice of the Peace at —— Sessions
whose name may perish with his cruelty once sitting as judge in
the absence of a wise and kinder hearted assosiate mixd up this
malicious sentence in his condemnnation of 2 Gipseys for horse-
stealing 'This atrosious tribe of wandering vagabonds ought to be
made outlaws in every civilizd kingdom and exterminated from
the face of the earth' and this perescuting unfeeling man was a
cler[g]yman)   I usd to spend my sundays and summer even-
ings among them learning to play the fiddle in their manner by
the ear and joining in their pastimes of jumping dancing and
other amusements   I became so initiated in their ways and
habits that I was often tempted to join them[95]   They are very
ignorant in the ways of the world and very loose in their morals
     they seem by their actions to be ignorant of any forms of faith
in religion and if they are questiond by a confident for they will

83

reveal nothing to strangers they will admit the existance of a god and say that a belief that there is a god is sufficient without any more trouble to get to heaven   they keep the sabbath like catholics by indulging in all manner of sports and pastimes but they show a knowledge how it ought to be kept by desisting from them when a stranger or suspic[i]ous person dressd in the color of a parson passes bye   I never met with a scholer amongst them nor with one who had a reflecting mind   they are susceptible of insult and even fall into sudden passions without a seeming cause   their friendships are warm and their passions of short duration but their closest friendships are not to be relied on   they are deceitful genneraly and have a strong propensity to lying yet they are not such dangerous characters as some in civilizd life for one hardly ever hears of a Gipsey committing murder   their common thefts are trifling depredations taking any thing that huswifes forget to secure at night hunting game in the woods with their dogs at night of which all are fish that come [to the] net except foxes   but some of them are honest   they eat the flesh of Badgers and hedge hogs which are far from bad food for I have eaten of it in my evening merry makings with them   they never eat dead meat but in times of scarcity which they cut into thin slices and throw on a brisk fire till it is scorchd black when it looses its putrid smell and does very well for a make shift providence   when they can afford it they wash the meat in vinegar which takes the smell out of it and makes it eat as well as fresh meat   they are more fond of vegetables then meat and seldom miss having tea in an affternoon when they can afford it

they are fond of smoking to excess both men and women there common talk is of horses lasses dogs and sports   I have often noticd the oddness of their names such as Wisdom Do[u]ghty Manners Lotty Let[t]ice Rover Ishma[e]l   these are not half the odd names but they have come easy to the common talk reccolection — and are the names of a well known tribe whose surnames are Smith   many of their names are Jewish but few christian ones are Israel [Viney, Liskey, Major   ][96]   they seem to be names that have decended from generation to generation as the

84

young ones bear similar names to their parents not generally but almost universaly   In my first acquantance with them I had often noticd that the men had a crooked finger on one hand nor woud they satisfy my enquireys till confidence made them more familiar and then I found the secret was that their parents disabled the finger of every male child in war time when infants to keep them from being drawn for Militia or being sent for soldiers for any petty theft they might commit which woud invariably be the case if they had been able men when taken before a magistrate as they lay under the lash of the law with the curse of a bad name

They had pretentions to a knowledge of medicine but their reciepts turnd more on mystic charms and spells   yet they had a knowledge of Plants — which they gave names too themselves   as I had a knowledge of wild plants I usd to be amusd with the names they calld them by   a little plant with a hard stem that grows in villages and waste places one sort bearing minute yellow flowers and another purple ones   these they calld burvine and reckond famous for the scurvey

Wasp weed is the water betony growing by brook sides which gaind their name by the wasps being invariably attachd to its blossoms getting therfrom a gluttinous matter for the cement of their combs   this is a celebrated plant with the gipseys for the cure and relief of deafness   Buckbane is the bogbean   husk head is the self heal a cure for wounds and furze b[ou]nd is the tormentill a cure for fevers adder bites etc[97]

In fortune telling they pertended to great skill both by cards and plants and by the lines in the hand and moles and interpretations of dreams but like a familiar Ep[i]stle among the common people that invariably begins with 'This comes with our kind love to you all hoping you are all well as it leaves us at present thank god for it'   the preface to every bodys fortune was the same that they had false frends and envious neighbours but better luck woud come and with the young that two was in love with them at the same time one living near and one at a distance   one was a dark girl and one a fair girl and he lovd the fair girl the best etc etc

85

The credulous readily belevd them and they extorted money by another method of mutterd over their power of revenge which fright[ened] the honest huswife into charity   I have h[e]ard them laugh over their evening fire at the dupes they had made in believing their knowledge in foretelling future events and trying each others wits to see who coud make a tale that might suceed best the next day   as I said before they have no scholars amon[g]st them but I have known people write letters for them to be read as I suppose by the same assistance   the men are very hot in their tempers and loose in their discourse delighting to run over smutty ribaldry but the women have not lost the modesty that belongs them so far as to sit and hear it without blushing the young girls are reservd and silent in the company of men and their love affections are seeming cold and carless of return

they somtimes marry with the villagers but its very rarely and if they do they often take to their wandering courses again village clowns are oftener known to go away with the gipsey girls which happens verry frequently   I had a great desire myself of joining the Smiths Crew and a young fellow that I workd with at a lime kiln did join with them and married one of the gipseys his name was James Mobbs and hes with them still   I usd to dislike their cooking which was done in a slovenly manner and the dread of winters cold was much against my inclinations their descriptions of summer revellings their tales of their yearly journeys to Kent and their rendevouses at Norwood were they got swarms of money by fiddling or fortune telling and them that coud do neither got a rich harvest by hop pulling which work they describd as being so easy were tickling temptations to my fancy   [A25, 11-14]

The gipseys in matters of religion are not so unfeeling as may be imagind   instruction seems to be all they want   a friend of mine told me last night that a methodist preacher preachd to a great company of them on Ketton heath a few miles distant when some few paid a disregard to his exortations but the rest listend with attention and some even shed tears

There is not so many of them with us as there usd to be   the inclosure has left nothing but narrow lanes were they are ill provided with a lodging   Langley Bush is the only place were they frequent commonly   they are very troublesome to those who are acquainted with them always calling to see them and never leaving the house without begging[98] something

[A25, 14-15]

Memorys of Love Chapter 6

As I grew up a man I mixd more in company and frequented dancings for the sake of meeting with the lasses for I was a lover very early in life my first attachment being a school boy affection but Mary ——[99] who cost me more ballads then sighs was belovd with a romantic or platonic sort of feeling   if I coud but gaze on her face or fancy a smile on her co[u]ntenance it was sufficient   I went away satisfied   we playd with each other but named nothing of love   yet I fancyd her eyes told me her affections   we walkd together as school companions in leisure hours but our talk was of play and our actions the wanton innosence of childern   yet young as my heart was it woud turn chill when I touchd her hand and trembled and I fancyd her feelings were the same for as I gazd earnestly in her face a tear woud hang in her smiling eye and she woud turn to whipe it away her heart was as tender as a birds but when she grew up to woman hood she felt her station above mine   at least I felt that she thought so for her parents were farmers and Farmers had great pretentions to somthing then so my passion coold with my reason and contented itself with another tho I felt a hopful tenderness one that I might one day renew the acqua[in]tance and disclose the smotherd passion   she was a beautiful girl and as the dream never awoke into reality her beauty was always fresh in my memory   she is still unmarried

[A25, 7]

87

That number three seems to have brought many things to a con-
clusion with me in love   I met th[r]ee full stops or three pro-
fessions of sincerity — my first was a school affection — Mary
J[oyce]   I am ashamed to go on with the name   I felt the dis-
paragement in our situations and fearing to meet a denial I carried
it on in my own fancies to every extreme writing songs in her
praise and making her mine with every indulgence of the fancy
       I cannot forget her little playful fairey form and witching
smile even now
       I remember an accident that roused my best intentions and hurt
my affection unto the rude feelings of imaginary cruelty when
playing one day in the church yard I threw a green walnut that hit
her on the eye   she wept and I hid my sorrow and my affection
together under the shame of not showing regret lest others might
laugh it into love — my second was a riper one   Elizabeth
N[ewbon][100] who laid open her own fancys or affections by writ-
ing too an unfinished sentence with chalk on a table at a lone cot-
tage where young people used to meet on sundays — I guessed
the rest in my own favour and met the confession of her esteem
by her not caring to deny it — this went on for years with petty
jealousies on both sides   at length giving ear to the world she
charged me with sins of changing affections and rambling fancys
— I felt the accusations as insults and my temper mastered my
affections — a short time after I met with Patty by accident fell in
love by accident married her by accident and esteemed her by
choice   and sure enough had I not met her I should have at this
day been a lonely solitary — feeling nothing but the worlds sorrows
and troubles and sharing none of its happiness — as it is in the
midst of trouble I am happy in having a companion whom I feel
deserves my best esteem   [A53, 3r, 13r-v, 3v]

After mixing into the merrymakings of Wakes Weddings House
warmings and Holliday [celebrations] I lost that lonely feeling
and grew dissapated   not that I was over fond of drink but I
drank for the sake of company and to stifle unpleasant feelings
which my follys often brought on me   perhaps the word

house warmings needs an explanation to be understood   it is a custom common in villages and is this   when a person shifts from an old habitation to a new one the gossips then old neighbours meet to have a tea drinking with any others that chuse to go and the men join them at night to drink ale and the young one[s] make up a dance and then they warm the new house as they call it by drinking and singing and other merriment   I spoke of follys   they were love follys that often made the heart ach a pain well known to lovers causd by rejected addresses to some one whom I felt a sudden affection for and who on my disclosing it woud affect to sneer and despise me   my first love reallity was with a girl of Ashton whose name was Elizabeth Newbon she was no beauty but I fancyd she was every thing and our courtship was a long one   I usd to meet her on sundays at a lodge house on Ashton Green at first and then went to her home

her father was a Weelwright and an old man who professd to be learned in the bible and was always trying my wisdom were such and such passages might be found   my silence generaly spoke my lack of religion and he shook his head at my ignorance

he thought that religion consisted of learning such scraps as a sort of curiosity by heart   he knew one book in the bible in which God was not once mentiond   it was Ezra[101]   and he knew the name of the Mountain were noahs ark rested and other bible curositys and he read it to search for these things to be able to talk about them and thought him self a religious man tho he never went church and he was so for he was happy and harmless

he possesd a Large bible with notes which he took in Numbers when a young man   it was Wrights Bible and he often spoke of the pleasure he felt in reading the first number one sunday night in a terrible thunder storm   he had another book on which he set a great value   it was Lord Napiers Key to the revelations[102]   he believd the explanations there given as the essence of truth and every newspaper occurence that happend in war and political governments he fancyd he coud find there and Boneyparte [   ] and the comet   he believd in Moors almanack[103] too with great reverence and unlockd its mystical

herigliphic with his revelation key yearly tho it was not so suit-
able a key as Moors who waited the events of the year and explaind
it afterwards   [A25, 7-8]

My fondness for study began to decline and on mixing more into
company [of] young chaps of loose habits that began by force and
growing into a custom it was continued by choice till [I] became
wild and irregular and poetry was for a season thrown bye
these habits were gotten when the fields were inclosed mixing
among a motly set of labourers that always follow after the News
of such employments   I usd to work at setting down fencing
and planting quick lines with partners whose whole study was
continual cont[r]ivances to get beer and the bottle was the general
theme from weeks end to weeks end and such as had got drunk
the oftenest fancied themselves the best fellows and made a boast
of it as a fame but I was not such a drinker as to make a boast of it
and tho I joind my sixpence towards the bottle as often as the rest
I often missd the tott that was handed round for my constitution
woud not have bore it — Saturday nights usd to be what they
calld randy nights which was all meeting together at the public
house to drink and sing and every new beginner had to spend a
larger portion then the rest which they calld colting a thing com-
mon in all sorts of labour   [B7, 91]

We usd to go on Sundays to the Flower pot a little public house at
Tikencoat a neighboring village and in one of these excursio[n]s I
first saw patty going across the fields towards her home   I was
in love at first sight and not knowing who she was or were she
came from I felt very ill at rest and clumb on the top of a dotterel
to see which way she went till she got out of sight — but chance
quickly threw[104] her again in my way a few weeks after one even-
ing when I was going to fiddle at Stamford   I then ventu'd to
speak to her and succeeded so far as [to] have the liberty to go
home with her to her cottage about 4 Miles off and it became the
introduction to some of the happiest and unhappiest days my
life has met with   after I left her to return home I had taken

90

such a heedless obsever[an]ce of the way that lead over a cow-
pasture with its thousand paths and dallied so long over pleasant
shapings of the future after I left her that twilight with its doubtful
guidance overtook my musings and led me down a wrong track
in crossing the common and as I coud not correct my self I got
over a hedge and sat down on a baulk between a wheat field were
my rhy[m]ing feelings again returnd and I composd while sitting
there the ballad inserted in the village minstrel and the song of all
the days etc[105]   when the moon got up I started agen and on
trying to get over the same hedge again as I thought to cross the
common I saw somthing shine very bright on the other side   I
fancyd it to be bare ground beaten by the cows and sheep in hot
weather but doubting I stoopd down to feel and to my terrord
surprise I found it was water and while in that stooping posture
I saw by the lengthy silver line that stretchd from me that it was
the river   if I had taken a step with out this caution my love
[would have met a sudden end]

I was frighted and sat under the hedge till daylight   what
a many times to a mans follys meet with those dangers and death

91

scapes in his heedless pleasure haunted youth   my reccolec-
tion can turn many in mine from boyhood   [B7, 81]

I usd to go on evenings in the week and every sunday to the
lodge[106] not at all times on love errands merely but to get out of
the way for the lodging house was generaly cumberd with
inmates and the Inn was continualy troubling me with new jobs
        the solitudes around the Lodge was plentiful and there were
places were the foot of man had not printed for years perhaps
        the scenery all round were beautiful   heaths and woods
swelled their wild and free vari[e]tys to the edges of the orison
        I usd to wander about them with my artless and interesting
companio[n] in more then happiness   a large wood in sum-
mer usd to be coverd with Lilys of the valley of which she usd to
gather handfulls for her flower pots and I helpd her to gather
them   in these woods were larg[e] caverns calld swallow pits
by the woodmen of an imense depth so that if a stone was thrown
in one might count [a] while befor one heard it echo
                                                    [B7, 83]

Casterton cowpasture which I usd to pass thro on my visits to
patty very frequently was a very favourite spot and I pland and
wrote some of the best of my poems in the first volume among its
solitudes[107]   [A34, 3]

After I had burnt lime at the kiln awhile Mrs Wilder of the New
Inn hearing that I had been at Burghley gardens got me to work
in the garden were I had a good time of it but the place led me into
all sorts of company   I workd here till the autumn and then
went with my old companion to Pickworth
        Pickworth is a place of other days   it appears to be the ruins
of a large town or city   the place were we dug the kiln was full
of foundations and human bones   we was about a stones
throw from the spot were the church had been which was entirely
swept away excepting a curious pointed arch perhaps the entrance
to the porch that still remains a stout defiance to the besiegings of

92

time and weather   it now forms a gateway to a stackyard
A new church has been built on the cite of the old one since I was
there at the sole expence as I have heard of the Revd Mr Lucas of
Casterton[108]   [A32, 13]

March to Oundle in the Local Militia

When the country was chin deep in the fears of invasion and
every mouth was filld with the terrors which Bouneparte had
spread in other co[u]ntrys a national scheme was set on foot to
raise a raw army of volunteers and to make the matter plausible
a letter was circulated said to be written by the prince regent
I forget how many was demanded from our parish but I remem-
ber the panic which it created was very great — no great name
rises in the world without creating a crowd of little mimics that
glitter in borrowd rays and no great lye was ever yet put in circu-
lation with[out] a herd of little lyes multipl[y]ing by instinct as it
were and crow[d]ing under its wings   the papers that were
circulated assurd the people of england that the French were on
the eve of invading it and that it was deemd nessesary by the

93

regent that an army from 18 to 45 shoud be raisd immediatly
this was the great lye and then the little lyes was soon at its heels
which assurd the people of Helpstone that the french had invaded
and got to London and some of these little lyes had the impu-
dence to swear that the french had even reachd northampton —
the people got at their doors in the evening to talk over the rebel-
lion of 45 when the rebels reachd Derby and even listend at inter-
vals to fancy they heard the french rebels at Northampton knock-
ing it down with their cannon   I never gave much credit to
popular storys of any sort so I felt no consern at these storys tho
I coud not say much for my valour if the tale had provd true
We had a cross graind sort of choise left us which was to be forcd
to be drawn and go for nothing or take on as Volunteers for the
bounty of 2 guineas   I accepted the latter and went with a
neighbours son W. Clark to Peterbro to be swore on and prepard
to join the regiment at Oundle   the morning we left home our
mothers parted with us as if we was going to Botaney Bay and
people got at their doors to bid us farewell and greet us with a sort
of Jobs comfort that they doubted we shoud see helpstone no
more — I confess I wishd my self out of the matter   by times
when we got to Oundle the place of quarters [we] was drawn out
into the fields and a more motly multitude of lawless fellows was
never seen in oundle before and hardly out of it   there was
1300 of us   we was drawn up into a line and sorted out into a
company   I was one of the shortest and therefore my station is
evident   I was in that mixd multitude calld the batallion which
they nick namd 'bum tools' for what reason I cannot tell
the light Company was calld 'light bobs' and the granadeirs
'bacon bolters'   these were names given to each other who felt
as great an enmity against each other as ever they all felt for the
french   some took lodgings but lodgings were very expensive
the people took advantage of the tide and chargd high so I
was obligd to be content with the quarters alloted me which was
at the Rose and Crown Inn kept by a widow woman and her 2
daughters which happend to be a good place   the girls were
modestly good naturd and the mother a kind hearted woman

behaving well to all that returnd it   our company was the 5th
and the Captain was a good sort of feelow using his authority in
the language of a friend advising our ignorance when wrong of
what we ought to do to be right and not in the severity of a petty
tyrant who is fond of abusing those beneath him merely for the
sake of showing authority   I was never wonderful clean in my
dress at least not clean enough for a soldier for I thought I took
more then nessesary pains to be so   I was not very apt at lear-
ing my exercise for I then was a ryhmer and my thoughts were
often absent when the word of comand was given and for this
fault I was terribly teazd by a little louse looking coporal who took
a delight in finding fault with me and loading me with bad jests
on my awkardness as a sold[i]er as if he had been a soldier all his
life   I felt very vext at the scurroulus coxcomb and retorted
which only added more authority in his language   he fou[n]d
fault with me when it belongd to others merely to vex me and if I
venturd to tamper with his mistake he woud threaten me with
the awkard squad for speaking   I grew so mad at last with this
fool that I realy think I shoud have felt satisfaction in shooting
him and I was almost fit to desert home and then agen I though[t]
my companions woud laugh at me so I screwd up my resolution
to the point at last and determind if he accusd me wrongfully for
the time to come I woud certanly fall out of the ranks and adress
him be the consequence what it woud   I had no great heart for
boxing but I saw little fear in him for he was much less in strength
then I was and the dread of the dark hole or awkard squad was
but little in comparison to the teazing insults which this fellow
daily inflicted so I was determind to act up to my vengance be the
consequenc[e] what it might and I soon found an oppertunity for
he was present[l]y at his pert jests and sneering meddling again

    madness flus[h]t my cheek in a moment and when he saw it
he rapt me over my knees in a sneering sort of way and said that
he woud learn me how such fellows as I was dealt with by sol-
diers   I coud stand it no longer but threw my[109] gun aside and
seizing him by the throat I twisted him down[110] and kickd him
when he was down which got the fellow fame for those that had

95

been against him before lifted him up and calld him a good fellow
and calld me a coward while they led me to the black hole but the
captain enqu[i]rd into the frey and the black hole was dispensd
with in serving an addition on guard in its stead   the fellow
th[r]ew a mortified eye on me ever after and never found his
tounge to tell me of a fault even when I was in one

[B7, R98-R96]

I was threatend with the b[l]ack hole by one and even the tying up
to the halbert by others who said the drummers were exce[rcis]ing
them selves and being able to use the whip with punishment
I thought I possest common sense in a superior degree as not to
feel fear at threatend sirmises of any sort for I always look'd on
such things as mere tampering for childern but I confess my com-
mon sense was overcome and I felt fearful that somthing was in
the wind till it blew over and got too late to [require me a flogging]

[B7, R96]

I once got into the awkard squad not for my own fault but that of
others which shows that bad company is not very commendable
      one morning an old pieman came up and taking as he fancyd
an advantage of our hunger like a crafty politician he askd an
increasd price for them thinking our nessesitys woud urge us to
buy[111]   [B7, 94]

The officers were often talking about Bounaparte in the field and
p[r]aising each other in a very redicilous manner very often   I
will repeat one anecdote   having found out that the common
men were more expert in making nightly plunders in orchards
then learing their exercise by day and as they coud not come at
the offenders being those who slept in out houses that coud go in
and out as they chusd they determind on a plan to harass them as
they calld it by taking them out in the field two additionel hours
in the morning from 6 to 8 but they was not aware that 6 was a
late hour with ploughmen who was usd to get up before the sun
all the year round so instead of harrising the men they quickly

harassd themselves and the scheme dropt   in one of these
early exercises one of the Officers ladys whose fears for her hus-
bands safty seemd very great even in little things sent the servant
maid after him with his breakfast and as she came simpering
along making her timid enquireys the captains of companys
declard that they thought M^r xxx had been too much of a soldier
to stand this and others swore upon their honours that he woud
not stand it   at length the enquiring maid found out her noble
master who sneeringly disdaind to[112] take it just as his brother
officers expected the maids only reason for bringing it being that
her mistress was afraid he woud take cold by being out of doors
in such unusual hours which to be sure was a mortifying dis-
closure to the pin featherd soldier   'Go home and teach your
mistress to know better girl' was the gallant replye and his
brother officers who were on the look out to watch the event
when they saw the maiden depart hastend up to congratulate his
valour and shake hands with him as a brother worthy the name
of a soldier   the very clowns coud not help seeing this as redi-
culous and burst into a hearty laugh as the farce ended   the
others got into a bye word and I itchd to do somthing with it and
wrote a ballad which I venturd to offer one evening at Bells the
printers for publication when a young man behind the co[u]nter
read it and laughd heartily saying he had heard of the circum-
stance but it was too personal to print and returnd it   I felt fear-
ful of being found out so I quickly destroyd it tearing it into very
small pecies as I went along and threw them away but I heard
nothing more of the matter   I can[n]ot remember much of it
now but I thought little of it when I wrote and more after it was
destroyd

[B7, R95-R94]

On the last time we was calld up there was a fresh bounty set on
foot of a further 2 guineas to those who woud enlist for extended
service as they calld it to be sent so many miles out of the county
to guard barracks castles or any other urgengys that might hap-
pen five shillings of which was to be paid down and the rest to

be given when they were wanted   I did not much matter an
extent of service but I felt purposes enew for the 5 shillings and
when it was offerd me I took it without further enquirey and
never heard further about it[113]   [*incomplete*]

[B7, R94]

My first feelings and attempts at Po[etry]
Chapter 4

I cannot say what led me to dabble in Ryh[me or] at what age I
began to write it but my first r[ude attempts took the form of]
imitations of my fathers Songs for he knew and sung a great
many and I made a many things before I venturd to comit them
to writing for I felt ashamd to expose them on paper and after I
venturd to write them down my second thoughts blushd over
them and [I] burnt them for a long while but as my feelings grew
into song I felt a desire to preserve some and usd to correct them
over and over till the last copy had lost all kindred to the first even
in the title   I went on some years in this way wearing it in my
memory as a secret to all   tho my parents usd to know that my
leisure was occupyd in writing yet they had no knowledge of
what I coud be doing for they never dreamd of me writing poetry
      at length I venturd to divulge the secret a little by reading
imatations of some popular song floating among the vulgar at the
markets and fairs till they were common to all but these imata-
tions they only laughd at and told me I need never hope to make
songs like them   this mortified me often and almost made me
desist for I knew that the excelling such doggerel woud be but a
poor fame if I coud do nothing better but I hit upon an harmless
deception by repeating my poems over a book as tho I was read-
ing it   this had the desird effect   they often praisd them
and said if I coud write as good I shoud do   I hugd my self over
this deception and often repeated it and those which they praisd
as superior to others I tryd to preserve in a hole in the wall but

98

my mother found out the hurd and unconscously took them for
kettle holders and fire lighters when ever she wanted paper not
knowing that they were any thing farther then attempts at learn-
ing to write for they were writing upon shop paper of all colors
and between the lines of old copy books and any paper I coud get
at for I was often wanting tho I saved almost every penny I had
given me on sundays or holidays to buy it instead of sweet meats
and fruit and I usd to feel a little mortified after I discoverd it but
I dare not reveal the secret by owning to it and wishing her to
desist for I feard if I did she woud have shown them to some one
to judge of ther value which woud have put me to shame so I kept
the secret dissapointment to myself and wrote on suffering her to
destroy them as she pleasd but when I wrote any thing which I
imagind better then others I preservd it in my pocket till the paper
was chafd thro and destroyd by a diff[er]ent and full as vain pre-
sevation   [A34, R10]

My mother brought me a picturd pocket hankerchief from Deep-
ing may fair as a fairing on which was a picture of Chatterton and
his Verses on Resignation[114]   chance had the choice of it
she was mentioning the singular circumstance to me yesterday
by asking me wether I rememberd it and saying that she little
thought I shoud be a poet then as she shoud have felt fearful if
she had for Chattertons name was clouded in mellancholly
memorys which[115] his extrodinary Genius was scarcly know[n]
     the common people knew he was a poet and that was all
they know the name of Shakespear as one but the ballad monger
who produces [and] supplys hawkers with their ware are poets
with them and they imagine one as great as the other   so much
for that envied emenence of common fame   I was fond of
imatating every thing I met with and therefore it was impossible
to resist the oppertunity which this beautiful poem gave me   I
am not certain that this was the name of the poem   my memory
was freshend some few years ago to believe so in reading the life
of Chatterton by (I think) someone of the name of Davy[116] as I
have the poem by me I will insert it[117]   [A34, 9]

99

I always wrote my poems in the fields and when I was out of work
I usd to go out of the village to particular spots which I was fond
of from the beauty or secre[c]y of the scenes or some assosiation
and I often went half a days journey from home on these excur-
sions   in one of these rambles I was in a narrow escape of
being taken up as a poacher   it was a fine day and I went to
wander on wittering heath with the double intention of ryhming
and seeking wild plants — I found a beautiful spot on the side of
a rivulet that ran crooking and neglected among the yellow furze
and misty green sallows that met on both sides   I sat down
nearly conseald in the furze and tall downy grass and began to
ryhme till I insensibly fell asleep and was awakend by muttering
voices on the other side of the thicket   I lookd thro and saw
they were keepers by their guns   one of the dogs came up and
peepd at me and the men made a stop as if they suspected som-
thing was in it   I felt very fearful but it was soon over for they
passd on   I was far away from any road and my account of
myself woud have seemd but an idle one   it woud have only
raisd their suspicions and I shoud have been taken up as a
poacher undoubtedly so as soon as they were safe off I made the
best of my way out of danger for the part I was in was enclosd
with a wall and belongd to the Marquis   [A32, 6]

Among these trifles are many keepsakes of my early days when I
used to drop down under a bush and scribble the fresh thoughts
on the crown of my hat — since the world has found me I feel it a
presumption to hide my self and fancy I feel as I felt then — I have
more knowledge — as I found nature then so I made her — if an
old pond with its pendant sallows fringing its mossy sides hap-
pened to be in the pleasant nook where I sat concealed among the
black thorns drawing its picture — I called it a pond and if it was
a flood wash in the meadows I called it a lake or imagined it one
or if I sat under the ragged sides of a stone pit I fancied my self
under the shadows of a rock and so my feelings were stirred into
praise and my promises were muttered in prose or ryhme as the
mood might suit at the moment and then these moods often

repeated grew unperceived into quantity on paper and then I indulged my vanity in thinking how they would look in print and then I selected what I thought best and hid the others out of shames way as laughing stocks for the crowd who think it a childs occupations to indulge in such feelings and inexcusable folly in a man but on flitting from my native place I hunted over my bundles of paper intending to save the trouble of carriage by destroying those I set least store bye and the bundle[s] from whence these were taken were among the first of my intentions but I read them and paused thinking of old days and old feelings and excuse my vanity gentle reader — if I did not think them worthy of your praise   I felt I could not burn them   [Pfz 198, 42]

I always wrote my poems in great haste and generaly finishd them at once wether long or short for if I did not they generaly were left unfinishd   what corrections I made I always made them while writing the poem and never coud do any thing with them after wards   [A25, 10]

There was an Elegy also on an old Cart Horse[118] an early poem which I alterd and made a tollerable thing of   the old Horse was in great fame in the Village for his gentleness and strength and readiness at all sorts of jobs   Another was a Tale of the Lodge house[119]   [B6, R81]

The Lodge house was a story of my mothers [I] put into ryhme   it was a current one in the village and the place were it was said to have happend was a lone house calld[120] the 'heath house' about 2 miles from the Village   it stood in a lone hollow in the ground northward below the present new one called Milton Farm   it was disinhabited and in ruins when I was a boy   it had been a farm house and one of the barns was kept up were my father used to thresh in winter for several years — there were sever[a]l dismal storys afloat of midnight murders done in this place in the days of its prosperity and of course a great many accounts of shrieking women and groaning men heard and seen

101

near the spot by passing shepherds and feast goers in the night
    I remember with what fearful steps I usd to go up the old
tottering stairs when I was a boy in the dinner hours at harvest
with other companions to examine the haunted ruins   the
walls were riddeld all over with names and dates of shepherds
and herdsmen in their idle hours when the[y] crept under its
shelter from showers in summer and storms in winter and there
were mysterious stainings on the old rotting floors which were
said to be the blood of the murderd inhabitants — it also was the
haunt of Gipseys and others who pulld up every thing of wood to
burn till they left nothing but the walls — the wild cat usd to hide
and raise its kittens in the old roof an animal that used to be
common in our woods tho rather scarce latly — and the owls usd
to get from the sun in its chimney and at the fall of evening usd
to make a horrid hissing noise that was often taken for the waking
noise of the hanting spirits that made it a spot shund desolat and
degected   [A34, 2]

so I determined on some plan or other to preserve what I wrote
and I went to Deeping to purchase a blank book of Henson the
printer and book[s]eller there   I believe it was at the fair   he
was rather inquisitive to know what I wanted it for and on getting
flushd with ale I dropt some loose hints about dabbling in ryhmes
and he expressd a desire to see some   I told him he shoud
somtime and it passd on   I gave eight shilling for the blank
book and inserted such of the poems I had bye me that I thought
better of then the rest and the others I left as they were   Edward
Drury has this Book   he got it out of me by impertinent inva-
sions of my secrets and kept it as all my other MSS are kept — for
some purpose unknown to me — there are several fragments in
it which I intended to have made use of as there are in all that are
scatterd about which prevents me [incomplete]   [A25, 10]

I had often thought of colecting my best poems in a book and I
went to Hensons to enquire the price of one   he told me 8
shillings and on being alowd to pay for it as I woud I had one

102

(this book is now in the possesion of Ned Drury)   he seemd puzzled to imagine what use I was going to make of it   he had know[n] me before by binding books for me taken in No[s] and by seeing me often at the chappel at Helpstone for I was then fond of hearing the Independants and was much happier then perhaps then I have been since — but his knowledge of me only served to darken the riddle of my purchase for my ignorant appearance and vulgar habits had nothing of literary [manners] about them

he urgd many side wind enquireys to pump and wide guesses but I had kept the secret too long to be so easily perswaded as to let it go — but it was the fair day and getting a little bold with ale on my going for the book before I started home I lost my sho[y]ness and dropt a few hints as to the use I inte[n]ded it and it wakend his guesses into the suppose that I dabbled in ryhme

I acknowledged it and he wishd to see them   I told him he shoud but it passd on with out further conversation about the matter till now   [B3, 80; A31, 214]

He [J.B. Henson] was a bookseller and printer in a small way at Market Deeping one of the lowest market towns in england and as full of ignorance of books as a village — he came to Deeping as a school master   he then tur[n]d to a bookbinder and bought and sold a few second hand books and finally he set up printing Auction Bills and songs and pamphlets for travellers and at last he ventured to print books   his first trial was the 'history of Joseph'[121] which was badly done   the next was Bunyans Pilgrims Progress Heavenly footman etc which he sold in six-penny Numbers   these was done much better nay tolearably well so as to procure him employment from the London Book-sellers and he printed several religious books for one Baine a London Puplisher and the last things I know of which he printed on his own account was The Golden Treasury — a small book of Arithmetic by a —— Pousnell a schoolmaster of Deeping and a political pamplet of wooden ingenuity by a Northamptonshire Farmer — he then broke and contented himself with his smaller beginnings of printing Ballads and Auction bills till last year when he left the place on the experimental adventuring of finding a better — when he first came to deeping he was a religious man belonging to the congregational dissenters or Independants and then did some dirty doings with sathan or at least the doings were exposd by accident for they are worldly doings and tho preachd and reprobated every sunday by religious of all persuasions they are common to her every family — tho the poluted stream flows by a secret passage — like the muddy one that emptys its self in the Thames — proffession in all religious opinions is a very meek pretending good lady clamourous against the world and its ways and always busy to abuse it — but in pra[c]tice of good she is a dead letter — he was turnd off from his profession of clerk to the Independants

The current coin that carrys a man at self interest thro the world is fair pretentions hollow friendships and false promises which are all of one value and but the reverse and tran[s]vers of a counterfit   [A31, 216-17]

I wrote several of my poems while I was here and formd a resolution of publishing them for I was head over ears in embarassments and knew not which way to get out   I had shown some to my first acquaint[a]n[c]e in the matter J.B. Henson of Market Deeping Among which was the Sonnet to the Setting Sun and the one to the Primrose two of the earliest I ever wrote and these two he approvd of very much and also a poem on the death of Chatterton which he wanted to print in a penny book to sell to hawkers but I was doubtful of its merits and not covetous of such fame so I declind it   he seemd very anxious to publish my poems   he said he woud write to his London booksellers to hear if they woud assist us or take a share in the matter   I forget their names   and we proposd to do it by subscription and as soon as an hundred subscribers was gotten he was to begin to print it and on our starting he was to print 300 prospectuses for one Pound and I wishd him to write the thing but he declind and urgd me to it   I was very loath and had a worse opinion of my prose abilitys then my poetry for I had never written a letter excepting the silly love epistles aluded [to] but I tryd what I coud do   we lodgd at a public house still if a mellancholy sign swinging in the wind by a solitary clump of some five or six houses coud give it a licence to be calld so that stood as if no passenger coud ever be supposd to find it and as tho the road had forgotten the few fragments of the town that mea[s]urd it

   it seemd to stand out of the worlds eye yet there was occasional droppers in that made it any thing but a place fit for study so I usd to think over it in my morning and night journeys too and from work   in one of the mellancholy mornings I wrote the two first verses of what is life[122]   having another lime kiln at royal[123] about two miles off and at this place I sat down one day on a coal skuttle and wrote my address to the Public on a piece of paper which I kept for the purpose   it gave me a deal of trouble and I was ill satisfied with what I had written but I wanted to do somthing to get out of debt so I wrote it and Directed it with a pencil and in the want of sealing wax seald it with pitch and took it to Stamford but my heart was in a thousand minds ere I got there   somtimes I thought I woud give up all though[t]s of poetry and again my hopes returnd and I resolvd to try the experiment thinking that if I got laughd at and reapd scorn instead of profit in the publication of my poems it woud only be a cure to all foolish fancys and scribbling follys for the future so I sat down upon a stone heap before I got into Stamford and lookd over it again to correct it and I felt as I went on as if every body knew my errand and my face reddend at the gaze of a passer bye   the post office was shut up when I got there and they wanted a penny with the letter but I had not got one so they took [it] with a loath kind of [attitude] an[d] bye and bye a letter returnd from Henson stating that he woud meet me at Stamford with 100 of the prospectuses and arrange for further matters   I accordingly went and for the first time saw a sonnet of mine in print and I scarcly knew it in its new dress and felt a prouder confidence then I had hither too done thinking it got merit by its dress   his mind was rather changd when I got there   he did not seem so urgent to print them and instead of a pound he had got 5 or 6 shillings more

105

one for his journey etc etc   I was not aware that promises was
a current coin among booksellers of all sizes from Henson the sale
bill printer to the city professor   I met him at the Dolphin Inn
     I found that he did not come on purpose on my er[r]and
but he had two old books to dispose of one a bible and we went
down to Adams the second hand bookseller to dispose of them
and left some prospectuse[s]   he wanted to go into Thompsons
shop but I declind as I owd him a small debt which I coud not dis-
charge and while we was drinking together a dull looking fellow
in a genteelish dress came in to whom Henson gave one of the
papers offering at the same time as a sort of apology a little account
[of] my profesion etc but the fellow just threw his eyes over it then
lookd at me and walkd out of the room without saying a word
the next person that came in was of a milder disposition tho his
profession is not a common assosiate at such places yet in spite of
foibles he was a good fellow   Henson[124] begd him to peruse
one   he did and made enquiries to me which I answerd in a
shoy [manner] but he wishd me success and gave the sonnet some
praise askd me to drink with him and bade Henson set his name
down as a subscriber wishing at the same time that he was able to
give me further assistence   this gave me heart and did me more
good then all I ever met with before or after   I felt it deeply and
never forgot the name of the Rev^d M^r Mo[u]nsey[125]   a short
[while] after I left pickworth and returnd home wher Henson pro-
posd to print the work as soon [as] he shoud have 100 Subscribers
     the[n] after I had got a good many things ready for him to begin
with he said he coud not do it unless I coud borrow £15 of any friend
in the village but there was not a frend in the village friendly
enough to lend me fifteen shillings and I told him so   then he
proposd £10 and in this shuffling from one proposal to another I
got very uneasy and my confidence in his promises shrunk to
nothing   I wishd then that I had never engagd in the matter
and felt ashamd as I went down the street scarcly daring to look
any one in the face for the prospectuses had filld every bodys
mouth with my name and prospects most of which was Jobs com-
forters and the cry was against me (see etc etc)   [A32, 14-17]

at the situation I found myself in after I had printed and distributed all my papers — I found not one subscriber and my hopes seemd lost — I knew not what course to take   I had got no work to go too and I hardly dare show my face to seek for any — every body seemd to jeer me at my foolish pretentions and seemd shony at my fallen hopes — enquirey stood on tiptoe with question go were I woud and I hated to hear them and evaded them as well as I coud   I felt uncommonly uneasy and knew not what to do

I sometime thought of running away and leaving home were I might be at peace among strangers (for my dissapointment was fast growing into a bye word) — and I went to Stamford twice to enlist in the attillery which was recruiting there but my variety of minds prevented me besides my love matters etc was a strong tether that I coud not easily break — I went so far at one time as to take the money from a recruit but the sergant was a better man then such usually are and said he took no advantage of a man in liquor for I was fresh at the time and let me off with paying the expences of the drink — but I was wanting in height which might be a better plea then the sergants honesty   [A32, 5]

in the midst of this dilemma a bookseller name Thompson sent in a bill for 15 shillings which he desired I woud pay him as he was going to leave the place   I was very willing to pay him but I was not able so I wrote a few lines to tell him the situation I was in sending at the same time a few prospectuses and wishing he woud do somthing to assist me while I promisd to pay the debt as soon as ever I was able which I hopd to be ere long   I got my companion T Porter of Ashton to take the letter but he treated all with contempt and abusd him   the debt was ran for some numbers of the boston enquirer which I never finishd — Ned Drury had enterd on the shop then and on seeing one of the prospectuse[s] he took it for a matter of profit and paid the 15 shillings for me before he enquird further   this matter he has translated into a lye in the Introduction which has another lye in it not of his insertion as he says and that is of my selling the poems for 26 Pounds   I never sold them at all is the fact of the matter   I

107

once signd an agreement of Drurys which alowd me a quarters
profit   I was fresh at the time but it got wind and others heard
of it that knew better then I did who calld it a villanous trick so
he sent it up to London to be destroyd as they say   I know
nothing   this I know that I have never signd an agreement of
any kind since and never will   when my friend Porter told me
of his success I was in a tetherd perplexity and knew not what to
do but Ned Drury with his friend R Newcomb publisher of the
Stamford Mercury they calld at a farmers of the name of Clerk to
dine and enquire into my character and merits as a poet   the
former was open to every meddler but the latter was a secret so
they came to enquire more about it with me   I was at a neigh-
bours house at Billings the bachelors hall when they came and
my sister ran for me and on telling me two gentlemen wanted to
see me I felt hopful and timidly went home when I found them
talking to my parents   Drury said little or nothing but New-
comb askd some questions as to how my writings was disposd of
and when I told him that I had made proposal for henson[126] to
print them he said they did not wish to take them out of his hands
but that instead of desiring money to print them they woud let
me have money for my nessesitys so I thought the difference of
advantage a good one and readily engagd to get my MSS from
Hensons   Mr Newcomb invited me to dine with him on the
monday as he prepard to start but cautiously opend the door
again to remind me that unless I brought the MSS I need not
come   I felt insulted with his kindness and never accepted the
invitation tho I took them   [A32, 16-18]

tho I took some of them the next day when Drury lookd over
them and gave me a guinea as a sort of earnest I suspect and
promisd to pay my debts   I remaind with him the whole day
and he gave me a poem in my hands to read of Lord Byrons   I
think it was the G[i]a[o]ur and the first time I had ever seen any
of them   I promisd to take him more of my poems when I got
them from Hensons (he making it a matter of speculation and try-
ing to be sure of his bargain before he enterd too far in it   so far

108

he was right) so I wrote to him and sent it by my mother to deliver up my poems as [he] had broken the engagments by wishing me to borrow £15   I told him that this was an impossib[ili]ty all along and mentiond my better prospects in the new engagment I had made with Drury   he gave them up with some reluctance and I took them to Drury[127]   [he] showd them to the Revd M\[r\] Towpenny[128] of Little Casterton who sent them back with a cold note stating that he had no objection to assist in raising the poor man a small subscription tho the poems appeard to him to posses no merit to be worthy of publication   Drury read this presious thing to me and as I fancyd all men in a station superior to me as learned and wise especialy parsons I felt my fortune as lost and my hopes gone and tho he tryd to cheer me I felt degected a long time and almost carried it too far   after prosperity shone out upon me I rememberd it keenly and wrote the following lines on his name and a letter which I never sent

Towpenny his wisdom is and towpenny his fame is
Towpenny his merit is and towpenny his name is
And as twopence is a trifle I well may do without him
Ill sing in spite of twopenny and not care towpence about him

soon after Twopenny sent his note Drury showd them again to Sir English Dobbin[129] who expressd a different opinion and left his name as a subscriber   this heartend me again and I ryhmd on and became pacified   in this winter I finis[h]d all the fragments that I thought worth it for most of what I had done hitherto was unfinishd   the earliest of such were Helpstone which I had intended for a long poem in the manner of Goldsmith and the fate of amy Address to a Lark[130]   the address to a Lark was made one cold winters morning on returning home from raking stubble as the ground was so froze that I coud not work   I frit the lark up while raking and it began to sing which suggested the poem that was written in a mellancholy feeling — the Lost Greyhound was made while going and returning from Ashton one Winters day   the fate of Amy was begun when I was a boy   I usd to be very fond of hearing my friend J Turn[ill] read the Ballad of

Edwin and Emma[131] in weeding time and as Ameys story was popular in the village I thought it might make a poem so tryd it and imitated the other as far as the ideas of it floated on my memory

Evening was alterd from a very early one of a great length made one evening after I had been cowtending on the common... Noon which I wrote very early and composd on a hot day in summer while I went to fill my fathers bottle with water at round oak spring and Evening etc and the sonnets to the Setting Sun the Primrose the Gipseys evening blaze and a Scene etc   these were begun when I was 14 or 15 and finishd and in some cases alterd throughout   I began to write Sonnets at first from seeing two very pretty ones in an old news paper   I think they were by charlotte Smith[132]   the rest in the first vol was written the next summer and winter while the book was going thro the press one at the latter end

Crazy Nell was taken from a narative in the Stamford Mercury nearly in the same manner it was related   I was very pleasd with it and thought it one of the best I had written and I think so still   the next spring my master Wilders sent for me to work in the Garden and I started when I renewd my acquantance with Patty which had rather broken off   I usd to seize the leiseur that every wet day brought me to go to Drurys shop to read books and to get new tunes for my fiddle which was a pleasure of a pastime   when ever I wrote a new thing I usd to take it to Drury very often on Sunday morning to breakfast with him and in one of these visits I got acquanted with D[r] Bell[133] a man of odd taste but a pleasant acquantance   he was fond of books and had edited a droll one Entitled the banisher of the blue devils a jest book   he usd to cut out all the curious and odd paragraphs out of the news papers and paste them on sheets of paste board

he had a great many of these things which [he] had collected for many years   he had been a docter in the army and in the east or west Indias [and] became acquainted with Peter Pindar then in the same capacity some of whose early poems he possesd which had never been published   he wrote to earl Spencer respecting me and succeeded in getting me a salary of £20 per

110

Annum — I was full of hopes at my present success but my money
matters were still precarious for Drury objected at times to paying
all my bills tho he did it afterwards[134]   my mistress wishd to
see some of my pieces and usd to be anxious to introduce me to
strangers whom she woud talk too about me and who woud
express a curosity to see me but I usd to get out of the way when
I coud   one of these who stopd there a day or two saw some of
them and said that the poem of evening was an imitation of
somthing which has slipt my memory now   I thought the man
shoud say somthing if he knew nothing and seeing we displayd
but a bookeless appearance he hazarded his make shift for learn-
ing as heedless as he pleasd   I know nothing of who or what
he was — Drury told me now that my poems was crownd with
the utmost success I coud wish for as they were in the hands and
met the favourable opinion of a gentleman who coud and woud
do them justice but he woud not tell me his name and a painter of
profiles was in the town whom he engagd to take my likness
these things were trifle[s] to remember but they were great at
their beginings   they made me all life and spirits and nothing
but hopes and prosperity was before me — (Pattys friends who
rather lookd coldly on my acquainten[ce] with her and who
seemd to take my [attentions] as more of intrusions then visits)
now began to be anxious after my [welfare] and courted my
acquaintance while I on the contrary felt their former slights and
now I felt my self on advantage ground I determind to take my
revenge and neglected to go or but slightly heeded their urgent
invitations and while I as at home in the winter I renewd my
acquaintance with a former love and had made a foolish con-
fidence with a young girl at Southorpe[135] and tho it began in a
heedless [flirtation] at Stamford fair from accompanying her
home it grew up in to an affection that made my heart ach to think
it must be broken for patty was then in a situation that marriage
coud only remedy   I felt awkardly situated and knew not
which way to proceed   I had a variety of minds about me and
all of them unsetteld   my long smotherd affections for Mary
revivd with my hopes and as I expected to be on a level with her

111

bye and bye I thought then I might have a chance of success in renewing my former affections   amid these delays pattys emergencys became urgent   she had reveald her situation to her parents when she was unable to conseal it any longer who upbraided her with not heeding thier advice and told her as she had made her bed hard she shoud lye on it for on my first arrival at Casterton a young shoemaker paid his addresses to her whose visits were approvd off more by her parents then her self and when I had disinherited him of his affections they encouragd him to come on and tryd and urgd to win her mind over to his and their wishes   when I reflected on these things I felt stubbornly disposd to leave them the risk of her misfortunes but when she complaind of their [coldness towards her] I coud stand out no longer and promisd that my prosper[i]ty shoud make me her friend and to prove that I was in earnest I gave her money to [bolster her] independance till we shoud be married   this behaviour pacified them and left her at peace — they were poor tho they had known better days and they fancyd that the memory of these things aught to be accou[r]ted for and make them above the level in the vulgar occupations of life like my profession their friends too still enjoyd prosperity and woud fancy it a stain to [unite] their family with a lime burner   such was the tide that bore strongly against us on our first acquaintance but when my book was publishd the wind changd and all were on my side courting my acquaintance and things will fall in their season wether they are wanted and expected or not   Autum seldom passes away without its tempest and friendship began upon speculation and self interest is sure to meet with a shock as chances and changes fall out   the man that built his house upon sand was run down by the tide — my friendship is worn out and my memorys are broken

I held out as long as I coud and then married her at Casterton church   her uncle John Turner was father and gave her the wedding dinner

I workd on at the New Inn till the winter and then returnd home on a disagreement in the wages as he promisd me nine

shillings a week the year round and then wanted to put me off
with seven   he was an odd man but a good Master and the
place on the whole was one of the best I ever met with   I left it
with regret and rather wishd to return as I liked the town and the
fields and solitudes were wild and far better then the fenny flats
etc that I [had] been usd but circumstances fell out to prevent me

I left Casterton on the Bullruning day at Stamford and on call-
ing on Drury I fell in with John Taylor whom I found was the
Editor of my poems then in the press and nearly ready for pub-
lishing   he was visiting M[r] Gilchrists and in the evening they
sent one of the servant maids to Drurys to invite me to go   I
felt loath but on his persuasion I started and he showd me the
door and felt very irksome while I stayd   M[r] Gilchrist read an
account of Woodcroft Castle from Woods Historys[136] and Taylor
talkd over some sayings and doings of the living authors   I
stopt a short time and when I got back to Drurys I wrote some
ryhmes which was publishd in the first [volume]   [A32, 18-22]

most of the Poems which I destroyd[137] were descriptive of Local
Spots about the Lordship and favourite trees and wild flowers
      one of these 'On the Violet' was inserted by Taylor in the
Village Minstrel and the 'Walk to Burghley Park'[138] is of the same
date   There was another on 'Round Oak Spring'[139] as good as
either of these which has not been publishd   Chauncy Hare
Townsend[140] saw the Book in Drury's possesion and told me he
was particularly pleased with this poem which made me think
more of them afterwards then I had done   the encouragment
my first Volume met with lifted me up into heartsome feelings
and ryhming was continually with me night and day   I began
the Village Minstrel a long while before attempting to describe
my own feelings and love for rural objects and I then began in
good earnest with it after the trial of my first poems was made
and compleated   it was little time but I was still unsatisfied
with it and am now and often feel sorry that I did not withold it a
little longer for revision   the reason why I dislike it is that it
does not describe the feelings of a ryhming peasant strongly or

113

localy enough   I began a second part to effect this and got a
good way in it and sent Taylor a specimen but he said nothing in
return either for it or against it and as I found the verses multi-
plied very fast and my intended correction of localitys growing
very slow I left off and destroyd a good part of it   the rest
remains as they were — all the poems in the Village Minstrel save
the early ones above mentioned were written after the publica-
tion of the first Vol and a many more unpublished yet   most of
the Poems now written were written in the three years preceding
the first publication   I have written nothing since I was taken
ill march was a twelvemonth in ryhme   I had many ryhming
projects in my head and often felt anxious to write a dramatic
Poem but perhaps the prevention by illness has been the means
of saving the fame I have gotten as they might have been such
failures in such matters [as to] have forfieted all

[B6, R81]

A pro[p]het is nothing in his own country

Envy was up at my success with all the lyes it coud muster
some said that I never wrote the poems and that Drury gave me
money to father them with my name   others said that I stole
them out of books and that parson this and Squire tother knew
the books from which they were stolen   pretending scholars
said that I had never been to a grammer school and there fore it
was impossible for me to write any thing and our parson[141] indus-
triously found out the wonderful discovery that I coud not spell
and of course his opinion was busily distributed in all companys
which he visited that I was but a middling success of a poet but his
opinion got its knuckles rapt — and then he excusd the mistake
by saying he did not read poetry and consequently knew little
about it   there he was right — one sunday the same prophet
caught me working a common problem in geometry with the
scale and compasses in which I was fond to dabble and after

114

expressing his supprise at my meddlings in such matters he said we do these things different at colledge   we make a circle without compasses and work a problem without a scale — the solution of this problem was somthing like a round lye — an old leistershire farmer and his family in a neighboring vill[a]ge was uncommonly against me   they declard it was impossible for me to do any thing and dis believd every thing but that which was against me — thus every kind loves its own color and on that principal the Indian believes the devil a white sprit and the europea[n]s a black one — the old man had a lubberly son whom he fancied to make a learned one by sending him to school till he was a man and his ten years wisdom consisted of finding that 2 and 2 makes 4 that a circle was round and a triangle had 3 corners and that poetry was nothing in comparison to such knowledge the old men believd it and though[t] like wise

[B3, R90]

The Critics speaks their guesses or opinions with such an authourity of certainty as tho they were the fountain of truth   some of them said I had imitated the old poets Raleigh Drumond etc and several of them complaind at my too frequent imitations of Burns   now the fact is that when my first poems was written I knew nothing of Burns not even by name for the fens are not a literary part of england   nay my ignorance was not only a wide guess from all these but they had no existance with me — and I know nothing of Drummond etc further then the name even now   I had an odd Volume of Ramsay a long while and if I imitated any it shoud be him to which I am ready to acknowledge a great deal

[B3, 81]

I have been accused of being a drunkard and of being ingratful towards my friends and Patrons by a set of meddling trumpery to whom I owe none who never gave me furether notice then their scandal which is too weak or foolish for me either to notice or replye to   they are a set of little curs without teeth whose barkings can do no harm and whose busy meddling rather serves to

115

create laughter then anger   the utmost breath of their satire tho blown up to bursting has not sufficient strength to bear up a soap bubble so let them rail   most of them have known me from childhood and coud never find that I had any faults till now — I possesd their good word 18 years and it did me no service — and if I shoud live to wear their bad one as long it will do me no harm so I care nothing about them tho their meddlings get the ears of some that believe them — I have felt all the kindness I have received tho I did not mak[e] a parade of it   I did not write eternal prases and I had a timidity that made me very awkard and silent in the presence of my superiors which gave me a great deal of trouble and hurt my feelings   I wishd to thank them and tell them that I felt their kindness and remained silent   neither did I trumpet the praises of patrons eteranly werever I went — I had found that great talkers were always reckond little liars and that eternal praisers in public were alowd to be whisperers of slander in secret so I thought that if I was always speaking of myself and patrons among such company I shoud be suspected and reckond as one of them — I was never utterly cast down in adversity   I struggled on   neither was I at any time lifted up above my prosperity   I never attempted to alter my old ways and manners   I asumed no proud notions nor felt a pride above my station   I was courted to keep company with 'the betters' in the village but I never noticed the fancied kindness

the old friends and neighbours in my youth are my friends and neighbours now and I have never spent an hour in any of the houses of the farmers since I met with my [success] or mixd in their company as equals   I visit none but an old neighbours with whom I was acquainted in my days of labour and [hardship]

I keep on in the same house that we always occupied and have never felt a desire to have a better — tho it has grown into a great inconvinience since my father first occupied it 35 years ago

it was as roomy and confortable as any of our neighbours and we had it for 40 shillings rent while an old apple tree in the garden generaly made the rent   the garden was large for a poor man and my father man[a]ged to dig it night and morning before and

after the hours of labour and lost no time   he then did well —
but the young farmer that succeeded our old Landlord raised
the rent and the next year made four tennements of the house
leaving us a corner of one room on a floor for 3 Guineas a year and
a little slip of the garden which was divided into 4 parts but as my
father had been an old tennant he gave him the choice of his share
and he retaind our old apple tree   tho the ground was good for
nothing yet the tree still befrended us and made shift to make up
the greater part of our rent till every misfortune as it were came
upon him to crush him at once for as soon as hee was disabled
from work the old tree faild to bear fruit and left us unable to get
up the rent and when Drury found me out we owd for 2 years and
was going to leave it the next year   my father was going to a
parish house and I was at Casterton in service were I intended to
remain and when I met with my unexpected prosperity I never
felt a more satisfied happiness then being able to keep on the old
house and to put up with all its unconven[i]enc[e]s and when I
was married the next door occupier happend to leave his tene-
ment so I took it and remaind on — I have often been urged and
advised to leave it and get a more roomey and better looking
house by visitors who gave me no better encouragement then
their words and whom I did not expect woud be of any service to
me in case their advice happend to lead me into greater inconvi-
nences in the end so I took no notice of them and lived on in the
same house and in the same way as I had always done following
my old occupations and keeping my old neighbours as friends
without being troubled or dissapoi[n]ted with climbing ambi-
tions that shine as fine as they may only tempt the restless mind
to climb so that he may be made dizzy with a mockery of splendor
and topple down headlong into a lower degradation then he left
behind him —

and as soon as he went to the parish for relief they came to clap
the town brand on his goods and set them down in their parish
books because he shoud not sell or get out of them   I felt
utterly cast down for I coud not help them sufficient to keep them
from the parish so I left the town and got work at Casterton with

117

Gordon   I felt some consolement in solitude from my distress
[by] letting loose my revenge on the unfeeling town officer in a
Satire on the 'Parish' which I forbore to publish after wards[142] as
I thought it [   ]

    and they remaind quiet spectators of my success and ceased to
meddle with my father when I did not care for their kindness
[nor] fear the[ir] resentment   [B3, 85-7]

In the beginning of January my poems was publishd after a long
waiting anxiety of nearly two years and all the reviews excepting
Philips waste paper Mag:[143] spoke in my favour   in the course
of the publication I had venturd to write to Lord Milton to request
leave that the vol might be dedicated to him but his Lordship was
starting into Italy and forgot to answer it so it was dedicated to
nobody which perhaps might be as well   as soon as it was out
my mother took one to Milton when his Lordship sent a note to
tell me to bring 10 more copys on the following sunday   I went
and after sitting awhile in servants hall were I coud eat and drink
nothing for thought his Lordship sent for me and instantly
expland the reasons why he did not answer my letter in a quiet
unaffected manner which set me at rest   he told me he had
heard of my poems by parson Mossop who I have since heard
took hold of every oppertunity to speak against my success or
poetical abilitys before the book was publishd and then when it
came out and others praisd it instantly turnd round to my side
    Lady Milton also askd me several questions and wishd me to
name any book that was a favourite expressing at the same time
a desire to give me one but I was confou[n]ded and coud think of
nothing so I lost the present   in fact I did not like to pick out a
book for fear of seaming overeaching on her kindness or else
Shakespear lay at my tongues end   Lord fitzwilliam and lady
fitzwilliam too talkd to me and noticd me kindly and his Lordship
gave me some advice which I had done well perhaps to have
noticed better then I have   he bade me beware of booksellers
and warnd me not to be fed with promises — on my departure
they gave me an handfull of money the most that I had ever

118

possesd in my life together   I almost felt that I shoud be poor
no more   there was seventeen pound

Af[ter]wards I was visited by the Hon[bl] M[r] Pierpoint[144] with an
invitation to go to burghly on the sunday but when sunday came
it began to snow too unmercifully for a traveller even to ventur
thus far so I coud not go till the monday tho it was not the weather
that prevented me   I felt fearfull that my shoes woud be in a
dirty condition for so fine a place   when I got there the porter
askd me the reason why I did not come before and when I spoke
of the weather he said 'they expected you and you shoud stand
for no weathers tho it rained knives and forks with the tynes
downward   we have been suspected of sending you away'
this was a lesson that I afterwards took care to remember   after
awhile his Lordship sent for me and went upstairs and thro wind-
ing passages after the footman as fast as I coud hobble almost fit
to quarrel with my hard naild shoes at the noise they made on the
marble and boarded floors and cursing them to myself as I set my
feet down in the lightest steps I was able to utter   his Lordship
recieved me kindly askd me some questions and requested to look
at the MSS which Mr Pierpont wishd me to bring in my pocket
after I had been about half an hour eyeing the door and now and
then looking at my dirty shoes and wishing myself out of the
danger of soiling such grandeur he saw my embarassments as I
suspect and said that I shoud loose my dinner in the servants hall
and said I had better go but it was no use starting for I was lost and
coud not stir a foot   I told his Lordship and he kindly opend
the door and showed me the way when he sudde[n]ly made a stop
in one of the long passages and told me that he had no room in his
gardens for work at present but that he woud alow me 15 gineas
a year for life which woud enabale[145] me to pursue my favourite
studys at least two days in a week (this bye the bye was far better)

I was astonishd and coud hardly believe that he had said it
he then calld a servant and I went off scarcly feeling the ground

I went on and almost fanc[y]ing myself as rich a man as his
Lordship   that night I calld at O. Gilchrists and he scarcly
belie[v]d it and I thought I was mistaken   [A55, 7-8; A32, 1]

119

good luck began to smile from all quarters and my successes made me almost beside myself   Lord Radstock wrote to me with the most feeling affections and has acted to me more of a father then a friend   Blairs Sermons[146] accompanied the letter and Mrs Emmerson[147] about the same time wrote with kind encouragments and accompanied it with a Youngs Night thoughts but the first letter I ever recievd was from a disguised name A.B. supposd to be Dawson Turner of Yarmouth[148] seasond with good advice which I did not heed as I ought and Captain Sherwell[149] wrote to me early and kindly   it was thro his friendship that I recievd the present from Walter Scott of 2 Guineas and the Lady of the Lake which was wrongly and sadly mistated in the gossip that appeard in the London Mag: intitld a Visit etc   I felt disapointed when I heard it was a present from the author but I said nothing   C.S. made an apology for the omision by saying that Walter Scott enjoyd such a high literary character that he did not wish to hazerd an opin[i]on or insert his name in the Vol   I cannot exactly say what the words were without refering to the letter but a little slip of paper was inserted in the vol by CS stating that Walter Scott presented the Lady[150] of the Lake to John Clare with the modest hope that he woud read it with attention   it was a foolish modesty at best — I told a friend of mine about the matter [and he] laughd and said that he rememberd the time when the author of the lady of the lake hazarded his reputation in a matter by courting the favour of the critics in stating that his livelihood consisted in his writings   wether this be true or false it rests in my mistake for Octave Gilchrist was the man that told me and I believe him —   [A32, 1-2; B3, 75]

[Visitors and Visits]

I was now wearing into the sunshine and the villagers that saw caraiages now and then come to the house filld with gossiping gentry that was tempted by curosity more then any thing else to seek me   from these I got invitations to corespond and was swarmd with promises of books till my mother was troubld and fancied that the house woud not hold them but her trouble was soon set aside for the books never came and one letter generally worded with extravagant praise courting a quick reply I replied warmly and there the matter ended   I had nothing but my dissapointment in return but I soon felt expierenc[e] growing over these deceptions and when such matters was palmd on me again I never answerd them   I had two or three of these things nay more from parsons — amid these successes I went to work as usual but was often tormented and sent for home to satisfye the gaze of strangers — Lord Radstock started a subscription that filld me with astonishment at his accounts of its success Taylor and Hessey inserted a hundred pounds in there names at the top of the List and the good Lord Fitzwilliams gave me a hundred pounds from a letter which Taylor sent who took the [opportunity] to kill two birds with one stone and mentiond Keats in his letter to whom his Lordship gave 50 pound and a short time after a tirade [was published in the] London Magazine

[A32, 2-3]

the first publication of my poems brought many visitors to my house out of a mere curosity to expect to know wether I realy was the son of a thresher and a laboring rustic as had been stated and when the[y] found it realy was so they lookd at each other as a matter of satisfied supprise askd some gossiping questions and on finding me a vulgar fellow that mimicd at no pretentions but spoke in the rough ways of a th[o]rough bred clown they soon turnd to the door and dropping their heads in a good morning attitude they departed — I was often annoyd by such visits and got out of the way when ever I coud and my wife and mother was often out of temper about it as they was often caught with a dirty house   then which nothing was a greater anoyance

[B7, R93]

some of them askd me if I kept a book to insert the names of visitors

121

and on my answering in the negative they woud often request to insert them on my paper and many of them left promises which they never performd so I soon learnd that promises was a good seed time but prefromances brought a bad harvest forgetfulness coming in between like pharoahs lean kine and swallowing them up[151]   I had the works of Lord Byron promisd by 6 different people and never got them from none of them   [B7, R93]

Among the many that came to see me there was a dandified gentleman of uncommon odditys of character that not only borderd on the ridicilous but was absully[152] smotherd in it   he made pretentions to great learning and knew nothing   on his first coming he began in a very dignified manner to examine the fruits of experience in books and said he hoped I had a fondness for reading as he wished to have the pleasure to make me a present of some   he then begd my walking stick and after he had got it he wanted me to write my name on the crook   I really thought the fellow was mad   he then asked me some insulting libertys respecting my first acquaintance with Patty and said he understood that in this country the lower orders made their courtship in barns and pig styes and asked wether I did   I felt very vext and said that it might be the custom of high orders for aught I knew as experience made fools wise in most matters but I assured him he was very wrong respecting that custom among the lower orders here   his wife said he was fond of a joke and hoped I shoud not be offended but I saw nought of a joke in it and found afterwards that he was but a scant remove from the low order himself as his wife was a grocers da[u]ghter   after he had gossiped an hour he said well I promised to give you a book   but after examining your librar I dont see that you want any thing as you have a great many more then I expected to find still I shoud make you an offer of somthing   have you got a Bible   I said nothing but it was exactly what my Father had long wanted and he instantly spoke for me and said we have a bible sir but I cannot read it the print is so small so I shoud thank you for one   the man lookd very confused and explaind by

his manner that he had mentioned the very book which he
thought we had to escape giving it   [A33, 1]

[Preston]

his name was Preston[153] and he made me believe that he was a
very great Poet and that he knew all the world and that almost all
the world knew him   he had a vast quantity of M.S.S. he said
by him but had not published much at present tho he had two
rather important works in the press at that time whose publica-
tion he anxiously awaited and on pressing him hard about their
size and contents he said that one was an Elegy on the death of
the Queen and the other some anecdotes that he had pickt up in
India which the religious tract society was printeing for him
he said he thought that the first woud be about 9^d and the other
3^d price but his grand work for he calld it so himself was yet to be
tried   it was 'The Triumph of Faith'   he had met with one
patron at Cambridge by accident as it were who admird a hymn
which had been sung and enquiring after the Author Mr Preston
present him self and the person invited him to sup with him were
he heard his himny again sung to the Pianaforte with excessive
gratification as him self expressd it — he had been a sailor and
pretended to be familiarly acquainted with Ireland the Shakes-
pear Phantom[154] whom he described as a great and unfortunate
Genius — he was for ever quoting beautys from his own poetry
and he knew all the living poets in England and scotland as famil-
iar as his own tongue — he was a living hoax — he had made two
or three visits to Bloomfield and talkd of him as familiar as if he
had been his neighbour half a life time   he calld him 'brother
bob'[155]
he was one who was very fond of asking questions and answer-
ing them him self by guesses before those whom he was talking
to had time to replye   'how large will your new book be — say
about 5 shillings   who is your first Patron   shall we say

Lord Radstock   how many are printed at an edition   we'll say a thousand eh' and these he woud utter and reply too in one breath without a break or hesitation to wait your reply or to know the correctness of his guesses and between the intervals of his discourse he woud[156] repeat some lines from Byron in mouthing drawl somthing like the growl of a mastiff — he askd me wether I was a good reader of poetry and on my saying that I was not he woud say come to London sir by all means 'come to London Sir'

we have sporting clubs Lectures and all manner of [exercises] to make you a perfect reader and reciter of poetry — he knew all the Painters and Royal Accademicians and coud critis[iz]e their various exellences and defects with great dexterity of tongue

he praised Hilton[157] and two or three others as the tops of the tree while a stood abusing a sketch of my head that hung by the wall and finding a thousand faults with it   I let him go on and then told him it was done by Hilton   he turnd himself round on his heel blamed his eyesight and discoverd nothing but beautys afterward

with 'well friend John you must give me so and so' he utterd a prayer expounded a chapter in the bible sung a hymn told a smutty story and repeated one of Mores Songs in quick succession   I felt quite wearied with his officious company for I had him the whole day and some months after he wrote me word that urgent busness had brought him to Peterbro and that if I wanted to see him I shoud write a welcome to tell him so   I thought this was an easy oppertunity to let silence inform him he was not welcome so I never wrote and he never came

[A33, 8; A18, 275, 269]

Another impertinent fellow of the Name of Ryde[158] who occupys a situation which proves the old Farmers assertion that the vilest weeds are always found in the richest soil

[A18, 269]

A Mr Frellingham of Peterboro came to see me with a painter[159]

[B6, R85]

124

Hopkinson

Mr Hopkinson[160] of Morton the magistrate sent an odd sort of invitation for he was an odd sort of man he sent a note saying that a horse woud be at my door at helpstone on such a morning at such a time of the clock leaving me no option wether I chused to go or not it was harvest and I was busy reaping wheat I told the man I was reaping for about the matter and he said I had better go so accordingly the poney came and I started the day after I got in his wife took me round the town to walk as she told me but I found it was to sho me to her parishioners I felt very much anoyd at the awkard situation it led me in for I found they did not want to be troubled either with one or the other her impertinent enquireys were often evaded with a carless indifference and a pretending business at their domestic labours they woud scarcley wait to hear her speak ere the weel was started into a quicker twirl or the pots and pans scoured with a more bustleing hand she was going to take me regularey round from door to door but I was obliged to tell her that I was not fond of such visitings so she desisted but not without seeming to be offended — she was one of the oddest and most teaseing ca[r]ds in her fancied kindness that I ever met with — as soon as I got in she took me up stairs to show me a writing desk which she told [me] to consider as my own and showd me at the same time all the draws and their contents of Paper Pens ink sealing wax sticks saying that she expected I shoud make use of it and hoped I woud write something every day as she woud find me plenty of paper but when the up shoot came and after I had exhausted my whole budget of thanks and compliments for the present she begd to caution me that I shoud not take it away that it was mine every time I came and as long as I staid but she coud not part with it out of the house as it was an old favourite — she proposed reading my poems over leaf by leaf to give her opinions of them and make observations etc etc for my benefit and advantage to correct in a second edition and she began with the introduction she read a few lines and then preached over an half hours comment she said the introduction was very well written but I must now think of improving it as I had met with many friends whom it woud be very rude of me not to mention as they certainly woud look for some compliment from me for the notice they had taken and she thought that I coud do it better in ryhme   when she got to the poems she woud remark this is a pretty poem but why did you not dedicate it some one of your friends as you did the woodman   she read in a loud confident voice like the head boy in a school who is reckond a good reader and whos consiet thinks he is so g[ood] and tho she met with words frequently in reading other books that she did not understand she woud jar them over with an unmeaning mutter as if she thought you woud take no notice or did not understand it — she[161] woud often lift up her eye from her book to see if I was attentive and on finding my attention occupied with other things she gave up the critisisms after commenting on a few passages   she appeard to be a woman of very little understanding and less learning to help it out — there were two daughters that were well read in books and of quiet and amiable disposition but they had quarreld with her and did not come down stairs while I stayd — the man was one of odd taste and habits and I found that tho a magistrate he woud tell lies — he had written a book with a design of instructing his parishoners in a pompous and long winded style   he never wishd to be seen ignorant of any[thing] not even in the gossip or news of the village — he woud not bear contradicting and therefore was well quallified for a country magistrate   if you told any thing at dinner as an interesting story or fact of any kind it woud not seem to move his attention to listen a moment but the next day he woud repeat your story word for word as his own and tell it to you with as much gravity as if you had been a stranger to it and never heard it before

He askd me some pointless questions about my patrons in a carless manner as if he did not need enquireys when one day or two after wards he woud talk about them as if he had been a familiar acquaintance and knew much more about them then I did nay he woud tell me about them as if I knew nothing   he

126

askd about the way in which Lord Milton and Exeter [behaved]
and after I had told him he said he woud mention me to them
as if they had never known or noticed me — he said he was
acquainted with Lord Waldgrave and showd me a vol of my
poems which he said Lady Waldgrave had given him — he took
me with him to see Falkingham jaol a good distance from Morton
and every one we met gentle or simple he woud stop to speak too
and almost ask their business nay he woud question those that
appeard his inferiors as if they were under going an examination
in a court of justice — once when we were going to see Belvoir
Castle while walking by a plantation a labourer happend to break
out into a brisk loud whistle of a song tune and he instantly stopt
to listen and swore they were poachers and bade me go on the
other side to watch which way they started   I tryd to convince
him that the whistle was a song tune but it was no use — and as
soon as the fellow heard or perhaps saw that he was suspected
tho hid from us I expect he felt fearful and stopt his whistle
this convinced the other that his opinion was right — so after
watching awhile the fellow made his appearance and met us to
know if we was waiting for him   He askd him his business
there and he said he was putting down fencing which satisfied
the magistrate — who I verily believe mistrusted every stranger
for thieves or vag[a]bonds   [A25, 20, 28-30]

I had several kind and gentlemanly [visitors] came to see me
Chauncy Hare Townsend came to see me   it was one evening
in summer and asked me if John Clare lived there   I told him I
was he and he seemd supprised and askd agen to be satisfied for
I was shabby and dirty   he was dissapointed I dare say at
finding I had little or nothing to say for I had always had a natural
depression of spirits in the presence of strangers that took from
me all power of freedom or familarity and made me dull and
silent for [if] I attempted to say any thing I coud not reccolect it
and made so many hums and hahs in the story that I was obliged
to leave it unfinished at last   I often tryd to master this con-
fusion by trying to talk over reasonings and arguments as I went

127

about in my rambles which I thought I did pretty well but as soon as I got before any body I was as much to seek as ever — C.H.T. was a little affecting with dandyism and he mimicked a lisp in his speech which he owd to affectation rather then habit   otherwise he was a feeling and sensible young man   he talkd about Poets and poetry and the fine scenery of the lakes and other matters for a good while and when he left me he put a folded paper in my hand which I found after he was gone was a sonnet and a pound bill   he promised and sent me Beatties Minstrel[162]

some letters passd between us and I sent him a present of my Village Minstrel when I never heard of him afterwards[163]   he has since published a Volume of Poems   [B6, R86]

I met with notice from the Bishop of Peterbro[164] who sent me a beautifully bound copy of Miss Aikins Elizabeth[165]   his Lady came to see me twice with the Revd Mr Parsons[166] and a young lady who presented me with a vol of sermons on the christian religion   Mr Parsons gave me a copy of the Oxford sausage[167]

they talkd awhile about my poems and then lookd in the garden at my flowers and started — Drury usd to be very fond of introdusing me to strangers when I was at his house and I went there very often and at one of these calls General Birch Reynardson[168] came into the shop to buy some books and made some enquireys about me   Drury told him I was at hand and he expressd a desire to see me when he invited me to come to Holywell (and expressd a regret that Lady Sophia his sister coud not see me being very ill and having sat up too long the day before on expecting my coming   I felt vext I did not go but it was no use her Ladyship gave me the pleasures of hope[169]) which I did in the beginning of April   it was a pleasant day for the season and I found the scenery of Holywell very beautiful   he showd me his library which was the largest I had seen then and he pulld out of the crammd shelves a thin Quarto beautifully bound in red morrocco   he said they were Love Elegys written by his father and of course in his mind were beautiful   I just glancd over them and fanc[i]ed they were imitations of Hammond[170]   at

128

the end were some in MS which I suspected to be written by himself   I then went to see the garden and strolld a little about the park   a little river ran sweeping along and in one place he was forming a connection with it to form an Island   in one sunny spot was a large dial and near it under the shadows of some evergreens was a bird house built in the form of a cage glass all round and full of canarys that were fluttering about busily employd in building their nests — in looking about these places with the general a young lady the governess to the child[e]r whom accompanyd us whom I mistook for his wife neither of whom unriddeld my mistake till I found it out and I felt ashamd and vexd when I started home the young lady wishd to see me again

after dinner the young lady came and requested I woud write a copy of Verses for her and an elderly woman wanted me to write an address to her son in imitation of Cowpers Lines on his mothers Picture   [A32, 3-4]

after looking about the gardens and the library I was sent to dinner in the Servants Hall[171] and when it was over the housekeeper invited me into her room were the governess came and chatted in a free manner and asking me to corespond with her gave me her address   the house keeper wishd me to write an address to her son in imitation of Cowpers lines on his mothers picture — the governess was a pretty impertinent girl and mischeviously familiar to a mind less romantic then my own   I felt startled into sudden supprises at her manner and in the evening on my return home I was more supprisd still when on getting out of the park into the fields I found her lingering in my path and on coming up to her she smiled and told me plainly she was waiting to go a little way home with me   I felt evil apprehensions as to her meaning but I was clownish and shoy and threatnd no[172] advantages to interpret it   she chatted about my poems and resumed the discourse of wishing me to correspond with her which I promised I woud   when we came to the brink of the heath that stands in view of Pattys cottage I made a stop to get rid of her but she lingerd and chatterd on till it grew very late when

129

a man on horseback suddenly came up and askd the road we had came from when she thinking it was the General hastily retreated but on finding her mistake she returnd and resumd her discourse till it grew between the late and early when I wishd her good night and abruptly started without using the courage of shaking her by the hand — I felt excessive[l]y awkard all the way home and my mind was filld with guesses and imaginings at her strange manner and meanings — I wrote one letter too her and intended to be very warm and very gallant in it but fearing that she only wanted me to write love letters to have the pleasure to talk about them and laugh at them so my second mind wrote a very cold one in which I inserted the second address to a Rosebud in humble life[173] in which I requested no Answer nor hinted a second adventure so there the matter or mystery ended for I never unriddeled its meanings tho it was one of the oddest adventures my poetical life met with   it made me rather consieted as I sometimes fancied the young lady had fallen in love with me and I expected [   ][174] — she came from Birmingham   I shall not mention her name here   [A25, 19-20]

I now recieved invitations to go to Milton not to visit Lord Milton but his servants but they were the first rate of the house and well informed men not unacquanted with books and I never met with a party of more happy and harti[e]r fellows in my life   There was Artis up to the neck in the old Norman Coins and broken pots of the Romans and Henderson[175] never wearied with hunting after the Emperor Butterfly and the Hornet Sphinx in the Hanglands wood and the Orchises on the Heath and West an upright honest man tho his delight in reading extended little further then the prices that fat sheep and bullocks fetchd and the rise of corn every week in the news paper — 'the mans the man for a that' and Roberts[176] who sung a song of Moor[e]s and admired his poetry as clever and as stoutly as most ametuers and Grill the Cook[177]   he was a french man and possesd a fund of patient good humour and a countenance inimitable in england his visage was a Ciracature in good earnest and woud heartily

130

repay Cruikshanks a journey from London to take it   Artis
drew an outline often of his countenance but they want the spirit
of the origional   they are only outlines — and there was
Hague the wine Butler whose library consisted of one solitary
book 'Browns reflections on a summers day'   he was an odd
good sort of fellow — there were two young maidens — Mrs Proc-
ter and Mrs Byron[178] who had not the womanly affectation about
them of even attempting showing some affinity of kindred from
the coinsidences of their names with two popular poets   they
were above pardonable vanity and one of them was a lover of
poesy   [A18, 273]

John Taylor came to see me merely I suppose to make up an arti-
cle for the London Mag: for he never came afterwards   he was
to have met a friend who came from the same place a hearty
fellow that called the day before — I was a going to Stamford and
met Taylor on the road   he spent most part of the day with me
in walking about the fields
    Taylor is a man of very pleasant address and works himself into
the good opinions of people in a moment but it is not lasting for
he grows into a studied carlessness and neglect that he carries
into a system till the purpose for so doing becomes transparent
and reflects its own picture while it woud hide it —[179] he is a very
pleasant talker and an excessive fluent on Paper currency and
such politics   he can talk on matters with a superficial know-
ledge of them very dexterously and is very fond of arguing about
the latin and Greek poets with the Reverends and the cambridge
[scholars] that drop in to his waterloo house   he assumes a
feeling and fondness for poetry and reads it well — not in the
fashionable growl of mouthing spouters but a sort of whine — he
professed a great friendship for me at my first starting and offerd
to correct my future poems if he did not publish them[180] so I sent
all my things up as I wrote them and neither got his opinion or
the poems back again his only opinion being that he had not time
to spare from other pursuits to revise and correct them for the
press and when I sent for the poems agen he was silent — he

wrote the Introductions to both my Vols of Poems — his manner
is that of a cautious fellow who shows his sunny side to strangers

he has written some pamphlets on polotics and the Identity of
Junius[181] a very clever book and some very middling papers in the
London Magazine and bad sonnets   Gilchrist told me that he
first displayd the schoolboy prodogy of translating some of
Horaces odes into ryhme which he sent to the Mirror that hot bed
of Indications — he askd me to correspond with him which I did
very thickly as I fancied he was the greatest frend I had ever met
with but after he had publishd 3 vols of my poems his correspon-
dence was laid by and I heard nothing more from him

he never asks a direct question or gives a direct reply but con-
tinualy saps your information by a secret passage coming at it as
it were by working a mine like a lawyer examining a witness and
he uses this sort of caution even in his common discourse till it
becomes tedious to listen or reply   he sifts a theory of truth
either true or false with much ingenuity and subtelty of argument
and his whole table talk is a sort of Junius Identified but his pati-
ence carrys it to such lengths in seeming consistency till the first
end of the ravelled skein which he winds up at the begining is lost
again and unwound in looking for the other — to sum up his
character he is a clever fellow and a man of Genius and his Junius
Identified is the best argument on circumstantial Evidence that
ever was written   [B6, R86-R85]

A Confession of Faith

My creed may be different to other creeds but the difference is
nothing when the end is the same — if I did not expect and hope
for eternal happiness I should be ever miserable — and as every
religion is a rule leading to good by its professor — the religions
of all nations and creeds where that end is the aim ought rather to
be respected then scoffed at — a final judgment of men by their
deeds and actions in life is inevitable and the only difference

between an earthly assize and the eternal one is that the final one needs no counsellors to paint the bad or good better or worse then they are   the judge knows the hearts of all things and the sentence may by expected to be just as well as final wether it be for the worst or the best — this ought to teach us to pause and think and try to lead our lives as well as we can   [N30, 3]

Opinions in Religion

I have not mentioned any thing about my opinions on religious matters and I am sorry to say I am much wanting   in my younger days I inclined to deism but on reading Pain[e]s Age of Reason lent me by a companion instead of hardening my opinion it broke it and I was doubtful of pain[e]s sub[t]eltys for he seemd determined to get over every obstacle with the opinion he set out with

after this I turned a methodist but I found the lower orders of this persuasion with whom I assosiated so selfish narrow minded and ignor[ant] of real religion that I soon left them [and] sank into m[ethodist] sects agen   they believed every bad [opi]nion [except about] themselv[es] [Henson] the preacher then of [Market Deeping][182]   [D2, 8]

I som times thought seriosly of religion and in one of my moral reflective moments found the Methodists but I found them [*incomplete*]

if every mans bosom had a glass in it so that its secret might be seen what a blotted page of christian profession and false pretentions woud the best of them display

My mind was always hung with doubts   I usd to fancy at times that religion was nothing and woud say to myself if there is a god let him dry up this pond of water or remove this stone and then I will believe and then on seeing things remain as they were I concluded that my doubts were true but after reflection

upbraided my foolish presumption and my conscence woud
struggle to correct my errors [A25, 17]

I feel a beautiful providence ever about me as my attendant deity
    she casts her mantle about me when I am in trouble to shield
me from it   she attends me like a nurse when I am in sickness
puts her gentle hand under my head to lift it out of pains way and
lays it easy by laying hope for my pillow   she attends to my
every weakness when I am doubting like a friend and keeps me
from sorrow by showing me her pictures of happiness — and
then offering them up to my service   she places herself in the
shadow that I may enjoy the sunshine and when my faith is sink-
ing into despondancy she opens her mind as a teacher to show
me truth and give me wisdom when I had it [A53, 43r]

A religion that teaches us to act justly to speak truth and love
mercy ought to be held sacred in every country and what ever the
differences of creeds may be in lighter matters they ought to be
overlookd and the principle respected [B4, 136]

First Visit to London

My Gilchrist often asked me if I shoud like to see London and as
I felt an anxiety he said I shoud go up with him the next time he
went which was early in March and I started with him in the old
Stamford Coach[183]   my mind was full of expectations all the
way about the wonders of the town which I had often heard my
parents tell storys about by the winter fire and when I turnd to
the reccolections of the past by seeing people at my old occupa-
tions of ploughing and ditching in the fields by the road side
while I was lolling in a coach the novelty created such strange
feelings that I coud almost fancy that my identity as well as my
occupations had changd that I was not the same John Clare but
that some stranger soul had jumpd into my skin — when we passd

134

thro Huntingdon Mr G. shewd me the House at this end of the town were Oliver Cromwell was born and the parsonage with its mellancholy looking garden at the other were Cowper had lived which was far the most interesting remembrance to me tho both were great men in the annals of fame   I thought of his tame hares and Johnny Gilpin[184]   as we glided along in the heavy sweeing coach I amusd myself with catching the varying features

of scenery   I remembere the road about Royston was very dreary   the white chalk like hills spread all round the cir[c]le and not a tree was to be seen   on[e] mellancholy thorn bush by the road side with a bench beneath it was all that my eye caught for miles   as we approached nearer London the coachmen pointed out 3 large round hills close by the road side and told a superstition about them which I forget

[A33, 9]

Here is one of the old Castles here that was in such requisition in the days of Cromwell and the holes in the wall then used for the cannon have never been filled up — it is a dreary looking building close to the turnpike

I have often read my self into a desire to see places which poets and novelists and Essayists have rendered classical by their descriptions of the[ir] presence and other localitys rendered sacred by genius — such is the parsonage house at Huntington with its old garden once the habitation of Cowper — such the brigs over the river Ouse ere you enter Huntington where he wandered with his dog which doubtless there cropt him the white water lily and won a song for its pains — then at the other end of

135

the town is the 'premises' were the english napoleon Oliver Cromwell followed the occupation of a brewer

but I had forgot the neat house and pleasant shrubbery of [Amwell] and the reading world has forgot him — as the wild bees honey is forgotten in the meadow grass yet the coachman had often seen a plain quaker like man wandering in a summers morning by the side the awthorn hedges in the pleasant grounds surrounding that house and that man was John Scott[185] the quaker poet   [A46, 153]

on the night we got into London it was announcd in the Play Bills that a song of mine was to be sung at Covent garden by Madam Vestris[186] and we was to have gone but it was too late   I felt uncommonly pleasd at the circumstance   we took a walk in the town by moonlight and went to westminster bridge to see the river thames   I had heard large wonders about its width of water but when I saw it I was dissapointed thinking I shoud have seen a fresh water sea and when I saw it twas less in my eye then Whittlesea Meer[187]   I was uncommonly astonished to see so many ladys as I thought them walking about the streets   I expressd my suprise and was told they were girls of the town as a modest woman rarely venturd out by her self at nightfall
[A33, 10]

Mem: ladys thronging the streets at night   [B3, 82]

I had often read of the worlds seven wonders in my reading Cary at school but I found in London alone thousands   Octave took [me] to see most of the curositys   we went to westminster abbey to see the poets corner and to both Play houses were I saw Kean and Macready and Knight and Munden and Emmery[188]
the two latter pleased me most of all but the plays were bad ones   they were [incomplete]   [A31, 58]

When I was in london the first time Lord Radstock introduced me to Mrs Emmerson   she has been and is a warm kind friend of

136

tastes feelings and manners almost romantic   she has been a
very pretty woman and is not amiss still and a womans pretty
face is often very dangerous to her common sense for the notice
she recievd in her young days threw an affectatious [air] about
her feelings which she has not got shut of yet for she fancys that
her friends are admirers of her person as a matter of course and
acts accordingly which appears in the eyes of a stranger ridicul-
ous enough but the grotesque wears off on becoming acquanted
with better qu[a]litys and better qualitys she certanly has to
counterballance them   she [was] at one word the best friend I
found and my expectations are looking no further   her cores-
pondence with me began early in my public life and grew pretty
thick as it went on   I fancyd it a fine thing to corespond with a
lady and by degrees grew up into an admirer some times writing
as I felt somtimes as I fancyd and sometimes foolish[l]y when I
coud not account for why I did it   I at length requested her
portrait when I reccolect ridicu[lous] enough alluding to Lord
Nelsons Lady Hamilto[n]   she sent it and flatterd my vanity in
return   it was beautifuly done by Behn[e]s the sculpter but bye
and bye my knowledge [of] the world sickend my roma[n]tic feel-
ings   I grew up in friends[hip] and lost in flattery afterwards
so she took to patronizing one of Col[e]ridges [sons] who had
written a visionary ode on Beauty in Knights quarterly
Magaz[in]e[189] in whom she discoverd much genius and calld him
on that stake one of the first Lyric poets in England — she then
whisht for her picture agen and I readily agreed to part with it —
for the artificial flower of folly had run to seed   [B3, 82]

the hills on the road to London — bare bleak awful misty and
beautiful[190]   [B3, 82]

I spent a good deal of time too with Rippingille[191] the painter
whom I first got acquainted with in meeting him at Mrs Emmer-
sons   he is a rattling sort of odd fellow with a desire to be
thought one and often affects to be so for the sake of singularity
and likes to treat his nearest friends with neglect and carlessness

on purpose as it were to have an oppertunity of complaining about it

he is a man of great genius as a painter and what is better he has not been puffed into notice like the thousands of farthing rush lights (like my self perhaps) in all professions that have glimmered their day and are dead   I spent many pleasant hours with him while in London   his greatest rellish is puning over a bottle of ale for he is a strong dealer in puns   we acted a many of lifes farces and crackt a many jokes to gether many of them bad ones perhaps and without kernels and we once spent a whole night at Offleys the Burton ale house[192] and sat till morning

he has some pretentions to ryhme and wrote An Address to Eccho which was inserted in the London Mag   most of his 'Trifles' in that way are satirical   I was to have gone over to Bristol to see him but illness prevented me   he affected to be little taen with worldly applause and was always fishing for it — he was very carless of money and squanderd it away as a thing of no other use but to spend   [B3, 56]

and from him I had learnd some fearful disclosures[193] of the place

he used to caution me if ever I happend to go to be on my guard as if I once lost my way I shoud [be] sure to loose my life as the street Ladys woud inveigle me into a fine house were I shoud never be seen agen and he described the pathways on the street as full of trap door[s] which dropd down as soon as pressd with the feet and sprung in their places after the unfortunate countryman had fallen into the deep hole as if nothing had been were he woud be robd and murderd and thrown into boiling chauldrons kept continualy boiling for that purpose and his bones sold to the docters — with these terrible jealousys in my apprehensions I kept a continual look out and fanci[e]d every lady I met a decoyer and every gentleman a pickpocket and if the[y] did but offer any civility my suspicions were confirmd at once and I felt often when walking behind Gilchrist almost fit to take hold of his coat laps
[A31, 59]

Burkhardt[194] took me to Vauxhall[195] and made me shut my eyes till I got in the midst of the Place and when I opened them I almost fancyd myself in fairey land but the repetition of the round about walk soon put the Romance out of my head and made it a faded reality — these were the scenes that he delighted in and he wishd to take me sometime to see the Beggars Opera[196] a public house so calld the resort of [thieves] but we had no time   I had had a romantic sort of notion about authors and had an anxious desire to see them fancying they were beings different to other men but the spell was soon broken when I became acquanted with them but I did not see many save at Taylors Dinner partys were Charles Lamb and young Reynolds and Allan Cunningham[197] and Carey with Wainwright the painter[198] often met and I saw Hazlitt

                                                                      [A31, 58]

One of my greatest amusments while in London was reading the booksellers windows   I was always fond of this from a boy and my next greatest amusment was the curiosity of seeing litterary men   of these all I have seen I shall give a few pictures just as they struck me at the time   some of them I went purposly to see   others I met in litterary partys that is the confind contributors dinners at Taylors and Hesseys   I had no means of meeting the constellation of Genius in one mass   they were mingld partys   some few were fixd stars in the worlds hemisphere   others glimmerd every month in the Magazine some were little vapours that were content to shine by the light of others   I mean dabling critics that cut monthly morsels from genius whose works are on the waters free for all to catch at that chuses   these bye and bye I coud observe had a self satisfaction about them that magnified molehills to mountains   I mean that little self was in its own eye a giant and that every other object was mere nothings   I shall not mention names here but it is evident I do not alude to friends

[I have heard it asserted that all critics are dissapointed ryhmsters there attempts for a name turning bankrupt as soon as they began business   this may be because of their general abuse of

139

the trade   this general opinion to the extent of my knowledge
holds good of every critic I know   were they were not poets by
profession I have found they had been ryhmers in their boyish
days and their librarys generaly conseald in one corner the thin
lean vollumne splendidly bound and dedicated to some young
friend a lover of poetry and of consequence a poet   this little
great pretending volume with its unasuming pretentions pleasd
the circle of friends for whom it was printed at the authors expence
and on getting no further they found it was easier to talk about a
book then make one so they turnd critics and sold their brain
dress of praise and abuse at market price][199]

Reynolds[200] was always the soul of these dinner partys   he
was the most good natured fellow I ever met with   his face
was the three in one of fun wit and punning personified   he
woud punch you with his puns very keenly without ever hurting
your feelings for it you lookd in his face you coud not be offended
and you might retort as you pleasd   nothing coud put him out
of humour either with himself or others   if all his jokes and
puns and witticisms were written down which were utterd at 2
or 3 of these dinner partys they woud make one of the best Joe
Millers that have ever passd under that title   he sits as a carless
listner at table looking on with quick knaping sort of eye that
turns towards you as quik as lightning when he has a pun joke or
story to give you   they are never made up or studied   they
are the flashes of the moment and mostly happy   he is a slim
sort of make som thing as you may conscieve of an unpretending
sort of fashionable fellow without the desire of being one   he
has a plump round face a nose somthing puggish and a forehead
that betrays more of fun then poetry   his teeth are always
looking through a laugh that sits as easy on his unpuckerd lips as
if he was borne laughing   he is a man of genius and if his
talents was properly applied he woud do somthing   I verily
believe that he might win the favours of fame with a pun but be
as it will wether she is inclind to smile or frown upon him he is
quite at home wi content   the present is all with him   he
carrys none of the Author about him   an hearty[201] laugh

which there is no resisting at his jokes and puns seems to be more
reccompence then he expected and he seems startld into wonder
by it and muses a moment as if he turnd the joke over agen in his
mind to find the 'merry thought' which made the laughter
they drop as it were spontaniously from his mouth and turn
again upon him before he has had time to conside[r] wether they
are good or bad   he sits in a sort of supprise till another joke
drops and makes him himself again...[202]   [B3, 68-70]

Reynolds is a near kin to Wainwright in openheartedness and
hillarity but he is a wit and a punster and very happy and enter-
taining in both pretentions for with him they are none for they
come naturally from his discourse and seem rather to flow from
his ink in his pen in his writings then from his mind   there is
nothing studied about them — and be the pun as severe as it may
his pleasant arch manner of uttering it forbids it to offend and it
is always taken in the same good natured way as it is intended —
he has written a great deal in Magazines and periodicals of all
names and distinctions and he is an author of no mean preten-
tions   as to quantity tho he has never acknowledged any with
his name   he wrote the Poem called the Naiad in imitations of
the old scotch ballad called the Mermaid of Galloway The
Remains of Peter Cocoran The Garden of Florence and a mock
Parody on Peter Bell all full of wit fun and real Poetry with a good
share of affectation and somthing near akin to bombast
    He is one of the best fellows living and ought to be a Poet of the
first order   himself is his only hinderance at present   Lord
Byron was his first Patron and corrected a poem and praised it
which has not been published   [B3, 58-9]

Hazlit[t] is the very reverse of this   he sits a silent picture of
severity   if you was to watch his face for a month you woud
not catch a smile there   his eyes are always turnd towards the
ground except when one is turnd up now and then with a sneer
that cuts a bad pun and a young authors maiden table talk to
atoms were ever it is directed   I look upon it that it carrys the

141

convi[c]tion with it of a look to the wise and a nodd to the foolish he seems full of the author too and I verily believe that his pockets are crambd with it   he seems to look upon M꞉ This and M꞉ Tother names that are only living on Cards of Morning calls and Dinner Invitations as upon empty chairs as the guests in Macbeth did on the vacancy were Banquos ghost presided they appear in his eye as nothings too thin for sight and when he enters a room he comes stooping with his eyes in his hands as it were throwing under gazes round at every corner as if he smelt a dun or thief ready to seize him by the colar and demand his money or his life   he is [a] middle sizd dark looking man and his face is deeply lind with a satirical character   his eyes are bright but they are rather turned under his brows   he is a walking satire and you woud wonder were his poetry came from that is scatterd so thickly over his writings   for the blood of me I coud not find him out that is I shoud have had no guess at him of his ever being a scribbler much more a genius   they say she is an odd lady and sure enough in him her odditys are strongly person[i]fied — then there is Charles Lamb a long remove from his friend hazlett in ways and manners   he is very fond of snuff which seems to sharpen up his wit every time he dips his plentiful finger into his large bronze colord box and then he sharpens up his head thro[w]s himself backward in his chair and stammers at a joke or pun with an inward sort of utterance ere he can give it speech till his tongue becomes a sort of Packmans strop turning it over and over till at last it comes out wetted as keen as a razor and expectation when she knows him wakens into a sort of danger as bad as cutting your throat but he is a good sort of fellow and if he offends it is innosently done   who is not acquanted with Elia and who woud believe him otherwise   as soon as the cloath is drawn the wine and he's become comfortable   his talk now doubles and threbles into a combination of repetitions urging the same thing over and over again till at last he — leans off with scarcly 'good night' in his mouth and dissapears leaving his memory like a pleasant ghost hanging about his vacant chair and there is his sister Bridget[203] a good sort of woman tho her kind cautions and tender admonitions are nearly lost upon Charles who like an undermined river bank leans carlessly over his jollity and recieves the gentle lappings of the waves of womans tongue unheedingly till it ebbs and then in the same carless posture sits and recieves it again tho it is all lost on Charles   she is a good woman and her cautions are very commendable for the new river runs very near his house and the path for a dark night is but very precar[i]ous to make the best of it and he jeanty fellow is not always blind to dangers so I hope the advice of his Sister Bridget will be often taken in time to retire with the cloth and see home by daylight

and there sits Carey the translator of Dante[204] one of the most quiet amiable and unasuming of men   he will look round the table in a peacful silence on all the merry faces in all the vacant unconser[n]ment imaginable and then he will brighten up and look smilingly on you and me and our next hand neighbour as if he knew not which to address first and then perhaps he drops a few words like a chorus that serve all together   his eyes are not long on a face   he looks you into a sort of expectation of discoursing and starts your tongue on tiptoe to be ready in answering what he may have to start upon when suddenly he turns from you to thro[w] the same good naturd cheat of a look on others

he is a tallish spare man with a longish face and a good forhead   his eyes are the heavy lidded sort whose easiest look seems to meet you half closd   his authorship and his priesthood sit upon him very meekly   he is one of those men which have my best opinions and of whom I feel happy with every oppertunity to praise   on my second visit to London I spent 2 very happy days with him at Chiswick (I was then in good health)

his wife is a good sort of person and of so young a look in his company that I mistook her a long while for his daughter   he lives [in] the house once occupied by Thorn[h]ill the painter[205] and he showd me the window thro which Miss Thorn[h]ill elopd with Hogarth and over the chimney piece were some heads sketchd on the wall by Hogarth but the servants being left to themselves to white wash the room in Mr Carey's abscen[c]e from home utterly defacd this precious relic and he greatly regretted

143

the loss when he told me   I also saw Hogarth[s] painting room at the end of the garden which is now a hay loft   you asend to it by a broad stept ladder   it has no prepossesing appearance about it and you almost feel to doubt memorys veracity when she whispers you this is the spot were Hogarth sat and painted pictures for the royal academy of fame but proofs as strong as holy writ meet your eye in a corner of the Garden were two narrow slips of stones stand close to the wall one [to] the memory of a bird with an inscription on it by Hogarth himself and the other to the memory of a dog with an inscription taken from Churchills poetry[206] by Mrs Hogarth 'Life to the last enjoyd here Pompey lies'

the Arbour of honey suckles or creepers hangs shadowy silence above them and in this corner Mr Carey pointed out the spot were Hogarth usd to play skittles and if my memory wears right impressio[n]s the frame is there still and then to wind up the curosity that such objects had excited we went to see the monument of Hogarth in the Church yard   I coud not help fancying when I walkd about the garden that the roses and cloves and other flowers were old tennants that knew Hogarth and his lady as well as their present occupants   bye the bye the translator of Dante will not deminish the classical memorys of the old mansion with his possesion of it   Poetry and painting are sisters — There was Col[e]ridge at one of these Partys   he was a man with a venerable white head fluent of speech not a 'silver tong[ue]d hamilton'[207] his words hung in their places at a quiet pace from a drawl in good set marching order so that you woud suppose he had learnt what he intended to say before he came it was a lecture parts of which [*then cut away*]

[B3, 70, 61-3]

A little artless simple seeming body somthing of a child over grown in a blue coat and black neckerchief for his dress is singular with his hat in his hand steals gently among the company with a smile turning timidly round the room — it is De Quincey the Opium Eater and that abstruse thinker in Logic and Metaphysics XYZ

144

Then there is Allan Cunningham (Reynolds calls him the dwarf) comes stalking in like one of [Spenser's] black knights but his countenance is open and his look is hearty   he hates puns and is fond of scotch ballads scotch Poets and every thing scottish down no doubt as far as scotch snuff — well he is a good fellow and a good poet and when the companys talk is of poetry he is ready to talk 2 ways at once but when puns are up his head is down over his glass musing and silent and nothing but poetry is the game to start him into hillarity again — There is a young man of the [*last seven words in different ink and then cut away*]   [B3, 64]

Southey

I never saw him but I heard somthing about him by meeting in company with 2 of his wifes sisters at Mrs Emmersons those 'Pretty milliners of Bath' as Byron calls them but I cannot say much for his judgment if these sisters are to be taken as a sample for the rest   they are sharp ready witted girls but rather plain

I learnd from them that Southey was a livly sort of man aways in gay spirits who wrote both in prose and verse with a great deal of ease but the Number of his publications woud almost tell us that this is the fact   he writes amid the noise of his childern and joins in their sport at intervals   Wordsworth on the contrary cannot bear a noise and composes with great difficulty   I shoud imagine he prefers the mossy seat on the mountains to the closet for study   at least his poems woud lead one to think so

Southy presents a copy of every work he publishes to his wife and he wrote a copy of Roderic[208] on french green paper on purpose to present to her   [B3, 84]

I stopt about a month in London and spent my time very pleasantly visiting about the town with those former wonders of Poets Painters and authors of most denominations that had worn out of my wonders into common men   I vis[i]ted Hilton Wainwright Lamb [and Hood] with Taylor[209]   Wainwright is a very comical sort of chap   he is about 27 and wears a quizzing glass and makes an excuse for the ornament by complaining of bad eyes   he is the Van Vink booms Janus Weathercock[210] etc of the Magazine   he had a picture in the exebition of 'Paris in the chamber of Helen' and the last time I was in London he had one there of 'the Milk maid' from Waltons angler both in my opinion very middling performances but my opinion is but of it self a middling one in such matters so I may be mistaken — he is a clever writer and some of his papers in the Magazine are very entertaining and some very good particularly the beginging of one a description of a Church yard —[211]   [B3, 54]

[Second Visit to London]

When Taylor came to see me he invited me to come to London and I took his invitation and started a second time   I spent most of my time at Taylors and Mrs Emmersons — I went up by my self as poor Gilchrist was very ill and coud not start just then tho he came up afterwards   he took me to see Gifford[212] who the first time we went up was too ill to see us but this time he was rather getting near neighbour to health and gave me welcome with a hearty shake of the hand and congratulated me on my last poems (the Village Minstrel) then just published which he said were far better then my first   he also bade me beware of the booksellers and repeated it several times[213]   he was sitting on his sofa surrounded with books and papers of all sorts   he chatted awhile to Gilchrist about Books and Authors and Pope and lent him a New Satire to read called the 'Mohawks'[214] in which he said he was mentioned   he supposed Lady Morgan was the Author and after Gilchrist had dipt into it here and there he prono[u]nced it worthless — the next day we went to call on Murray[215] in Albemarle street who flatterd me with some

146

compliments on my success and hoped that I woud always call on him when ever I came to London   he is a very pleasant man   he showed us the English Bards and Scotch Reviewers illustrated with Portraits which we turned over and departed and as we got at the door Giffords carriage drove up and on leaving the shop he gave each of us a copy of his Translation of Persius

[B3, 88]

altho I had conquered the old notion of kidnappers or men stealers being a common trade in London and staid long enough to find that this was a tale on my first visit I found that another very near kin to it on my second visit that I had not expected to find in the places were it was most practised was very common among all professions — they are a sort of genteel Purse knappers that tho they do not want the carcass will quickly lighten the pockets in exchange for bad bargains and they seem to know and pounce on a countryman as a raven on carrion — I wanted several things while there as curoisitys or presents to take home with me and I used to think that by going into the best looking shops in the most thorough fare streets I shoud stand the least risk to be cheated so in I went and gave every farthing they set upon the article and fancied I had got a good bargain till experience turned out to the contrary   when I first got up being rather spare of articles of dress I went into a shop in fleet street and purchased as a first article a pair of stockings for which the man asked 3/6 and on my giving it without a word of contrariety he made a pause when I asked him the price of another article and told me as he kept nothing but first rate articles they were rather high in the price and laying a redy made shirt on the counter he says that is 14 Shillings   I told him it was too high for me and with that he instantly pretended to reach me another which was the very same article agen   this was 6^s / 6^d I paid it and found afterwards that the fellows fine cloth was nothing but callico — I obse[r]ved it was always a custom in most shops that when you went in to ask for an article the thing they first shew you was always put a one side and another recommend[e]d as superior

147

which I found was always to the contrary — so experience taught
me always in future to take the one they did not reccommend —
on my last visit to London I wanted to take somthing home for
Patty and thinking that Waithman[216] had been a great stickler for
freedom and fair dealing among the citizens his news paper
notoriety reccomended me to his shop at the corner of Bridge
street as the hope that I might come in for a fair bargain but here
I was more decieved then ever for they kept the best articles aside
and reccomen[d]ed the worst as soon as they found out their
customer was of the country   when I took the things home I
found that they were a bad bargain still and a great deal dearer
then they might have been bought for at home — so much for
Patrons of Liberty and news paper passports for honest men — I
saw more in the way of wonders this time then I did at first but
they did not leave such strong impressions on my memory as to
be worth remembrance — I usd to go with Thomas Bennion
Taylors clerk or head porter about the city when he went out on
errands and very often went into each curosity that came in our
way such as [   ] A[nd] [   ] and other hard names for clap-
traps to ease the pocket of its burthen   I remember going into
Bullocks Mexico[217] with the Editors Ticket that Taylor gave me
and the fellows at their several posts of money catching fancying
I dare say that I was the critisizing editor looked with much sup-
prise at my odd clownish appearance and asked me so many
pumping questions that I was glad to get out agen without paying
much attention to the wonder of the show — Tom was very fond
of introducing me to the booksellers were he had business who
were too busily occupied in their own conserns to take much
heed of mine

[D2, 1; B3, 54-6][218]

I did not know the way to any place for a long while but the royal
academy and here I used to go almost every day as Rippingille the
painter had told the ticket keeper who I was and he let me come
in when ever I chose which I often made use of from nessesity

[B3, 54][219]

I do not know how the qualms of charity come over those who have plenty of riches to be charitable but I often feel it so strongly myself when objects of compassion pass me that its the only thing that makes me oftenest wish I had plenty for the pleasure of relieving their wants and when I was in London I often parted with my little money so freely that I was often as bad off as those I relieved and needed it perhaps as bad that is I felt[220] as bad or worse inconvinience then they from the want of it   I remember passing St Pauls one morning where stood a poor Affrican silently soliciting charity but the sincerity of his distress spoke plainer then words   I felt in my pockets but I had only fourpence in all and I felt almost ashamed to recieve the poor creatures thanks for so worthless a pittance and passed him but his looks spoke so feelingly that even a trifle would be acceptable that I ran back a long way and put the fourpence into his hand and I felt worse dissapointment when I saw the poor creatures heart leap to thank me and the tears steal down his cheeks at the gratification of the unlooked for boon for his thanks and supprise told me he had met with little of even such charity as mine — and I determind the next day to get my pocket recruited if possible and give him a shilling and my first walk was to St Pauls but the poor affrican was gone and I never saw him again —   [B5, R93]

My [Third] Visit to London

'Nothing set down in malice'[221]

A journey for pleasure is a precarious sympathy soon robd of its enjoyments by unforeseen dissasters but a journey for the improvment of ill health undertaken by that smiling encourager hope hath little to make it palatable tho the joys of the one are as much to be relied on as the other

Upon this last matter my Journey to London was made   I went for the benefit of advice to a celebrated scotch phisic[i]an Dr Darling[222]   the complaint lay in my head and chest   I was

149

very ill when I first went but I gradualy recievd benefit   some
reccolections of this visit shall be the subject of this chapter
they are observations of men and things thrown together in a
myscellaneous manner   this was the third time I had been up
so the vast magnitude [of] that human ant hill that strikes every
stranger with wonder had lost its novelty   the first time I went
up was in company with a first friend of old long syne memory
Octavius Gilchrist now gone to the land of uncertainty   poor
Octave   I still remember how we went sweeing along the road
on the heavy reeling coach   London was no novelty with him
but with me every thing was a wonder   I had read in my read-
ing [made] easy of the worlds seven wonders but I found in lon-
don alone thousands   as we approachd it the road was lind wi
lamps that diminishd in the distance to stars   this is London I
exclaimd   he laughd at my ignorance and only increasd my
wonder by saying we were yet several miles from it   when we
got in it was night and the next morning every thing was so
uncommon to what I had been usd to that the excess of novelty
confou[n]ded my instinct   every thing hung round my con-
fusd imajination like riddles unresolvd   while I was there
I scarcly knew what I was seeing and when I got home my
remembrance of objects seemd in a mass one mingld in another
like the mosiac squares in a roman pavement   on my second
visit things became more distinct and seperate on the memory
and one of my greatest wonders then was the continual stream of
life passing up and down the principal streets all the day long and
even the night and one of my most entertaining amusments was
to sit by Taylors window in Fleet Street to see the constant succes-
sions throng this way and that way and on this my last visit I
amusd my illness by catching the most beautiful women['s] faces
in the crowd as I passd on in it till I was satiated as it were with
the variety and the multitude and my mind lost its memory in
the eternity of beautys successions and was glad to glide on in
vacancy with the living stream   one of the greatest curiositys I
saw then was Devilles the Phreneologists[223] collection of heads
himself excepted   he is a kind simple hearted good humourd

150

man   Phrenenology is with him somthing more then a System
     it seems the life and soul of his speculations   he is never
weary of talking about it or giving 'Lectures on heads'   Stran-
gers of all exceptions Poets Philosophers Mathematicians and
humble unknown beings that with the world have no name are all
welcomd up his stairs and led to his matchless head gallery while
he with smiling politness satisfys ever eager enquirey as readily
as it is askd for   they have only to pull off their hats and drop
half hints and then the lecture on heads commences   he
mostly begins with 'Why Sir I shoud say heres order very strong
— or wisa wersa the want of it   heres plenty of constructivness
— I shoud say your fond of mathematics and heres ideality   I
shoud say that you have a tallent for poetry   I dont say that
you are a poet but that you have a tallent for it if applied   heres
the organ of collor very strong   I shoud say you are fond of
fine colors and wisa wersa   were theres the organ of form with
out color nothing showy is likd of   here is benevolence wery
prominent   I shoud say you seldom pass a beggar or street
sweeper without dropping a copper   heres weneration very
high   I shoud say you are religious   (the subject perhaps is
worldly minded and remains silent)   I dont say your a chris-
tian mind but you have a veneration for the deity thats sufficient
for our system   heres combativness very large   I shoud say
you are not slow at revenging an insult particulary if it be offerd
to a female for the armorous propensitys are large also   I
shoud say you have a love for the fair sex but not so as to make it
troublsome   aye aye sir   now I look agen heres order very
strong sure enough   I shoud say that things being put out of
order displeases you very much and that you are often tempted
while at table to put a spoon or knife and fork in its place   I
shoud say its the most likly thing to create disturbances in your
family   heres form very strong   I shoud say you are a
painter or that you have talents for painting if applied   heres
construction very large   I shoud say you are fond of mathema-
tics and I shoud say you have a great talent that way if the mind
was turnd to it   heres ideality too (he is a poet)   no I shoud

151

not say that   I shoud say he has a talent for it if put into action
      are you a poet Sir (yes)   aye aye the systems right but I
shoud not venture so far as to decide upon that as a many heads
develop poetry very stron[g]ly were it has never been applyd
      well sir you see the system is correct   he then in smiling
silence waits your de[c]ision of his remarkable prophecy and
hard and earthlike is that soul who can return an harsh and
unbelieving opinion on the system but I believe his is seldom
paid so unkindly for his good naturd trouble   his perdictions
are so cautiously utterd with so many causes for the liklihood of
failures in nice points that even failings them selves in his lectures
strike as convictions   when he lecturd on my head I coud not
help likening him to a boy (perhaps he had no existance but in my
friends Reynolds fancy for it was he that told the story) who was
so cautious as not to be out in any thing   he was once askd
wether the earth went round the sun or the sun round the earth
      the boy said he believd they took it by turns one going round
one day and the other the next — Deville then leads your eye to
his collection [and] points out on particular heads the most con-
vincing proof of his system in the characteristics of Murderers
Poets Painters Mathematicians and little actors of all work were
his wisa wersas become very frequent   he then takes you
below were the apparatus is all ways ready to bury you in plaster
if you chuse and if Literary men and Artists he politly hints that
he shoud like a cast of them   they cannot do less then comply
and the satisfaction of adding fresh materials to his gallery doubly
repays him for all his trouble   [B3, 65-8]

After I had been in London awhile Rippingille came down from
Bristol with Mr Elton[224] and as I was much improved in health
under Dr Darling I indulged in some of the towns amusements with
my old comrade for he was fond of seeking after curiosity and
brancing about the town   he was always for thinking that con-
stant exercise taking all weathers rough and smooth as they came
were the best phisic for a sick man and a glass of Scotch Ale only
seemed to strengthen his notions   the first jaunt that we took

together was to see the 'Art of Self Defence' practiced at the fives court[225]   it was for the Benefit of Oliver[226] and I caught the mania so much from Rip for such things that I soon became far more eager for the fancy then himself and I watch'd the appearance of every new Hero on the stage with as eager curosity to see what sort of a fellow he was as I had before done the Poets — and I left the place with one wish strongly in uppermost and that was that I was but a Lord to patronize Jones the Sailor Boy[227] who took my fancy as being the finest fellow in the Ring — I went with Rippingill and Elton to see Deville the Phrenologist and a very clever fellow in his own profession we found him   after he found who I was he instantly asked me permission to take my bust in plaister which I consented to as Rippingill and Elton wanted a copy — the operation was stifling and left a strong dislike on the [subject] not to do it again — Rippingille also introduced me to Sir T.L.[228] who was a very polite courtouis and kind man which made the other matters sit very agreeable about him — just as we got up to the door Prince Leopold was going in to sit for his picture — and we took a turn up the Square for a while and did not offer to venture till we saw him depart   Rip sent in his card and we was instantly sent up into his painting gallery were we amused ourselves till he came and kindly shook me bye the hand and made several enquireys about me   he paid Rip several fine compliments about his picture of the breakfast at an Inn and told him of his faults in a free undisguised manner but with the greatest kindness   after he had shown us about his painting room and chatted a considerable time we prepared to start when he followed up and said he coud not let me go without showing me a brother poet and took us into another room were a fine head of Walter Scott stood before us — I left his house with the satisfactory impression that I had never met with a kinder and better man then Sir T.L. and I dare say Rip was highly gratified with the praise he had received for S[ir] T[homas] told him that the Royal family at a private view of the Exebition before it opened to the public took more notice of his picture then all the rest — but Rip woud not own it for he affects a false appearence

153

of such matters — we went to F Freelings[229] the same day who had expressed a desire to have a copy of his picture of the 'post office' but he was 'not at home' so I had not the pleasure of seeing him and when Rip went the next day I coud not go with him

[B3, 12, 18]

Rip was very fond of seeming to be amused [and] talking and looking at things of which he understood nothing[230] and with this feeling we went 2 or 3 times to the french Playhouse[231] somewere in tottenham court road   none of us understood a word of french and yet we fancied ourselves delighted for there was a very beautiful actress[232] that took our fancys and Rip drew a Sketch of her in penc[i]lling for me which was somthing like her tho he stole none of her beauty to grace it   still

we also went to see Astleys Theatre[233] were we saw morts of tumbling

Rip stopt about 3 weeks this time and hastened home to get ready some Lectures on painting which he intended to deliver at the Bristol Institution[234]   [B3, 20]

I got acquainted this time with Van Dyk[235] a young man whose literary matters sat very quietly about him   he was of a very timid and retreating disposition before strangers but to a friend he was very warm hearted   he published a little vol of Poems called Theatrical Portraits   he was very ready at writing an impromtu which he woud often do very happily   he went with me to M^rs E[mmerson]s were we met with Lord R[adstock] who was very friendly with him   [B3, 18]

Etty the Painter

I went with Hessey to visit a very odd sort of character at the corner of St Pauls Church yard   he was a very simple good sort of man with a troublesome sort of fondness for poetry which

154

was continually uppermost and he wrote ryhmes himself which he thrust into any ones notice as readily as if they were anothers
    he had two daughters who seemd to be very amiable girls one of which kept an album in which her fathers productions were very prominent   he seemed to be very fond of translating Davids Psalms into ryhme   he was a friend and acquaintance to Miss Williams to whom he said he had sent a copy of my poems   at his house I met with Etty the painter[236] he was a man of a reserved appearance and felt as awkardly situated I dare say as myself when M[r] Vining[237] proposed healths and expected fine speeches in reply for tho Etty replyed he did it very shortly and when mine was drank I said nothing and tho the companys eyes were expecting for some minutes I coud not say a word tho I thought of some several times and they were wishes that I was out of the house — M[r] Vining appeared to be a sort of patron to Etty   [B3, 20, 30]

for 3rd Visit to London

When I used to go any were by my self especially Mrs E[mmerson]s I used to sit at night till very late[238] because I was loath to start not for the sake of leaving the company but for fear of meeting with supernatural [apparitions] even in the busy paths of London and tho I was a stubborn disbeliever of such things in the day time yet at night their terrors came upon me ten fold and my head was as full of the terribles as a gossips — thin death like shadows and gobblings with soercer eyes were continually shaping in the darkness from my haunted imagination and when I saw any one of a spare figure in the dark passing or going on by my side my blood has curdled cold at the foolish apprehension of his being a supernatural agent whose errand might be to carry me away at the first dark alley we came too and I have often contrived to catch his countenance by the windows or lamps which has only satisfied me to undergo the terrors of a fresh [apprehension]

155

I have often cursed my silly and childish apprehensions and woud disbelieve it tho I coud not help thinking so on — I coud not bear to go down the dark narrow street of Chancery lane   I[t] was as bad as a haunted spot to pass and one night I resolved to venture the risk of being lost rather then go down tho I tryd all my courage to go down to no purpose for I coud not get it out of my head but that I shoud be sure to meet death or the devil if I did

so I passd it and tryd to find fleet street by another road but I soon got lost and the more I tryd to find the way the more I got wrong so I offerd a watchman a shilling to show me the way thither but he said he woud not go for that and asked a half a crown with I readily gave him when he led me down many narrow alleys and I found myself in Chancery lane at last

I believe I may lay this foolish night feeling to a circumstance in my youth when I was most terribly frightend[239] I coud never forget it nor yet be thoroughly pacified tho I always boasted of a disbelief of such matters in the day time to keep up a forced courage to keep one from being laughd at as I often do now for the same reason [*incomplete*]   [B3, 16]

while I was in London the melancholly death of Lord Byron was announ[c]d in the public papers and I saw his remains born away out of the city on its last journey to that place were fame never comes — tho it lives like a shadow and lingers like a sunbeam on his grave it cannot enter   therefore it is a victory that has won nothing to the victor   his funeral was blazd forth in the papers with the usual parade that accompany the death of great men

one ostentatious puff said to be written by Walter Scott which I dont believe was unmercifully pompous   Lord Byron stood in no need of news paper praise those little wirl puffs of praise   I happend to see it by chance as I was wandering up Oxford street on my way to Mrs Emmersons when my eye was suddenly arested by straggling gropes of the common people collected together and talking about a funeral   I did as the rest did tho I coud not get hold of what funeral it coud be but I knew it was not a common one by the curiosity that kept watch on

156

every co[u]ntenance   bye and bye the grope collected into
about a hundred or more when the train of a funeral suddenly
appeard on which a young girl that stood beside me gave a deep
sigh and utterd poor Lord Byron   there was a mellancholy
feeling of vanity — for great names never are at a loss for flat-
tere[r]s that as every flower has its insect — they dance in the sun-
beams to share a liliputian portion of its splendour — upon many
countenances — I lookd up in the young girls face   it was dark
and beautiful and I coud almost feel in love with her for the sigh
she had utterd for the poet   it was worth all the News paper
puffs and Magazine Mournings that ever was paraded after the
death of a poet since flattery and hypocr[is]y was babtizd in the
name of truth and sincerity — the Reverend the Moral and fastidi-
ous may say what they please about Lord Byrons fame and damn
it as they list — he has gaind the path of its eterni[t]y without
them and lives above the blight of their mildewing censure to do
him damage — the common people felt his merits and his power
and the common people of a country are the best feelings of a
prophecy of futurity — they are below — or rather below[240] the
prejudices and flatterys the fancys of likes and dislikes of fashion
— they are the feelings of natures sympathies[241] unadulterated
with the pretentions of art and pride   they are the veins and
arterys that feed and quiken the heart of living fame   the
breathings of eternity and the soul of time are indicated in that
prophecy   they did not stand gaping with suprise on the trap-
pings of gaudy show or look on with apathisd indefference like
the hir[e]d mutes in the spectacle but they felt it   I coud see it
in their faces   they stood in proufond silence till it passd not
enquiring what this was or that was about the show as they do at
the shadow of wealth and gaudy trappings of a common great
name — they felt by a natural impulse that the mighty was fallen
and they mournd in saddend silence   the streets were lind as
the procession passd on each side but they were all the commonest
and the lowest orders   I was supprisd and gratified   the
windows and doors had those of the higher [orders] about them
but they wore smiles on their faces and thought more of the

spectacle then the poet — tho there was not much appearance of that   it lookd like a neglected grandeur   the young girl that stood by me had cou[n]ted the carriages in her mind as they passd and she told me there was 63 or 4 in all   they were of all sorts and sizes and made up a motly show   the gilt ones that lede the procession were empty — the hearse lookd small and rather mean and the coach that followd carried his em[bers] in a urn over which a pawl was thrown tho one might distinguish the form of the [urn] underneath and the window seemd to be left open for that purpose — I believe that his liberal principals in religion and politics did a great deal towards gaining the notice and affections of the lower orders   be [that] as it will it is better to be beloved by the low and humble for undisguisd honesty then flattered by the great for purchasd and pensiond hypocrisy were excuses to win favours are smmuggeld on the public under the disguise of a pretended indifference about it[242]   [B3, 71-2]

he stood in no need of News paper praise not even from Walter Scott   the public did not think of looking for the imortality of his name among Warrens Blacking Princes Kalador and Atkissons Bears Greese[243] the universal occupiers of News papers that emblazon their columns with flourishing and colored deceptions like so many illuminated M.S.   when they looked for Lord Byrons popularity they sought it among more deserving and more respectable company   they expected to see it among the immortal Memorys of the Bards of Old England were they find it occup[y]ing one of the [highest places]   [B3, 72]

I woud advise young authors not to be upon too close friendships with booksellers that is not to make them bosom friends – they may all be respectable men tho respectability is but a thin garment in the worlds eye of pretending claims that often 'covers a multitude of sins' — and their friendships are always built on speculations of profit like a farmer shewing his sample   if a book suits them they write a fine friendly letter to the author   if not they neglect to write till the author is impatient and then comes a note declining to publish mixd with a seasoning of petulance in exchange for his anxiety   therefore like all other matters of trade interested friendships too close and hastily made must meet some time or other a drop in the market and leave one side dissapointed   when I first began with the world a fair promise was a sufficient pledge to trust my heart in the opinion and a warm friendship was soon kindled   as I grew older in them some of these began to dissapoint me and I regretted but leaping out of the frying pan into the fire I remain were I began   When I began with the world I felt as much worldly faith in fair words and seasoning promises as woud have loaded a car[a]van to mecca but as soon as I mixd up with it I felt the mistake and reformd a little   I knew of some little trea[c]herys in low life of mock friendships that spoke fair words to the face and soon as the back was turnd joind in the slanders against him who told lyes for a purpose and acted the hypocrite in matters of religion friendship gain or an ruling passion that might be uppermost but I was not aware that these dwarfs had grown up with fashions and other life to giants   on my first visit to London I had a glimpse of things as they are and felt doubtful   on my second I had more dissapointments and in my last I saw so much mistey shuffling that my fa[i]th of the world shrunk to a skeleton and woud scar[c]e fill a nutt shell or burthen a mouse to bear it — the vastest of wisdoms hath said 'put no confidence in men for they will decieve you'   [B7, 77-8]

near conclusion

Many people will think me a vain fellow perhaps for attaching or fancying such importance to these memoirs as to think they will repay my vanity or labour in dwelling on them to this length and in many instances the manner in which they are written may draw on me a juster [criticism] for some of my remarks ar[e] very weak and some of the anecdotes very trifling and the expressions

159

impertinent but most of the naritive was written in severe illness which may be a sufficient appology for defects *in the author tho not perhaps for their being thrust on the reader*[244]   As to the humble situation[245] I have filled in life it needs no appology for all tastes are not alike   they do not all love to climb the Alps but many content themselves with wanderings in the valleys — while some stand to gaze on the sun to watch the flight of the towering eagle — others not less delighted look down upon the meadow grass to follow the fluttering of the butterflye   in such a lattitudde I write not without hopes of le[a]ving some pleasures for readers on the humble pages I have here written

[D2, 8; cf. A32, 11]

I may be thought a vain fellow by acknowledging things that others keep secret but I care not for I am proud of the notice I have met with and he that gets a name or fame for both is one be the duration what it may and affects to despise it or treat it with car-lessness is a liar and a hypocrite for the meanest nature will exert itself to be noticd one way or other — the clown tries all his might to be the heroe of the restling ring   this is the lowest species of fame yet it brings with it a satisfaction and reward equal to the highest   [A25, 10]

I shoud imagine that my low origin in life will not be a mote in the eye of literature to bear against me and I will not urge it as an excuse for what I have written   [B3, 59]

As we grow into life we leave our better life behind us like the image of a beauty seen in a looking glass   happiness only dis-semminates happiness while she is present and when she is gone we retain no impression of her enjoyments but a blank of cold imaginings and real dissapointments[246] unless we are deter-mined to shape our conduct to her approval and then she is ever with us [and n]ot her picture but her perfection not in shadow but reality — read this over again and profit by it

[D14, 9r]

160

Like the poor purgatorial convict of the grecian mythology I have for these nine years been rolling hopes to that mountain of promise pointed out to me in the beginning by friendly inte[r]ferences and often I have seemed as if I had accomplis[h]ed to the very top when down went hopes and all together to the bottom again — in the shape of broken promises stinging impositions and other trouble unaccounted for and unknown till they made their appearance — and as yet I am but as an alien in a strange land

[Pfz 198, 48; cf. A49, preceding p.1]

My family has increased and my affections also grow with them — and the old love for parted places the heaths and woods and cowcommons around my native place wears out — whenever I am surrounded by my family there is my comfort and if I was in the wilds of america with them for my companions there would my home be — but I am too old fashioned for the times   I have no taste for the rage for emigration — if I cannot find peace at home I dare not venture to look for it out of my own country and therefore my emigration is but a short way

[Pfz 198, 47]

Charity is is said covers a multitude of sins — but avarice is a cruel beast — it would throw water on a drowned mouse — cheat an adam out of his fig leaved apron and paint the very devil with lamp black — with a visage all the while as sincere and sanctified as if it was preaching a charity sermon

[B5, 41]

With not a few 'envy hatred and malice' is a trinity and with many self interest is a god and with the rest I think misrepresentation and hypocrisy is an idol — or the world is still a mistery for from boyhood I have been going on fools errands and my whole life has been a first of april — the veriest lout that can scarcely muster wit enough to tell his right hand from his left has been able to out wit me and make me believe his deceptions — I have been bandied from pillar to post with every assurance of fair play to be

161

further cheated — and every imposture is coloured into friend-
ship as if a thief should say 'poh man what offended at help and
assistance' when he had pickt his pocket

[B5, R41]

The world seems eager of the oppertunity to discomfort one[s]
feelings under the indulgence of imagined friendship — but I
have no animosity of any kind about me — even insult could not
burn me into anger melt me into tears or curdle my feelings into
scorn but it would sink into my heart like a stone and I fear that if
envy hatred or malice owes me any ill will they are gratified for
my spirits are nearly broken and my condition sadly out of repair

[B6, R146]

We had a very uncomfortable occurence indeed in the death of
Lady Milton[247]   she was such an amiable woman and so well
beloved that our whole neighbourhood is in mourning not in
dress but in heart and I fear the loss will never be supplied — she
must have been an excellent woman for she has left no public
enemies behind   all join in her praise at least all that I hear of

[B5, R83]

Poverty has made a sad tool of me by times — and broken into
that independance which is or ought to belong to every man by
birthright — the travellers situation is no riddle to me now — tho
I used to wonder over it when I had no friends — A traveller who
had been questioned as to what he had seen and where he had
been declared that [he] had been so far as to be able to get no
further [to] see the greatest of wonders and being at last forced to
turn back as not being able to place even a sixpence between the
earth and the sky and altho the earth and sky did not actualy
grow together
     I have been so long a lodger with difficulty and hope and so
often looked on the land of promise without meeting with it —
that I have often felt myself in the midst of Solomons advice to
his son — 'My son it is better to die then to be poor — for the

162

honesty of a poor man is ever suspected while the rich "makes
faults graces"

> And on the finger of the throned queen
> The basest jewel will be well esteemed'[248]

[A53.49r, 64v]

some bring in a [plea] on the reader that have had an eye to mod-
esty that they have written nothing no not even a syllable that she
need even blush to read   another says that they have kindled
their musings at the coals of the alter and that they breath in toto
the true spirit of religion as if writing about religion was the test
of Poetry   another urges the persuasion of friends and quotes
the proofs of their judgments praises to be sure — these are the
cants and excuses of prefaces   [B6, R83]

I might have inserted several praises from friends in extracts from
their letters mentioning my poems etc but I leave the books I have
published and the poems that may yet be published to speak for
themselves   if they cannot go without leading strings they
will never go far with them so let them fall and be forgotten —
they have gained me many pleasures and friends that have
smoothed the rugged road of my early life and made my present
lot sit more easily on the lap of life and I am proud of the notice
they have gained me and I shall feel a prouder gratification still if
my future publications be found worthy of further encouragment
and if nothing I have written be deemed worthy the notice of
posterity I have neither the power nor the wish to save them from
the fate that awaits them[249]

[B3, 68 and A31, 51]

When a person finds fault with every body but himself it may be
rightly infered that self is the only pleasant thing in life with him
and that the credit of every body is sacrifised to mentain that
opinion — but when one speaks with the same freedom of him-
self as of others it can never be doubted that there is any other

163

cause or interest attached to it then the one that he writes as he
feels — impartiallity is not always truth as it sometimes and often
mistakes its own opinion for it but it never can be construed into
pergury as uttering a false opinion for the interest of itself or
others — I have attempted to do so throughout this narative
I have described things as I thought they were without feeling a
dislike to this person or a love for that — I have exposed my own
faults and feelings with the same freedom as tho I was talking of
an enemey   I have not hesitated about the interpretations that
they may give birth too but related them as they are and were
ever   [if] I am mistaken in my opinion of others it is my Judg-
ment and not my will that misled me

[B3, 59]

I have provd the world and I feel disapointed   the hollow pre-
tendings calld friendships have deadend my feelings and broken
my confidence and left me nothing and perhaps the fault is not in
the world but in me   every friendship I made grew into a vain
attachment   I was in earnest always or I was nothing and I
believd every thing that was utterd came from the heart as mine
did   I made my opinions of people the same to their faces as I
did behind their backs reserving nothing   I spoke as freely of
their faults as I did of their merits and lovd everybody the better
for serving me like wise   if I tryd to disemble my real opinion
in my inosc[ence]ness woud break thru and betray me so I spoke
as I thought and [not for the deceiving][250] and when I made a
familiar friend I gave him my confidence and unbosomd my
faults and failings to him without hesitation and reserve putting
my all into his hands and there bye making my self bare to his
with out caring to enquire into his own as a holdfast or earnest to
keep secrets   on the other hand I have a fault that often hurts
me tho I cannot master it   I am apt to mistake some foibles that
all men are subject to into breaches of friendship and therebye
grow hessitant and loose my sincerity for them and when I feel
dissapointed in my opinions of them I never can recover my
former attachment tho I often try and I always see the silent

164

enmity of an enemey when I can no longer feel the sincerity of a friend   I know I am full of faults tho I have improvd and temperd my self as well as I was able but these that stick to me were born with me and will dye with me   if ever any body did or does me a foul barefacd wrong that memory grows with my life and break[s] out with every oppertunity and if there is a resurection quickning with the dust it is such a vivid spark in my nature that I believe I shall not forget it in my grave

[D2, 7]

APPENDIX

CLARE'S NOTES FOR HIS AUTOBIOGRAPHY

Carrying fathers dinner to the hayfield — filling his bottle at the
  fountain house warmings — E.C.
Weddings
[Pilf]ering the sticking etc
living a year at Gregorys
refusing to be a shoe maker
tending horses of a sunday
getting peas to boil
old bibles
muddying ponds out for fish in meadow
Bathing
chalking names under brig arch with firsticks
Playing at soldiers — nine peg Morris
making cockades etc of corn poppys and bluebottles
Buying Isaac Walton at Stamford
Buying Leonidas of Cue[1]
childish games
making house of sticks clay and stones
gathering broken pots   getting mallow seeds and calling them
  cheeses when playing at feasts etc

Playing soldiers
Mallows etc   Mallow prizes Berys etc for keeping sunday well
  and going church
Love Memorys
Acquaintance with Mary at school
Going to T. Porters Cottage at Ashton every sunday
Meeting E Newbon there — her fathers bible
meeting with E: Sells at Stamford fair – going to Southorp
  living at Casterton
Acquaintance wi patty   going to work at Casterton —

166

Burning lime at Pickworth

Playing the fiddle —
Gardening at Wilders etc
Pattys Lodge
Beautiful Scenery
Huge caverns in the woods
    there
My first visit to London

Marriage etc etc

living at Wilders — acquain-
tance with Patty first acquain-
tance with Henson Deeping

Drury   Lincoln
Taylor   London
Gilchrist   Stamford
Rev[d] Holland — M[rs] Emmerson
    London
Lord Radstock

Going to Lord Milton to get him
    to procure me a writers place
his failure
his long enduring kindness to my father
the wish to dedicate my first poems to his Lor[d]ship
the reasons for not doing so
first Visit to Milton
Visit to Burghley

cutting pictures from books
Pomfrets poems etc

Old Hopkinson and wife — Morton
their characters
'Rumour and the popular voice'
'Some look to more then truth and so confirm Opinion'
Carey's Dante

first visit to London — going to M[r] Carys chiswick — Visiting
    Thompsons grave at Richmond church — Wainwright
Visit to holliwell house   mistake in —— a young governess
spending sundays in woods
fetching bags flower maxey
robbing orchards nights
love affairs
Trip to Oundle
Local Militia

167

Visit to Wisbeach
Garden boy at burghley
Runaway to Newark
Return home
Old B[urbidge] Journey from London wi4[d2]   [B3,75-6]

Waithmans shop   Sir M.B. Clare[3]
Visit to Carys   West Indies

Drury and Songs by Crouch[4]   Sir T. Lawrence
Dedications
etc Writing for Every day book and for   [B3, 88]
    Receptacle

Van Dyk
Sir T. Lawrence
F. Freeling
Lord R[adstock]
Mrs E[mmerson]   [B3, 12]

Pooty Hunting
Visiting favorite spots
Hopkinson   Morton
Boyish reccolections
French girl[5]   [A18, 273]

Saw — Darley   J. Emmerson
        Cunningham   J.K. Hervey
        A.A. Watts
        F. Howard — Painter[6]   [A9, 6]
Heads
Beginnings with the world
Amusing friends
Opinions on religion   [A32, 11]

Boys standing on the bridge throwing crumbs down to the fish
— Ants and their manners and customs how they form new
colonies
— Bees swarming description of Birds build nests a peculiar
instinct — plough
Woodmans Fireside boys dropping in from birds nesting   some
tear their cloaths etc etc —
The gossips Tale
The ploughman & dithcher have their extacys and imagine and
picture to themselves while at toil $\frac{\text{hopes}}{\text{dreams}}$ of happiness of
what they may be   [A31, 21]

Orchis hunting
Gipsies
Lilies of the Valley
Old Stone pits befringed with Ivy
Gathering Cows lips for wine
pleasures of waiting in a spot to hear the song of a nightingale
— waiting for a lover — successive growth of flowers
Pleasures of fair going in boys — returning — pleasures of
cutting open a new book on a spring morning
                                   [A31, 22]

Christmas Boxes
promised my childern
Anna — Valentine and Ornson
Eliza — Cock Robin
Frederic — Peacock at Home and Butterflyes Ball
John   Dame Trott and Her Cat
William — Mother Hubard and her Dog
Sophy   House that Jack built   [D14, 7r]

John and William started to school — september
Frederick — September
Anna — Oct[r] 29.[7]
                                   [A57, R72b]

Anna Maria Clare	Born June 2nd	1820
Eliza Louisa Clare	Born June 13th	1822
Frederic Clare	Born January 6th	1824
John Clare	Born June 16th	1826
William Parker Clare	Born April 29.	1828
Sophia Clare	Born July 24th	1830
Charles Clare	Born January 4th	1833

[N30, 4]

THE JOURNAL

Monday   I have determind this day of beginning a sort of
journal to give my opinion of things I may read or
see and set down any thoughts that may arise either
in my reading at home or my musings in the Fields
and this day must fill up a sort of Introduction for I
have nothing else to set down   all I have read to
day is Moores Almanack for the account of the
weather which speaks of rain tho its very hot and
fine.

Tuesday   I have read Foxes book of Martyrs[1] and finishd it to
day and the sum of my opinion is that Tyrany and
Cruelty appear to be the inseperable companions
of Religious Power and the Aphorism is not far from
truth that says 'All priests are the same' — The great
moral prescept of a meek and unoffending teacher
was 'Do as ye would be done unto' and 'love those
that hate you'[2]   if religious opinions had done
so her history had been praiseworthy

Wednesday The rainy morning has kept me at home and I have
amusd my self heartily sitting under Waltons Syca-
more tree hearing him discourse of fish ponds and
fishing   what a delightful book it is the best
English Pastoral[3] that can be written   the des-
criptions are nature unsullied by fashionable tastes
of the time   they are simply true and like the
Pastoral Ballads of Bloomfield[4] breath of the common
air and the grass and the sky   one may almost
hear the water of the river Lea ripple along and the
grass and flags grow and rustle in the pages that
speak of it   I have never read a happier Poem in
my time

171

Thursday   Took a pleasant walk to day in the fields but felt too
weak to keep out long   tis the first day of shoot-
ing with the sportsmen and the poor hares part-
ridges and pheasants were flying in all directions
panic struck   they put me in mind of the inhabi-
tants of a Village flying before an invading enemy
        the dogs runs with their sleek dappld sides
rustling in the crackling stubbs and their noses close
to the ground as happy as their masters in the sport
tho they only 'Mumble the game they dare not bite'[5]
as Pope says — I forcd to return home fearing I might
be shot under the hedges and wrote 2 letters One to
Cunningham[6]

Friday   My health woud permit me to do nothing more
then take walks in the garden to day   what a
sadly pleasing appearence gardens have at this
season   the tall gaudy holliock with its mellan-
choly blooms stands bending to the wind and bid-
ding the summer farwell while the low Asters in
their pied lustre of red white and blue bends beneath
in pensive silence as tho they musd over the days
gone by and were sorrowful   the swallows are
flocking to gether in the sky ready for departing and
a crowd has dropt to rest on the wallnut tree were
they twitter as if they were telling their young
stories of their long journey to cheer and check fears

Saturday   Written an Essay to day 'on the sexual system of
plants' and began one on 'the Fungus tribe and on
Mildew Blight etc' intended for 'A Natural History
of Helpstone' in a Series of Letters to Hessey[7] who
will publish it when finishd   I did not think it
woud cause me such trouble or I shoud not have
began it.
Recievd a kind letter from C.A. Elton[8] — Read the

172

september Nº of the London Mag: only 2 good
articles in it — 'Blakesmore in H——shire' by Elia and
review of 'Goethe' by De Quincey   these are
exelent and sufficient to make a bad Nº interesting.

Sunday   A wet day   wrote a letter to Rippingille and to
H.F. Carey[9] and finishd another Page of my Life
which I intend to bring down to the present time
      as I did not keep a journal earlier I have inserted
the names of those from whom I have recievd letters
and to whom I have written in cronological order as
near as I can reccolect   see the *Appendix no 1*[10]
I have read the first chapter of Genesis the begin-
ning of which is very fine but the sacred historian
took a great deal upon credit for this world when he
imagines that god created the sun moon and stars
those mysterious hosts of heaven for no other pur-
pose then its use 'the greater light to rule the day
and the lesser light to rule the night' 'and the stars
also to give light upon the earth'[11] — it is a harmless
and universal propens[i]ty to magnify consequences
that appertain to ourselves and woud be a foolish
thing to try the test of the scriptures upon these
groundless assertions — for it contains the best
Poetry and the best morality in the world

13th Day of Sep: 1824

Monday   Wrote two or three pages of my life — read some of
the Sonnets of shakspear which are great favourites
of mine and lookd in to the Poems of Chatterton[12]
to see what he says about flowers and have found
that he speaks of the Lady smock
      'So have I seen the lady smocks so white
      'Bloom in the morning and mowd down at night'
as well as my favourite line of
      'The king cups brasted with the morning dew'

173

Tuesday	Continued the reading of Chatterton in search for extracts to insert in my natural history inserted them in the Appendix see N° 2[13] — I was struck with the many beautifull and remarkable passages which I found in them what a wonderful boy was this unfortunate Chatterton I hate the name of Walpole for his behaviour to this Genius and his sneering and cold blooded mention of him afterwards when his gossiping fribble had discoverd them to be forgeries why did he not discover the genius of the author — no because they surpassd his Leadenhall[14] forgery of 'Otranto'[15]
Wednesday	Finishd the reading of Chatterton admire his tradegy of Elia and Battle of Hastengs noticd a good description of a Thunder storm in the Ballad of Charity. v.29 etc and a beautiful one of a ladye[16] inserted it in Appendix No 3 Chatterton seemd fond of taking his similes from nature his favourite flower seems to be the 'kingge coppe' and his favourite bird the 'pied Chelandrie' (Red cap) the only trees he speaks of are the oak and elm[17]
Thursday	Had a visit from my friend Henderson of Milton who brought 'Don Juan'[18] in his Pocket I was very ill[19] and nursing my head in my hand but he revivd me and advisd me to read 'Don Juan' we talkd about books and flowers and Butterflyes till noon and then he discanted on Don Juan which he admird very much I think a good deal of his opinion and shall read it when I am able
Friday	Began Don Juan 2 verses of the Shipwreck very fine and the character of Haidee is the best I have yet met it is very beautiful the Hero seems a fit partner for Tom and Jerry fond of getting into

174

scrapes and always finding means to get out agen
for ever in the company of ladys who seem to watch
at night for oppertunitys for every[20] thing but say-
ing their prayers   perhaps they are as good as
their neighbours   nay better they do with out
that fas[h]ionable veil hypocrisy

Saturday   Bought the John Bull Magazine[21] out of curosity to
see if I was among the black sheep   it grows in
dullness   thats one comfort to those that it nick-
names 'Humbugs'   I have seen a boy group in a
sink for the hopes of finding a lost halfpenny but I
have been worse employd then that boy for I have
dabbld in filth and found nothing — abuse without
wit is dullness double distilld — the John Bull News
is keen and witty and in consequence entertaining
— have writ 5 letters[22] — J. Henderson — Rev[d] M[r]
Carey — A. Cunningham. H.S. Vandyke. and
Hessey

Sunday   I wish I had kept a journal sooner not of facts only
but opinions of books when one rises fresh from the
reading and thoughts that may rise at the moment
for such a collection woud be an entertaining medley
of the past out of which tho there might be a many
weeds one might cull a few flowers if not can[di]-
dates for eternity yet too good to be totally lost in
the black unreckonings of days gone bye
Took a walk about the fields a deep mist in the
morning hid every thing till noon returnd and read
snatches in several poets and the Song of Solomon
thought the supposd illusions[23] in that lucious
poem to our Saviour very overstraind far fetchd and
conjectural   it appears to me an eastern love
poem and nothing further   but an over heated
religious fancy is strong enough to fancy any thing

175

I fancy that the Bible is not illustrated by that suposision   tho it is a very beautiful Poem it seems nothing like a prophetic one as it is represented to be

20th Day of Sep: 1824

Monday   A very wet day: an occurence has happend in the village tho not very remarkable yet very singuler for I have not heard of a former one in my days   tis a Gipseys wedding Israel Smith and Lettyce Smith   what odd names these people have   they are more frequently from the Bible then the testament for what reason I know not and more common from their own fancys then either — the Fiddle accompanyd them to church and back   the rest part of it was nothing different to village weddings — Dancing and Drinking — Wrote a Song for them being old friends

Tuesday   The Statute[24] and a very wet day for it   the lasses do not lift up their gowns to show taper ancles[25] and white stockings but on the contrary drop them to hide dirty ones   wrote a poem on the 'Statute' last year lookd it over and think it a good one Taylor is of another opinion and thinks it not but it is true like the 'Lodge house' and others he dislikes and I shall one day publish them and others he has in his possesion under the title of 'A Living poets remains'[26]

Wednesday Very ill and did nothing but ponder over a future existance and often brought up the lines to my memory said to be utterd by an unfortunate nobleman when on the brink of it ready to take the plunge
'In doubt I livd in doubt I dye
'Nor shrink the dark abyss to try
'But undismayd I meet eternity'[27]

176

the first line is natural enough but the rest is a rash courage in such a situation

Thursday   A wet day   did nothing but nurse my illness Coud not have walkd out had it been fine   very disturbd in consience about the troubles of being forcd to endure life and dye by inches and the anguish of leaving my childern and the dark porch of eternity whence none returns to tell the tale of their reception

Friday   Tryd to walk out and coud not have read nothing this week   my mind almost over weights me with its upbraidings and miserys my childern very ill night and morning with a fever — makes me disconsolate and yet how happy must be the death of a child   it bears its sufferings with an innosent patience that maketh man ashamd and with it the future is nothing but returning to sleep with the thoughts no doubt of awaking to be with its play-things again

Saturday   Read some of the Odes of Collins   think them superior to Grays[28]   there is little pomp about them and much lucious sweetness   I cannot describe the pleasure I feel in reading them neither can I posses discrimination enough in Critisism to distinguish the different merits of either both are great favourites of mine yet their perusal gives me different pleasures   I find in the same Vol Odes by a poet of the name of Ogilvie[29] — 'full of pomp and fury signifying nothing' they appear to me bold intruders to claim company with Gray and Collins

Sunday   Took a Walk in the fields   heard the harvest

Cricket[30] and shrew mouse uttering their little
clickering Songs among the crackling stubbles
the latter makes a little earpiercing noise — not
unlike a feeble imitation of the sky lark and I verily
believe this is the very noise which is said to be
made by the little swift footed bird calld the cricket
lark   came home and read a chapter or two in the
New Testament   I am convincd of its sacred
design and that its writers were inspird by an
almighty power to benefit the world by their writ-
ings that was growing deeper and deeper into
unfruitful ignorance like bogs and mosses in neg-
lected countrys for want of culture — but I am far
from being convincd that the desird end is or will
be attaind at present while cant and hypocrisy is
blasphemously allowd to make a mask of religion
and to pass as current characters   I will not say
that this is universal   God forbid —

27th Day of Sep: 1824

Monday   Read in Milton: his account of his blindness[31] is very
pathetic and I am always affected to tears when I
read it   the opening and end of 'Paradise Lost' I
consider sublime and just as the beginning and
finish of an Epic Poem shoud be   I never coud
read 'Paradise regaind' thro tho I have heard it
praisd highly   'Comus' and 'Allegro' and 'Pen-
serose' are those which I take up the Oftenest
what a beautiful description at the shut of evening
is this
'– – – – – – – What time the labourd ox
'In his loose traces from the furrow came
'And the swinkt hedger at his supper sat'[32]

Tuesday   Wrote another chapter of my Life   read a little in
Grays Letters great favourites of mine   they are

178

the best letters I have seen and I consider Burns
very inferior to all the collections I have met with
    tho they have gaind great praise they appear
to me when I read them as the letters of a man who
was looking further then his corespondent and
straining after somthing fine till he forgets both
his boast of independance is so often dwelt upon
till it becomes tiresome and seems more like the
despair of a dissapointed man then the content of a
happy one

Wednesday Took a walk in the fields   saw an old woodstile
taken away from a favourite spot which it had occu-
pied all my life   the posts were over grown with
Ivy and it seemd so akin to nature and the spot were
it stood as tho it had taken it on lease for an undis-
turbd existance   it hurt me to see it was gone for
my affections claims a friendship with such things
      but nothing is lasting in this world   last year
Langly bush was destroyd an old white thorn that
had stood for more then a century full of fame
the Gipseys Shepherds and Herd men all had their
tales of its history and it will be long ere its memory
is forgotten

Thursday   Lookd over the 'Human heart'[33]   the title has
little connection with the contents — it displays the
art of book making in half filld pages and fine paper
— 'The Murderers Death bed' is very poor the worst
thing in the Newgate Calendar is as interesting —
'Thou shalt not do Evil etc' is a new version of the
old tale of Colonel Kirks Cruelty better told in history
then prose poetry — 'Amy Wilton' is an immitation
of the scotch novelists and of course inferior — 'The
Lucrese of France' is good

179

Friday   Had a new will made as the old one was not right
proving nothing that I wishd and every thing con-
trary — this I dont like   I leave C Mossop E.T.
Artis[34] and J.A. Hessey Executors and all monies
arising from book profits etc in their trust with that
in the funds and what ever may be put out to Interest
      the money in the funds to be drawn out and
shard equaly among my childern when the youngest
is 21   I dont understand the expression in it of
my 'Sons and daughters and *their respected Represen-
tatives'* and shall have it alterd — it was signd by
W. Bradford and Taylor[35]

Saturday   Read the poems of Conder[36] over a second time
like some of them very much   there is a many
quiet and unpretending beautys among them
the Imitations of the Psalms are good   the Ode
to the Nightingale is good but the expression of 'Sir
Nightingale' is bad and spoils it — The principal
poem is like many such attempts poor   the best
poems on religion are those found in the Scriptures
which are inimetable and therefor all imitations
cannot but be inferior — the first Sonnet on Autumn
is a good one and the Song 'Twas not when early
flowers was springing' is beautiful   I am much
pleasd with many more which I shall read anon

Sunday   Began to read the 'Garden of Florence' by Reynolds[37]
      it is a beautiful simple tale with a few consiets
      it begins prettily 'In the fair City of Florence
ther did dwell' etc and ends sweetly
      'The lonly nighti[n]gale and watching star
      'At eve for ever their companions are'
there is a many beautys in it   the Romance of
Youth is too romantic that is the youth it describes
is[38] not a general character — yet there are several

180

beautys in it of true poesy — the Red cap is a beauti-
ful comparison *'It self a featherd flower'* the com-
paring the white stem of the Birch to a serpent is
bad taste somthing like the serpents wreathing
round the artificial trees in Vauxhall gardens —
Verse 32 about the king fisher turns on a consiet and
verse 66 about the faireys boddice is a worse consiet
still — 'May the rose of months the violet of the
year' is very pretty the volume is full of beautys
of the best sort — the verse about the two childern
is another addition to the many from Chantrys
monument.[39]
Let C. Mossop take my new Will home with him for
lawer Taylor to alter — read in the testament the
Epistle of St John I love that simple hearted
expression of 'little childern'[40] it breaths of
brotherly affection and love

4th Day of Oct[r]: 1824

Monday
I have again reflected over my new will and I believe
the expression of *'and their respective legal represen-
tatives'* is wrong so I shall alter it as soon as it is
returnd — I had several memorandums which I
intended to have inserted in the will but I was told
it woud cost too much in proving if it was long so I
will insert them in the Appendix No 4[41] that my
desires may be known and as I anxiously hope
attended too tho it often happens otherwise
theres little trust in the world to leave faith behind
us upon promises

Tuesday
One can scarcly trust fame on credit in these days of
misrepresentation and deception this morning
a Play Bill was thrown into my house with this
pompous Blunder on the face of it
'Theatre Market Deeping'

'On Thursday Evening, October 7, 1824
'Will be presented the popular new Comedy
(never acted here) calld
'Pride shall have a Fall or the twentieth Hussar
'Written by the *Revd G. Groby*
'and now Performing at the Theatre Royal
Covent garden with increasd Attraction and
Applause' —
In the 'Times Telescope'[42] they rechristend me
Robert Clare   there went the left wing of my
fame

Wednesday   Recievd the London Magazine[43] by my friend
Henderson who brought it from town with him
a very dull No the worst of Magazines is waste
papers repetitions for humbug is the Editor of them
all   in the June No Dequincey had a paper on
'false distinctions' which contended quite right
enough that women had an inferior genius to men
in July 'Surry' put up a little clever petition
against it which read very well but provd nothing
in the lions head a little unknown[44] stuck a
letter to Ed: on the same side in August another[45]
popt a plea for female genius   between the two
opinions of middling stuff in September 'Surry'
popt in another push for his opinion and in October
the middling middle one is pushing a go between
agen   when will it end — the article on Byron[46]
carrys ignorance in the face of it — Recievd a letter
from Carey[47]

Thursday   Got a parcel from London 'Eltons Brothers' 'Allins
Grammer'[48] gifts of the Authors: and Erskines
Internal Evidences of Religion the Gift of Lord
Radstock one of my best friends   a very sensible
book   this passage struck[49] me which I first

182

opend — 'To walk without God in the world is to walk in sin and sin is the way of danger. Men have been told this by their own consiences and they have partially and occasionly believd it but still they walkd on'. — too true — Recievd 3 letters[50] from Vandyk, M[rs] Emmerson — and Hessey — Done nothing

Friday   Very ill to day and very unhappy   my three Childern are all unwell   had a dismal dream of being in hell   this is the third time I have had such a dream — as I am more and more convincd that I cannot recover I will make a memorandum of my temporary conserns for next to the Spiritual they ought to come and be attented too for the sake of those left behind   I will insert them in No 5 of the Appendix[51] — Neglect is the rust of life that eateth it away and layeth the best of minds fallow and maketh them desert[52] — Done nothing

Saturday   Observd to day that the Swallows are all gone when they went I know not   saw them at the beginning of the week   a white one was seen this season by M[r] Clark in the fields while out a shooting — Patty has been to Stamford and brought me a letter from Ned Drury[53] who came from Lincoln to the Mayors Feast on thursday   it revives old reccolections   poor fellow he is an odd one but still my reccolections are inclind in his favour — what a long way to come to the Mayors Feast   I woud not go one Mile after it to hear the din of knifes and forks and to see a throng of blank faces about me chattering and stuffing 'That boast no more expression then a muffin'

Sunday   A wet day   have finished the life of Savage in

183

Johnsons Lives of the Poets[54]   it is a very inter-
esting piece of biography but the critisisms are
dictated by friendship that too often forgets judg-
ment ought to be one of the company   to leave
this and turn to the Life of Grey what a contrast
it almost makes the mind dis believe critisism and
to fancy itself led astray by the opinions of even the
wisest of men — I never take up Johnsons lives but
I regret his beginning at the wrong end first and
leaving out those beautiful minstrels of Elizabeth
— had he forgot that there had been such poets as
Spencer Drayton Suckling etc etc   but it was the
booksellers judgment that employd his pen and we
know by experience that most of their judgments
lye in their pockets — so the Poets of Elizabeth are
still left in *cobwebs* and mystery   Read in the
afternoon Erskines Evidences of revealed Religion
and find in it some of the best reasoning in favour of
its object I have ever read   I think a doubting
christian may be set right at a first perusal and a
reasoning Deist loose doubts sufficient to be half a
christian in some of the arguments and a whole one
ere he get to the end

11th Day of Octr: 1824

Monday   I have been dipping into the Miserys of human Life[55]
here and there   the petty troubles are whimsical
enough and the thing is a novel one which is suffi-
cient to ensure sucess now and I understand it ran
thro a many editions and that the Author made £1500
by it clear profit — so much for fashion   Collins
poems woud not pay for the printing and the price
Milton got for his Paradise lost is well known
so fashions taste is still the same   her out side
only alters upon her foolereys

Tuesday   Began to learn a poor lame boy the common rules of
              arithmetic etc   find him very apt and willing to
              learn
              Began an Enquirey into the Life of Bloomfield with
              the intention of writing one and a critisism on his
              genius and writings   a fellow of the name of
              Preston pretended to know a great deal about him
              but I must enquire into its authenticity — Capel
              Loft[56] did not improve on the account given by his
              brother George by altering it — Editors often commit
              this fault

Wednesday   Feel rather worse   lookd over the Magaz[in]e for
              amusment for Magazines are the best things in
              Literature to pass away a mellancholy hour
              their variety and the freshness of their subjects
              wether good or bad never fail of amusment to
              reccomend them   Blackwood has had a hard hit
              on Taylor   there is no more Editor Scotts[57] at
              present to check them
              The letter on Mackadamizing[58] is good — the Review
              on Walladmor[59] is 30 pages long   I wish Dequin-
              cey had better subjects for his genius tho there is
              some parts of the novel that seems alive with action

Thursday   Wrote a letter to Lord Radstock[60] — Read some
              passages in the Poems of Tannahill[61]   some of
              his Songs are beautiful particulary 'Loudons Bonny
              woods and braes' 'We'll meet beside the dusky glen'
              and 'Jessey'   his poems are poor and appear as
              if they were written by another — The scotch Poets
              excell in song writing because they take their images
              from common life were nature exists without
              affectation

Friday   Read in Eltons Poems   some passages in the

brothers are very good and appear to be the utterance of feeling   the small poems are middling
    'Rob roy' and 'A Fathers reverie' are two of the best   the epithet 'virgin voice' is odd and this line sounds namby pambily 'and therefore love I thee'[62]   there is a pleasant sound lingers on the ear while reading these lines
    '— the bare trees with crashing boughs aloft
    Rock and reecho and at whiles are hushd
    I commune with my spirit and am still'[63]

Saturday   Wrote 2 more pages of my life   find it not so easy as I at first imagind as I am anxious to give an undisguisd narative of facts good and bad   in the last sketch which I wrote for Taylor I had little vanitys about me to gloss over failing which I shall now take care to lay bare and readers if they ever are publishd to comment upon as they please   in my last 4 years I shall give my likes and dis likes of friends and acquaintance as free as I do of my self —

Sunday   Recievd a letter from Mrs Gilchrist[64] — read some passages in my Shakspear   took a walk   the hedges look beautiful with their crimson hips bright red awes and glossy sloes   lookd in the Poems of Colridge Lamb and Loyde[65] — Colridges monody on Chatterton is beautiful but his sonnets are not happy ones   they seem to be a labour after exelence which he did not reach   some of those by his friend Lloyd are exelent and seem to have attaind it with out trouble   'Craig Millar Castle' and 'to November' are the best with my opinicn — Lambs best poetry is in 'Elia'   its a sufficient fame in a late harvest — I wish he woud write on

18th Day of Octr: 1824

Monday   Lookd again into 'Don Juan'   like it better and
feel a wish that the great poet had livd to finish it
tho he appears to have lost his intended plan on
setting out and to have continued it with any pur-
pose that came uppermost — Don Juans visit to
England reads tiresome and one wishes at the end
that he had met with another shipwreck on his
voyage to have sent him else were

Tuesday   Lookd over a New vol of provincial poems by a
neighbouring poet   Bantums 'Excursions of
Fancy'[66] and poor fancys I find them   there is not
a new thought in them   four years ago a poet
was not to be heard of with in a century[67] of Help-
stone and now there is a swarm — 'Roses Early Muse'
'Wilkinsons Percy' both of Peterbro — 'Messings
Rural Walks' of Exton — 'Adcocks Cottage Poems'
of Oakam — 'Bantums Excursions of fancy' of Teigh
'Strattons Poems' — of Abbots Ripton etc etc etc
and all of a kin wanting in natural images etc

Wednesday Workd in the garden at making a shed for my
Ariculas   the Michaelmass daisey is in full flower
both the lilac-blue and the white thick set with its
little clustering stars of flowers   I love them for
their visits in such a mellancholy season as the end
of autumn — the Horse chesnutt tree is loosings
large hand shapd leaves that litter in yellow heaps
round the trunk — the walnutt is compleatly bare
and the leaves are tand brown and shr[i]veld up as
if scorchd — the elms are as green and fresh as the
oak

Thursday   Recievd a letter from Hessey[68] — and wrote one —
took a walk in the fields — gatherd a bunch of wild

187

flowers that lingerd in shelterd places as loath to dye — the rag wort still shines in its yellow clusters — and the little heath bell or harvest bell quakes to the wind under the quick banks and warm furze — clumps of wild Marjoram are yet in flower about the mole hilly banks and clumps of meadow sweet linger with a few bunches yet unfaded

Friday   Read Hazlitts Lectures on the Poets[69] — I admire his mention of the daisy as reminding him of his boyish days when he usd to try to jump over his own shadow — he is one of the very best prose writers of the present day and his works are always entertaining and may be taken up when ever one chuses or feels the want of amusement — his political writings are heated and empty full of sound and fury — I hate polotics and therefore I may be but a poor judge

Saturday   Continued to read Hazlitt[70] — I like his Lectures on the Poets better then those on the comic writers and on Shakspear   his 'view of the English stage' is not so good as either   they might have remaind in their first places without any loss to the world viz the News papers for which they was written — his other works I have not seen — Read in Shakspear 'the midsummer nights dream' for the first time — I have still got 3 parts out of 4 of the Plays to read yet and hope I shall not leave the world without reading them

Sunday   Recievd a letter from Lord Radstock[71] — finished another chapter of my life read some passages in Blairs Sermons — lookd into 'Maddox on the culture of flowers' and the 'Flora Domestica'[72] which with a few improvments and additions woud be one of the most entertaining books ever written — If I live I will write one on the same plan and call it a garden of wild Flowers as it shall contain nothing else with quotations from poets and others   an English Botany on this plan woud be very interesting and serve to make Botany popular while the hard nick- namy sy[s]tem of unuterable words now in vogue only overloads it in mystery till it makes darkness visable[73]

25th Day of Octbr: 1824

Monday   Old Shepherd Newman dyd this Morning an old tenant of the fields and the last of the old shepherds   the fields are now left desolate and his old haunts look like houses disinhabited   the fading woods seem mourning in the autumn wind how often hath he seen the blue skye the green fields and woods and the seasons changes and now he sleeps unconsious of all   what a desolate mystery doth it leave round the living mind — the latter end of Grays Elegy might be well applied to this tenant of the fields 'Oft have we seen him' etc etc[74]

Tuesday   Recievd a letter from Allan Cunningham[75] — Looked into Pope   I know not how it is but I cannot take him up often or read him long to gether   the uninterrupted flow of the verses wearys the ear — there are some fine passages in the Essay on Man — the Pastorals[76] are nick[n]amed so for daffodils breathing flutes beachen bowls silver crooks and purling brooks and such like everlasting sing song does not make pastorals   his prologue to the satires is good — but that celebrated Epitaph on Gay ends burlesqly 'Striking there pensive bosoms etc'[77]

Wednesday   I have been very much struck with some passages in the Poems of Aaron Hill with many happy expressions and origional images   I have inserted a few of them in the Appendix N° 6[78]   he seems to struggle to free his ideas from the turnpike hackneyhisms of sounding ryhmes and tinkling periods[79] then in fashion for most of the ryhmers of that day seem to catch their little inspirations from Pope

Thursday   Wrote a letter to Mrs Gilchrist[80] — read some pages in Shakspear — turnd over a few leaves of Knoxes Essays[81] — Read Bacons Essay[82] on the idea of a compleat garden divided into every month of the year in which the flowers bloom   what beautiful Essays these are   I take them up like Shakspear and read them over and over and still find plenty to entertain me and new thoughts that strike me as if I had not seen them before

Friday   Read some poems of Wordsworth   his 'Susan Gray' or 'Solitude' 'The pet lamb' 'We are seven' 'the Oak and broom' 'the Eglantine and the fountain'[83] 'two April Mornings' 'Lucy' etc are some of my greatest favourites — when I first began to read poetry I dislikd Wordsworth because I heard he was dislikd and I was astonishd when I lookd into him to find my mistaken pleasure in being delighted and finding him so natural and beautiful   in his 'White doe of Rylston' there is some of the sweetest poetry I ever met with tho full of his mysterys

Saturday   Recievd a present of two Volumns[84] of Sermons 'On the Doctrines and practice of Christianity' from Lord Radstock — he is one of my best friends and not of much kin with the world — the chrisanthymums are just opening their beautiful double flowers   I have Six sorts this year the claret colord the buff the bright yellow the paper white the purple and the rose color   lost one the jocolate or coffe color — promisd more from Milton[85]

Sunday   Took a walk   got some branches of the spindle tree with its pink colord berrys that shine beautifully in the pale sun — found for the first time 'the herb true love' or 'one berry'[86] in Oxey Wood   brought a root home to set in my garden — Lookd into the two Vols of Sermons from Lord R.   the texts are well selected and the sermons are plainly and sensibly written   they are in my mind much superior to Blairs popular Sermons and that is not going great lengths in their praise for Blairs are queit and cold and his study seems more in the eloquence and flow of Style then in the doctrine of religion for the language is beautiful but it is studied like D[r] Johnsons musical periods

1st, Day of Nov[r], 1824

Monday   Took a walk to lolam brigs[87] to hunt for a species of fern that usd to grow on some willow tree heads in Lolham lane when I was a boy but coud find none — got some of the yellow water lily[88] from the pits which the floods had washd up to set in an old water tub in the garden and to try some on land in a swaily corner as the horse blob thrives well which is a water flower — listend in the evening to glinton bells at the top of the garden   I always feel mellancholy at this season to hear them and yet it is a pleasure
    'Im pleasd and yet Im sad'[89]

Tuesday   Set some box edging round a border which I have made for my collection of ferns — read some pas-

sages in Blairs Grave a beautiful poem and one of
the best things after the manner of Shakspear
its beginning is very characteristic of the subject —
there are crowds of beautiful passages about it —
who has not markd the following aged companions
to many such spots of general decay
    'A row of reverend elms
    'Long lashd by rude winds. Some rift half down
    '– – – – – – – – Others so thin a top
    'That scarce two crows can lodg in the same tree'[90]

Wednesday   Took a walk with John Billings to swordy well to
gather some 'old mans beard' which hangs about
the hedges in full bloom   its downy clusters of
artificial like flowers appear at first sight as if the
hedge was litterd with bunches of white cotton —
went into hilly wood and found a beautiful species
of fern on a sallow stoven in a pit which I have not
seen before — there are five sorts[91] growing about
the woods here the common brake the fox fern the
harts tongue and the polopody two sorts the tall
and the dwarf

Thursday   Recieved a letter and prospectus from a School-
master of Surfleet wishing me to become a cores-
pondent to a periodical publications calld 'the Sci-
entific Receptacle'[92]   what a crabbed name for
poesy to enlist with   it professes to be a kins
man to the 'Leeds Corespondent' and the 'Boston
Enquirer' the latter of which I remember to have
been much pleasd with — in which was a pretty
song by poor Scott

Friday   Read in Bishop Percys Poems the 'Relic of ancient
poetry'   take them up as often as I may I am
always delighted there is so much of the essence

192

and simplicity of true poetry that makes me regret I
did not see them sooner as they woud have formd
my taste and laid the foundation of my judgment
in writing and thinking poeticaly   as it is I feel
indebted to them for many feelings[93]

Saturday   Took a walk in the fields   the oaks are beginning
to turn reddish brown and the winds have stript
some nearly bare   the under woods last leaves
are in their gayest yellows   thus autumn seems
to put on bridal colors for a shroud — the little har-
vest bell is still in bloom trembling to the cold[94] wind
almost the only flower living save the old mans
beard or travellers joy on the hedges

Sunday   Recieved a packet from London[95] with the Mag: and
some copys of M.S.S. that come very slowly and a
letter very friendly worded but I have found that
saying and doing is a wide difference[96] too far very
often to be neighbours much less friends — Recievd
a letter too from Vandyke   Lookd into Words-
worths Poems and read Solomons Song and beauti-
ful as some of the images of that Poem are some of
them are not reconsilable in my judgment above the
ridicilous   I have inserted them in a blank verse
fashion in the Appendix Nº 7[97]   yet the more I
read the scriptures the more I feel astonishment at
the sublime images I continualy meet with in its
Poetical and prophetic books nay every were about
it all other authors diminishes to dwarfs by their
side

8th Day of Novr, 1824

Monday   Read over the Magazine[98]   the Review of Lord
Byrons Conversations is rather entertaining   the
pretendery letter of James Thompson is a bold lye

193

I dislike those lapt up counter fits mantld in truth like a brassy shilling in its silver washings — those brimingham half pence passd off as matter of fact moneys Elia can do better — the rest of the articles are motly matters some poor and some middling Magazines are always of such wear

Tuesday   Read Shakspears Henry the Fifth[99] of which I have always been very fond from almost a boy   I first met with it in an odd Vol which I got for 6[d] yet I thought then that the welch officer with two other of his companions were tedious talkers and I feel that I think so still   yet I feel such an interest about the play that I can never lay it down till I see the end of it

Wednesday Read Macbeth   what a soul thrilling power hovers about this tradegy   I have read it over about twenty times and it chains my feelings still to its perusal like a new thing   it is Shakspears masterpiece — the thrilling feelings created by the description of lady Macbeths terror haunted walkings in her sleep sinks deeper then a thousand ghosts   at least in my visions of the terrible she is a ghost herself and feels with spirit and body a double terror

Thursday   Recievd a letter from Inskip[100] the friend of Bloomfield full of complaints at my neglect of writing what use is writing when the amount on both sides amounts to nothing more then waste paper   I have desires to know somthing of Bloomfields latter days but I can hear of nothing further then his dying neglected so its of no use enquiring further — for we know that to be the common lot of genius

194

Friday

Burnt a will which Taylor of Deeping made for me by Mossops Orders as it was a jumble of contradictions to my wishes — wrote the out line for another In which I mean to leave every thing both in the copy right and fund money etc etc of all my Books M.S.S. and property in the power of my family at le[a]st in the trust of those I shall nominate trustees and Lord Radstock is one that I shoud like to trouble for the purpose

Saturday

Lookd into Thompsons Winter[101]   there is a freshness about it I think superior to the others tho rather of a pompous cast   how natural all his descriptions are   nature was consulted in all of them   the more I read them the more truth I discover   the following minute descriptions are great favourites of mine and prove what I mean describing a hasty flood forcing thro a narrow passage he says

'— — — — — — — — — — — — — — — rapid and deep
'It boils and wheels and foams and flounders
      through'
'Snatchd in short eddies plays the witherd leaf
'And on the flood the dancing feather floats'

Sunday

Read in old Tusser[102] with whose quaint ryhmes I have often been entertaind   he seems to have been acquainted with most of the odd measures now in fashion   he seems to have felt a taste for inclosures and Mavor that busy notemaker and book compiler of school boy memory has added an impertinent note to tussers opinion as an echo of feint praise   so much for a parsons opinion in such matters — I am an advocate for open fields and I think that others expirience confirms my opinion every day — there is two pretty sonnets in Tusser

195

and some natural images scatterd about the book
the four following lines are pretty
'The year I compare as I find for a truth
'The spring unto child hood the summer to youth
'The harvest to manhood the winter to age
'All quickly forgot as a play on a stage'
some of the words in the glossary have different
meanings with us — To addle means to earn wages
— eddish with us is the grass that grows again af[103]
it is mown — staddle bottom of a stack etc etc etc

15th, Day of Nov[r] 1824

Monday   Went out to gather pootys on the roman bank for a
collection   found a scarce sort of which I only
saw two in my life one pickd up under a hedge at
peakirk town end and another in bainton meadow
    its color is a fine sunny yellow larger then the
common sort and round   the rim of the base is a
black edging which extends no further then the rim
it is not in the collection at the British Museum[104]

Tuesday   My friend Billings told me to day that he saw four
swallows about the second of this month flying
over his house   he has not seen them since and
forgot to tell me at the time — now what becomes of
these swallows for the winter   that they cannot
go into another country now is certain and that they
must abide or perish here is certain but how or were
is a mystery that has made more opinions then
proofs and remains a mystery on

Wednesday The Chrisanthums are in full flower   what a
beautiful heart cheering to the different seasons
nature has provided in her continual successions of
the bloom of flowers — ere winters bye the little
acconite peeps its yellow flowers then the snow drop

196

and further on the crocus dropping in before the
summer multitude and after there departure the tall
hollioak and little aster blooms in their showy colors
then comes the michael mass daisy and lastly the
Chrisanthemum while the china roses
    '— — — — — — — — — — — — all the year
   'Or in the bud or in the bloom appear'[105]

Thursday   Read in Southeys Wesley[106]   he has made a very
entertaining book of it but considering the subject I
think he might have made more of it   the charac-
ter of Wesley is one of the finest I have read of
they may speak of him as they please but they can-
not diminish his simplicity of genius as an author
and his piety as a christian   I sincerly wish that
the present day coud find such a man

Friday   Had a visit from my friend Henderson and I felt
revivd as I was very dull before: he had a pleasing
News to deliver me having discoverd a new species
of Fern a few days back growing among the bogs on
Whittlesea Mere and our talk was of Ferns for the
day   he tells me there is 24 different species or
more natives of England and Scotland   one of
the finest of the latter is calld the Maiden hair fern
growing in rock clefts

Saturday   Went out to hunt the harts tongue species of fern
and fell in with the ruins of the old Castle in Ashton
lawn[107] but found none   its commonest place is
in Wells in the crivices of the walls but I have found
it growing about the badger holes in open Copy
wood[108]   got very wet and returnd home —
finishd the 8th Chapter of my life[109]

Sunday   Paid a second visit to the old castle in ashton lawn

with my companion J. Billings to examine it — we
strum it and found it 20 yards long fronting the
south and 18 fronting eastward   we imagind
about 12 foot of the walls still standing tho the rub-
bish has entirely coverd them except in some places
were about a foot of the wall may be seen   it is
coverd with in and without with black thorn and
privet and s[p]urge laurel so that it is difficult to get
about to view it   I broke some of the cement off
that holds the stones together and it appears harder
then the stone it self   brought some home in my
pocket for my friend Artis   there is some rabbits
haunts it and the earth the[y] root out of their bur-
rows is full of this cement and perishd stone — part
of the moat is still open

22nd, Day of Novr 1824

Monday
Lookd into Miltons Paradise lost   I once read it
thro when I was a boy   at that time I liked the
Death of Abel[110] better   what odd judgments
those of boys are   how they change as they ripen
when I think of the siender merits of the Death
of Abel against such a jiant as Milton I cannot help
smiling at my you[n]g fancys in those days of happy
ignorance

Tuesday
Some months back I began a system of profiting by
my reading at least to make a show of it by noteing
down beautiful odd or remarkable passages and
immitations in the poets and prose writers which I
read and I have inserted some liknesses of Lord
Byrons in the Apendix No 8[111] about which there
has been much batteling and ink shed — I never
saw some of them noticed before

Wednesday I have often been struck with astonishment at the

198

tales old men and women relate on their remembrances of the growth of tree[s]   the Elm groves in the Staves acre Close at the town end were the rooks build and that are of jiant height   my old friends Billings says he remembers them no thicker then his stick and saw my fathers uncle set them carr[y]ing a score on his back at once   I can scarcly believe it

Thursday   Recievd a letter from Hessey[112]   I have not answerd his last and know not when I shall   the worlds friendships are counterfits and forgerys on that principal   I have provd it and my affections are sickend unto death and my memorys are broken while my confidence is grown to a shadow — in the bringing out the second Edit of the Minstrel they was a twelvmonth in printing a title page —

Friday   Went to see if the old hazel nut tree in lea close was cut down and found it still standing   it is the largest hazel tree I ever saw being thicker then ones thigh in the trunk and the height of a moderate Ash — I once got a half peck of nutts when in the leams off its branches when a boy — the Inclosure has left it desolate its companions of oak and ash being gone

Saturday   Recieved a parcel of Ferns and flowers from Henderson[113] the common Polipody growing about the thorp park wall the harts tongue growing in a well at Caistor the Lady fern[114] growing at whittlesea Meer and tall white Lychnis with seven new sorts of Chrysanthemums — the Paper white the bright lemon 3 sorts of lilac and 2 others — I like these flowers as they come in the melacholy of autumn

Sunday A gentleman came[115] to see me to day whose whole talk was of Bloomfield and Booksellers he told me to put no faith in them and when I told him that all my faith and M.S.S. likewise was in their hands already he shook his head and declared with a solemn bend of his body 'then you are done by G–d — they will never print them but dally you on with well managed excuses to the grave and then boast that they were your friends when you are not able to contradict it as they have done to Bloomfield' he then desird me to get my MSS back by all means and sell them at a markets price at what they woud fetch — he said that Bloomfield had not a £100 a year to mentain 5 or 6 in the family why I have not £50 to mentain 8 with this is a hungry difference

29th, Day of Novr 1824

Monday Lent Henderson 5 Nos of 'London Mag:' from July to November and the 'Human Heart'

Tuesday An excessive wet day — Recd[116] the Literary (Butterflye) Souvenir for 1825[117] in all its gilt and finery what a number of candidates for fame are smiling on its pages — what a pity it is that time shoud be such a destroyer of our hopes and anxietys for the best of us are but doubts on fames promises and a century will thin the myriad worse then a plague

Thursday One of the largest floods[118] ever known is out now an old neighbour Sam Sharp out last night at Deeping Gate and attempting to get home was drownd

Friday Found a very beautiful fern in Oxey wood suppose it the White Maiden Hair of Hill[119] it is very scarce here

Sunday   I have been thinking to-day of all the large trees about our neighbour hood and those that have curious historys about them — there was a Walnutt tree (now cut down) stood in Loves yard[120] a[t] Glinton of which this is the history — old Will Tyers[121] now living says while going to Peakirk one day when a boy he pickd up a walnutt and took it home to set it in his garden were it throve well and bore nutts before he left the house it[s] present occupier got great quantitys of nutts most seasons and a few years back it was cut down and the timber sold for £50

6th Day of Dec[r], 1824

Monday

Tuesday   Another Gipsey Wedding of the Smith family fiddling and drinking as usual

Wednesday   Found the common Pollopody on an old Willow tree in Lolham Lane and a very small fern in hilly wood scarcly larger then some species of moss and a little resembling curld parsley   I have namd it the Dwarf Maiden hair[122] and I believe it is very scarce here

Friday   Began to take the Stamford Mercury Newspaper with Bradford and Stephenson[123]

13th, Day of Dec[r], 1824

Monday   Bought a Moors Almanack with its fresh budget of wonderful predictions on the weather and the times utterd with such earnest ambition of pretending truth that one shoud think the motto 'The voice of the heavens' etc means nothing more or less then the voice of Moors Almanack etc — saw two 'Will o whisps'[124] last night   see Appendix N[o] 9.

201

Tuesday   A coppled crownd Crane [i.e. a heron] shot at
Billings pond on the green — twas 4 foot high from
the toes to the bill — on the breast and rump was a
thick shaggy down full of powder which seem[ed]
to be a sort of pounce box to the bird to dress its
feathers with to keep out the wet — its neck and
breast was beautifully staind with streaks of watery
brown its wings and back was slate grey the crown
on its head was of the same color

Wednesday Went to Milton   saw a fine Edition of Leniuses
Botany[125] with beautiful plates and find that my fern
which I found in Harrisons close dyke by the wood
lane is the 'thorn pointed fern'   saw also a beauti-
ful book on insects[126] with the plants they feed on
by Curtis — found Artis busy over his 'fossil plants'
and 'Roman Antiquitys' but his complaints of the
deceptions of publishers are akin with mine

Thursday   Saw Hendersons collection of Ferns which is far
from compleat tho some of them are beautiful —
learnd from him of a singular instinct in plants of
the creeping or climbing kind some having a prop-
ensity to twine to the left in their climbing and
others to the right — the wood bine seems to twine
to the left and the travellers joy to the right but this
is not an invariable fact

Friday   Recievd a letter from Lord Radstock[127]

Sunday   Returnd from Milton[128]

20th, Day of Decr, 1824
Monday

Wednesday A coppled crownd hen pheasant shot very large

and colord about the breast and back like the cock but the head was plain

Thursday   Recievd a letter from Mrs Emmerson[129] and the 'Observer' after a long Absence in France — Wrote a letter to Mrs E. and to Francis Freeling Esqr —

Saturday   Christmass day   gatherd a hand ful of daiseys in full bloom — saw a wood bine and dog rose in the woods putting out in full leaf and a primrose root full of ripe flowers — what a day this usd to be when a boy how eager I usd to attend the church to see it stuck with evergreens (emblems of Eternity) and the cottage windows and the picture ballads on the wall all stuck with Ivy holly Box and yew — such feelings are past — and 'all this world is proud of'

Sunday   Found at the bottom[130] of a dyke made in the roman bank some pootys of varied colors and the large garden ones of a russet color with a great many others of the meadow sort which we calld 'badgers' when I was a school boy   found no were now but in wet places — there is a great many too of a water species now extinct — the dyke is 4 foot deep and the soil is full of these shells — have they not lay here ever since the romans made the bank and does the water sorts not imply that the fields was all fen and under water or wet and uncultivated at that time I think it does — I never walk on this bank but the legions of the roman army pass bye my fancys with their mysterys of nearly 2000 years hanging like a mist around them   what changes hath past since then — were I found these shells it was heath land above 'swerdy well'

27th Day of Dec^r, 1824-5

Monday

Wednesday Went with neighbour Billings to Southey Wood and Gees Holt to hunt ferns — found none — met with a new species of moss fern shapd growing on a common species like the missletoe on the thorn — it is a sort of moss missletoe[131] — preserved a specimen — saw a branch of black thorn dog rose and eldern in full leaf all in one hedge row — saw a bumbarrel with moss as if building a nest

Thursday Recievd an answer from F. Freeling[132] to my enquirey wether the charge of a penny is legal at Deeping office for post paid and frankd letters and News papers and I find that it is for letters but no mention is made about News papers so I am as ignorant as ever on that head but I will enquire further

Friday Recieved a letter from Hessey[133] containing a Draft for £20 being the fund money and Earl Spencers half yearly salary — nothing further about my new poems is mentiond — wrote to Rev^d H F Carey — Gatherd a Crow flower in full bloom

Saturday Saw a Reciept to mend broken china in the Stamford Mercury[134] — 'Gloucester cheese softend by warm water and mixed with quick lime is a good cement for china-ware etc etc' —
News papers have been famous for Hyperbole and the Stamford Mercury has long been one at the head of the list of extravagance — in an article relating an accident at Drury lane Theatre is the following 'A *large piece of timber* fell on Miss Poveys head and wounded her severly *She was of course incapable of performing* etc — who woud not of course believe Miss Poveys head harder then a statues after this

Sunday Recieved a parcel from Mrs Emmerson[135] — took a

Walk to 'Simons wood' found 3 distinct species of the 'Bramble' or mulberry — Henderson will have it there is but 2 but I am certain he is wrong and believe there is 4 — the common one that grows in the hedges — the larger sort that grows on commons bearing larger fruit — calld by childern 'black berry' the small creeping 'dew berry' that runs along the ground in the land furrows and on the brinks of brooks and a much larger one of the same kind growing in woods   botanists may say what they will — for tho these are all of a family they are distinctly different — there are 2 sorts of the wild rose the one in hedges bearing blush colored flowers and the other much smaller in woods with white ones

3rd, Day of Jany, 1825

Monday	
Wednesday	Jiliflowers Polanthuses Marigolds and the yellow yarrow in flower and the double scarlet Anemonie nearly out — crocuses peeping out above ground swelling with flower — the authoress (Miss Kent) of the 'Flora Domestica' says the snow drop is the first spring flower she is mistaken the yellow winter aconite is always earlier and the first on the list of spring
Thursday	My dear boy Frederick is one yeer old this day
Friday	Bought some cakes of colors with the intention of trying to make sketches[136] of curious snail horns Butterflys Moths Sphinxes Wild flowers and what ever my wanderings may meet with that are not too common

Saturday A ryhming school master is the greatest bore in literature   the following ridicilous advertizement proves the assertion taken from the 'stamford mercury'[137]

'Boston

'Mr Gilberts boarding and day school will reopen on Monday January 17th 1825'

'For favours past his heart *must flow*
'And kind regard to youth shall show
'That Gilbert feels and grateful will
'The noble art "to learn" instill'

Sunday News paper Miracles Wonders Curositys etc etc   under these heads I shall insert any thing I can find worth reading and laughing at — 'Two extraordinary large eels were last week taken upon the saltings at Steeple in Dengie hundred Essex — these monsters of their species ([138]and there is every reason to believe them to be the fresh water silver eel — One was *seven feet* in length twenty one inches in surcumferance and weighd *fifty seven pounds* the other was six feet long larger round then the former and weighd sixty two pound — twenty years back one was taken nearly six feet long close to portman marsh wall — in Essex a quarter of a mile from Maldon bridge — a part of one of [the] eels was eaten by our correspondent who speaks highly of its flavour' — Essex herald[139]   'A parish clerk 115 years old is now able to read without spectacles and dig graves' etc etc — Stamford Mercury

10th, Day of Jan^y, 1825

Monday Saw a white thorn bush yesterday in Oxey-wood in the leaf all over and by next Sunday no doubt the knots of may may be seen — the winter ackonite just peeping out with its yellow flowers — the Aron

206

just appearing under the hedges as in april and the Avens (a common hedgrow plant) has never lost its leaves but appears as green as at spring —

Tuesday — Began to fetch maiden earth from molehills for my flower beds — heard the Mavis thrush sing for the first time this winter — it of[ten] sings earlier and has been heard on christmass day when the weather has been open

Thursday — Help'd Billings to take in Beans

Friday — A scarlet daisey in flower in the Garden — Recieved a letter from C.A. Elton[140] who tells me there is a many plants and ferns about Bristol downs and valleys and 'some rathe[r] peculiar to the country.' I hope I shall be able to go in spring

Saturday — This day is my Fathers birthday who is 60 years old — 'Thus runs the world away'[141]

Sunday — Took a walk in 'Porters snow close' to hunt ferns in the morning and in Turnills 'heath wood' in the afternoon   found nothing but the fox fern which is the commonest of all about here — Recieved a letter from Mrs Emmerson[142] and answered it

17th Day of Jan^y, 1825

Monday

Wednesday — A slight storm of snow for the first time this winter — just compleated the 9th Chapter of my Life — corrected the poem on the 'Vanitys of the world' which I have written in imitation of the old poets on whom I mean to father it and send it to Montgomerys paper the 'Iris' or the 'Literary Chronicle' under that character[143]

Thursday   Wrote a letter to Hessey[144]

Friday   A robin whistling on the plumb trees by the window I never heard one so early before

Saturday   'A new vegetable called the "Asparagus Potatoe" has been introduced into this country   it comes into season just as the asparagus goes out' — 'So little wind prevails in Italy that not a wind mill is to be seen in any part of it, there were two in venice but were taken down as usless for want of wind' — 'An elm tree suppos'd to be a thousand years old was blown down near ludlow castle' — 'A black birds nest with four young ones was found a few days ago in Yorkshire' — Stamford Mercury[145]

Sunday   News paper wonders — 'There is now living at Barton an old lady of the name of Faunt who has nearly attained the great age of 105 years — she has lately cut *new teeth* to the great supprise of the family' Stamford Mercury[146] — Took a walk to hilly wood brought home another plant of the white maiden hair fern that grows on a sallow stoven in a sort of spring — wrote to Mr Sharp[147] of the dead letter office — finished my 'two ballads to Mary'[148] which I intend to send to the 'Litterary Gazette' as also my three Sonnets to Bloomfield[149] and I am weary of writing for the London Magazine   these recent refinings are petty and trifling at best[150]

24th, Day of Jany 1825

Monday

Tuesday   A fine day   the bees were out busily flying as if seeking flowers   the sky was hung with light flying clouds and the season appeard as if the beginning of april

Wednesday	Fetchd some soil from Cowper green for my ferns and flowers — the sharpest frost for this winter which woud not bare [i.e. bear] a boy to slide on — From what cause sprung the superstition of making the No 3 a fatal No? — it is so much so — that ghosts use it and never pay a visit without giving their (fashionable) signal of 3 raps to anounce their arival
Thursday	Recieved a letter from M[r] Sharp[151] and one from Lord Radstock — and answerd his Lordships sending in it the 'Vanitys of Life' a poem — heard the buzz of the black beetle or cockchaffer[152] that flyes about in the autumn evenings and early in spring — it is different to the brown or summer beetle which is described by Collins — 'the beetle winds

'His small but sullen horn' [153]

and is not so common

Sunday	Recieved a letter from M[rs] Emmerson[154] and a 'Litterary Gazette' from somebody in which is a Review of an unsuccessful Attempt to reach Repulse Bay etc By Captain Lyon[155] from which the following curious incident is extracted speaking of some graves of the Esquemaux he says 'Near the large grave was a third pile of stones covering the body of a child which was coiled up in the same manner. A snow bunting had found its way thro the loose stones which composed this little tomb, and its now forsaken neatly built nest was found placed on the neck of the Child. As the Snow bunting has all the domestic virtues of our English Red breast it has always been considerd by us as the Robin of these dreary wilds and its lively chirp and fearless confidence have renderd it respected by the most hungry sports men — I coud not on this occasion view

its little nest placed on the breast of Infancy without wishing that I possesed the power of poeticaly expressing the feelings it excited'

31st, Day of Jan^y, 1825

Monday — Went to Simons Wood for a succor [i.e. sucker] of the Barberry bush to set in my Garden — saw the Corn tree putting out into leaf — a yellow crocus and a bunch of single snow drops in full flower — the mavis thrush has been singing all day long Spring seems begun — The wood bines all over the wood are in full leaf

Tuesday — A beautiful morning   took a walk in the fields saw some birch poles in the quick fencing and fancyd the bark of birch might make a good substitute for Paper   it is easily parted in thin lairs [i.e. layers] and one shred of bark round the tree woud split into 10 or a dozen sheets and I have tryd it and find it recieves the ink very readily

Wednesday — Went to walk in the fields and heard Ufford bells chimeing for a funeral   when I enquired I found it was for poor old John Cue of Ufford a friend of mine with whom I workd some seasons at turnip hoeing for which he was famous — he knew my Grandfather well and told me many reccolections of their young day follys — John Cue was once head Gardener for Lord Manners of Ufford hall — he was fond of flowers and books and possesd a many curious ones of the latter among which was 'Parkinsons H'

Thursday — Recieved a letter from Hessey[156] with £5 enclosed and a parcel containing 2 Nos of the New Series of London Mag: and 'Waladmor' a German-scotch

210

Novel — if Job was living now he woud stand a chance to gain his wish 'O that mine enemey woud write a book'[157] for this is the age of book-making — and like the small pox almost every body catches the plague

Friday

The first winters day   a sharp frost and a night fall of snows drifting in heaps by a keen wind — there has been a deal of talk about the forwardness of this season but last season was not much behind — on the third of this month I found an hedge sparrows nest in Billings Box trees before the window with three eggs in it   I lookd again in March and found two young ones pin featherd starved to death — she laid agen in the same nest and brought off a fledgd brood in april

Saturday

Severe frost – Recieved a joint letter from Lord Radstock and M[rs] Emmerson[158] under a Frank which was put into post too soon for which a charge of 1 py was made — 'knaves in office' watch chances as the cat watches mice and are of that species of animals that catch their prey by supprise

Sunday

Severe frost – Recieved a letter from M[rs] Gilchrist[159] — heard by Ned Simpson[160] of Stamford that a bird of the hawk kind was shot at a fountain in hollywell Park of a large size which he calls the *'hair legd falcon'*   heard by the same of a white mole being caught in Stamford field

7th, Day of Feb[y], 1825

Monday

Thursday

Fine day   the bees are out and busily seeking for wax among the little flowers of the yellow acconite

211

— a sparrow is building its nest in a hole in the old wallnut tree in the Taylors Gardens

Friday   Saw the first young Lamb this season — saw a blue violet on the Ivy bank next the lane in Billings Close

Saturday   Recieved a letter from Van dyke[161] in which he appears as the Editor of my Poems   they chuse who they please this time but my choice comes next and I think I shall feel able to do it my self   he wishes me to alter the title of my song written in imitation of Peggy Band to Peggy Bland because the old ballad is bad   I did it in memory of the music and shall not alter it

Sunday   Recieved a letter from Dr Darling[162] — an odd sort of fellow came to day with a bag full of old school summing books wanting me to buy them and vowing that he was the author of them and that I might make a good bargain by publishing them   what odd characters there are in the world   the fellow fancied that I was excessive ignorant to palm such ignorant impudence upon me for truth   after he found that his scheme woud not take he begd two pence and departed — he is the son of an odd fellow at Baston — he is a little foolish in his nature and they put him along while to school to compleat what she began — my dear Anna taken very ill[163]

14th Day of Feb^y, 1825

Monday   Wrote to Vandyk and Dr Darling[164]   in my letter to Vandyk I inserted the tune 'Peggy Band' there is a many beautiful tunes to these provincial Ballads   such is the 'White Cockade' 'Wars alarms' 'Down the Burn Davy' old and new 'Through the Wood laddy' 'Dusty Miller' 'Highland Laddie'

212

and a very beautiful one I forget the title it begins 'A witherd old gipsey one day I espied Who bade me shun the thick woods and said somthing beside' but the old woman that sung it is gone — the 'old Guardian Angels' 'Banks of Banna' and a thousand others

Tuesday   Heard the Black bird sing in Hilly wood — received a *Valentine* from Mrs Emmerson[165]   this new thing of affections flowering in such things is a sort of fishing for Wales in buckets — My Anna is somthing better[166]

Wednesday   Heard the Skylark sing at Swordy well — saw a piece of bayonet and gun barrel found while digging a stone pit   this proves the story that superstition tells of a battle fought here by the rebels in Cromwells time[167] — it is said were there is smoke there is fire and I often think were superstition lingers with her storys there is always some truth in them — brought home a bush of Ling or heath to plant in the garden

Thursday   Saw a large bunch of blue violets in flower and a root of the Bedlam Cowslip

Saturday   Received a News paper from Montgomery in which my poem of the 'Vanitys of Life'[168] was inserted with an ingenius and flattering compliment past upon it   praise from such a man as Montgomery is heart stirring and its the only one from a poet that I have met with — went to Turnills Heath close to get some furze bushes to set in the Garden

Sunday   Found several pieces of roman pot[169] in Harrisons top close on the hill over which the road crosses to the Tindhills at the north east corner of Oxey wood one piece was the letter V   Artis says they are Roman and I verily believe some Roman camp or pottery was made there

21st, Day of Feby, 1825

Monday   A Robin busy at building its nest in the Garden —

Tuesday   A hedge Sparrow building its nest in one of Billingss Box trees

Saturday   Recieved a Letter from Lord Radstock[170] filld with scraps of News paper Poetry among which was a pretty Valentine by Montgomery and some verses said to be written by Lord Byron   they are in his manner — the rest after the perusal of the News papers are 'nothings' — when his Lordship sees any thing he fancys better then the rest he always attributes it to Mrs Emmerson or some of his friends as he has done now   one to her and one to Van-dyke

Sunday   Recieved a letter in ryhme from a John Pooley[171] a very dull Fooley who ran me 10d further in debt as I had not money to pay the postage   I have often been botherd with these poet pretenders...pilfered ...the ryhmes...

28th, Day of Feby, 1825

Monday

Tuesday   Saw to day the largest piece of Ivy I ever saw in my life mailing a tree which it nearly surpassd in size in Oxey wood   it was thicker then my thigh and its cramping embraces seemd to diminish the tree to a dwarf — it has been asserted by some that Ivy is very injurous to trees and by others that it does no

214

injury at all — I cannot deside against it — the large pieces were covered all over with root like fibres as thick as hair and they represented the limbs of animals more then the bark of a tree

Wednesday Found A Mavis Thrushes nest with 3 eggs these birds always build early they make a nest like a black birds but instinct has taught them a lesson against the cold which the other has no occasion for and that is they never line their nests without wool which keeps the nest warm at this early season they always begin to sing as soon as the male blossoms of the hazel or (Trails) make their appearance and build their nests when female flowers put forth their little crimson threads at the end of the buds to recieve the impregning dust of the male dangling trails

Thursday This is Pattys Birth day

Friday Went to Ailsworth heath to fetch ling or common heath and furze bushes to set in my garden — went in Bates spinney to hunt the black maiden hair[172] found none but saw some of the largest furze and common brakes I had ever seen my friend Billings measured a furze bush which was 11 foot and a ½ high and a brake branch 8 foot and a ¼ — found a curious sort of Iris[173] or flag growing in a pond in the wood and fancy it not a common one brogth a bit home to set

Saturday Recieved a letter from Lord Radstock and M[rs] Emmerson[174] — also one from a M[r] Weston the Editor of poor Bloomfields Letters and Remains requesting me to send him the letters I have of the poet and asking permission to publish those of

215

mine   poor Bloomfield I wish that death had left me a little longer the pleasures of his friendship — Went to see the Fox cover in Etton field sown with furze some years ago which now present a novel appearance and thrive better then on their native heath tho the place is low ground

Sunday

Recieved a parcel from Hessey with the Magazine and a leaf of the new poems also a present of Miss Kents Sylvan Sketches[175]   she seems to be a thorough book maker and tis a thorough book sellers failure to see the point of a new history of birds[176]

Parish Officers are modern Savages as the following fact will testifye — Crowland Abbey — 'Certain surveyors have lately dug up several foundation stones of the Abby and also a great quantity of stone coffins for the purpose of repairing the parish roads!!' Stamford Mercury[177] — Anna taken agen for the worse yesterday had a terrible fever all night and remains in a doubtful state —

7th, Day of March 1825

Monday

Wrote to E.T. Artis[178] — M[rs] Gilchrist and M[rs] Emmerson — enclosing one in Artis's Letter (to get it Frankd) for M[rs] W. Wright of Clapham[179] — requesting her to give me a bulb of the 'Tyger lily' and a sucker of The 'White Province Rose'

Tuesday

Wrote to Hessey and to Jos Weston[180] of 12 Providence Row Finsbury Square London enclosing my letters of Bloomfield for his use in a forth coming Vol of his Corespondence — went to Royce wood to get some Service trees to set in Billings close

Wednesday

I had a very odd dream last night and I take it as an ill omen for I dont expect that the book[181] will meet

216

a better fate — I thought I had one of the proofs of the new poems from London and after looking at it awhile it shrank thro my hands like sand and crumbled into dust — The birds were singing in Oxey wood at 6 oclock this evening as loud and various as at May

Thursday Heard an Anecdote yesterday of D[r] Dodd[182] which is well known and considerd authentic among the common people   it is said that D[r] Dodd was taunted on his way to the place of execution by a lady who had envied his popularity and looking out of a window as he passd she exclaimd 'Now D[r] Dodd weres your God' when he bade her look in the last Chapter of Micah and read the 8th 9th and 10th verses for an answer which she did and dy'd soon afterwards of a broken heart

Friday Intend to call my Natural History of Helpstone 'Biographys of Birds and Flowers' with an Appendix on Animals and Insects — The frogs have began to croke and spawn in the ponds and dykes

Saturday Received the first proof of the Shepherds Calender from Hessey to correct — and a letter from Lord Radstock[183] in which he seems to be offended at a late opinion of mine of some News paper Poems that he sent me as specimens of the beautiful — and he thanks his stars that his taste is not so refined as to make him above admiring them — the word refinement has lost its origional use and is nothing more then a substitute for fashionable coquette which I thank my stars for keeping me too ignorant to learn

Sunday Recieved a letter from the Editor of Bloomfields

Correspondence[184] inclosing the return of my letter of Bloomfield and a scrap of his hand writing written in his summer house at Shefford an Inscription in it which I hear is now defaced   what a sad thing it is to see the relics of such poets destroyed   who woud not have made a pilgrimage to have seen the summer house and its inscription as left by the Bard — in the same letter also was a pretty unaffected letter from Hannah Bloomfield his daughter   she seems to inherit the gentle unasuming manners and feelings for which her father was loved and esteemd — lent Henderson 3 Nos of the New 'London Mag: and Review'   took a walk to open copy to see the Nutt trees in flower which promise a great nutting season

14th Day of March 1825

Monday	My double Scarlet Anemonie in full flower — A sharp frosty morning
Tuesday	I have been reading over Mrs Barbaulds Lessons for Childern[185] to my eldest child who is continually teazing me to read them I find by this that they are particulary suited to the tastes of childern as she is never desirious of hearing anything read a second time but them
Wednesday	Took a walk to hunt pootys about Royce close and the Tindhills — went to visit an old favourite spot in Oxey wood that used to be smotherd with Ferns — got some sallow trees[186] to set in Billings Close and a stoven of Black alder to set in my garden
Thursday	Recieved a letter[187] and present of Books from Lord Radstock containing Hannah Moores 'Spirit of Prayer' — Bp Wilsons 'Maxims' Burnets 'Life of

God in the soul of Man' — 'A New Manual of Prayer' and 'Watsons Answer to Paine' a quiet unaffected defence of the Bible and an example for all contro-vertialists[188] to go bye were railing has no substitute for argument — I have not read Tom Paine but I have always understood him to be a low blackguard

Friday   The sharp frosty mornings still continue

Saturday   Had from Drakards[189] a folio book price 9s/d. to insert the best of my poems in that Hessey says he will send down

Sunday   Still sharp frosty mornings — Recieved a letter from Mrs Emmerson[190] with an Ode to Spring — Spring is a wonderful mother for ryhmes

21st, Day of March 1825

Monday   Had a double Polanthus and single white Hepatica sent me from Stamford round which was rapped a curious prospectus of an 'Every day book' by W. Hone.[191] if such a thing was well got up it woud make one of the most entertaining things ever pub-lished — and I think the prospectus bids fair to do something   there is a fine quotation from Her-rick for a Motto   how delightful is the freshness of these old poets   it is meeting with green spots in deserts

Tuesday   A cold wintry day

Wednesday   Recieved a parcel from Holbeach[192] with a Letter and the Scientific Receptacle from J.Savage — they have inserted my poems and have been lavish with branding every corner with 'J.Clares' — how absurd are the serious meant images or attempts

219

at fine writing in these young writers   on[e] of them concludes a theme on a dead school master with a very pathetic and sublime wish as he fancys perhaps 'wishing that the tear he leaves on his grave may grow up a marble monument to his memory'[193] — this is the first crop of tears *I have ever heard of sown with an intention to grow.*

Thursday	Recievd a letter from Lord Radstock[194] with a packet of News papers from Mʳˢ Emmerson
Sunday	This is Palm Sunday — I went to the woods to seek some branches of the sallow palms for the childer calld by them 'geese and gosslings' and 'Cats and Kittens' — Susan Simpson and her brother[195] came to see me — lent her the 2 Vols of 'Walladmor'

28th, Day of March 1825

Monday	
Wednesday	Recieved a letter from Vandyk[196] which proves all my suspicions are well founded I suspected that he had not seen those M.S.S. which I considerd my best poems and he says in his letter that he has not — they have often pretended to be very anxious after my success etc and to appear...and that has put them always in the hands of...[197]
Thursday	Artis and Henderson came to see me and we went to see the Roman Station agen Oxey wood which he says is plainly roman — he told me that he went three times and sent oftener for the M.S.S. which they did not send at last —[198]
Friday	My Sister Sophy is 27 year old to day Recieved from Wilson[199] Vyse's 'Tutors Guide' 2 Vols

Saturday   'The Lingfield and Crowhurst[200] choir sung several select[201] pieces from Handel in the Cavity of a Yew tree in the church yard of the latter place   The tree is 36 feet in Circumference and is now in a growing state — The hollow was fitted up like a room and sufficiently large to contain the performers — On clearing out the interior of the tree some years since a 7 lb cannon ball was discovered which no doubt had been fired into it; it was cut out from the solid part of the tree' — Stamford Mercury[202]

Sunday   Two gentlemen came to see me from Milton one of them appeard to be a sensible and well informd man   he talkd much of the poets but did not like Wordsworth and when I told him I did he instantly asked me wether I did not like Byron better
            I dont like these comparisons to knock your opinions on the head with — I told him that I read Wordsworth oftener then I did Byron and he seemd to express his supprise at it by observing that he coud not read Wordsworth at all

4th, Day of April 1825

Monday

Friday   Recieved a letter from Lord Radstock[203] and one from Mrs Emmerson with an offer that Mr Clutterbuck the Attorney will draw up my will if I chuse which oppertunity I shall certainly take hold of

Sunday   Found a branch of white thorn in Porters Snow close knotted and nearly in flower   it is considerd very early if a branch of May as it is called can be found on the first of new May[204]

11th, Day of April 1825

Monday

221

Wednesday   The black thorn showing flower

Thursday   My mother is 67 years old this day[205]   she has
been afflicted with a dropsy for this 20 years[206] and
has for all that out lived a large family of brothers
and sisters and remains 'the last of the flock'
The Snake head or Frittellary in flower also the light
blue, Pink, and White Hyacinths — Bluebell or
Harebell in flower — the Primrose Violet and Bed-
lam Cowslips fading out of flower

Friday   Recievd a letter from Lord Radstock[207] in which his
Lordship says that VanDyk is going out of town for
a while   this is the man that was to get my new
book thro the press in 6 weeks and with the assis-
tance of Taylor and Hessey has been a month about
one proof of it[208]

Saturday   Took a walk in the field a birds nesting and botanizing
and had like to have been taken up as a poacher in
Hillywood by a meddlesome consieted keeper
belonging to Sir John Trollop[209]   he swore that
he had seen me in act more then once of shooting
game when I never shot even so much as a sparrow
in my life — what terryfying rascals these wood
keepers and gamekeepers are   they make a
prison of the forrests and are its joalers

Sunday   I have waited 3 weeks for a new proof of the Shep-
herds Calender and nothing has come which was to
be in 3 days — I have sent ten times[210] for some
rough copys of Poems which I sent up to Taylor
when the 'Village Minstrel' was in the press and I
have not got them yet and never shall I expect — I
want them to finish some for a future publication
and correct others — if I had known the pretending

222

and hypocritical friendship of booksellers...I woud not have put such large quantitys of faith in them to want to...[211] I have never as yet had a settling as every friday is over with them[212] — Recieved a letter from D[r] Darling[213] — no proofs yet — Saw a solitary Field fare in Oxey wood   I never observed one so late before — Wrote to Hessey in a manner that I am always very loath to write but I coud keep my patience no longer

18th, Day of April 1825

Monday   Resumed my letters on Natural History in good earnest and intend to get them finished with this year if I can get out into the fields for I will insert nothing but what comes or has come under my notice

Tuesday   The Swallows have made their appearan[ce]   I saw one to day and I heard by a cow boy that they were come three days ago

Wednesday Recieved a letter from Taylor[214] in answer to mine to Hessey of last Sunday — He is very pettish respecting my anxiety and irritation and says that if my friends who gave me the advice and cautions etc respecting the neglect and mystery of booksellers or myself can find a Publisher who can do better by them then he does he will readily return the M.S.S. — but he throws a river in the way for me to cross by saying that tho mine and their distrust can do no good it may do harm — now if it can do harm to find fault with actions that deserve no commendation I am sure it can do no good to speak in their praise

Thursday   Heard the Nightingale for the first time this season in Royce wood

Friday   Went to Milton — saw the red headed brown linnet[215] smaller then the brown do [i.e. ditto] — saw a Pettichap or hover bird — and a large flock of Field fares — brought home a white Primrose heard a many Nightingales — in the evening I heard a bird make a long continued noise for a minute together like a childs skreeker or a cricket but much louder — Henderson promises to give me some information respecting the birds about Milton

Saturday   Saw the red start or Firetail to day and little Willow wren[216] — the black thorn tree in full flower that shines about the hedges like cloaths hung out to dry — Saw in the Stamford paper[217] that the lost leaf of Dooms day book was found and had no time to Copy out the account

Sunday   No Proofs of the New Poems yet — Recieved a Letter from Lord Radstock and Mrs Emmerson[218]

25th, Day of April 1825

Monday   Heard a terrible kick up with the Rats in the cieling last night and might have made up a tollerable faith to believe them ghosts — A Thunder storm several claps very loud in the distance came from south west

Tuesday   This used to be 'Break day'[219] when the Fen commons used to be broke as it was calld by turning in the stock   it used to be a day of busy note with the villagers but inclosure has spoiled all

Wednesday Heard the Cuckoo for the first time this Season — it was said to be heard a week back by a shepherd — Saw the large Grey Wag tail   I think it a bird of passage as I have never seen it in winter — some

224

young Plants of Ash and Maple showing leaf — saw a bird with a dark line over each ear   I think it one of the flycatchers

Thursday   Hedge sparrow finished her nest in Billings Box tree and laid one egg — Wallnutt showing leaf — Sycamore and Horse chesnutt nearly cover'd — I observed a Snail on his journey at full speed and I markd by my watch that he went 13 Inches in 3 minutes which was the utmost he coud do without stopping to wind or rest   it was the large Garden snail

Friday   The hedge Sparrow in the Box tree has been about 12 days building her nest the Robin in the wall about 14 and the Jenny wren near 3 Weeks — Heard all thro last night the sort of watch ticking noise calld a death watch and observed there was one on each side the chamber and as soon as one ceased ticking the other began I think it is a call that the male and female use in the time of cohabiting — A Jenny wrens nest with the out side just built I mean to see how long she is about the lining

Saturday   Received another letter[220] from the Editor of Bloomfields Correspondence requesting me to alter a line in my Sonnets on Bloomfield 'Thy injured muse and memory need no sigh' and asking permission to publish only two of them which I shall not agree with either way   Editors are troubled with nice amendings and if Doctors were as fond of Amputation as they are of altering and correcting the world woud have nothing but cripples

Sunday   'A Salmon *near* 20 lbs weight was caught about a fortnight ago by Robt Nassau Sutton Esq[r] while

225

trolling in the river Trent near Kelham Hall' —
Stamford Mercury[221]

2nd, Day of May 1825

Monday   Bradfords Club[222] feast next door never went into
the Yard to see them a thing I never did in my life
before — illness makes the merriest pastimes of life
as tiresome foolerys and turns the sweetest offer-
ings of pleasure to gall —

Tuesday   Wrote a letter to Taylor and one to Mrs Emmerson[223]

Friday   Coud not sleep all night   got up at three oclock
in the morning and walkd about the fields — the
birds were high in their songs in Royce wood and
almost deafning   I heard the Cricket bird[224]
again in full cry in Royce wood it is just like a childs
screeker — saw a Hawk like bird that made an odd
noise like one of the notes of the Nightingale as if to
decoy his prey in sight

Saturday   Sent some Pootys and Ferns to Henderson yester-
day

Sunday   Went to Walk in the fields   saw the white thorn
in some places about the hedges covered over with
May and the Wilding or Crab also was smothered
with blossom   the Maple was in full flower

9th, Day of May 1825

Monday   Wrote another portion of my Life and took a Walk
to seek a Nightingales nest — found a Song thrushes
in bushy close by the side of a young oak with 4
eggs   never saw one of this kind in such a place
before

226

Tuesday	Saw a male and female of the Tree sparrow (as I supposed them) in Royce close hedge next the lane the cock bird had a very black head and its shades of brown were more deep and distinct then the house sparrow the female when flying showd two white feathers in her tail — they seemd to have a nest in the hedge row but I coud not find it — saw a Pettichap in Bushy close its note is more like 'Chippichap' it keeps in continual motion on the tops of trees uttering its note
Wednesday	Recieved a letter last night from Henderson[225] with a plant of the Double Marsh marigold — the male flowers of the Wallnutt ripe and falling off
Thursday	It is often reported that the Sky lark never sings but on the Wing this report is worth little truth like a many others I saw one this morning sing on the ground
Friday	Met with an extrodinary incident to day while Walking in Open wood to hunt a Nightingales nest — I popt unawares on an old Fox and her four young Cubs that were playing about she saw me and instantly approachd towards me growling like an angry dog I had no stick and tryd all I coud to fright her by imitating the bark of a fox hound which only irritated her the more and if I had not retreated a few paces back she woud have seized me when I set up an haloo she started
Saturday	Recieved the April and May Ma[ga]zine from London with a letter from Hessey and one from Vandyke[226] that has lain ever since 15th of march the Magazine is very dull . a Note also from Miss Kent accompanied the parcel to request my assistance to

give her information for her intended History of Birds but if my assistance is not worth more then 12 lines it is worth nothing and I shall not interfere

Sunday

Extracts from the Stamford Mercury[227]

'Coals were first used in England in the reign of Edward the 1st. the smoke was supposed to corrupt the air so much that he forbad the use of them' — A fellow who passes himself off on the ignorant as a prophet is extorting money from the ignorant by telling them that a flying serpent will come to destroy them against whose venom he sells spells that ensure their safety — 'The delusion respecting the flying serpent still continues: The fatal days were stated to be thursday last the 18 and 28th The Prophet has been travelling thro Dorset and the adjoining counties offering his charms for sale and has not found a deficiency of dupes   yet of those who demur he asks 'If you will not recieve the servant how will you recieve the master when he comes'[228]

16th, Day of May 1825

Monday

Tuesday   At a meeting of Florists held at the Kings Head at Newark last week prizes were adjudged as follows

Auriculas

First	–	Grimes Privateer	–	Mr Ordoyns[229]
Second	–	Stretches Alexander	–	Mr Ordoyns[229]
Third	–	Wilds Black and Clear	–	Mr Welby

Polyanthuses

First	–	Twineys Princess of Wales	–	Mr Ordoyns[229]
Second	–	Fillinghams Tantararia	–	Mr Taylor
Third	–	Englands Defiance	.	–	Mr Clark

Sunday   News paper Odditys[230]
'A spirited London bookseller announces that he is
printing the Duke of Yorks Speech against the Cath-
olics in *letters of gold* ' — this is shining fame at least
— 'The total population of America is 34,280,000. of
which 11,287,000. are Protestants 22,177,000, Roman
Catholics and 820,000. Indians not Christians' 'At
Wieland in Poland The imajination is confoundeded
at the idea of finding after a desent of 850 steps in
the salt mines vast Halls (the Hall of Klosky is 360
feet high and 180 feet wide) stabling for 80 horses
store houses Offices for Clerks and three Chappels
the whole of the fittings alters crusifixes tables
desks and seats worked in salt!' Stamford Mercury
— Recieved a letter from Lord Radstock with one
enclosed of a Mr Boilau with a flattering compliment
on my poems calling me a pretty flower

23rd Day of May 1825
Monday   More Wonders from the Mercury[231]
'A Clergy man of the established Church name Ben-
son now attracts larger congregations at St Giles'
church then the celebrated Mr Irving once did at the
Caledonian   Mr Bensons Chief Characteristic is
calm and dignified reasoning Mr Irvings powerful
eloquence and vehement action'
'211 Stage Coaches pass weekly through Daventry
Northamptonshire' Stamford Mercury

Tuesday and Wednesday   The Catholics have lost their bill[232]
once more and its nothing but right they shoud
when one beholds the following Sacred humbugs
which their religion hurds up and sanctifys — 'A list
of Catholice relics in a church at Dobberan[233] a Vil-
lage in Mecklenburg' — From Nugents Travels[234] —
'A small quantity of flax which the Virgin Mary had

for spinning — A bundle of hay which the three wise men of the east had for their cattle and left behind them at bethlehem — A bone of Ignatius Loyola the founder of the jesuits — A piece of poor lazaruses Garment. — A bone of St Christopher and first joint of his thumb — A piece of linnen cloth which the Virgin Mary wove with her own hands — A piece of the head belonging to the fish mentioned in Tobit — The napkin which the bride groom made use of at the marrige of Cana of Galilee — A hair of St Jeromes Mustachios — Part of Judas bowels which gushed out as he burst asunder — The Sissars with which Delila cut off Sampsons hair — A piece of the apron which the butcher wore when he killed the calf upon the return of the prodigal son — One of the five smooth stones which David put into his bag when he went to encounter the jiant Goliah — A branch of the tree on which Absalom hung by the hair — The heads of St Thomas the Apostle of St Paul and of St Peter — A piece of St Peters fishing net — the Priest told the traveller that one of the relics had been stolen in the last Century and it was no less then a quill of the Angel Gabriels Wing'

Thursday   Took up my Hyacinth bulbs and laid them in ridges of earth to dry — made a new frame for my Ariculas — found a large white Orchis[235] in Oxey Wood of a curious species and very rare — I watched a Blue cap or Blue Titmouse feeding her young whose nest was in a wall close to an Orchard   she got caterpillars out of the Blossoms of the apple trees and leaves of the plumb — she fetchd 120 Catterpillars in half an hour — now supposing she only feeds them 4 times a day a quarter of an hour each time she fetches no less then 480 Catterpillars and I shoud think treble the number

230

Friday   Recieved a letter and a packet of News papers yesterday from M[rs] Emmerson[236] in which she promises to send me some Polyanthuses from Bath and Carnations also —

Saturday   Found the old Frog in my garden that has been there this four years   I know it by a mark which it recieved from my spade 4 years ago   I thought it woud dye of the wound so I turnd it up on a bed of flowers at the end of the garden which is thickly covered with ferns and blue bells and am glad to see it has recoverd — in Winter it gets into some straw in a corner of the garden and never ventures out till the beginning of May when it hides among the flowers and keeps its old bed never venturing further up the garden —

Sunday   The following Advertisment is from the Observer of Sunday May 22. 1825. 'Just published The Speech of his Royal Highness the Duke of York in the house of Lords the 25 April 1825 Printed by J. Whittaker (with the same splendour as the account of the Coronation of his Majesty) in letters of Gold on the finest Card paper price 10[s] /6 Sold by Septimus Prowett 23 Old Bond Street'   Well done Septimus Prowet the speech is an open and honest one and well deserves it — Heard the most severe thunder clap yesterday that I ever heard in my life   it was heard instantly (only 3 pulses) after the flash — Found a very scarce[237] and curious orchis of an iron grey color or rather a pale rusty tinge with a root like the pile wort   I cannot make out its name — I found last week a fine white piegon Orchis which is seldom found

30th Day of May 1825

231

Monday   Took a Walk yesterday to Bassetts close at the bottom of the worm stalls to see the Ash tree that the lightning struck on Saturday   it took off the large top and splinterd the body to atoms driving large pieces of it in all directions round the tree to the distance of fifty yards   the stump of the trunk left standing was pilled of the bark all round and split to the bottom   I never saw such terrible power of lightning in my life before; people came to see it from all the neighbouring villages and took away the fragments as curositys

Tuesday   My dear Child Eliza was taken ill of a fever on Sunday night and is as yet no better — Sent a Letter and parcel to Mrs Emmerson[238] with the 'Parish' and my new Will for Mr Clutterbuck to draw up — Mrs Bellairs of Woodcroft Castle came to see my garden — Artis told me he fancied that the place in Harrisons close was a Roman Pottery   I have since reccolected that there used to be a large hole about two stones throw from it calld 'Potters Hole' when I was a boy and filld up since the inclosure   this may go far for [i.e. to support] his opinion

Thursday   This is my Darling Annas Birth day who is 5 years old a weakling flower fast fading in the bud — 'withering untimlessly'[239] — Recieved a parcel from Hessey with the Mag: and the first proof agen corrected for good with a note from Hessey and a long letter from Taylor[240] very kindly worded in which he speaks of disolving partnership with Hessey on Midsummer next

Friday   Finished planting my Ariculas — went a Botanizing after Ferns and Orchises and caught a cold in the wet grass which has made me as bad as ever — Got the tune of 'Highland Mary' from Wisdom Smith a gipsey and pricked another sweet tune with out name as he fiddled it

Saturday   Saw three fellows at the end of Royce wood who I found were laying out the plan for an 'Iron rail way'[241] from Manchester to London — it is to cross over Round Oak Spring by Royce Wood Corner for Woodcroft Castle   I little thought that fresh intrusions woud interupt and spoil my solitudes after the Inclosuıe   they will despoil a boggy place that is famous for Orchises at Royce Wood end

Sunday   Returned the proof to Hessey   wrote a note to Hessey[242] and one to Mrs Wright of Clapham accompanied with some flowers viz — 'Lilies of the Valley' 'Shepherds Goldy locks' 'Jerusalem Cows lips' 'Yellow flowerd Yarrow' 'Lilac flowerd Cranes bill' 'Black flowered Cranes bill' and 'Pencil flowerd Dᵒ', [i.e. ditto] — Read a continuation of a good paper in the London on 'A poor Students struggles thro Cambridge etc'[243]   the rest are moderates among the middlings

6th, Day of June 1825

Monday   Went to see Mrs Bellairs Garden at Woodcroft with Anna   saw a Scarlet Anemonie and White Piony both very handsome   the Mote round the Garden has a very fine effect and the long Bridges that cross it made of planks and railed with crooked pieces of oak — I thought of the time of Cromwell while walking about it and felt the difference — Swallows had several nests under the bridge

Tuesday   Recieved another parcel from Hessey with another

proof of the Poems Viz the 'Sorrows of Love'[244]
Taylor has cut out a great deal and some things
which I think might have stood   the parcel also
brought a present of 'Aytons Essays'[245] a young
writer of great promise which was killed in the bud
        these Essays are exelent and contain a deal
more of the Human heart then an affectedly written
book with that Title

Wednesday   Poor old Coz. Day the Mole Catcher dyed to night
             after a short illness — he has been a tennant of the
             Meadows and fields for half a Century

Thursday   Recieved a letter from Mrs Emmerson[246] and wrote
             an answer to it — Returned the proofs of January
             and the Broken Heart and wrote to Taylor — sent
             some flowers to Mrs Bellairs and am promised the
             'Scarlet Anemonie' 'White Piony' and 'Pink Bromp-
             ton Stocks'

Friday   Saw the Blue Grey or lead colored Flycatcher for
             the first time this season   they are called 'Egypt
             Birds' by the common people from their note which
             seems to resemble the sound of the word 'Egypt'
                 they build in old walls like the red start and
             Grey Wagtail

                    13th, Day of June 1825
Monday   My dear Eliza is 3 years old to day — I feel anxious
             to insert these memorandums of my affections as
             Memory tho a secondary is the soul of time and life
             the principal but its shadow — Observed an Eclipse
             or some other Phenomen of the Sun this Morning
             not noticed in the Almanack   I first saw it about
             half past four and it continued till after five   it
             had exactly the same appearance as an Eclipse and
             I believe it was nothing else[247]

234

Sunday   Recieved a Letter from Taylor[248] in which he says
                that there is twice as much more as he wants for the
                Shepherds Calender and a few months back one of
                his causes for delay was that there was not enough
                to begin with   nothing has made a wide differ-
                ence here but[249] time and left a puzzling Paradox
                behind it which tells that he is a very dillatary chap
                — Recieved a Letter from Mrs Emmerson with a
                Parcel containing a present of a Waiscoat and some
                fine Polyanthus Brompton Stock and Geranium
                Seed

                    20th, Day of June 1825
Monday

Tuesday   Wrote a letter to Taylor[250] — found a birds nest in
                the thatch of a hovel gable end in Billings yard
                think it a Fly catchers   it resembles in color and
                shape somthing of the chat or White throat or more
                like the sedge bird then either   the female sits
                hard and the cock feeds her with catterpillars from
                the leaves of trees

Thursday   Wrote to Mrs Emmerson[251] and sent a letter to Hones
                Every day book with a poem which I fatherd on
                Andrew Marvel

                    27th, Day of June 1825
Monday

Saturday   Recieved a letter from Hessey[252] with the Dividend
                or half yearly payment of the money in the funds
                and Lord Spencers Anuity — they always send it in
                written drafts to be drawn on their bankers for what
                reason I cannot tell unless it is to make a safe car-
                rige[253]   I wanted £10 more then my sallarys but

                    235

they have not sent it this time and have only sent me the £15 which belongs me — Wrote to Mrs Emmerson and sent some verses in imitation of the old Poets to Hones Every Day Book 'On Death' — The Baloon with Mr Green and Miss Stocks[254] passd over our garden opposite the wallnutt tree

Sunday   To day is Helpstone feast[255]   Wrestling and fighting the ploughmans fame is still kept up with the usual determined spirit

4th, Day of July 1825

Monday

Thursday   Wrote an answer to Hesseys letter of the 30th of June[256] which contained a draft for my dividend and salary and enquired after the stoppage of the new poems   also was forced to solicit them anew to send me £10 which I want to pay off my half yearly accounts

Saturday   Mr Sharp from London called on me

Sunday   Recieved a letter from Hessey[257] with the £10 which I wanted more then my Sallary came to — and with the News also that they have sold the London Mag:

11th, Day of July 1825

Monday   Started to Milton — a very pleasant morning saw a bird that was an entire stranger to me about the size and shape of a green linnet with wings of a brown grey color and the crown of the head of a deep black that extended downwards no further then the eyes   it had an odd appearance and tho Artis looked thro Pennant[258] he coud not find any thing resembling it and believes it to be an unnoticed species of the linnet tribe

236

Tuesday   Went to day to see Artis   found him busy over
             his antiquitys and Fossils — he told me a curious
             thing about the manner in which the Golden crested
             wren builds her nest   he says it is the only english
             bird that suspends its nest which it hangs on three
             twigs of the fir branch and it glews the eggs at the
             bottom of the nest with the gum out of the tree to
             keep them from being thrown out by the wind
             which often turns them up side down with out
             injury

Wednesday   This day I am thirty two[259] — and my health was
             drank at Milton by two very pretty girls M[rs] P——r
             and M[rs] B——n[260] who wishd I might treble the
             number — I had my wish in turn but I did not drink
             it in return —[261] Henderson has promised me a curi-
             ous 'Everlasting Pea' a Climbing Rose the Monkey
             Flower Feather Hyacinth and some Chrisanthemums

Thursday   Recieved a letter from Lord Radstock[262] in which his
             Lordship has made another troublesome request
             for his letters which he has written to me   I can-
             not hunt them up at present

Friday   Recieved a letter from M[rs] Emmerson[263] in which she
             tells me that Rippengille is come up and she wants
             me to start tomorrow — this is one of the hottest
             days I have known and all my ferns is nearly scorchd
             up — Began to teach Eliza Holmes the common
             rules of Arithmetic at the restless request of her
             parents who are anxious for me to learn her

Saturday   Still uncommonly Hot

                      18th, Day of July 1825
Monday

Thursday   Paid Stevenson[264] for the Stamford Mercury and gave it up as too expensive

Sunday   Found a species of Broom[265] in Bushy Close of a dwarf kind   the like sort grows in great quantitys on Casterton Cow pasture — the weather changed very cold but still dry

25th, Day of July 1825

Monday   'A hive of Bees natives to New South Wales has been recently brought to this country — The bees are very small and have no Sting but their honey is peculiarly fine' Stamford Mercury[266]

Wednesday   Recieved the 28 No of the Every day book in which is inserted a Poem of mine which I sent under the assumed name of 'James Gilderoy' from Surfleet as being the production of Andrew Marvel and printed in the Miscellanys of the Spalding Antiqurarys — I shall venture agen under another name after awhile — Viz 'Poem on Death'[267]

Friday   Recieved a proof from Taylor — the plan is again altered[268] and he now intends to print the Months only and leave out the Tales   this plan is one that puts the worst first and leaves the best for a future oppertunity — this proof contains Febuary and April — the last is good for nothing and is not worth troubling the printer with — the poem on Spring is the best in the bundle and woud supply its place well

Saturday   Sharp came to bid me good bye before he started to London   a young Lady was with him of very amiable and pleasing manners who was very fond of Poetry and flowers

238

Sunday   Recieved a letter from M[rs] Emmerson[269] in which she has discovered me to be the Author of the Verses on Death in the every day book signed Marvel she has oftener been wrong in her guesses and I think if I had not given her some hints of it before I sent it she woud not have found it out now

1st Day of Aug[st] 1825

Monday   Heard an old Fen Farmer say to day that on his farm he finds a great deal of wood perticularly Oak Hazel and Yew in the earth   he says that the earth is actually nothing else but a decomposition of wood and that it will grow nothing but Oats   he says that the Hazel will burn well as fire wood but the oak dyes out unless continually blown — he also talkd of great quantitys of shells being found as white as Dogs teeth

Tuesday   Wrote a Letter to William Hone[270] 'Every day book' signd Roberts with a copy of Verses which I have titled 'A Farwell and Defiance to Love' and fatherd on Sir John Harrington but I dont suppose they will get inserted

Wednesday   A person of the name of Clay[271] came to see me the 'Editor of the Scientific Receptacle'   he stopt with me all the rest day   he talked much of poetry and Poets but the latter were such names that nobody knew but himself the correspondents of Diarys Mathematical companions etc etc — he told me an odd circumstance of a farmer in the fen growing nothing but 'Teazles' for the purpose of carding a nap on cloth   they are stronger he says then the wild made so perhaps by cultivation

Thursday   Recieved a letter from M[rs] Gilchrist[272] in which she

says that Baron Field[273] has offered to edit Octaves
miscellaneous papers

8th, Day of Aug[st], 1825

Monday

Tuesday Sowed my Anemonie and Bath Polyanthus seed —
lent Miss Fanny Knowlton[274] Bloomfields Hazle-
wood Hall and Remains[275] and Aytons Essays —
Got a look at Gilleads of Spaldings 'Alworth Abbey'
and I never saw such a heap of unnatural absurditys
and ridiculous attempts at wit and Satire strung
together in my reading existance

Wednesday a news paper lye[276] of the first order — 'M[r] Gale of
Holt in the parish of Bradford Wilts has at present a
Pear of the jagonel kind in his possesion which was
taken by himself from the tree in 1776, *49 years ago
and is now as sound as at the first moment it was gathered.*
it is hung up by the stalk and no means what ever
has been adopted to preserve it. — it must have
been a wooden one

Saturday Went to Milton   wrote a Letter to Miss Kent[277] —
and corrected and sent the Proof back to Taylor —
saw the Transactions of the Horticultural society

Sunday Returned from Milton   brought home some
flower seeds and roots — saw two very large catter-
pillars which a man found among the Potatoes in
his garden   one was about 3 Inches long and the
other 4 the smaller one was green with triangular
marks of black, light blue, and yellow, the other
was yellow with triangular marks of the same colors
as the other save that were the other was yellow this
was white

240

15th Day of Augst, 1825

Monday

Saturday   Wrote a letter to Henderson[278] and sent one with it to get frankd for A A Watts Esqr Editor of the 'Literary Souvenir' with a Ballad 'First Loves Reccolections' for insertion in that Work

Sunday   Recieved a letter from Mr Emmerson[279] which tells me that Lord Radstock dyed yesterday   he was the best friend I have met with — tho he possesed too much of that simple heartedness to be a fashionable friend or hypocrite yet it often led him to take hypocrites for honest friends and to take an honest man for an hypocrite —

22nd, Day of Augst,

Monday

Tuesday   Found a beautiful Deaths head Moth catterpillar in Billings Potatoes   it is about 4½ Inc[h]es long of most beautiful rainbow colors

Friday   Recieved a letter from the Editor[280] of a new annual Almanack of the Muses or Souvenir or Forget me not or some such thing intended to be published by Messrs Bains and Son of Paternoster Row requesting me to send a contribution

Saturday   James Billings shot a Cuckoo to day on one of his Plumb trees — it was very like the sparrow hawk in color but it had a strait bill and very thin short yellow legs neither of which seemed able to turn assailants in its own defence for it had only its wing broke and lived a long while   it peckd at the hand that was held out to it but it coud not peck so hard as a

241

black bird — the inside of its mouth was of a fine red which led us to think it was a Cuckoo

Sunday   Yesterday I found another of those deaths head Moth catter pillars in Billings Potatoes

29th, Day of Augst, 1825

Monday   Went to Milton   turned out a very wet day took the two large catterpillars which I found in Billings Potatoes and find they are the Deaths head Moth

Tuesday   The account of Lord Radstocks death was thus mentioned in 'Bells Weekly Messenger' of August 29th — 'On the 17th instant Admiral Lord Radstock was seized at his house in Portland Place with a sudden attack of apoplexy.   The strength of his constitution struggled with that of the malady till the 20th when the hopes which had been entertained of his recovery vanished and his Lordship expired — Admiral Lord Radstock G.C.B. aged 72 was the second son of John third Earl of Walgrave by the Lady Elizabeth Leveson Gower sister of the Marquis of Stafford'

Friday   Recieved a letter from Mrs Emmerson[281]

Sunday   Wrote a letter to Mrs Emmerson[282] and one to Mrs Gilchrist and one also to Baynes and son Publishers in Pater noster row respecting some contributions solicited for a new Poetical Almanack

5th, Day of Sepr 1825

Monday

Wednesday   Recieved a letter from Hessey[283] telling me that

242

Taylor has been very ill also one from Messrs Baynes and son and one from Allaric A Watts of Manchester — Recieved in October a letter from J.Power of the Strand requesting permission to publish 'Brooms grove' with music for which he gave me 2 Sovereigns

Thursday   Met old Dacon the Jew of Cliff[284] at Billings who has the odd notion to believe himself the saviour of the world and in spite of all this is a very sensible and remarkable man — about 5,, 10 Inches high with a pleasing countenance   his hair and beard is never cut or shaved

Sunday   Went to meet M^r and Mrs Emmerson[285] at the New Inn at Deeping and spent three days with them

Feby 6. 1828[286]

Sunday   Read in the Examiner the Bankrupt of W.Baynes and Son   so there goes £5 which I was to have had for writing for the 'Amulet'

7th, Day of Feb^y, 1825

Monday   1828
Greatly distressed to day and uncommonly ill
O what a blessing is health   we know not how to prize it till we loose it   Dr Darling restored me to health but my foolish follys has compelled her to leave me again and I fear for ever

Tuesday   1828

Wednesday   1828
Went to Stamford to day with Patty in great distress to Dr Cooper   I have set it down here to see if I shall live till 1829 to see it again   I fear not but so be it   I am not my own maker

[N15, 10-115]

243

SOME BRIEF OBSERVATIONS

1807   In the field called the Barrows as a man was digging a Grip over one of the lands he found the remains of a human body one foot deep — lying with the legs doubled up beneath it and a short time after I found several beads of a variety of beautiful colours   there was also a fine locket found and the remains of several other ornaments

Some men digging along on Copper [i.e. Cowper] green found several bones of the human species lying all their length in one grave — 1813 May   [A48, R43]

Monday 10th August 1828   A Favourite Tabby Cat Got killed to day either purposly or by accident I cannot make out which

Jany 3rd 1829   Paid to Joseph Henderson Milton The sum of 12s/. on account and for J. Taylor for roman coins
                                                [N17, inside front cover]

Oct 8th   Friday 1830 –
Recieved 6 sets of Poems
6 Do of Village Minstrel
And 12 Do of Shepherds Calender   [N29, 10]

April 19   The last of my Poor Stock Doves got murdered in the cage under the Eldern Tree in the Garden by a Dog after I had kept it seven years   [N29, 21]

244

MEMORANDUMS

[Clare's Appendix no. 5]

There is £400 in the Funds or at least was before it was put in said to be in the joint Names of Taylor and Hessey   I know nothing more

I have had no settlement with Taylor and Hessey yet for neither of the Volumnes and have gone on in a very foolish manner   I am sorry now tho its not too late — one of the best Counselors tells me to 'put no confidence in Man' and I believe Expirience is reminding me that wroldly faith is of less worth then nothing but Experience sells her advice very dear and makes every body pay for it. I understand that 7000 of the Poems on Rural Life and Scenery and the Village Minstrel was struck off up to the 4 Edition of the one and 2nd Edition of the other 5000 of the first and 2000 of the Second   I was to have half the profits but I wish I had sold them out and out as others do and then I shoud have had the principal out at use and the interest to live on and now I get nothing as it were

Edward Drury has most of my M.S.S. and Taylor and Hessey has copys and origionals of them all   I have got few or none myself   this hurts me very often   no doubt they will do the right thing and yet there is many doubts they may not

I will have the Shepherds Calender out directly — I will set down before I forget it a Memorandum to say that I desire Mrs Emmerson will do just as she pleases with any M.S.S. of mine which she may have in her possesion to publish them or not as she chuses but I desire that any living names mentiond in my letters may be filld up by * * * and all objectionable passages ommited a wish which I hope will be invariably complied with by all   I also intend to make Mr Emmerson one of the Executors in my new will

I wish to lye on the North side the Church yard just about the middle of the ground were the Morning and Evening Sun can

linger the longest on my Grave   I wish to have a rough un-
hewn stone somthing in the form of a mile Stone so that the play-
ing boys may not break it in their heedless pastimes with nothing
more on it then this Inscription.

I desire that no date be
inserted there on as I wish
it to live or dye with my
poems and other writings   October
which if they have merit   8th
with posterity it will and   1824
if they have not it is not   "Vanity of vanity's
worth preserving   all is Vanity."

Memorandums Continued

I once signd an agreement made out by Drury a long while back
but I was repentant afterwards of it and it was burnt   I have
made nor signd none since and never will   Drurys was to
allow me a quarters profit   bravo I was drunk at the time and
therefore heeded not the bargain till I heard about it from my lost
Friend Octavius Gilchrist   the agreement of Drury was said to
be burnt and I know nothing further but this I know that there is
no other agreement in existance beyond what I have wishd in my
last will of Sep   1824

[N15, 122-3]

246

CLARE'S WILL AND RELATED OBSERVATIONS

In the name of God amen, I John Clare of the Parish of Helpstone in the County of Northampton do make this my last Will and Testament   I give to my Sister Sophia Kettle[1] the Sum of £10, and leave the Sum of 4 shillings a week to my Parents both out of the Copy right of my works if in case they make as much money in interest as here specified if not the sum that they shall make is to be applied as above and if they make more the overplus goes to my childern   the £16 interest from the 4 per Cents is to be paid to my family as usual and the principal divided amongst the Childern at the youngests coming of age tho my wife is to have the benefit of the interest not only to bring up the childern but so long as she continues unmarried   all My Books are to be published on the origional terms of half profits to my family   I wish Taylor and Hessey to be the Publishers and I further wish that my friend John Taylor shoud be the Editor of my Remains and that all my writings be submitted to him   he was one of the first friends I met and I wish to leave him one of the last
I wish my Library to be sold save those books which I shall name as presents   the others I entrust to Messrs Taylor and Hessey to be disposd of as they shall judge proper
     I give to my friend Eliza Louisa Emmerson my Byron in 4 Vols. 8vo also my writing desk and ink stand I give to Lord Radstock my Picture in water colors painted by W. Hilton as a present to my Father who requests the same to be done[2]

[N29, 4]

BUSINESS DEALINGS WITH EDWARD DRURY
AND JOHN TAYLOR

Ned Drury has got my early Vol of M.S.S.   I lent it him at first but like all my other M.S.S. elsewere I coud never get it agen — he has a great quantity of Songs written purposly for an intended publication with music by Crouch[1]   5 or 6 of them was publishd but what profit they made I cannot tell   I got nothing — he has copys of all my M.S.S. except those written for the Shepherds Calender — the 'early M.S.S. Book' was the one which I bought of J.B.Henson of Market Deeping   it is a thin Folio in parchment covers   I gave 8 shillings for it

[D14, 6r]

To E. Drury

As I expect the words of the dead are venerably noticed which they leave behind let me hope then from you (if my survi[v]er) that my wishes may be complied with in publishing no poems which are against my inclination in any improved form what ever but to utterly condemn them to oblivion M.S.S. excepted   if I knew such things I dissaprove of shoud appear in print in part after my death it woud be the greatest torture possible   therefore all you find in these books mark wi a cross an[y] of the above description   this is the only thing I wanted to[2] look the books over for and this is a thing which as a friend I hope one day or other you will see acted according to my wishes

John Clare
[BL, Add.MS.54224,fol.143r]

There is one thing which I do not like in this matter and that is the trumpeting my difficulties in the papers and the fact is they are made much worse then they are — I have had small sums of money at different times from Taylor which may imperceptibly amount to a larger sum then one is aware of but there is no settling in the matter and no disposition to settling and as I wish not to leave my family in any shadow where the world can have any apology by way of kindness to make any mistatements of money charges on their little property I am anxious it should be settled

the worst is the first bookseller to whom my trifles were intrusted turned round upon me with a meaness that I never dreamed of and cheated me out of all profit connected with the first Vol — he said I sold it for 26 pound and then made a charge on T[aylor] and H[essey] on my account for £20 as copy right — I should have been glad then to have sold it for £10 but the fact is I never recieved a farthing in that shape for of all the little sums I recieved from him every farthing was placed against my account with Taylor and to mend the matter as I objected to the account as being a great deal too much his conscience took off a portion

yet avarice is never conquered and in a bye way after the other was paid without acquainting me with the matter he presented a bill of £20 a fiction to the fraction of a farthing and Taylor without acquainting me untill it was paid — paid it — this compleatly upset my faith in the honesty of professions and when my bother was over for this Drury threatened me with law in the first instance and I in too much haste to escape an idle threat which he dare not have put in force wrote to T[aylor] and H[essey] to get them to settle it and to secure my property as a turn over but nothing of that kind was done and I was never settled in my mind   but always wishing for a settling I wrote to Taylor to correct the errors in the accounts and he said they should be looked into but as yet I have heard nothing   I wrote to Drury asking him how he could make such mistakes to my injury and also for the trifles in MS he possessed of mine — of the copy right fiction he was silent and made no reply   of the invented bill for £20 he 'wrote' I had it in 'money and goods' and of the MSS he said I had given them to him — perhaps I might — but I thought not   but as to the other lies I was sure of it which was the only part of the loss that injured me — I could hardly bear patience enough to contradict such a barefaced lie — and when I did it was to no purpose so I was done out of £40 which from the difference of right had it been mine to recieve make £80 less — here is the fact of the matter — and tho I know I am cheated such is the cunning of avarice like the tricks of a conjeror it defies detection

[A57, 67-9]

THE WILL O WHISP OR JACK A LANTHORN

[Clare's Appendix no. 9]

I have often seen these vapours or what ever philosophy may call them but I never wit nessd so remarkable an instance of them as I did last night which has robd me of the little philosophic reason-[in]g which I had — about them I now believe them spirits but I will leave the facts to speak for themselves — There had been a great upstir in the town about the appearance of the ghost of an old woman who had been recently drownd in a well — it was said to appear at the bottom of neighbour Billings close in a large white winding sheet dress and the noise excited the curosity of myself and my neighbour to go out several nights together to see if the ghost woud be kind enough to appear to us and mend our broken faith in its existance but nothing came   on our return we saw a light in the north east over eastwell green and I thought at first that it was a bright meoter   it presently became larger and seemd like a light in a window   it then moved and dancd up and down and then glided onwards as if a man was riding on hors back at full speed with a lanthorn light   soon after this we discoverd another rising in the south east on 'dead moor' they was about a furlong asunder at first and as if the other saw it it danced away as if to join it which it soon did and after dancing together a sort of reel as it were — it chaced away to its former station and the other followd it like things at play and after suddenly overtaking it they mingled into one in a moment or else one dissapeard and sunk in the ground   we stood wondering and gazing for a while at the odd phenomenon and then left the will o wisp dancing by itself to hunt for a fresh companion as it chose — the night was dusky but not pitch dark and what was rather odd for their appearance the wind blew very briskly it was full west — now these things are gennerally believd to be vapours rising from the foul air from bogs and wet places were they are generaly seen and being as is said lighter then the common air they float about at will — now this is all very well for Mrs Philosophy

251

who is very knowing but how is it if it is a vapour lighter then the air that it coud face the wind which was blowing high and always floated side ways from north to south and back — the wind afected it nothing but I leave all as I find it I have explaind the fact as well as I can — I heard the old alewife at the Exeters arms behind the church (Mrs Nottingham[1]) often say that she has seen from one of her chamber windows as many as fifteen together dancing in and out in a company as if dancing reels and dances on east well moor   there is a great ma[n]y there — I have seen several there myself one night when returning home from Ashton on a courting excursion   I saw one as if meeting me   I felt very terrified and on getting to a stile I determi[n]d to wait and see if it was a person with a lanthorn or a will o whisp   it came on steadily as if on the path way and when it got near me within a poles reach perhaps as I thought it made a sudden stop as if to listen me   I then believed it was some one but it blazd out like a whisp of straw and made a crackling noise like straw burning which soon convincd me of its visit   the luminous haloo that spread from it was of a mysterious terrific hue and the enlargd size and whiteness of my own hands frit me   the rushes appeard to have grown up as large and tall as walebone whips and the bushes seemd to be climbing the sky   every thing was extorted out of its own figure and magnif[i]ed the darkness all round seemd to form a circalar black wall and I fancied that if I took a step forward I shoud fall into a bottomless gulph which seemd garing all round me so I held fast by the stile post till it darted away when I took to my heels and got home as fast as [I] coud so much for will o whisps.

[N15, 129-32]

A REMARKABLE DREAM

Last night oct^r 13.1832 I had a remarkable dream — that [my] Guardian spirit in the shape of a soul stirring beauty again appeared to me with the very same countenance in which she appeared many years ago and in which she has since appeared at intervals and moved my ideas into extacy — I cannot doubt her existance — I thought I was in a strange place and in a rather fine room among strange people yet the host who appeared so paid me much attention and kindness   yet I was in low spirits and in despondancy when on a sudden a lovely creature in the shape of a young woman with dark & rather disordered hair and eyes that spoke more beauty then earth inherits came up to me in a familiar way and leaning her witching face over my shoulder spoke in a witching voice and cherishing smiles sentences that I cannot reccolect   yet I instantly knew her face and the reccolections of her appearance in former dreams came vivid in sleep

The first dream in which she appeared to me was when I had not written a line — I thought she suddenly came to my old house led me out in a hurried manner into the field called maple hill and there placed me on the tope where I could see an immense crowd all around me — in the south west quarter of the field towards hilly wood & swordy well appeared soldiers on horse back moving in evolutions of exercise   the rest were crowds of various descriptions on foot as at a large fair where ladies in splendid dresses were most numerous but the finest ladie in my own hearts opinion was the lady at my side — I felt shamed into insignificance at the sight and seemed to ask her from my own thoughts why I had been so suddenly brought into such immense company when my only life and care was being alone and to my self — you are the only one of the crowd now she said and hurried me back and the scene turned to a city where she led me to what appeared to be a book sellers shop where I reluctantly followed

she said somthing to the owner of the place who stood behind a counter when he smiled and at his back on a shelf among a vast crowd of books were three vols lettered with my

253

own name — I see them now   I was astonished and turning to look in her face I was awake in a moment but the impression never left me and I see her still   she is my good genius and I believe in her ideality almost as fresh as reality —

many years after this I dreamed I was in the long close   it seemed morning where all the people in the village seemed passing by me in one mind northward towards the west end — I felt anxious to know their purpose but they were all silent both in look and speech   the sun seemed of a pale moon struck light — the sky had a dull unnatural hue and a sudden conviction struck me that all was called to judgment so I instinctively followed with the rest feeling great depressions and rather uneasiness of mind   the crowd went on to the church yard and then into the church   as soon as I entered the gate I heard a loud humming as of the undertones of an organ and felt so affraid that before I got opposite to the school door I shrunk back and felt a wish to return to my reccolections of home and at that moment somthing of a delightful impulse took me seemingly by the arm and led me forward — I see the yellow grave stone which I stood opposite when she came to my side just at the school door — I looked sideways for hope and fear — she was in white garments beautifully disorderd but sorrowful in her countenance yet I instantly knew her face again — when we got into the church a light streamed in one corner of the chancel and from that light appeared to come the final decision of mans actions in life   I felt awfully affraid tho not terrified and in a moment my name was called from the north east corner of the chancel — when my conductress smiled in extacy and uttered somthing as prophetic of happiness   I knew all was right and she led me again into the open air when I impercievenly[1] awoke to the sound of soft music — I felt delighted and sorrowful and talked to her awake for a moment as if she were still bending over me — these dreams of a beautiful presence a woman deity gave the sublimest consceptions of beauty to my imagination and being last night with the same presence — the lady-divinity left such a vivid picture of her visits in my sleep dreaming of dreams that I could no longer doubt her existance so I wrote them down to prolong the happiness of my faith in believing her my guardian genius — the cause I cannot tell   the fact is truth if so be it may be said of dreams

[MS B5, 50-1]

'CLOSES OF GREENSWARD...'

Closes of greensward & meadow eaten down by cattle about harvest time & pieces of naked water such as ponds lakes & pools without fish make me melancholly to look over it & if ever so cheerfull I instantly feel low spirited depressed & wretched — on the contrary pieces of greensward where the hay has been cleared off smooth & green as a bowling green with lakes of water well stocked with fish leaping up in the sunshine & leaving rings widening & quavering on the water with the plunge of a Pike in the weeds driving a host of roach into the clear water slanting now & then towards the top their bellies of silver light in the sunshine — these scenes though I am almost wretched quickly animate my feelings & make me happy as if I was rambling in Paradise and perhaps more so then if I was there where there would still be Eves to trouble us

[N6, 20]

JOURNEY OUT OF ESSEX

Journal Jul 18 — 1841 — Sunday — Felt very melancholly — went a walk on the forest in the afternoon — fell in with some gipseys one of whom offered to assist in my escape from the mad house by hideing me in his camp to which I almost agreed but told him I had no money to start with but if he would do so I would promise him fifty pounds and he agreed to do so before saturday   on friday I went again but he did not seem so willing so I said little about it — On sunday I went and they were all gone — an[1] old wide awake hat and an old straw bonnet of the plumb pudding sort was left behind — and I put the hat in my pocket thinking it might be usefull for another oppertunity — as good luck would have it, it turned out to be so

July 19 Monday — Did nothing

July 20 Reconnitered the rout the Gipsey pointed out and found it a legible one to make a movement and having only honest courage and myself in my army I Led the way and my troops soon followed but being careless in mapping down the rout as the Gipsey told me I missed the lane to Enfield town and was going down Enfield highway till I passed 'The Labour in vain' Public house[2] where A person I knew comeing out of the door told me the way

I walked down the lane gently and was soon in in Enfield Town and bye and bye on the great York Road where it was all plain sailing and steering ahead meeting no enemy and fearing none I reached Stevenage where being Night I got over a gate crossed over the corner of a green paddock where seeing a pond or hollow in the corner I forced to stay off a respectable distance to keep from falling into it for my legs were nearly knocked up and began to stagger   I scaled some old rotten paleings into the yard and then had higher pailings to clamber over to get into the shed or hovel which I did with difficulty being rather weak and to my good luck I found some trusses of clover piled up about 6 or more feet square which I gladly mounted and slept on   there was some trays in the hovel on which I could have reposed had I not found a better bed   I slept soundly but had a very uneasy dream   I thought my first wife[3] lay on my left arm and somebody took her away from my side which made me wake up rather unhappy   I thought as I awoke somebody said 'Mary' but nobody was near — I lay down with my head towards the north to show my self the steering point in the morning

July 21   [— when I awoke][4]   Daylight was looking in on every side and fearing my garrison might be taken by storm and myself be made prisoner I left my lodging by the way I got in and thanked God for his kindness in procureing it (for any thing in a famine is better then nothing and any place that giveth the weary rest is a blessing)   I gained the north road again and steered due north — on the left hand side the road under the bank like a cave I saw a Man and boy coiled up asleep which I hailed and they woke up to tell me the name of the next village[5]

Some where on the London side the 'Plough' Public house[6] a Man passed me on horseback in a Slop frock and said 'here's another of the broken down haymakers' and threw me a penny to

JOURNEY OUT OF ESSEX

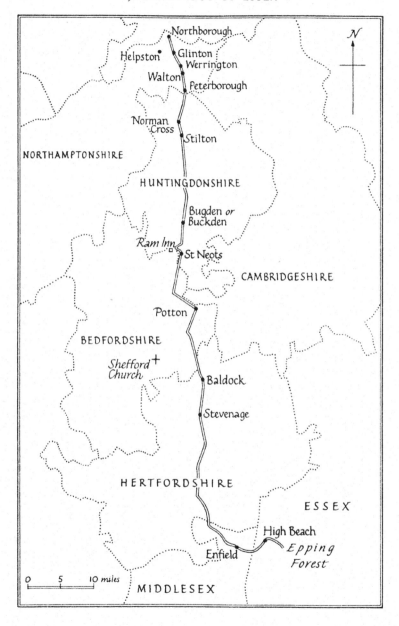

Northborough
Helpston
Glinton
Werrington
Walton
Peterborough

Norman
Cross
Stilton

NORTHAMPTONSHIRE

HUNTINGDONSHIRE

Bugden *or*
Buckden
Ram Inn
St Neots

CAMBRIDGESHIRE

Potton

BEDFORDSHIRE

Shefford
Church
Baldock

Stevenage

HERTFORDSHIRE

ESSEX

High Beach
*Epping
Forest*
Enfield

0   5   10 miles

MIDDLESEX

N

get a half pint of beer which I picked up and thanked him for and when I got to the plough I called for a half pint and drank it and got a rest and escaped a very heavy shower in the bargain by having a shelter till it was over — afterwards I would have begged a penny of two drovers who were very saucey so I begged no more of any body meet who I would

— I passed 3 or 4 good built houses on a hill and a public house on the road side in the hollow below them   I seemed to pass the Milestones very quick in the morning but towards night they seemed to be stretched further asunder   I got to a village further on and forgot the name   the road on the left hand was quite over shaded by some trees and quite dry so I sat down half an hour and made a good many wishes for breakfast but wishes was no hearty meal so I got up as hungry as I sat down — I forget here the names of the villages I passed through but reccolect at late evening going through Potton in Bedfordshire where I called in a house to light my pipe in which was a civil old woman and a young country wench makeing lace on a cushion as round as a globe and a young fellow all civil people — I asked them a few questions as to the way and where the clergyman and overseer lived but they scarcely heard me or gave me no answer*

I then went through Potton and happened with a kind talking country man who told me the Parson lived a good way from where I was or overseer I do'n't know which so I went on hopping with a crippled foot for the gravel had got into my old shoes one of which had now nearly lost the sole   Had I found the

* Note   On searching my pockets after the above was written I found part of a newspaper vide 'Morning Chronicle' on which the following fragments were pencilled soon after I got the information from labourers going to work or travellers journying along to better their condition as I was hopeing to do mine in fact I believed I saw home in every ones countenance which seemed so cheerfull in my own — 'There is no place like home' the following was written by the Road side — 1st Day — Tuesday — Started from Enfield and slept at Stevenage on some clover trusses — cold lodging
Wednesday — Jacks Hill is passed already consisting of a beer shop and some houses on the hill appearing newly built — the last Mile stone 35 Miles from London got through Baldeck and sat under a dry hedge and had a rest in lieu of breakfast [Clare has written: 'This Note should be placed at the bottom of the page']

overseers house at hand or the Parsons I should have gave my
name and begged for a shilling to carry me home but I was forced
to brush on pennyless and be thankfull I had a leg to move on — I
then asked him wether he could tell me of a farm yard any where
on the road where I could find a shed and some dry straw and he
said yes and if you will go with me I will show you the place — its
a public house on the left hand side the road at the sign of the
'Ram'[7] but seeing a stone or flint heap I longed to rest as one of my
feet was very painfull so I thanked him for his kindness and bid
him go on — but the good natured fellow lingered awhile as if
wishing to conduct me and then suddenly reccolecting that he
had a hamper on his shoulder and a lock up bag in his hand cram
full to meet the coach which he feared missing — he started hastily
and was soon out of sight — I followed looking in vain for the
country mans[8] straw bed — and not being able to meet it I lay
down by a shed side under some Elm trees between the wall and
the trees being a thick row planted some 5 or 6 feet from the
buildings   I lay there and tried to sleep but the wind came in
between them so cold that I lay till I quaked like the ague and quit-
ted the lodging for a better at the Ram which I could hardly hope
to find — It now began to grow dark apace and the odd houses on
the road began to light up and show the inside tennants lots very
comfortable and my outside lot very uncomfortable and wretched
— still I hobbled forward as well as I could and at last came to the
Ram   the shutters were not closed and the lighted window
looked very cheering but I had no money and did not like to go in
      there was a sort of shed or gighouse at the end but I did not
like to lie there as the people were up — so I still travelled on
the road was very lonely and dark in places being overshaded
with trees   at length I came to a place where the road branched
off into two turnpikes one to the right about and the other straight
forward and on going bye my eye glanced on a mile stone stand-
ing under the hedge so I heedlessly turned back to read it to see
where the other road led too and on doing so I found it led to Lon-
don   I then suddenly forgot which was North or South and
though I narrowly examined both ways I could see no tree or

bush or stone heap that I could reccolect I had passed so I went on
mile after mile almost convinced I was going the same way I came
and these thoug[h]ts were so strong upon me that doubt and
hopelessness made me turn so feeble that I was scarcely able to
walk yet I could not sit down or give up but shuffled along till I
saw a lamp shining as bright as the moon which on nearing I found
was suspended over a Tollgate[9]   before I got through the man
came out with a candle and eyed me narrowly but having no fear
I stopt to ask him wether I was going northward and he said
when you get through the gate you are; so I thanked him kindly
and went through on the other side and gathered my old strength

as my doubts vanished I soon cheered up and hummed the
air of highland Mary[10] as I went on   I at length fell in with an
odd house all alone near a wood but I could not see what the sign
was though the sign seemed to stand oddly enough in a sort of
trough or spout   there was a large porch over the door and
being weary I crept in and glad enough I was to find I could lye
with my legs straight   the inmates were all gone to roost for I
could hear them turn over in bed as I lay at full length on the
stones in the poach — I slept here till daylight and felt very much
refreshed as I got up — I blest my two wives and both their familys
when I lay down and when I got up and when I thought of some
former difficultys on a like occasion I could not help blessing the
Queen[11] — Having passed a Lodge on the left hand within a mile
and half or less of a town I think it might be St Ives but I forget the
name[12] I sat down to rest on a flint heap where I might rest half an
hour or more and while sitting here I saw a tall Gipsey come out
of the Lodge gate and make down the road towards where I was
sitting   when she got up to me on seeing she was a young
woman with an honest looking countenance rather handsome I
spoke to her and asked her a few questions which she answered
readily and with evident good humour so I got up and went on to
the next town with her — she cautioned me on the way to put
somthing in my hat to keep the crown up and said in a lower tone
'you'll be noticed' but not knowing what she hinted — I took no
notice and made no reply   at length she pointed to a small

262

tower church which she called Shefford Church[13] and advised me
to go on a footway which would take me direct to it and I should
shorten my journey fifteen miles by doing so   I would gladly
have taken the young womans advice feeling that it was honest
and a nigh guess towards the truth but fearing I might loose my
way and not be able to find the north road again I thanked her and
told her I should keep to the road when she bade me 'good day'
and went into a house or shop on the left hand side the road   I
have but a slight reccolection of my journey between here and
Stilton for I was knocked up and noticed little or nothing — one
night I lay in a dyke bottom from the wind and went sleep half an
hour when I suddenly awoke and found one side wet through
from the sock in the dyke bottom so I got out and went on — I
remember going down a very dark road hung over with trees on
both sides very thick which seemed to extend a mile or two
I then entered a town and some of the chamber windows had
candle lights shineing in them — I felt so weak here that I forced
to sit down on the ground to rest myself and while I sat here a[14]
Coach that seemed to be heavy laden came rattling up and stopt
in the hollow below me and I cannot reccolect its ever passing by
me   I then got up and pushed onward seeing little to notice for
the road very often looked as stupid as myself and I was very
often half asleep as I went   on the third day I satisfied my
hunger by eating the grass by the road side which seemed to taste
something like bread   I was hungry and eat heartily till I was
satisfied and in fact the meal seemed to do me good   the next
and last day I reccollected that I had some tobacco and my box of
lucifers being exausted I could not light my pipe so I took to chew-
ing Tobacco all day and eat the quids when I had done and I was
never hungry afterwards — I remember passing through Buckden
and going a length of road afterwards but I dont reccolect the
name of any place untill I came to stilton where I was compleatly
foot foundered and broken down   when I had got about half
way through the town a gravel causeway invited me to rest
myself so I lay down and nearly went sleep   a young woman
(so I guessed by the voice) came out of a house and said 'poor

creature' and another more elderly said 'O he shams' but when I
got up the latter said 'o no he don't' as I hobbled along very lame
    I heard the voices but never looked back to see where they
came from — when I got near the Inn at the end of the gravel walk
I met two young women and I asked one of them wether the road
branching to the right[15] bye the end of the Inn did not lead to
Peterborough and she said 'Yes' it did so   as soon as ever I was
on it I felt myself in homes way and went on rather more cheerfull
though I forced to rest oftener then usual   before I got to Peter-
borough a man and woman passed me in a cart and on hailing me
as they passed I found they were neighbours from Helpstone
where I used to live — I told them I was knocked up which they
could easily see and that I had neither eat or drank any thing since
I left Essex   when I told my story they clubbed together and
threw me fivepence out of the cart   I picked it up and called at
a small public house near the bridge were I had two half pints of
ale and twopenn'oth of bread and cheese   when I had done I
started quite refreshed only my feet was more crippled then ever
and I could scarcely make a walk of it over the stones and being
half ashamed to sit down in the street I forced to keep on the
move and got through Peterborough better then I expected
when I got on the high road I rested on the stone heaps as I passed
till I was able to go on afresh and bye and bye I passed Walton and
soon reached Werrington and was making for the Beehive[16] as
fast as I could when a cart met me with a man and woman and a
boy in it   when nearing me the woman jumped out and
caught fast hold of my hands and wished me to get into the cart
but I refused and thought her either drunk or mad but when I was
told it was my second wife Patty I got in and was soon at North-
borough but Mary was not there neither could I get any informa-
tion about her further then the old story of her being dead six
years ago which might be taken from a bran new old Newspaper
printed a dozen years ago but I took no notice of the blarney
having seen her myself about a twelvemonth ago alive and well
and as young as ever — so here I am homeless at home and half
gratified to feel that I can be happy any where

'May none those marks of my sad fate efface
'For they appeal from tyranny to God'   Byron[17]

July 24th* 1841   Returned home out of Essex and found no
Mary — her and her family are as nothing to me now though she
herself was once the dearest of all — 'and how can I forget

        To Mary Clare – Glinton
                        Northborough July 27 1841
My dear wife
    I have written an account of my journey or rather escape from
Essex for your amusement and hope it may divert your leisure
hours — I would have told you before now that I got here to
Northborough last friday night but not being able to see you or to
hear where you was I soon began to feel homeless at home and
shall bye and bye feel nearly hopeless but not so lonely as I did in
Essex — for here I can see Glinton Church and feeling that Mary
is safe if not happy and † I am gratified‡ though my home is no
home to me my hopes are not entirely hopeless while even the
memory of Mary lives so near me   God bless you My dear Mary
    Give my love to your dear and beautifull family and to your
Mother — and believe me as I ever have been and ever shall be
                        My dearest Mary
                    Your affectionate Husband
                                    John Clare
                            [N6, 1-4; N8, 22-6]

* N8 has 'July 23rd'.
† Followed by the deleted words: 'I shall be the same'.
‡ Followed by the deleted words: 'to believe so'.

ASYLUM OBSERVATIONS

God almighty bless Mary Joyce Clare and her family now and
forever — Amen
God almighty bless Martha Turner Clare and her family now and
forever — Amen   [N8, 21]

Fern hill
at the back of the chapple a beautifull retreat from a mad house
                                                                  [N8, 25]

Jack Randalls Challange To All The World
Jack Randall[1] The Champion of the Prize Ring Begs Leave To
Inform The Sporting World That He Is Ready To Meet Any Cus-
tomer In The Ring Or On The Stage To Fight For The Sum Of £500
Or £1000 Aside   A Fair Stand Up Fight half Minute Time Win
Or Loose   he Is Not Particular As To Weight Colour Or Country
    All He Wishes Is To Meet With A Customer Who Has Pluck
Enough To Come To The Scratch
                          Jack Randall
May 1st 1841[2]   [N8, 42]

Note for 'Child Harold'
Easter Sunday — 1841   Went In The Morning To Buckhurst
Hill Church And Stood In The Church Yard — When A Very
Interesting Boy Came Out While Organ Was Playing Dressed In
A Slop Frock Like A Ploughboy And Seemingly About Nine
Years Of Age   He Was Just Like My Son Bill When He Was
About The Same Age And As Stout Made — He Had A Serious
Interesting Face And Looked As Weary With The Working Days

As A Hard Working Man   I Was Sorry I Did Not Give Him The
Last Halfpenny I Had And Ask Him A Few Questions As To His
Age And Name And Parents But Perhaps I May See Him Agen
Byron   [N8, 43]

Easter Monday — At The Easter Hunt I Saw A Stout Tall Young
Woman Dressed In A Darkish Flowerd Cotton Gown As A Milk-
maid Or Farm Servant And Stood Agen Her For Some Minutes
Near A Small Clump Of Furze — I Did Not Speak To Her But I
Now Wish I Had And Cannot Forget Her — Then I Saw Another
Get Out Of A Gig With A Large Scotch[3] Shawl On And A Pretty
Face
Note for 'Child Harold'   [N8, 44]

April 21st 1841
1 Weeks Labour — 2s/6d — Drawn 1s — 1s left 6d
April 27th Recieved 1s
May 1st   Do   1s 6
May 3rd   Do   6
Mathew Gammons over 5d a day —
worked all the week and recieved only 6d — due or left 2s
May 10 Recieved 6d
May 14 Do for Song of Deborah 1s
May 18 Recieved 1s
May 22   Do   1
  Do for Child Harold — 1s 0
May 24 Recieved 1s
  Do 29   Do   1s
May 30 Recieved 1s
Monday   [N8, 46]

267

Recieved from C.Redding[4] while in Prison on Leopards Hill
Eleven books two Given and the rest returnable — viz — Child
Harold — Reddings Poems — and following lent viz Don Juan
1 Vol 5 Cantos — 2nd Part Cants 6.7.8   Part 3rd Cants 9,10,11
— Part 4th 12,13,14 — Part 5th Cants 15,16,

[N8, 60]

LETTER TO MATTHEW ALLEN

To MATTHEW ALLEN

[c.27 August 1841]

My dear Sir

Having left the Forest in a hurry [I h]ad not time to take my
leave of you and your family but I intended to write and that
before now but dullness and dissapointment prevented me for I
found your words true on my return here having neither friends
or home left but as it is called the 'Poets cottage' I claimed a lodg-
ing in it where I now am — one of my fancys[1] I found here with
her family and all well — they meet me on this side Werrington
with a horse and cart and found me all but knocked up for I had
travelled from Essex to Northamptonshire without ever eating or
drinking all the way save one pennyworth of beer which was
given me by a farm servant near an odd house called the plough
         one day I eat grass to humour my hunger — but on the last
day I chewed Tobacco and never felt hungry afterwards — where
my poetical fancy is I cannot say for the people in the neighbour-
hood tells me that the one called 'Mary' has been dead these 8
years[2] but I can be miserably happy in any situation and any place
and could have staid in yours on the forest if any of my friends
had noticed me or come to see me — but the greatest annoyance
in such places as yours are those servants styled keepers who
often assumed as much authority over me as if I had been their
prisoner and not likeing to quarrel I put up with it till I was weary
of the place altogether so I heard the voice of freedom and started
and could have travelled to York with a penny loaf and a pint of
beer for I should not have been fagged in body only one of my old
shoes had nearly lost the sole before I started and let in the water
and silt the first day and made me crippled and lame to the end
of my journey

I had Eleven Books sent me from How and Parsons Booksellers
some lent and some given me — out of the Eleven I only brought
5 vols here and as I dont want any part of Essex in Northampton-
shire agen I wish you would have the kindness to send a servant

269

to get them for me   I should be very thankfull not that I care about the books altogether only it may be an excuse to see me and get me into company that I do not want to be acquainted with — one of your labourers Pratts Wife borrowed — 'Child Harold' — and Mrs Fishs Daughter has two or three or perhaps more all Lord Byrons Poems and Mrs King[3] late of the Owl Public house Leppits Hill and now of Endfield Highway has two or three all Lord Byrons and one is The 'Hours of Idleness'[4]

you told me somthing before haytime about the Queen alowing me a yearly sallary of £100 and that the first quarter had then commenced or else I dreamed so[5] — if I have the mistake is not of much consequence to anyone save myself and if true I wish you would get the Quarter for me if due[6] as I want to be independant and pay for board and lodging while I remain here — I look upon myself as a widow or bachellor I dont know which — I care nothing about the women now for they are faithless and decietfull and the first woman when there was no man but her husband found out means to cuckold him by the aid and assistance of the devil but women being more righteous now and men more plentifull they have found out a more godly way to do it without the divils assistance and a man who possesses a woman possesses losses without gain — the worst is the road to ruin and the best is nothing like a good Cow — man I never did like much and woman has long sickened me   I should [like] to be to myself a few years and lead the life of a hermit — but even there I should wish from one whom I am always thinking of and almost every Song I write has some sighs and wishes in Ink about Mary — If I have not made your head weary by reading thus far I have tired my own by writing it so I will bid you good bye

and am My dear docter yours very sincerely   John Clare

give my best respects to Mrs Allen and Miss Allen and to Dr Stedman also to Campbell[7] and Hayward and Howard at Leopards Hill or in fact to any of the others who may think it worth while to enquire about me   [Bodleian Don.a.8][8]

270

SELF IDENTITY

A very good common place counsel is *Self Identity* to bid our own hearts not to forget our own selves and always to keep self in the first place lest all the world who always keeps us behind it should forget us all together — forget not thyself and the world will not forget thee — forget thyself and the world will willingly forget thee till thou art nothing but a living-dead man dwelling among shadows and falshood

> The mother may forget her child
> That dandled on her lap has been
> The bridegroom may forget the bride
> That he was wedded to yestreen[1]

But I cannot forget that I'm a man and it would be dishonest and unmanly in me to do so

Self Identity is one of the finest principles in everybodys life and fills up the outline of honest truth in the decision of character — a person who denies himself must either be a mad man or a coward

I am often troubled at times to know that should the world have the impudence not to know me but willingly forget[2] me wether any single individual would be honest enough to know me — such people would be usefull as the knocker to a door or the bell of a cryer to own the dead alive or the lost found   there are two impossibillities which can never happen — I shall never be in three places at once nor ever change to a woman and that ought to be some comfort amid this moral or immoral 'changing' in life — truth has a bad herald when she is obliged to take lies for her trumpeters — surely every man has the liberty to know himself

> Tis Liberty alone that gives the flower
> Of fleeting life its lustre and perfume
> And we are weeds without it.

[N6, 23]

271

AUTUMN

Autumn hath commenced her short pauses of showers calms
and storms and sunshine and shadow and with all her bustle she
is nothing but a short preface before a large volume of 'Winter'
though not yet come to drive us to the fireside   He is giving us
daily notice by dirty paths brimming dykes and naked fields that
he is already on the way — it is now very pleasant to take walks
in the morning and in fact at any time of the day though the morn-
ings are misty and 'the foggy dew'[1] lies long on the grass — here
is a drove leads us on its level sward right into the flaggy fens
shaded on each side with white thorn hedges covered with awes
of different shades of red   some may be almost called red-
black others brick red and others nearly scarlet like the coats of
the fox hunters — now we have a flaggy ditch to stride which is
almost too wide for a stride to get over — a run and jump just
lands on the other side and now a fine level bank smooth as a
bowling green curves and serpentines by a fine river whose wood
of osiers and reeds make a pleasant rustling sound though the
wind scarcely moves a single branch — how beautifull the bank
curves on like an ornament in a lawn by a piece of water the map
of ploughed field and grass ground in small alotments on the left
hand with an odd white cottage peeping some where between
the thorn hedges in the very perfection of quiet retirement and
comfort and on the right hand the clear river with its copses of
reeds and oziers and willow thickets and now and then a house
peeps through where the willows are not so thick and showing
trees loaded with apples of a dull red and too thick for lodges
shows we are near the approach of a town and now the church
spire[2] looking rather large dimensions catches the eye like a jiant
overtopping trees and houses and showing us his magnitude
from half way up the tower to the weathercock and looks noble
above his willow woods   nothing looks so noble among coun-
try landscapes as church steeples and castle towers as fine houses
and public edifices do among city scenery — tis pleasant as I have
done to day to stand upon a length of Bridges[3] and notice the

objects around us   there is the fine old Northborough castle[4]
peeping through the scanty foliage of orchards and thorn hedges
and there is the beautifull Spire of Glinton Church towering high
over the grey willows and dark wallnuts still lingering in the
church yard like the remains of a wreck telling where their fellows
foundered on the ocean of time — place of green Memorys and
gloomy sorrows — even these meadow arches seem to me some-
thing of the beautifull   having been so long a prisoner and
shut up in confinement they appear somthing worthy of notice —
to a man who has had his liberty they would appear nothing more
then so many tunnels thrown over a few puddles that are dry
three parts of the year but to me they are more interesting then a
flight of arches thrown over a cascade in a park or even the
crowded bridges in a great city — yonder is Maxey Tower church
looking as if it was lighting up with sunshine when the Autumn
sky is as gloomy as summer twilight and on the right peeping
between the trees may be seen West Deepings crocketed Spire and
on the left Glinton Mill goes sweeing away to the wind — how
sweet and green the banks wind along on each side the meadow
with now and then a single arch crossing the meadow drain
through which one can see a bit of the bank on the other side and
being weary looking out for steeples I will take the path down the
north bank   its green slopes look so pleasant though the wind
blows chilly and the rustics face looks purple with cold — men are
occupied in cutting the weeds from the drains to make a water
course for the autumn rains — solitary persons are sideing up the
hedges and thrusting the brushwood in the thin places and
creeps which the swine made from one ground or field into
another and stopping gaps made in harvest by gleaners and
labourers — the larks start up from the brown grass in the
meadows where[5] a couple of flutters and f[l]ights and drops out
of sight as suddenly again into the grass — now a flock of redcaps
seven or eight together take flight from the sides of the bank and
settle again in the hedges which are almost crimson with awes
seeming as if they fed on the seeds of the ragwort as no thistles
are near — a solitary crow and sometimes a pair fly with heavy

273

wing just over head now and then uttering a solitary croak to warn their tribes around that a man is approaching and then make a sudden wheel round at the sight of the stick in ones hand perhaps mistaking it for a gun — the top stones of the walls of all the bridges I pass are full of two letter names rudely cut with a knife — spread hands — and feet — often true love knotts and sometimes figures meant for houses churches and flowers — and sheep hooks and some times names cut in full — the idle amusements of cowtending boys horse-tenders and shepherds — now a snipe with its pointed wings hurries up from the meadow dyke into the fields — the meadow lakes seen from the bank puts me in mind of school adventures and boyish rambles the very spots where I used to spend the whole sundays in fishing while the bells kept chiming in vain — I cannot make out where all these feelings and fancys are gone too — The plot of meadows now dont look bigger then a large homestead and the ponds that used to seem so large are now no bigger then puddles and as for fish I scarcely have interest enough to walk round them to see if there is any — yon arches yonder with trees peeping above them and between them and where the traveller is hopping away wearily over them on the narrow road is Lolham Bridges — time makes strange work with early fancys   the fancied riches and happiness of early life fades to shadows of less substance even then the shadows of dreams   I sigh for what is lost and cannot help it — yet there is even calm spots in the stormiest ocean and I can even now meet happiness in sorrow   the rural pictures or objects in these flats and meadows warms ones loneliness such as a rustic driveing his little lot of cows or sheep down the plashy droves and plucking a handfull of awes from the half naked hedges to eat as he goes on — The rawky mornings now are often frosty — and the grass and wild herbs are often covered with rime as white as a shower of snow — in the fen greensward closes the pewet or lapwing may be seen in flocks of two or three hundred together about Waldram Hall[6] dabbling on the hedges [i.e. edges] of the lakes left by the rains — it is pleasing to see the woods of osiers by the river side fading yellow   There are a few willow trees by

274

the Hall or Cottage — where the crows sit in the old nests as if it was spring though perhaps they may do it to get from the cold for there is a little crizzling ice on the edges of the water in some places such as ruts and horsefeetings — Now the man is putting off his boat to ferry over the water where an odd passenger may now and then call to be ferried over the lake to the other bank or high road — the ozier hedges and holts are[7] with yellow and the white thorn hedges are getting thin of leaves and so crowded with awes that bye and bye the fields will be dressed in nothing but crimson and scarlet — nature like simplicity is beautifull in every dress she chuses to put on with the seasons — even winter with his doublet of snows & hoar frost can make himself agreeable when he chuses to give people leave to go out of doors — I love to clamber over these bridge walls and when I get off the banks on the road I instinctively look both ways to see if any passengers are going or coming or carts or waggons passing — now here is a stile partitioning off somebodys portion of the bank but the middle rail is off so I stoop under to get through instead of climbing over it — there is a pair of harrows painted red standing on end against the thorn hedge and in another ground an old plough stands on its beam ends against a dotterel tree   sometimes we see a roll lying in on one corner and broken trays and an old gate off the hooks waiting to be repaired till repairs are useless — even these rustic implements and appendages of husbandry blend with nature and look pleasing in the fields

[N6, 46-8]

LETTERS AND NOTES OF
THE NORTHAMPTON PERIOD

To CHARLES CLARE

Northampton Asylum June 15 1847

My dear Boy

I am very happy to have a letter from you in your own hand writing and to see you write so well   I am also glad that your Brothers and Sisters are all in good health and your Mother also   besure to give my love to her but I am very sorry to hear the News about your Grandfather but we must all die — and I must [say] that Frederic and John had better not come unless they wish to do so for its a *bad Place* and I have fears that they may get trapped as prisoners as I hear some have been and I may not see them nor even hear they have been here   I only tell them and leave them to do as they like best — its called the Bastile by some and not with [out] reasons — how does the Flowers get on   I often wish to see them — and are the young Childern at home   I understand there are some I have not yet seen   kiss them and give my love to them and to your Mother and Brothers and Sisters and my respects To John Bellars and to your Neighbours on each side of you Mr and Mrs Sefton[1] and Mr and Mrs Bellars and others who enquire after me   I have never been ill since I have been here save a cold now and then of which I take no notice

    Believe me my dear Boy

        that I remain your Affectionate Father   John Clare[2]

[N30, 14]

To CHARLES CLARE

Northampton Asylum Feby 1848

My dear Son

I was very happy to recieve your Letter to hear you was all in good health — your Mother and Brothers and Sisters and as satisfactory tell you I am as well myself thank God for it

When I first came here I saw some of your little Brothers and Sisters little Boys and Girls with Red heads and others also — dirty and healthy which satisfied me very well   some of them were with your own Sisters which left home before you was born — my dear Boy it does not signifye to a good boy or Girl how they are drest or of what colour the hair is   when you are men you will know so — the warmth of our cloathing and not the show is all thats required — Pride is an unnessesary evil — I readily excuse your Brothers John and William for not coming here and in fact beg them not to trouble them selves at all about it unless it would give them pleasure to do so — I tell you all Brothers and Sisters to Love truth be Honest and fear Nobody — Amuse yourselves in reading and writeing — you all have the Bible and other suitable books — I would advise you to study Mathematics Astronomy Languages and Botany as the best amusements for instruction — Angling is a Recreation I was fond of myself and there is no harm in it if your taste is the same — for in those things I have often broke the Sabbath when a boy and perhaps it was better then keeping it in the Village hearing Scandal and learning tipplers frothy conversation — 'The fields his study nature was his book'[3]   I seldom succeeded in Angling but I wrote or rather thought Poems made botanical arangements when a little Boy which men read and admired   I loved nature and painted her both in words and colours better then many Poets and Painters and by Preseverance and attention you may all do the same — in my boyhood Solitude was the most talkative vision I met with

Birds bees trees flowers all talked to me incessantly louder then the busy hum of men and who so wise as nature out of doors on the green grass by woods and streams under the beautifull

277

sunny sky — daily communings with God and not a word spoken
— the best books on Angling[4] are by Piscator and Henry Phillips
and Sir Humphry Davies though we must not over look the
Father of Anglers Isaac Waltons 'Art of Angling or the Contem-
plative Mans Recreation' a choice book with all Fishermen and
there is many others every way as good — I had hopes I should
have seen the Garden and Flowers [before] now — but we cannot
reckon on any thing before hand — the future is with providence
and unknown till it comes to pass — Like old Muck Rake in the
Pilgrims Progress I know nothing in other peoples business and
less in whats to come or happen — 'There is nothing like home'
    give my love to Mr and Mrs Bellars and Mrs Sefton and
remember me to all your neighbours who enquire after me par-
ticularly old John Green whose words came true and who was the
only Person who persuaded me not to come here — you never
mentioned your Grandfather   give my love to him and believe
my love to you all while I remain my dear Childern
              your affectionate Father   John Clare
                                              [N30, 16]

To MARTHA CLARE (W.F. Knight's hand)

                Northampton Asylum July 19th 1848
My dear wife,
    I have not written to you a long while but here I am in the Land
of sodom where all the peoples brains are turned the wrong way
    I was glad to see John yesterday and should like to have gone
back with him for I am very weary of being here — You might
come and fetch me away for I think I have been here long enough
    I write this in a green meadow by the side of the river agen
Stokes Mill [i.e. Spokes Mill] and I see three of your daughters
and a Son now and then   the confusion and roar of Mill dams
and locks is sounding very pleasant while I write it and its a very
beautiful Evening   the meadows are greener than usual after

278

the shower and the Rivers are brimful   I think it is about two
years since I was first sent up in this hell and not allowed to go out
of the gates   there never was a more disgraceful deception
than this place   It is the purgatoriall hell and French Bastile of
English liberty   Keep yourselves happy and comfortable and
love one another   by and bye I shall be with you perhaps
before you expect me   There has been a great storm here with
Thunder and hail that did much damage to the glass in the Neigh-
bourhood   hailstones the size of Hens Eggs fell in some places
    Did your brother John come to Northborough or go to Barn-
oak   his Uncle John Riddle came the next morning but did not
stay.   I thought I was coming home but I got cheated   I see
many of your little Brothers and Sisters at Northampton weary
and dirty with hard work some of them with red hands but all in
ruddy good health   some of them are along with your Sister —
Ruth Dakker who went from Helpstone a little girl   Give my
love to your Mother Grandfather Brothers and Sisters and believe
me my dear Children
    hers and yours very affectionately   John Clare
[N20, ii, 103-4]

To CHARLES CLARE

                    Asylum near Northampton June 1st 1849
My dear Boy
    I was very happy to have so long a Letter from you and to hear
that you was all well and to hear that the Garden is prosperous
and that You and Your Neighbours are all well and happy —
Spring and Summer came in beautifull and the crops of Grass and
corn are plentifull and give promise of Haytime and Harvest and
Plenty
    You told me to enquire of you about my old Neighbours and
Labouring Companions of my single Days — There is William
and John Close   do they live at Helpstone yet and how are

279

they — how is John Cobbler of Helpstone   I worked with him when a single Man and Tom Clare we used to sit in the Fields over a Bottle of Beer and they used to Sing capital Songs and we were all merry together   how is John and Mary Brown and their Daughter Lucy and John Woodward and his Wife and Daughter William Bradford and his Wife and A. and E. Nottingham and old John Nottingham and his Wife Sally Frisby[5] and James Bain and old Otter the Fiddler and Charles Otter and John and Jim Crowson — most of us Boys and Girls together — there is also John and James Billings and Will Bloodworth and Tom and Sam Ward and John Fell and his Wife and John King and Mr and Miss Large and Mr and Miss Bellars on the Hill and Mr Bull and all enquiring Friends and Mrs Crowson   many are dead and some forgotten and John and Mrs Bullimore[6] the Village Schoolmistress and Robin Oliver and his wife and Will Dolby and his Wife and Henry Snow and his Wife and Frank Jackson and his Wife Richard Royce and his Wife and Daughter and Jonothan Burbidge and his Wife and Daughter and all I have forgotten remember me kindly to — for I have been along while in Hell — how is Ben Price and Will Dolby for I liked Helpstone well — and all that lived in it and about it for it was my Native Place — how is Thomas Porter of Ashton   he used to be my Companion in my single Days when we loved Books and Flowers together and how is Charles Welsh of Bainton — my fondness for Flowers made me acquainted with him which has wore many Years and his Wife too and Daughters for they are all old Friends — Give my Love to your Brothers and Sis[ters] and Grand Father and Neighbours and ever [believe] me

your Affectionate Father   John Clare

[N30, 22]

280

To MARTHA CLARE

[1849-50]

My dear Wife

I have wrote some few times to enquire about yourself and the Family and thought about yourself and them a thousand othe[r] things that I use to think of the childern — Freddy when I led him by the hand in his childhood — I see him now in his little pink frock — sealskin cap — and gold band — with his little face as round as a apple and as red as a rose — and now a stout Man both strangers to each other the father a prisoner under a bad government so bad in fact that its no government at all but prison disapline where every body is forced to act contrary to their own wishes 'the mother against the daughter in law and the daughter against the mother in law'[7] 'the father against the son and the son against the Father' — in fact I am in Prison because I wont leave my family and tell a falshood — this is the English Bastile a government Prison where harmless people are trapped and tortured till they die — English priestcraft and english bondage more severe then the slavery of Egypt and Affrica while the son is tyed up in his manhood from all the best thoughts of his childhood bye lying and falshood — not dareing to show love or remembrance for Home or home affections living in the world as a prison estranged from all his friends

still Truth is the best companion for it levels all distinctions in pretentions   Truth wether it enters the Ring or the Hall of Justice shows a plain Man that is not to be scared at shadows or big words full of fury and meaning nothing   when done and said with them truth is truth and no further and the rights of man — age of reason and common sense are sentences full of meaning and the best comment of its truth is themselves — an honest man makes priestcraft an odious lyar and coward and a filthy disgrace to Christianity — that coward I hate and detest — the Revelations has a placard in capitals about 'The Whore of Babylon and the mother of Harlots'[8]   does it mean Priestcraft I think it must — this rubbish of cant must soon die

— like all others — I began a letter and ended a Sermon — and the paper too

I am dear Wife yours ever   John Clare

[N19, R129-R127]

The Humbug called the 'Ring or the 'Fancy[9] owes Me as Forfiets £1800 and I have been 9 Years without a Shilling and in this Prison still

Ben Caunt[10]

[N10, 90]

Jany 23rd 1850   Saw my Wife Patty in a Dream   she looked well — with little Billy and an Infant carried by someone else all looked healthy and happy — John Clare

[N10, inside back cover]

To SOPHIA CLARE (copy)

Northampton 8th Octr 1852

My dear daughter Sophy,

I am very glad to hear from you, and that the family are in good health — I hope that Charles[11] will be soon better, and that he will be very soon able to write me a letter, and give me the same good news of my family which will be always dear to me   I am happy at all times to hear of their welfare

I am very happy to inform, that I also am in very good health, and I think that I never have felt myself in better

You must not suppose me to be all ailing, because this is not in my own writing but a Gentleman who is here is very fond of writing, and therefore I have given him a copy and thank him for writing for me — You will understand it is only, that I do not

282

write so fluent and quick as he does that I have asked him to write
for me
    Give my love to your Grandfather your Mother and brothers
and sisters and believe me My dear Sophy
                Your affectionate Father   John Clare
                (Clare's signature)
                                          [N30, 36]

To JAMES HIPKINS [12]

                            March 8th 1860
Dear Sir
    I am in a Mad house and quite forget your Name or who you
are   you must excuse me for I have nothing to commu[n]icate
or tell of and why I am shut up I dont know   I have nothing to
say so I conclude [13]
                yours respectfully   John Clare
                                        [N40] [14]

To his WIFE and CHILDREN

                            March 9th 1860
My dear Wife and Childern
    I answer my dear Daughters Sophias Letter as soon as I can
I am not quite so well to write as I have been so I delayed it a few
days In hopes that I might be more able to answer your enquiries
      how is your Mother Grandfather and Grandmother and
Aunt Sophy and Mary — I want nothing from Home to come here
— I shall be glad to see You when you come — God bless you all
      Northboro is a quiet place — give my Love to my neighbours
and Friends and to your Grandfather and grandmother and to all
enquiring Friends, and believe me ever your affectionate
                Father   John Clare   [N422]

NOTES

Introduction

1   See above, p.39.

2   J.W. and A. Tibble, *The Prose of John Clare* (London, 1951; repr. 1970), p.3. Hereafter referred to as *Prose*.

3   Oddly enough, Clare did write one poem where the courtship takes place in a pig-sty — see *The Rivals*, l.372; note in E. Robinson and D. Powell (eds), *John Clare: Poems of the Middle Period* (Oxford, 1996), i. p.229. His story of the magistrate Hopkinson and his wife is a brilliant satire upon condescension gone wrong (see above, pp.125-7). The satirical tone of these passages conforms with *The Parish*, never published in Clare's day. See E. Robinson (ed.), *John Clare: The Parish* (Penguin, 1986).

4   Edmund Blunden (ed.), *Sketches in the Life of John Clare written by himself* (London, 1931), p.12. Hereafter referred to as 'Blunden'.

5   See above, pp.3-4.

6   See above, p.29.

7   See also Anne Tibble, *John Clare: A Life* (1972) and E. Storey, *A Right to Song: the Life of John Clare* (1982).

8   Mark Storey (ed.), *The Letters of John Clare* (Oxford, 1985), pp.78-9. Hereafter referred to as *Letters*.

9   Ibid., p.86.

10   Ibid. p.90.

11   Ibid. p.94.

12   Ibid., pp.333-4 and notes, p.398; and see above, pp.120-4.

13   See 'The Disabled Soldier' in E. Robinson and D. Powell (eds), *The Early Poems of John Clare* (Oxford, 1989, 2 vols — hereafter *Early Poems*), i, pp.125-7; 'Death of the Brave', i, pp.248-50; 'To the Welland', i, pp.102-3; 'Burthorp Oak' in A. Tibble and R.K.R. Thornton (eds), *John Clare: The Midsummer Cushion* (Manchester, 1978 — hereafter *M.C.*), p.429; 'On Dr. Twopenny', *Early Poems*, i, p.234; 'The Quack and the Cobler', i, pp.164-70; 'On the Death of a Quack', i, pp.330-32; 'Shakspear the Glory of the English stage', i, pp.336-7; 'Lord Byron', *M.C.* p.389; 'To the Memory of Keats', *Early Poems*,

ii, pp.476-7; 'To the Memory of James Merrishaw a Village School-master', *Early Poems*, i, pp.456-7; 'Lines on the Death of Mrs Bulli-more', i, pp.197-9.

14   'To Obscurity Written in a fit of despondency', *Early Poems*, i, p.386.

15   *Early Poems*, i, p.424-31.

16   'Dawning of Genius', *Early Poems*, i, pp.451-2; 'Some Account of My Kin...' ibid., ii, pp.607-8; 'In shades obscure...', ibid., ii, p.382.

17   *Letters*, p.133.

18   Ibid., p.138; Clare to Taylor, 7 January 1821.

19   Ibid., p.147.

20   Ibid., p.161.

21   Ibid., p.161 note 4.

22   Ibid., p.173; Clare to Taylor, 3 April 1821.

23   M. Storey, 'Edward Drury's "Memoir" of Clare', *The John Clare Society Journal*, no.11, July, 1992, pp.14-16.

24   *Letters*, p.172 note 2; Taylor to Clare, 7 April 1821.

25   F. Martin, *The Life of John Clare* (1865), p.vi.

26   Blunden, pp.11-12.

27   J. and A. Tibble, *John Clare: His Life and Poetry* (1956), p.10 note 1.

28   *Letters*, p.208. In note 9 on this page, Storey identifies this Literary Life with the 'Autobiographical Fragments' as printed in E. Robinson (ed.), *The Autobiographical Writings of John Clare* (Oxford, 1983), but see above, p.xviii.

29   Ibid., p.311.

30   Ibid., p.311 note 2.

31   *Prose*, p.2.

32   *Letters*, p.311.

33   See above, pp.173, 178 and 197.

34   *Letters*, p.380.

35   He seems to have obliterated remarks critical of Taylor in his Jour-nal for 30 March 1825, 15 April 1825 and 17 April 1825, but it should be pointed out that the Journal does not actually begin until Sep-tember 1824.

36   *Letters*, p.491.

Sketches in the Life of John Clare

1   Clare has heavily deleted this last sentence.

2   *John Cue of Ufford*: He was buried, aged 84, on Wednesday, 2 February 1825, as we are told in Clare's *Journal* for that date. He had been head gardener for Lord Manners of Ufford Hall. Clare worked with him for some seasons at turnip-hoeing. From him (see p.166) Clare acquired a copy of Leonidas. Victor Hatley in *A Northamptonshire Miscellany* (1983) identifies him with John Cew, servant, on the Ufford Militia List, 1762.

3   *old Nixons Prophesies*: Robert Nixon, *A True Copy of Nixon's Cheshire Prophecy* (London, 1715). A chapbook of the same kind as *Mother Shipton's Legacy*, see below. Such books were published by the Aldermary Churchyard Press, owned by the Dicey family. Mentioned by Clare at B5,82. Several editions are in the Harding Collection, Bodleian Library, Oxford.

    Mother Bunches Fairey Tales: See G.L. Gomme (ed.), *Mother Bunch's Closet Newly Broken Open and The History of Mother Bunch of the West* (London, 1885). *Mother Bunch's Fairy Tales*, printed for S. Maunder, 10 Newgate St. Price Sixpence, 1830, and many editions, several in the Harding Collection.

    Mother Shiptons Legacy: See W.H. Harrison, *Mother Shipton Investigated* (1881): also K.M. Briggs, *A Dictionary of British Folk Tales* (1970), Part A, vol.2, p.549 and Part B, vol.2, pp.690-1. Mentioned by Clare at B5,82. See also *The History of Mother Shipton* [Ursula Sonteil], (Coventry, 1815). There are several editions in the Harding Collection.

4   Clare has heavily deleted the preceding ten words.

5   *the sister that was born with me*: There is no mention of her baptism at Helpston but such occurrence was not uncommon. She was called 'Bessey' by Clare. See 'To a Twin Sister who Died in Infancy' (*Early Poems*, i,598-9).

6   *adam and Eve*: This bible story was very significant to Clare.

7   a master at a distance: John Seaton who held classes in the church vestry at Glinton.

8   *the flower and honour*: Admiral the Hon. William Waldegrave,

second son of the third Earl Waldegrave, later Baron Radstock, had been a friend of Nelson, quelled a mutiny on HMS *Latona* at the Mutiny of the Nore. He was an ardent evangelical and became Clare's patron. See pp.54-5.

9   *the bible*: Clare's work is deeply marked by his knowledge of the Bible. In particular he wrote many verse-paraphrases of biblical passages. See *Later Poems*, i,105-58.

10   *Sixpenny Romances*: See G. Deacon, *John Clare and the Folk Tradition* (1983). These pamphlets sold by hawkers were an important part of Clare's literary tradition. Some of the books to which Clare refers, e.g. Thomson's *Seasons*, Defoe's *Robinson Crusoe* and Kirke White's *Remains,* were published in chapbook editions and it may be to these that he refers.

    'Zig Zag': probably refers to the story entitled 'The Man with a Long Nose' (see Briggs, op. cit., Part A, vol.i, pp.408-9) in which occurs the rhyme:

> Did you see a maid running zigzag
> And in her hand a long leather bag
> With all the gold that e'er I won
> Since the time I was a boy yet?

    'Prince Cherry': The same story as 'Prince Darling'. See A. Lang, *The Blue Fairy Book* (New York, 1966), pp.278-89.

11   *'Father forgive...'*: Luke 23:24.

12   *'a little learning...'*: Pope, *An Essay on Criticism*, l.215.

13   *Bonnycastles Mensurationn*: J. Bonnycastle, *An Introduction to Mensuration and Practical Geometry*, 10th edn (1807).

14   *John Turnill*: Elder brother of Richard Turnill, Clare's schoolfellow and first close friend. They were the sons of a neighbouring farmer for whom both Clare and his father worked at various times. There are other testimonies (see pp.49-50 and 68) to John Turnill's intellectual aspirations.

15   *a shoemaker*: Will Farrow, see pp.63-5

16   *Francis Gregory*: Proprietor of the Blue Bell Inn, kept a few animals and had about six acres of land under the plough. He suffered

from ill health and died in 1811 soon after Clare left his service. See pp.66 and 72.

17 *Thompsons Seasons*: James Thomson's *Seasons* (1730).

18 *Come gentle Spring, ...*: The opening lines of 'Spring'.

19 *the words Lord and God*: See p.307 note 181.

20 *Burghly Park*: Burghley House, just South of Stamford, the home of the Marquis of Exeter, one of Clare's patrons.

21 *'the morning walk'*: 'A Morning Walk: Ah, sure it is...'. See *M.C.* pp.153-8.

22 *the evening walk*: 'Recollections after an Evening Walk: Just as the even bell rung...'. See *Early Poems*, ii. 326-8.

23 *the Master of the Kitchen Garden*: See pp.73-4 and 76.

24 Clare has written 'his'.

25 *on this ramble*: See pp.76-7.

26 *Pomfrets 'Love triumphant over reason'*: Revd John Pomfret, *Poems on Several Occasions* (London, 1746), pp.15-33.

27 *'Abercrombies Gardiners Journal'*: John Abercrombie, *The Gardener's Pocket Journal or Every Man his own Gardener*. In Clare's library, items 89 and 90 are Abercrombie's *The Gardener's Companion* (1818), and his *Practical Gardener* (1823). See D. Powell, *Catalogue of the John Clare Collection in Northampton Public Library* (Northampton, 1964, hereafter referred to as Powell).

'Wards Mathematics': E. Ward, *The Elements of Arithmetic...In five parts* (Liverpool, 1813).

Fishers 'Young mans companion': George Fisher, *The Instructor: or Young Man's Best Companion* (1763).

'Robin Hoods Garland': This was a popular chapbook containing songs and had many publishers. One copy is no.29 in the John Johnson collection in the Bodleian Library. It was published at price 6d. by Dicey who also published the *Northampton Mercury*. His distribution routes for chapbooks ran through Peterborough, Stamford, and Boston.

'Death of Abel': S. Gessner, *Death of Abel*, trans. F. Shoberl, n.d. but

probably 1814. Much of Clare's Eden imagery may have been derived from this work. Selections from Gessner were also published as a chapbook.

'Joe Millers Jests': Another famous chapbook, e.g. *Joe Miller's Jest Book; forming a rich Banquet of Wit and Humour* (1834). It dates from the Elizabethan period.

'Collection of Hymns': Perhaps John Wesley, *A Collection of Hymns, for the use of people called Methodists* (1825). See Powell, item 393.

28   *grammer*: see p.33.

29   '*Universal Spelling Book*': Daniel Fenning, *The Universal Spelling Book; or, a New and Easy Guide to the English Language* (1756) was a popular textbook and reached its 71st edition in 1823.

30   *Mr Arnold M.D.*: Thomas Graham Arnold practised at St Martin's, Stamford and attended Clare at John Taylor's request in spring, 1824. See *Letters*, pp.290-2.

31   *Thomas Porter*: See also pp.51, 67 and 107. Thomas Porter of Ashton, with the Turnill brothers, were Clare's closest boyhood companions.

32   *a Bookseller*: J.B. Henson of Market Deeping. See pp.55-6 and 102-6. He was also a preacher and a publisher of chapbooks, though we have not been able to find surviving specimens of his work. There was a Henson, printer of broadsides (see Northampton Public Library and Madden Collection, Cambridge University Library), of 81 Bridge St, Northampton, but he seems to have been George Henson, possibly a relation of Clare's would-be publisher.

33   '*The setting Sun*': See *Early Poems*, i, 150.

'*To a primrose*': See *Early Poems*, i. 182.

34   *Stephen Gordon*: Drakard's Stamford News, 18 April 1823, records his death, 'On Monday, in St. John's, Stamford, Stephen Gordon, lime-burner, aged 45.'

35   *Mr Wilders*: Wilders kept the New Inn at Casterton and had kilns there and at Ryhall and Pickworth.

36   *Pickworth*: The lime kiln at Pickworth was restored in 1992.

37 Clare has heavily deleted 'for the first time'.

38 *'What is Life'*: See *Early Poems*, i, 392-3.

39 *'Enquirer'*: The *Boston Enquirer*, 1811-13 (see Powell, item 199). This subscription is mentioned, p.107.

40 *Mr Thompson*: Thompson was an attorney and married the daughter of Richard Newcomb, owner of the *Stamford Mercury*. Edward Drury acquired his bookselling business in 1818.

41 *M' Drury*: Edward Drury of Lincoln, bookseller, publisher, friend of Peter De Wint and William Hilton and cousin of Taylor. After a brief stay in Stamford he returned to Lincoln in 1822.

42 *'Bachellors Hall'*: The scene of many a convivial evening for Clare, it still stands No 17 Woodgate, Helpston.

43 *John and James Billings*: See pp.51-3. They shared Clare's fondness for chapbooks. Clare wished to raise money for them from some of his writings.

44 *gentlemen*: Edward Drury and Richard Newcomb. See pp.107-8.

45 *John Taylor*: (1781-1864) Publisher and bookseller, he had served with James Lackington and with Vernor and Hood. He had previously assisted in the publication of Robert Bloomfield. He founded the *London Magazine* and was also the publisher of Keats, Hazlitt, Reynolds, Cary, De Quincey, and Landor. See E. Blunden, *Keats's Publisher* (1936) and T. Chilcott, *A Publisher and his Circle* (1972).

46 *Patty*: Martha Turner, whom Clare married in 1820.

47 *Mary*: Mary Joyce, daughter of a farmer at Glinton, and Clare's first love.

48 *ranters*: Primitive Methodists. See Mark Minor, 'John Clare and the Methodists: A Reconstruction', *Studies in Romanticism*, 19, Spring 1980.

49 *Robspiere*: Robespierre (1758-94), instrumental in 1793 in sending many to the guillotine, met the same fate in 1794.

50 *'Tell truth . . . the devil'*: This quotation could be attributed to Hugh Latimer, Ben Jonson, Rabelais or Shakespeare.

Autobiographical Fragments

1   *I was*: Clare has written 'I way'.

2   *eastwell spring*: A natural spring near Helpston which became a local meeting-place.

3   *harvest home*: The harvest celebrations. The harvest supper was once a grand occasion when all the harvest workers were invited to the farmer's groaning table.

4   *in man hood*: Clare has written 'mad'.

5   *shepherds and herd boys*: See Clare's poem 'A Sunday with Shepherds and Herdboys'.

6   *Emmonsales*: Emmonsales, or Ailsworth, Heath — now a nature reserve.

7   *a new world*: Followed by the deleted words: 'and expected the worlds end bye and bye but it never came'.

8   *Langley Bush*: A favourite meeting-point for gypsies near Helpston and originally the site of the open courts. A gibbet once stood at the spot. Clare tells us that the bush was destroyed by vandalism.

9   *splashing steam*: ? steam for 'team' or 'stream'.

10 *but*: Clare has written 'by'.

11 *the old woman*: Clare originally wrote 'milk maid'.

12 *the Marquis*: Clare is referring to Lord Milton.

13 *poor cade foal*: This story of the cade, or pet, foal is so near to Robert Bloomfield's poem, 'The Fakenham Ghost', that one wonders once again whether fact and fiction may not have become intertwined in Clare's mind.

14 *'Rotten Moor', 'Dead Moor', Eastwell moor, Banton green, Lolham Briggs, Rine dyke*: Many of these spots are identified in Daniel Crowson's pamphlet, *Rambles with John Clare* (1978), and in Peterborough City Council's two booklets of *Country Walks Around Peterborough*.

15 *how many days*: This passage originally began: 'I never had much relish for noisey games such as hunt the stag'.

16 *Northborough*: This legend is clearly connected with the chapbook, *History of Gotham*.

17 *a young lady being killd...by a shield ball*: This may be connected with the unidentified book, *The Female Shipwright*. Stories of young girls going to sea in search of their lovers were common.

18 *the old man and his ass*: A chapbook. Several editions in the Harding Collection, Bodleian Library, Oxford.

19 *Lilys astrology*: William Lilly (1602-81), *Christian Astrology* (1647) reprinted as *An Introduction to Astrology* (1835).

20 *Culpeppers Herbal*: Nicholas Culpeper, possibly the edition by John Hill (London, 1792).

21 *Noells of Walcott Hall*: The Noel family owned the Hall in the nineteenth century.

22 *Sandys travels*: George Sandys, *Travels*, 7th edn (London, 1673).

    Parkinsons Herbal: John Parkinson, *Theatrum Botanicum* (1640).

23 *to read them*: Followed by the deleted words: 'for his parents woud let him lend nothing'.

24 *his*: Clare has written 'he'.

25 *to pill oaks*: Followed by the deleted words: 'and some times to shoot crows'.

26 *the king and the cobler*: A chapbook. Several editions in the Johnson and the Harding Collections, Bodleian Library, Oxford, e.g. *The Comical History of the King and the Cobler, the Two Parts in One*, Liverpool, Printed for W. Armstrong, Banaster-Street. See also Briggs, op. cit., Part A, vol.2, p.437.

    Seven Sleepers: A chapbook. Several editions in the Harding Collection, Bodleian Library, Oxford. See also R. Johnson, *The Most Famous History of the Seven Champions of Christendom*.

27 *the Pleasant art of money catching*: An anonymous publication, 1816-51. See *The Pleasant Art of Money-Catching and the Way to Thrive by Turning a Penny to Advantage*...Falkirk, Printed for the Booksellers, 1840, in the Harding Collection.

28 *Randolph*: Thomas Randolph (1605-35), poet and dramatist. Born in Newnham, Northamptonshire, he led a boisterous life in London, and returned to his native county in 1634, broken in health

and heavily in debt. His works include *Amyntas*, a pastoral comedy, and the poem *The Muse's Looking-glasse* both published postumously in 1638.

29   *Tarlton*: Richard Tarlton (d.1588), comic actor, wit, and hero of the anecdote collection *Tarlton's Jests*.

30   *insert them here*: Not yet identified among Clare's manuscripts.

31   *Lord Radstock*: Admiral the Hon. William Waldegrave, second son of the third Earl Waldegrave, became the first Baron Radstock. Friend of Nelson and Naval Governor of Newfoundland, he quelled a mutiny on board HMS *Latona* at the mutiny of the Nore. He was an ardent evangelical and a very kindly man. See J. Marshall, *Royal Naval Biography* (1823-5), 8 vols, *The Annual Biography and Obituary* (1825), and D.W. Prouse, *A History of Newfoundland* (1896). He died in 1825.

32   *Behnes*: Henry Burlow Behnes (d.1837), the sculptor. Also made a bust of Clare now in Northampton Public Library. He tried to get S.C. Hall and others to pay Clare for his work.

33   *Lord fitzwilliam*: Charles William Wentworth Fitzwilliam (1786-1857), third Earl Fitzwilliam, a man noted for his probity and independence of mind. See also pp.118-19 and 121.

34   *Revd Holland*: Revd Isaiah Knowles Holland (d.1873). Presbyterian minister at Northborough and then St Ives, Huntingdon. Clare dedicated 'The Woodman' to him.

35   *'Village funeral'*: *Early Poems*, i, 223-7.

36   *the Woodman*: *Early Poems*, ii, 287-96.

37   *Kirk White*: The poet, Henry Kirke White, author of *Remains* (1824). See Powell, items 396-7. The book was also published as a chapbook.

38   *or*: Clare has written 'of'.

39   *Drakards*: John Drakard (1775?-1849), bookseller, proprietor of the *Stamford News* from 1809 and the *Stamford Champion* in January 1830. Renowned for his radicalism, he was once horsewhipped by Lord Cardigan in his own shop.

40   Cf. B3,83 for another version of the second paragraph. There are no significant variants.

41 *the Scotch Rogue*: A chapbook. Several editions in the Harding Collection, Bodleian Library, Oxford.

42 *Mr Gee*: Edward Gee, a retired farmer, who bought Clare's original cottage in 1778. He died in 1804.

43 *Tannahills song of Jessey*: See Journal, 14 Oct. 1824. Passage followed by 'Sir Michael B. Clare West India'.

44 Another version of this paragraph appears at B4, R99: As to my learning if I was to brag over it I might make shift to say a little about mathematics Astronomy Botany Geography and others of the Abst[r]use Arts and sciences for I puzzled over such matters at every hour of leisure for years as my curosity was constantly on the enquiry and never satisfied and when I got fast with one thing I did not despair but tryd at another tho with the same success in the end   yet it never sickend me   I still pursued knowledge in a new path and tho I never came off victor I was never conquored

45 *Lord Milton*: Charles Fitzwilliam, usually so-called by Clare in his father's lifetime. See note 33 above.

46 *Milton*: The Fitzwilliam estate near Peterborough.

47 *good luck and success*: Followed by the deleted words: 'it raind hard before we got there and when we got there we was put into the peterboro room'.

48 Identified titles include: *Dilworths Wingates Hodders Vyses and Cockers Arithmetic*: Thomas Dilworth, *The Schoolmaster's Assistant: being a compendium of arithmetic, both practical and theoretical* (London, 1744); Edmund Wingate, *Arithmetique made easie*, (London, 1652: 18th edn by 1751); James Hodder, *Arithmetick* (London, 1702): Powell, item 242; Charles Vyse, *The Tutor's Guide: being a complete system of Arithmetic...* (1770); Edward Cocker, *Cocker's Arithmetic* (London, 1688): Powell, item 159.

Horners Mensuration and Wards Mathematics Leybourns and Morgans Dialling: Horner: not identified. E. Ward, *The Elements of Arithmetic* (Liverpool, 1813); William Leybourne, *The Art of Dialling, by a Trigonal Instrument* (1699); Sylvanus Morgan, *Horologiographica: Dialling Universal and Particular* (London, 1652).

Female Shipwright: Unidentified chapbook. But see W. Clark Russell, *A Book for the Hammock* (1887), pp.91-114, for stories of women going to war in search of missing lovers or husbands.

Martindales Land Surveying and Cockers Land surveying: Alan Martindale, *The Country Survey-Book, or Land Meeter's Vade Mecum* (London, 1682), Unidentified book by Edward Cocker, author of *Arithmetic* (1678).

Hills Herbal: John Hill, *The British Herbal* (1756). Clare requested the Revd Charles Mossop in a letter dated January 1832 to send back his copy of Hill's *Herbal*. (*Letters*, p.565).

Balls Astrology: Richard Ball, *An Astrolo-Physical Compendium: or a brief introduction to astrology* (London, 1697).

Rays History of the Rebellion: James Ray, *A Compleat History of the Rebellion . . . in 1745* (1749).

Sturms Reflections: Christopher Christian Sturm, *Reflections on the Works of God*, trans. from the German in 1788. Clare was presented with the same author's *Morning Communings with God* (1825), by Herbert Marsh, Bishop of Peterborough, on 24 August 1827 (Powell, item 370). Selections from Sturm were also published as a chapbook.

Harveys Meditations: James Hervey, *Meditations among the Tombs* (1746), and many subsequent editions.

Thompsons Travels: Charles Thompson, *The Travels* (1744). See Powell, item 376.

Life of Barnfield: Probably *The Apprentices Tragedy or the History of George Barnwell*. A chapbook. See the Harding Collection, Bodleian Library, Oxford.

more: Probably Thomas Moore, the Irish poet, unless he means Hannah More, whose *Spirit of Prayer* (1825) was given to him by Lord Radstock (Powell, item 312).

Duty of Man: Richard Allestree, *The Whole Duty of Man* (1659). It was also published as a chapbook.

Lees Botany: James Lee, the elder, *An introduction to botany . . . extracts from the works of Linnaeus* (London, 1760).

Kings Tricks of London laid open: Richard King, *The new Cheats of London exposed; or, the frauds and tricks of the town laid open to both sexes* (Manchester, 1795).

The Fathers Legacy or seven stages of Life: A chapbook called 'The Seven Stages of Life' occurs in the Harding Collection, Bodleian Library.

49   *O. Gilchrist*: Octavius Graham Gilchrist (1799-1823). Grocer of Stamford, wrote on Clare in the *London Magazine*, January 1820. He was editor of *Drakard's Stamford News*, which included an obituary of him 1 July 1823.

50   We have chosen to insert paragraphs from B3, 73 (cf. A18, 271) and from B5, 46 into this account of Clare's reading which continues with 'I also was fond'.

51   *Ray*: John Ray (1627-1705), author of the famous *Historia Plantarum* (1686-1704, 3 vols), also a *Synopsis stirpium Britannicarum* (1690). It may be the shorter work to which Clare refers. Ray's interest in English words and proverbs would also have endeared him to Clare. See C.E. Raven, *John Ray Naturalist: His Life and Works* (Cambridge, 1950).

      Parkinson: John Parkinson, *Theatrum Botanicum* (1640).

      Gerrard: John Gerard, *The Herball, or generall Historie of Plants...* (1630).

52   *classing*: Clare has written 'calassing'.

53   *my friend Artis*: Edmund Tyrell Artis (1789-1847). Steward to Lord Milton but famous as an archaeologist. Published the beautiful *Durobrivae of Antoninus* in 1828. Clare helped him with his digs.

54   *Docter Touch*: Possibly the man described in a 'Copy of a letter received by a gentleman in Hull, dated Market Raisen, October 21' and printed in *Drakard's Stamford News*, 24 November 1809:

      Market Raisen has been crowded for these last ten days, past all belief; hundreds of people have come from all parts of the country to witness the far-famed skill of a *Quack Doctor*, whose account of himself is, *that he was never born, but taken out of the side of his mother, that he is the seventh son of a seventh son*, for seven generations, and that his mother was a seventh daughter. Many very genteel people even come to him, and positively assert that he cures all disorders by *his touch*; he licks their sores, breathes into their mouths, etc etc makes the blind see, the dumb speak, and the deaf hear. He is such a figure as perhaps you never beheld;

he parades the streets accompanied by a fiddle, a fife, a drum, and several men with ribbons to their hats; he has a long black beard, walks without his coat, with his waistcoat unbuttoned, and his stockings about his heels; he takes very little money of his patients, and yet spends a great deal; he gives a dinner or supper every day to the poor; he has six attendants, to each of whom he gives a guinea a day; his daily expences are supposed to be about twenty pounds. All the inns here are very much crowded, many people have been obliged to sleep on the floors; he generally has about two hundred patients a day, many have been here a week, and have not been able to see him. He went in a post-chaise and four, a few days ago, to visit a patient out of town; when he got to the town-end on his return, the horses were taken from the chaise, and he was dragged into the town by men amidst the huzzas and acclamations of the mob, ringing of bells, etc etc   indeed, they look upon him as something more than human; he pretends to much religion. I understand he was taken up at Lincoln, and committed to the house of correction as a vagrant, but they were obliged to give him his liberty. He will leave this place in a few days.

55   *Pool of Bethsheba*: Bethesda. See John 5:2-9.

56   *mentiond awhile back*: Clare either had another order in mind for his observations on Farrow or a passage about him is missing from the MSS.

57   *following Epitaph*: Clare is referring to 'On the Death of a Quack' (*Early Poems*, i, 330-2).

58   *another long tale*: 'The Quack and the Cobler', which appears in Pforzheimer Misc. MS 197, where Clare refers to it as 'a true tale', and is printed in *Early Poems*, i, 164-70).

59   *on an old woman*: Clare is referring to 'On the Death of a Scold' (*Early Poems*, i, 245-6).

60   *in dispair*: This is followed by Clare's description of two alternative endings: 'when the phantom of liberty in[s]tantly appears to cheer the lean figure with prophetic' and 'when the bloated pha[n]tom shrinks from its presence and fades away'.

61   *shoe maker*: Followed by the deleted words: 'to a man in the Village who woud have took me for nothing out of kindness to my Father'.

62   *Mrs Bellairs*: Owner of Woodcroft Farm. Clare was still enquiring after her as late as 1 June 1849. See p.278 below.

63   *'the milking pail'*: There are many songs of this name. This may be related to a chapbook entitled 'The Milk Pail' published by Aldermary Churchyard Press.

      'Jack with his broom': To be found most easily as 'The Green Bloom' in Lucy E. Broadwood, *English Country Songs*, pp.88-9. It may also be found as 'The Jolly Broom-man: or, the Unhappy Boy turnd Thrifty' in Thomas d'Urfey, *Wit, and Mirth; or Pills to Purge Melancholy* (1719-20), 16 vols, vol.IV, p.100.

64   Cf. A34,9, a shorter version.

65   *and then*: Followed by the deleted words: 'and longd to be a trade but I'.

66   *it was usless*: Followed by the deleted words: 'a little time after his abilitys and'.

67   Page torn off here, but the passage is clearly continued at A34, R7 below, which was originally the same MS.

68   *for fireing*: Followed by the deleted words: 'and I was often sent to take my fathers dinner when he was mowing were I often dallyd on the way with it'.

69   *'Little red riding hood'* etc.: Most of these chapbooks stories are familiar even to the modern reader, but see K.M. Briggs, *A Dictionary of British Folk Tales* and G. Deacon, *John Clare and the Folk Tradition*. R. Holmes, *The Legend of Sawney Bean* (1975), p.18 identifies four broadsheet versions in the National Library of Scotland. *The Seven Sleepers* appears in the Harding Collection, Bodleian Library. It is also printed in William Hone, *The Every-day Book*, vol.1, cols.1034-7, for 27 July 1838. *The History of Gotham* is discussed in J.E. Field, *The Myth of the Pent Cuckoo* (1913). See Clare's passage about Northborough, pp.47-8 above. Clare made a note to purchase *Valentine and Orson* as a Christmas present for his daughter Anna, and *Cock Robin* for Eliza (see p.69 above). 'Old mother Bunch and 'old Nixons Prophecys' are identified above, note 3 on p.36. Robin Hoods Garland was a 'special chapbook' published by the Aldermary Churchyard Press. It was a collection of songs and can be found as no.29 in the John Johnson Collection at the Bodleian Library. *The History*

of Thomas Hickathrift, Aldermary Churchyard Press (London, 1790), is also to be found, with other editions, in the Harding Collection, Bodleian Library, Oxford. *The History of Tom Long the Carrier, The History of Johnny Armstrong* and *The History of Lawrence Lazy* were all Aldermary Churchyard chapbooks.

70   *Oliver Cromwell memory*: This passage continues with a description very similar to that given above, from B8,101, and here omitted.

71   *over to try*: Followed by: 'so after — (insert here the Journey to Wisbeach'.

72   *a*: Clare has written 'and'.

73   *Rippingille*: Edward Villiers Rippingille (1798-1859), painter of rural scenes. He worked in Bristol. These paintings have not yet been identified.

74   This is line 76 of 'Summer' in Robert Bloomfield's *The Farmer's Boy*.

75   *destroyd them*: Followed by the deleted words: 'all save some of the woods and dingles   I livd at this place a twelvmonth'.

76   No words are omitted, but we have interrupted this passage, which continues below at '...the man was of so harsh a temper', in an attempt to preserve some continuity in the narrative.

77   The last five words are chemically faded.

78   *Tant Baker*: See *Drunken Barnaby's Four Journeys to the North of England* (1822), edited by Gilchrist for an account of Baker's 'Hole in the Wall' or 'Hole of Sarah', the 'drunkard's cave'. His death was announced in *Drakard's Stamford News*, 15 March 1822.

79   Cf. 'Ale', *Early Poems*, ii, 280-6.

80   *George Cousins*: The death of George Cousins, labourer, by accidental poisoning, aged 65, was announced in *Drakard's Stamford News*, 25 March 1821.

81   *Grantham*: Clare has a very damaged passage which appears to refer to their arrival in Grantham: '[by the time we go]t there it was night   when we [woke at last on] the next day it appeard to me [the air was full o]f rattling repetition noise as if all [the people in the] streets was turning skreekers and knocking at shutters [   ] we learnd since that they were stocking weavers' [A34, R9]. The condition of this passage has deteriorated still further (1995).

82   *Newark on trent*: The following passage seems to refer to Newark.

It will be noticed that the account of the enlisting in the milita does not seem to square with that at A34, R11-10 which follows: 'While here we went to a little village feast calld Baldwick and the Nottingham shire Militia was then very brief in getting substitutes or recruits   we got fresh' [A34, R13]. (Baldwick is unidentified.)

83   *so we*: Followed by the deleted words: 'returnd home and my parents was very happy to see me'.

84   *with the world*: Followed by the deleted words: 'I did not know what to be at'.

85   The confusion over this militia episode is increased by a deletion after 'ill at rest' which reads: 'the Nottinghamshire Militia was then recruiting in the town and I woud have listed but was', and by the single name, Moulton, which appears after the phrase 'I fled my toils and listed'.

86   *in the day*: Followed by the deleted words: 'Fame is very cheaply gained in a village and a pert fool with a little impudence'.

87   *Peter Pindar*: The pseudonym of John Wolcot (1738-1819), author of *The Lousiad* (1785), in which he ridiculed the King, Pitt, and others.

88   *ever*: Clare has written 'every'.

89   *to be saving*: Followed by the deleted words: 'for I had been measured at the Taylors for a new olive green coat a color which I had long aimd at'.

90   *Tycho Wing*: (1696-1750). Astrologer and editor of *Olympia Domata*.

91   Clare's note: 'wild ducks etc'.

92   *Smiths*: Well-known gypsy name. See Clare's Journal, 3 June 1825, and note 10 to *Journey out of Essex* on p.338.

93   *Boswells*: Another well-known gypsy name. Tyso Boswell's daughter, Sophia, married John Grey, who taught Clare the fiddle. See Sylvester Boswell, *The Autobiography of a Gipsy*, ed. John Seymour, 1970, and Claire Lamont, 'John Clare and the Gipsies', *The John Clare Society Journal*, no.13, July 1994, pp.19-31.

94   *king Boswell*: 'On Friday last an interesting funeral took place at Wittering, a village three miles South of Stamford. The individual, whose remains were consigned to the earth, was in life no less a

personage than Henry Boswell, well known as the Father or *King* of the Gipsies resorting to this part of the country. The old man was encamped on Southorpe Heath with several of his family and subjects on Sunday s'ennight, when death put an end to his reign and his earthly wanderings. He has been ill for a few days, but his complaint was really a decay of nature, for the patriarch was nearly a hundred years of age...' (*Stamford Mercury*, 15 October 1824).

95   *to join them*: Followed by the deleted words: 'I woud join in their slang terms almost as ready as them selves'.

96   The first square bracket is Clare's, the second ours.

97   Clare has written in the margin: 'Bur vine Wasp weed Buck bane husk head Furze bound Viney Liskey'.

98   Clare has corrected 'robbing' to 'begging'.

99   *Mary ——*: Mary Joyce.

100 *Elizabeth N[ewbon]*: Elizabeth, or Betty, Newbon. Wrongly identified as 'Newton' in F. Martin's *Life of John Clare*.

101 *Ezra*: Actually it is Esther.

102 *Lord Napiers Key to the revelations*: John Napier, *A Plaine Discovery of the whole Revelations of Saint John* (1593).

103 *Moors almanack*: Old Moore's Almanack. An example is reproduced in L. James, *Print and the People, 1819-1851* (1976), p.156.

104 *threw*: Clare has written 'thro'.

105 The ballad would appear to be 'When natures beauty shone compleat' and the song 'Of all the days in memoreys list' (*Early Poetry*, ii, 201-2 and 395-6).

106 *the lodge*: Walkerd Lodge, home of Patty (Martha Turner).

107 *first volume*: *Poems Descriptive of Rural Life and Scenery* (1820).

108 *Revd Mr Lucas of Casterton*: Richard Lucas, Rector of Great Casterton with Pickworth 1784-1827.

109 *threw*: Clare has written 'thro'.

110 *I twisted him down*: Followed by the deleted words: 'and I never felt dissapointment more keenly then I did in not thumping him'.

111 *to buy*: Followed by the deleted words: 'cut trousers' and 'awkard squad   ducking in plantations'.

112 *disdaind to*: Followed by the deleted words: 'join in such wifish follys'.

113 *about it*: Followed by the deleted words: 'bad lodgers etc'.

114 *Chatterton*: Thomas Chatterton (1752-70) who tried to pass off his poems as old MSS. He killed himself at the age of seventeen. See 'The Resignation', Donald S. Taylor and Benjamin B. Hoover, *The Collected Works of Thomas Chatterton* (Clarendon Press), pp.84-6.

115 *which*: Clare's mistake for 'while'?

116 *Davy*: Presumably John Davis, *The Life of Thomas Chatterton* (1806).

117 'The Resignation' (*Early Poems*, i, 325-7).

118 'The Death of Dobbin' (*Early Poems*, i, 84-90).

119 'The Lodge House' (*Early Poems*, i, 233-47).

120 *calld*: Clare has written 'callded'.

121 *'history of Joseph'*: *The History of Joseph and his Brethren*, a popular chapbook, was reprinted in J. Ashton, *Chapbooks of the Eighteenth Century* (1882). There is an edition (no.41) in the Johnson Collection at the Bodleian Library, Oxford, and several in the Harding Collection in the same library. Most editions are embellished with woodcuts.

122 'What is Life?' (*Early Poems*, i, 392-3).

123 *royal*: Variant of 'Ryhall'.

124 *Henson*: Clare has written 'Henderson' in error.

125 *Revd Mr Mounsey*: Revd Thomas Mounsey, second master at Stamford Free Grammar School.

126 *henson*: Clare has written 'henderson' in error and five lines later has amended 'Hendersons' to 'Hensons'.

127 *Drury*: Followed by the deleted words: 'when I reminded him of his engagment to pay my debts'.

128 *Revd Mr Towpenny*: Clare's mistake for 'Twopenny'. Revd Richard Twopenny (1757-1843) was vicar of Little Casterton from 1783 until his death. See *Early Poems*, i, 234.

129 *Sir English Dobbin*: Sir John English Dolben of Finedon Place, Northamptonshire, ancestor of Robert Bridge's friend.

130   The subsequent passage from 'the address to a Lark' down to 'on the common' also appears at A32,7 but it is there followed by: 'The lost Greyhound was made while going and returning from Ashton
                I saw one lye quaking under a haystack in the snow   I supposd it was lost and wrote the above
            some of the sonnets a short poem or two are early   the rest was written at later periods and most of them at Casterton   the one on the Fountain was written one sunday evening while sitting bye a brook on Casterton cowpasture with patty'.

131   *Edwin and Emma*: David Mallet's 'Ballad of Edwin and Emma' was published as a chapbook. See also *Journal of the Folk Lore Society*, June 1909, no.13 and no.3.
       The poems mentioned by Clare in this section, 'Helpstone', 'The Fate of Amy', 'Address to a Lark', 'The Lost Greyhound' or 'On a lost Greyhound lying on the Snow', 'Crazy Nell' and others can be found in *Poems Descriptive of Rural Life and Scenery* (1820). They are also included in *Early Poems*, i. These poems represent the genre of story-telling ballads describing pathetic rural events to which Clare was always strongly attracted. John Taylor, his publisher, while favouring them at first seems to have become increasingly critical of such poems.

132   *charlotte Smith*: Charlotte Smith (1749-1806). Her popular *Elegiac Sonnets* appeared in 1784.

133   *Dr Bell*: It was Dr J.G. Bell who secured a half yearly annuity from Earl Spencer for Clare. See *Letters*, pp.132 and 205.

134   *afterwards*: Followed by the deleted words: 'I pursued my avocations at Casterton in gardening etc till the latter end of'.

135   *a young girl at Southorpe*: Betty Sell, daughter of a labourer at Southorpe.

136   *Woods Historys*: This was the story of the king's chaplain, Dr Michael Hudson, who was trying to escape from Woodcroft Castle and had his hands cut off as he hung from the battlements. The story was told in Sir Walter Scott's *Woodstock* and in Clare's original version of 'The Village Minstrel' (see *Early Poems*, ii, 163-7).

137   *which I destroyd*: This passage amplifies a statement in *Sketches in the Life of John Clare* (see p.13 above).

303

138 'To the Violet' (*Early Poems*, ii, 10-11) and 'Narrative Verses written after an Excursion from Helpston to Burghley Park' (*Early Poems*, ii, 4-10).

139 *'Round Oak Spring'*: Published in *M.C.*, p.442.

140 *Chauncy Hare Townsend*: The Revd Chauncy Hare Townsend (1798-1868), friend of Dickens. *Great Expectations* was dedicated to him. He published *Poems* in 1821 (Powell, item 379) and *Sermons in Sonnets* in 1851. His letters to Clare are in the Egerton MSS, The British Library.

141 *our parson*: Revd Charles Mossop, Vicar of Helpston 1817-53.

142 *after wards*: Clare has written 'words'. See *Early Poems*, ii, 'The Parish', lines 1230-1369.

143 *Philips waste paper Mag*: Sir Richard Phillips (1767-1840), who founded the *Monthly Magazine* in 1796. Clare criticised him in a letter to Taylor 6 November 1821 (*Letters*, p.217) for his unsigned review of *The Village Minstrel* in the November issue.

144 *Hon^bl Mr Pierpoint*: Henry Manvers Pierrepont, brother-in-law to the Marquis of Exeter.

145 *enabale*: A32,1 starts here.

146 *Blairs Sermons*: Hugh Blair, *Sermons* (1819). See Powell, item 117. See also Clare's Journal for 31 October 1824.

147 *Mrs Emmerson*: Eliza Louisa Emmerson (1782-1847). See pp.136-7. She was a poet and a keen admirer of Clare's work. Unfortunately most of Clare's letters to her have disappeared. She was a friend of Lord Radstock and an evangelical.

148 *Dawson Turner of Yarmouth*: Dawson Turner (1775-1858), botanist and antiquary. Three of his letters to Clare survive in F1 on the first of which Clare has written 'This is the first letter I recieved'.

149 *Captain Sherwell*: Captain Markham E. Sherwill, author of *Ascent to the Summit of Mont Blanc* (1826) and *Poems* (1832).

150 *the Lady*: This passage onwards used to be attached to B3, 75, but is now missing.

151 At B7, 90 Clare has the couplet:
A lean mouthd fellow whose dead visage seems
Akin to pharoahs hunger hanted dreams

152 *absully*: Clare presumably intended to write 'absurdly' or 'absolutely'.

153 *Preston*: Edward Preston. F. Martin, *The Life of John Clare*, ed. E. Robinson and G. Summerfield (1964), p.124 says of him: 'The first of the tribe [of writers of unpublished books visiting Clare] was an individual of the name of Preston, a native of Cambridge, and author of an immense quantity of poetic, artistic and scientific works — none of them printed...'.

154 *Ireland the Shakespear Phantom*: William Henry Ireland (1777-1835) wrote verse imitations of early authors and then graduated to forging Shakespearian plays. When discredited he wandered almost penniless through Wales and Gloucestershire, visiting at Bristol in the autumn of 1796 the scenes connected with Chatterton's tragic death. He also wrote in imitation of Robert Bloomfield.

155 *'brother bob'*: Followed by: 'he made some enquireys after some'.

156 *he woud*: Followed by the deleted words: 'truth over somthing'.

157 *Hilton*: William Hilton, painter, RA (1819) and Keeper of the Academy (1820). He painted portraits of both Clare and Keats.

158 *Ryde*: Henry Ryde, estate-agent at Burghley. He was accused of assault on Mrs Woods in *Drakard's Stamford News*, 12 June 1829.

159 *a painter*: Clare has written below: 'Sir T Lawrence'   Sir M B Clare'.

160 *Mr Hopkinson*: Hopkinson may have been the religious magistrate denounced by Clare for his unfeeling denunciation of gypsies. See p.83. He was Vicar of Morton with Hacconby, Lincs, 1795-1841, also Rector of Etton, 1786-1828. Clare once wrote to Taylor 'if I had an enemey I coud wish to torture I woud not wish him hung nor yet at the devil my worst wish shoud be a weeks confinement in some vicarage to hear an old parson and his wife lecture on the wants and wickedness of the poor...' (7 January 1821; *Letters*, pp.137-8).

161 *she*: Clare has written 'you'.

162 *Beatties Minstrel*: James Beattie, *The Minstrel* (1819), presented by Chauncy Hare Townsend, 6 May 1820 (Powell, item 113).

163 *never heard of him afterwards*: Clare was in fact to receive further letters from him.

164 *the Bishop of Peterbro*: Herbert Marsh, Bishop 1819-39.

165 *Miss Aikins Elizabeth*: Lucy Aikin, *Memoirs of the Court of Queen Elizabeth* (1819). See Powell, item 93.

166 *his Lady...Revd Mr Parsons*: Marsh's wife, Marianne, who was a regular correspondent of Clare's...Revd Joseph Parsons, Prebendary of Peterborough Cathedral.

167 *Oxford sausage*: An occasional publication, principally of 'poems of *humour* and *burlesque*'. The Revd Joseph Parsons gave Clare a copy (Powell, item 325).

168 *General Birch Reynardson*: Thomas Birch married Etheldred Ann Reynardson, eldest daughter of Jacob Reynardson of Holywell Hall in the county of Lincoln, and in 1801 assumed the additional surname of Reynardson. *Drakard's Stamford News*, 18 April 1823, shows Reynardson and W. Hopkinson (note 159) on the same bench of magistrates sitting at Folkingham.

169 *pleasures of hope*: Thomas Campbell, *The Pleasures of Hope* (1816). See Powell, item 146.

170 *Hammond*: James Hammond (1710-42), poet. His *Love Elegies* were written in 1732 and published anonymously in 1743. They were condemned by Dr Johnson for 'frigid pedantry'. Perhaps this was the book General Reynardson showed Clare.

171 *the Servants Hall*: Followed by the deleted words: 'were I recognized an old enemey in a letter boy who had often anoyd me while passing to Stamford by our Kiln at Royal' (i.e. Ryhall).

172 *threatnd no*: Before 'no' Clare has tried to obliterate? 'threatnd' by writing 'John Clare' in bold letters through it.

173 'Second Address to the Rose Bud in humble Life': (*Early Poems*, ii, 331-2).

174 This hiatus is sufficient for four or five words.

175 *Henderson*: Joseph Henderson, head gardener at Milton, a keen botanist friend of Clare's.

176 *Roberts*: Frederic Roberts, servant at Milton Hall. See Clare's Journal, 2 August 1825. In a letter dated '15th March — at Milton' he thanked Clare for sending him 'A Comic song' (BL, Egerton 2250, fol. 295r – 6v).

177 *Grill the Cook*: Monsieur Grilliot, head cook at Milton Hall, better

known to the servants as 'Grill'. See Martin, *Life of John Clare*, pp.190-1, 195-7.

178 *Mrs Procter and Mrs Byron*: See Clare's Journal, 13 July 1825.

179 *it woud hide it* —: Followed by the deleted words: 'he invited me to come up to London before he left me'.

180 *publish them*: Followed by the deleted words: 'and wrote to Lord Radstock (in answer to one from his Lordship'.

181 *the Identity of Junius*: John Taylor, *The Identity of Junius with a Distinguished Living Character Established* (1816 and 1818).

182 Incomplete and bady torn reference to Henson, the bookseller. Clare regarded him as an arch hypocrite and may have been thinking of him when he wrote the second sentence that follows. A further reference to methodists occurs at B3,81; it may refer to a brother of Stephen Gordon of Kingsthorpe: 'insert account of Oliver who woud not suffer a book to be in the house unless the name of Lord or God was in it'.

183 *Stamford Coach*: Followed by the deleted words: 'but I felt very awkard in my dress'.

184 *Johnny Gilpin*: Clare has deleted the words between 'which was far' and 'Johnny Gilpin'.

185 *John Scott*: John Scott (1730-83), the Quaker poet, whose *Elegy written at Amwell, in Hertfordshire* appeared in 1769 and the *Poetical Works* in 1782.

186 *Madam Vestris*: John Clare's 'The Meeting', set to music by Haydn Corri, was sung by Madame Vestris and was published as a broadsheet. See Deacon, *John Clare and the Folk Tradition*, pp.64-5.

187 *Whittlesea Meer*: In Clare's day undrained and an attractive stretch of inland water.

188 *Kean and Macready and Knight and Munden and Emmery*: Edmund Kean was playing at Drury Lane in *The Hebrew*, a drama based on *Ivanhoe*, Macready at Covent Garden in *Ivanhoe, or The Jewess*, a musical play. Edward Knight was playing on the London stage in the early 1820s. Munden and Emery were in a farce at Covent Garden.

189 *Knights quarterly Magazine*: Charles Knight (1791-1873), author and publisher, edited unsuccessfully *Knight's Quarterly Magazine*

between 1823 and 1825. The 'visionary ode on Beauty' was titled 'Beauty; a lyrical poem' and appeared in the June-October 1823 number, pp.77-84. It is dated 1821 and above the initials D.C. Derwent Coleridge (1800-83), S.T. Coleridge's second son, contributed to the magazine under the same initials, but as 'Davenant Cecil'.

190   *bleak...misty*: These two words could equally well read 'blea[c]hd' and 'rusty'.

191   *Rippingille*: Cf. the passage at A31,54 which says that Clare met Rippingille 'on my first visit to London'.

192   *Offleys the Burton ale house*: Martin, op. cit., p.151, writes: 'After staying punctually through the performance in the Tottenham Court Road Theatre, sighing over the enchanting looks of Mademoiselle, the friends adjourned to a neighbouring public-house, and from thence to a tavern known as Offley's, famous for its Burton ale'.

193   *fearful disclosures*: These stories suggest the chapbook *Sweeney Todd*.

194   *Burkhardt*: J.C. Burkhardt, a London jeweller, and Gilchrist's brother-in-law.

195   *Vauxhall*: The spacious pleasure gardens were a source of merriment and romance.

196   *Beggars Opera*: Clare means Beggars Bush, a public house and vaudeville in Holborn.

197   *Allan Cunningham*: Writer and poet (1784-1842), collector of Scots tales and poems. He wrote to Thomas Hood, 28 May 1840: '...now how wellcome were your recollections of the Taylor and Hessey days when Lamb scattered his bright though dilatory jokes about, and Hazlitt sat with his fox like eyes looking direct at nothing and yet seeing all...' (National Library of Scotland archives, Edinburgh MSS.583, fol.739).

198   *Wainwright*: Thomas Griffiths Wainewright (1794-1852). Friend of Charles Lamb, author, painter, forger. See J. Curling, *Janus Weathercock* (1938). Did paintings from Walton's *Angler*.

199   We have chosen to insert this paragraph from D2, 3-4 into the discussion of writers meeting at John Taylor's.

200 *Reynolds*: John Hamilton Reynolds (1796-1832), friend of Keats and Byron, most famous for his *Peter Bell* (1819), a very witty parody of Wordsworth. It is interesting to find him satirizing Wordsworth for mentioning the number of eggs in a nest since this would seem more appropriate as a criticism of Clare. ('Look! *five* blue eggs are gleaming there'). Reynolds published *The Naiad* (1816), a book of literary forgeries *The Fancy: A Selection from the Poetical Remains of Peter Corcoran* (1820), and *The Garden of Florence* (1821). He contributed to the *London Magazine* under the name of Edward Herbert but eventually quarrelled with Taylor.

201 *hearty*: Clare has written 'heartly'.

202 We have interrupted this passage which, in the original MS, continues uninterrupted with 'Hazlitt is the very reverse of this' below, to include two further paragraphs headed 'Reynolds' occurring at B3, 58-9.

203 *Bridget*: Mary Ann Lamb, Charles Lamb's sister, was also known as Bridget Elia. Cf. the end of Lamb's essay 'Dream Children' (1822): 'and immediately awaking, I found myself quietly seated in my bachelor armchair, where I had fallen asleep, with the faithful Bridget unchanged by my side — but John L. (or James Elia) has gone for ever.'

204 *Carey the translator of Dante*: The Revd H.F. Cary (1772-1844). The following description of the crane in Clare's *The Shepherd's Calendar* derives at least in part from Cary's *Dante* which Clare owned (Powell, item 151).

> the solitary crane
> Swings lonly to unfrozen dykes again
> Cranking a jarring mellancholy cry
> Thro the wild journey of the cheerless sky

See E. Robinson, G. Summerfield, and D. Powell, *John Clare; The Shepherd's Calendar* (Oxford, 1993), p.33.

205 *Thornhill*: Sir James Thornhill (1675-1734), painter, was employed by Queen Anne on important works at St Paul's Cathedral, Hampton Court, Greenwich and Windsor. His daughter Jane married William Hogarth clandestinely on 23 March 1729.

206 *Churchills poetry*: Charles Churchill (1731-64), poet and satirist, who attained fame with the publication in 1761 of *The Rosciad* and

The Apology. Cowper found *Gotham* (1764) 'a noble and beautiful poem'. 'Life to the last enjoy'd, here Churchill lies' is line 152 of 'The Candidate' (1764).

207 *'silver tongued hamilton'*: John Hamilton Reynolds who published *The Garden of Florence and Other Poems* (1821) under the name of John Hamilton (Powell, item 233).

208 *Roderic*: Robert Southey, *Roderick; the Last of the Goths* (1814).

209 *Wainwright Lamb... Taylor*: In all probability the missing name is Hood.

210 *Van Wink booms Janus Weathercock*: T.G. Wainewright wrote for the *London Magazine* under the name of 'Janus Weathercock'. Lamb enquired of Hessey in the spring of 1822: 'What is gone of the Opium Eater, where is Barry Cornwall, and above all what is become of Janus Weathercock — or by his worse name of Vink — something? He is much wanted!' (E.V. Lucas, ed., *The Letters of Charles and Mary Lamb*, 1935, vol.11, p.323).

211 *Church yard —*: This passage is followed by: 'I was often puzzled to [?see] Hood'.

212 *Gifford*: William Gifford, editor of the *Quarterly*. His translation of *The Satires of Aulus Persius Flaccus* was published in 1821 (see Powell, item 221).

213 *several times*: At this point, in the margin: 'Mem: Wainwright Hood'.

214 *'Mohawks'*: A satirical poem by Sydney Owenson, later Lady Morgan.

215 *Murray*: John Murray, the publisher.

216 *Waithman*: Robert Waithman, Lord Mayor of London in 1823, was a political reformer. He was a linen-draper.

217 *Bullocks Mexico*: An exhibition of Mexican curiosities at the Egyptian Hall.

218 The first fifteen words are at B3,54 and the passage continues down to 'home with me' in what is now D2,1, though originally the same MS. B3,55 begins with 'and I used to think'.

219 There are two other versions at B6, R80 and R82.

220 *I felt*: Clare has written 'felt I'.

221 *'Nothing set down in malice'*: Cf. *Othello* 5.2.346.

222 *D' Darling*: Dr George Darling (1782-1862), friend of John Taylor, physician to Keats, Wilkie, Haydon, Chantrey and others.

223 *Devilles the Phreneologists*: Deville was one of the most respected 'professional' phrenologists in London, from the 1820s to the 1840s. See Clare's letter to Sir Charles Elton, (*Letters*, pp.309-11).

224 *Elton*: Sir Charles Abraham Elton (1778-1853), 6th baronet, was a scholar and author. His novel, *The Brothers* was published in 1820 (see Powell, item 197).

225 *fives court*: See Tom Bates, 'John Clare and "Boximania"', *The John Clare Society Journal*, no.13, July 1994, pp.5-13.

226 *Oliver*: Tom Oliver, famous pugilist.

227 *Jones the Sailor Boy*: A famous pugilist with whom Clare identified himself in his years of madness.

228 *Sir T.L.*: Sir Thomas Lawrence (1769-1830), painter and President of the Royal Academy from 1820. Clare always remained appreciative of his kindness.

229 *F Freelings*: Sir Francis Freeling (1764-1836), Secretary to the General Post Office.

230 *he understood nothing*: At A25, R27 Clare writes: 'Rip was very fond of seeming to be amused by sympathy and looking at things of which he understoo' [*incomplete*].

231 *the french Playhouse*: The Royal West London in Tottenham Court Road was known as the 'French Theatre'. See C.V. Fletcher 'The poetry of John Clare, with particular reference to poems written between 1837 and 1864', M.Phil. thesis, University of Nottingham, 1973.

232 *a very beautiful actress*: The leading actress in 1824 was known as 'Mlle. Delia'.

233 *Astleys Theatre*: A low vaudeville in London.

234 *Bristol Institution*: Followed by the deleted words: 'and he sent home for these that we shoud look over them together but no time was found for the purpose except one morning after breakfast'.

311

235 *Van Dyk*: Harry Stoe Van Dyk helped Taylor to edit Clare's *Shepherd's Calendar*. He was the author of *English Romances and Songs of the Six Minstrels*. He also published the poem *The Gondola* in 1827 (Powell, item 382) and *Theatrical Portraits* in 1822 (Powell, item 383).

236 *Etty the painter*: William Etty, R.A. (1787-1849), whom Clare classed alongside Hilton and Rippingille, as one of the neglected geniuses of the age.

237 *Mr Vining*: Possibly James Vining (1795-1870), actor.

238 *till very late*: Followed by the deleted words: 'for as soon as it began'.

239 Over this passage are the deleted words: 'knocking at odd looking houses at night'.

240 *or rather below*: Did Clare intend to write 'above'?

241 *sympathies*: Clare has written 'symptays'.

242 *were...about it*: These last nineteen words appear at B3,87 but, we believe, belong here.

243 *Warrens Blacking Princes Kaladar and Atkissons Bears Greese*: Warrens Blacking was one of the most widely advertised commodities in the 1820s and 1830s and few newspapers failed to carry their rhyming adverts. In a letter to Taylor, October 1831, Clare refers to 'puffers of Blacking and Bearsgreese' (*Letters*, p.550). Also advertised in the papers were such products as Rowland's Kalydor for the complexion and Atkinson's curling fluid and vegetable dye for the hair.

244 Italicized words written in different ink.

245 *situation*: Clare has written 'situtation'.

246 *real dissapointments*: Followed by the deleted words: 'that is if we do not build our'.

247 *Lady Milton*: Lady Milton died 1 September 1824.

248 *And on the finger...*: Shakespeare, Sonnets XCVI.

249 *from...them*: These last six words are at A31,51.

250 Torn away leaving a few incomplete letters, perhaps 'not for the deceiving'.

Appendix: Clare's notes for his autobiography

1   *Buying Leonidas of Cue*: Possibly Richard Glover, *Leonidas, A Poem* (1737). In Napoleonic England did Clare think of himself as resisting the might of Xerxes? Perhaps Clare had seen the following unconnected lines in Hone's *The Every-day Book*, vol.2, 21 March 1825, cols. 509-10:

> 'Cling to thy home! If there be the meanest shed
> Yield thee a hearth and shelter for thine head,
> And some poor plot, with vegetables stored,
> Be all that pride allots thee for thy board,
> Unsavoury bread, and herbs that scatter'd grow,
> Wild on the river's brink or mountain's brow,
> Yet e'en this cheerless mansion shall provide
> More heart's repose than all the world beside.'
>
> Leonidas of Tarentum.

2   *Old B . . .*: Clare has written at the side of A33,9 a note indicating that he is referring to Burbidge. We have not identified this work, entitled, according to Clare in MS A33, *Old Burbidge's Journey to London*.

3   *Sir M.B. Clare*: Sir Michael Benignus Clare, a rich West Indian, sent five guineas to Clare in September 1823, for the name's sake.

4   *Drury and Songs by Crouch*: At Edward Drury's suggestion, Clare's songs were set to music by Crouch who sold them on sheets embellished in a rather flamboyant manner. He never paid Clare for his work and Clare was reproved by John Taylor for entering into the arrangement with Drury. Crouch dedicated the songs to various notable people. F.W. Martin in *The Life of John Clare* (1864) was the first to comment on this business. A single example of one of Crouch's settings of Clare survives in the British Library Music Collection. It is of 'Sweet the Merry Bells Ring Round'.

5   *French girl*: These words also occur at B3,73. No account has survived in the autobiographical writings of Clare's meeting with this girl who was probably connected with the French prisoners-of-war at Norman Cross. The following sonnet occurs, however, at A61.40:

> I cannot know what country owns thee now
> With frances fairest lillies on thy brow

When england knew thee thou wert passing fair
I never knew a foreign face so rare
The world of waters roll and rushes bye
Nor let me wander where thy vallies lie
But surely france must be a pleasant place
That greets the stranger with so fair a face
The english maiden blushes down the dance
But few can equal the fair maid of france
I saw thee lovely and I wished thee mine
And the last song I ever wrote is thine
Thy countrys honour on thy face attends
Man may be foes but beauty makes us friends

6   *F. Howard*: Frank Howard (1805-66), designer and draughtsman, who first exhibited at the Royal Academy in 1825.

7   *Anna – Octr 29.*: Accompanied by a sketch of a church.

The Journal

1   *Foxes book of Martyrs*: Clare presented his father with an 1824 edition (Powell, item 207).

2   *'Do as ye would . . . that hate you'*: Matthew 7:12, 5:44.

3   *the best English Pastoral*: Izaak Walton, *The Compleat Angler* (1822); Powell, item 387. The river Lea in Hertfordshire was Walton's favourite river for angling.

4   *Pastoral Ballads of Bloomfield*: See *Wild Flowers* (1819) and *Rural Tales, Ballads and Songs* (1820); Powell, items 124 and 123. Clare to Thomas Inskip, 10 Aug. 1824: 'the greatest Pastoral Poet England ever gave birth too' (*Letters*, p.300).

5   *'Mumble the game they dare not bite'*: 'Epistle to Dr Arbuthnot', l.314.

6   *2 letters One to Cunningham*: *Letters*, pp.302-3 (letter to Cunningham only).

7   *Written an Essay . . . Letters to Hessey*: All printed in Grainger.

314

8   *letter from C.A. Elton*: 8 Sept. BL Egerton 2246, fol.379r-80v.

9   *letter to Rippingille and to H.F. Carey*: Neither letter has survived.

10   *Appendix no 1*: Not included here.

11   *'the greater light...upon the earth'*: Genesis 1:16.

12   *Poems of Chatterton*: Rowley's *Poems* (1777); Powell, item 152. The couplet is ll.79-80 of 'The Battle of Hastings No 1' and the single line is l.6 of 'Songe to Aella'.

13   *Appendix N° 2*: Not included here.

14   *Leadenhall*: Clare to Taylor, April 1821: 'I have often thought of trying at a novel taking all the scenes from low life for the silly stuff that comes out of leaden hall Street — gives good elbow room for doing it and leaves fair oppertunitys of advantage for success — but mine might be leaden as theirs so its safer to be silent' (*Letters*, p.179).

15   *'Otranto'*: The first edition of Horace Walpole's Gothic novel *The Castle of Otranto* (1764) was published as a translation from an Italian manuscript of 1529. The true authorship was only revealed in the second edition in 1765.

16   *a ladye*: On pp.119-20 of MS 15 Clare copied out selected lines from 'The Battle of Hastings N° 2' and headed them 'Description of a beauty'.

17   *'kingge coppe'...elm*: All these are mentioned in 'Aella: A Tragycal Enterlude'.

18   *'Don Juan'*: Byron's *Don Juan* (1823) and *Continuation of Don Juan* (1825); Powell, items 138 and 139.

19   *I was very ill...*: Clare wrote to Cunningham, two days later: 'I must end this letter for I can get no further   my head is so stupid and my hand so feeble and trembling' (*Letters*, p.304).

20   *watch...every*: This phrase is written through the deleted words 'be ready for any jobbery...and...'.

21   *John Bull Magazine*: No mention of Clare in the August or September issues. 'The Humbugs of the Age' series featured De Quincey in July, Dr Kitchiner in August, Sir Humphrey Davy in September.

22   *writ 5 letters*: Only the letter to Cunningham has survived (*Letters*, pp.303-4, quoted in note 19).

23   *illusions*: For 'allusions'.

24   *The Statute*: By 1824 the 'statute' had become only an agricultural holiday feast for re-hiring at Michaelmas.

25   *taper ancles*: Cf. ll.13-14 of 'Helpstone Statute or the Recruiting Party': 'They graceful lifted up their gowns/To show a taper ancle'. For 'Helpstone Statute' see *M.C.*, pp.65-70 and for 'The Lodge House' *Cottage Tales*, pp.1-9.

26   *'A Living poets remains'*: Grainger suggests that this title may have been suggested by Kirke White's *Remains* and/or John Hamilton Reynolds' subtitle to *The Fancy*: 'The Poetical Remains of the late Peter Corcoran', but more likely it was prompted by Clare's current concern with Bloomfield's *Remains* (1824) which had just been published (Powell, item 122).

27   *'In doubt... meet eternity'*: Unidentified quotation.

28   *Grays*: There are two volumes of Gray (1809 and 1826) in Clare's library (Powell, items 228 and 229), but no Collins.

29   *Ogilvie*: John Ogilvie (1733-1813) is represented in Clare's library by 'Ode to Melancholy' in *The Lady's Poetical Magazine; or Beauties of British Poetry* (Powell, item 276) and by 'Destruction of the World' in *The Parnassian Garland* (Powell, item 328). The quotation is from *Macbeth* 5.5.27-8 with 'pomp' for 'sound'.

30   *harvest Cricket* etc: Probably the dark bush cricket, *Pholidoptera griseoaptera*. The 'shrew mouse' could be either the common shrew, *Sorex araneus* or the pigmy shrew, *S. minutus*. The 'cricket lark' is probably the grasshopper warbler, *Locustella naevia*.

31   *account of his blindness*: The sonnet 'On His Blindness'.

32   *'What time... supper sat'*: 'Comus', ll.291-3.

33   *the 'Human heart'*: An anonymous collection of short tales just published by Taylor and Hessey (Powell, item 258).

34   *E.T. Artis*: In September 1824 Clare sent Artis 'the *"will"* the *London one* to look over' (*Letters*, p.305).

316

35   *W. Bradford and Taylor*: The signatories were William Bradford, licensee of the Bluebell Inn, and Taylor, a Deeping lawyer.

36   *the poems of Conder*: Josiah Conder, *The Star in the East*, just published by Taylor and Hessey (Powell, item 161). Conder (1789-1855) was the editor of the *Eclectic Review* 1814-17. 'To the Nightingale' begins:
   'O rare Sir Nightingale, what love-sick bard,
   Keeping in vain his nightly guard,
   Did first mistake for notes of kindred sadness
   Thy song of love and gladness?'

37   *the 'Garden of Florence' by Reynolds*: John Hamilton, *The Garden of Florence*, just published by Taylor and Hessey (Powell, item 233).

38   *is*: Clare has written 'in'.

39   *Chantrys monument*: 'Sleeping Children' in Lichfield Cathedral by Sir Francis Chantrey (1781-1842), the famous sculptor.

40   *'little childern'*: 1 John 2:1: 'My little children, these things write I unto you, that ye sin not'.

41   *Appendix No 4*: Not included here.

42   *'Times Telescope'*: See *Times Telescope*, 1821, p.195.

43   *Recievd the London Magazine*: Henderson to Clare, 'I send you the Magazine' (5 Oct., BL Egerton 2246, fol.393r).

44   *a little unknown*: H.N.T.S. in The Lion Head, the correspondence section in the *London Magazine*, July 1824.

45   *another*: 'Julius', probably George Darley, August 1824.

46   *article on Byron*: the anonymous 'Personal Character of Lord Byron', October 1824, which stressed the bad side of Byron's character.

47   *Recieved a letter from Carey*: Cary to Clare, 23 Sept., BL Egerton 2246, fol.387r-8v.

48   *Got a parcel...'Allins Grammer'*: Sent by Hessey 5 Oct., BL Egerton 2246, fol.395r-6v. Charles A. Elton, *The Brothers* (1820), Powell, item 197; W. Allen, *The Elements of English Grammar* (1813), acquired for Clare's library since The Northampton Collection was catalogued; Thomas Erskine, *Remarks on the Internal Evidence for the*

Truth of Revealed Religion, 7th ed. (Edinburgh, 1823), inscribed 'God Grant that he may make the proper use of it', by Lord Radstock on 11 September 1824 (Powell, item 200). The lines quoted are on p.65.

49   *struck*: Clare has written 'sturck'.

50   *Recievd 3 letters*: The letters from Van Dyk and Mrs Emmerson have not survived, the one from Hessey accompanied the parcel.

51   *No 5 of the Appendix*: See pp.245-6.

52   *Neglect is the rust of life . . .*: Cf. Matthew 6:19: 'Lay not up for yourselves treasures upon earth, where moth and rust doth corrupt'.

53   *a letter from Ned Drury*: 8 Oct., BL Egerton 2246, fol.397r-8v.

54   *Johnsons Lives of the Poets*: (1818); Powell, item 266. The story of Savage's birth and ill treatment as given by Johnson has been largely discredited.

55   *Miserys of human Life*: The Miseries of Human Life; or the Groans of Samuel Sensitive, and Timothy Testy. with a few supplementary sighs from Mrs Testy, anonymously published but in fact by James Beresford (1764-1840) (A New and Improved Edition, 1806), presented to Clare by Mrs Emmerson in 1822 'with the hope that its witty and clever contents may serve to beguile his occasional melancholy hours!' (Powell, item 115). Collins' *Odes on Several Descriptive and Allegoric Subjects* (1747) made little impression at the time, and Milton received £5 down for *Paradise Lost* (1667) and £5 two years later, in 1669.

56   *Capel Loft*: Capel Lofft (1751-1824), the Suffolk squire who promoted *The Farmer's Boy* in 1800.

57   *Scotts*: (1783-1821), editor of the *London Magazine* before Taylor, died in February 1821 after a duel with Jonathan Christie. 'Is poor Scott gone' (*Letters*, p.159). Scott was an early editor of *Drakard's Stamford News*.

58   *The letter on Mackadamizing*: 'Billy O'Rourke', 'Macadamization', *London Magazine*, October 1824, p.350, possibly by George Darley.

59   *the Review on Walladmor*: 'Walladmor: Sir Walter Scott's German Novel', October 1824, pp.353-82. *Walladmor* (1825), Powell, item 185, was in fact written by G.W. Haering and translated by De Quincey.

60 *Wrote a letter to Lord Radstock*: This letter has not survived.

61 *Poems of Tannahill*: Robert Tannahill (1774-1810), the Paisley weaver, *Poems and Songs, Chiefly in the Scottish dialect*, 4th ed. (1817); Powell, item 372.

62 *'and therefore love I thee'*: The last line of 'To a Young Lady'; 'virgin voice' is at l.2.

63 *'— the bare trees . . . and are still'*: ll.3-5 of 'The Brothers'.

64 *Recievd a letter from Mrs Gilchrist*: 16 Oct., BL Egerton 2246, fol.399r-400v. Mrs Gilchrist corresponded with Clare after her husband's death in 1823.

65 *Poems of Colridge Lamb and Loyde*: A copy of Coleridge's *Poems. To which are now added Poems by Charles Lamb, and Charles Lloyd* (1797) was presented to Clare by Lord Radstock and sold by the Northampton Public Libraries Committee in 1902.

66 *Bantums 'Excursions of Fancy'*: John Banton, *Excursions of Fancy* (1824); Powell, item 106. See *Letters*, p.334 for another list of upstart poets. In Clare's library are the anonymously published *The Early Muse* (Peterborough, 1822), item 190; S. Messing's *Rural Walks* (1819) and *Poems on Various Subjects* (1821), forming item 300; Nicholas Stratton, *Poems on Various Subjects* (1824), item 369. Rose and Wilkinson remain unidentified. Anna Adcock's *Cottage Poems* (1808) is not in Clare's library, but see his poem 'To Mrs Anna Adcock Author of "Cottage Poems"' (*Early Poems*, i, 34-5).

67 *a century*: Clare has amended 'fifty miles' to 'a century'.

68 *Recievd a letter from Hessey*: 18 Oct., BL Egerton 2246, fol.401r-2v. Clare continues 'and wrote one', but there are no October letters by Clare in *Letters*.

69 *Hazlitts Lectures on the Poets*: William Hazlitt, *Lectures on the English Poets* (1819); Powell, item 239. See Lecture 11, 'On Thomson and Cowper', p.204: 'The daisy that first strikes the child's eye in trying to leap over his own shadow, is the same flower that with timid upward glance implores the grown man not to tread upon it'.

70 *Continued to read Hazlitt*: *Lectures on the English Comic Writers* (1819), *Characters of Shakespeare's Plays* (1818), and *A View of the English Stage* (1818) are Powell, items 238, 237, and 240. For further comment on Hazlitt see *Letters*, p.178.

71   *Recievd a letter from Lord Radstock*: This letter has not survived.

72   *Blairs Sermons...'Flora Domestica'*: Hugh Blair, *Sermons* (1819),
      James Maddock, *The Florist's Directory* (1822), and Elizabeth Kent,
      Flora Domestica (1823); Powell, items 117, 293, 271.

73   *darkness visable*: *Paradise Lost*, i, 63: 'No light; but darkness visible'.

74   *'Oft have we seen him' etc etc*: The stanza continues
                                at the peep of dawn
                    Brushing with hasty steps the dews away
                    To meet the sun upon the upland lawn.

75   *Recieved a letter from Allan Cunningham*: This letter has not survived,
      but there is a transcript in N62.

76   *the Pastorals*: Clare is referring to Pope's 'Pastorals' (1709) and not
      to 'Windsor Forest' (1713).

77   *'Striking...etc'*: 'Epitaph on Mr. Gay. In Westminster Abbey,
      1732' ends 'Striking their pensive bosoms — "Here lies Gay!"'

78   *Appendix N⁰ 6*: Aaron Hill, *The Poems of Aaron Hill* (1822). Here
      Clare brings together some of his favourite passages.

79   *...tinkling periods*: Clare may have had in mind 1 Corinthians 13:1:
      '...I am become as sounding brass, or a tinkling cymbal!'

80   *Wrote a letter to Mʳˢ Gilchrist*: This letter has not survived.

81   *Knoxes Essays*: Vicesimus Knox, *Essays Moral and Literary* (1819);
      Powell, item 274. See *Letters*, p.97.

82   *Bacons Essay*: 'Of Gardens'.

83   *'the Eglantine and the fountain'*: i.e. 'The Waterfall and the Eglantine'.

84   *two Volumes*: Presumably *Eighteen Sermons* (1822) and *Eighteen
      Additional Sermons* (1823); Powell, items 192 and 193.

85   *promisd more from Milton*: Which arrived on 27 Nov.; see Journal for
      that date.

86   *'one berry'*: herb-Paris, *Paris quadrifolia*, no longer in Oxey Wood.

87   *lolam brigs*: Clare cut his initials in one of the Lolham Bridges.

88   *yellow water lily*: horse blob or brandy bottle, *Nuphar lutea*.

89   *'Im pleasd and yet Im sad'*: See Kirke White's 'I Am Pleased, And Yet

I'm Sad' which begins 'When twilight steals along the ground' in *Remains* (1824), p.38 (Powell, item 396).

90 *'A row of reverend elms... in the same tree'*: Robert Blair, 'The Grave', ll.45-9:

> ...a row of reverend elms,
> Coeval near with that, all ragged show
> Long lash'd by the rude winds; some rift half down
> Their branchless trunks, others so thin a-top
> That scarce two crows could lodge in the same tree.

91 *five sorts*: Clare to Artis, Sept. 1824: 'I have sent you two specimens of ferns if you have not got them I will send the roots by Moor before next weeks out — the dark one grows by "Wood lane" side in a dyke and the other in "Oxey wood"' (*Letters*, p.305).

92 *'the Scientific Receptacle'*: See *Letters*, pp.306-8 for Clare's reply of 20 Nov. to John Savage's letter (3 Nov., BL Egerton 2246, fol.404r-v): 'I have been ill ever since last March and tho a little better now I am far from well'. *The Leeds Correspondent, a Literary, Mathematical, and Philosophical Miscellany* (5 vols, 1815-23) and *The Enquirer* (3 vols, Boston, 1811-13) are items 279 and 199 in Powell. There is no Scott in the latter.

93 *Read in Bishop Percys Poems...for many feelings*: Thomas Percy (1729-1811), Bishop of Dromore, published *Reliques of Ancient English Poetry* in 1765. Clare to Hessey, 4 July 1820: 'D[rury] has sent me 3 vols calld "Percys Relics"   there is some sweet Poetry in them and I think it the most pleasing book I ever happend on   the tales are familiar from childhood' (*Letters*, p.82).

94 *cold*: Clare has written 'cold' through 'morning'.

95 *Recieved a packet from London*: James Hessey, 3 Nov., BL Egerton 2246 fol.405r-6v. The letter from Van Dyk is 30 Oct., F1, pp.117-20.

96 *difference*: Clare has written 'defference'.

97 *Appendix N⁰ 7*: Not printed here.

98 *Read over the Magazine*: 'Conversations of Lord Byron' and the letter headed 'Original Letter of James Thomson' (genuinely Thomson's) were published in the November *London Magazine*. Clare may have written 'pretending' rather than 'pretendery'.

99 *Henry the Fifth*: A reference to a chapbook version. The Welsh officer is Fluellen.

100 *Recievd a letter from Inskip*: Undated, BL Egerton 2250, fol.238r-9v. Thomas Inskip (1779-1849), Shefford watchmaker, friend to Bloomfield, Clare's most regular correspondent during his early asylum years (N 52).

101 *Thompsons Winter: The Seasons* (1818); Powell, item 377. Clare quotes ll.104-5, 130-1 of 'Winter' with 'flounders' for 'thunders'.

102 *Read in old Tusser*: William Mavor's new edition of Thomas Tusser's *Five Hundred Points of Good Husbandry* (1812); Powell, item 380. William Fordyce Mavor (1768-1837) was a clergyman and a compiler of educational works. The passage quoted is from 'December's Husbandry', 'A Description of Time and the Year', chap. XXIV, stanza 3, p.66.

103 *af*: For 'after' or 'if'.

104 *British Museum*: H.F. Cary showed Clare round the British Museum in 1828, but it is likely that he became familiar with it on his earlier visits to London.

105 *'all the year ... bloom appear'*: Quotation unidentified.

106 *Southeys Wesley*: Robert Southey, *The Life of Wesley* (1820); Powell, item 364.

107 *Ashton lawn*: See 'Ashton Lawn' (*M.C.* p.448) and Clare's letter to Sir John Trollope (*Letters*, p.553).

108 *open Copy wood*: Copy Wood or Open Wood or Open Copy are the same place, i.e. opposite Oxey Wood and Simon's Wood.

109 *finishd the 8th Chapter of my life*: Clare also wrote a letter on this day to John Savage (*Letters*, pp.306-8).

110 *Death of Abel*: See p.289, note 27.

111 *Apendix No 8:*: Headed '"Coincedences" – Lord Byron', not printed here.

112 *Recievd a letter from Hessey*: 22 Nov., BL Egerton 2246, fol.407r-8v.

113 *Recieved a parcel ... from Henderson*: 27 Nov., BL Egerton 2246, fol.409r-10v.

114 *Lady fern* and *white Lychnis*: Grainger suggests *Thelypteris palustris*, marsh fern, for the former, and *Lychnis chalcedonica* rather than white campion for the latter.

115 *A gentleman came*: He is unidentified.

116 *Recd*: Possibly 'Read'.

117 *Literary (Butterflye) Souvenir for 1825*: Clare's 'First Love's Recollections' and 'Song. Love, practice not those wily ways' appeared in the *Literary Souvenir* for 1826 and 'Ballad. There is a tender flower' in 1827.

118 *One of the largest floods*: We have been unable to confirm this flood from local newspapers or to identify Sam Sharp.

119 *White Maiden Hair of Hill*: Wall-rue, *Asplenium ruta-muraria*. For Hill's *Adiantum album* see John Hill's *The British Herbal* (1756), p.528.

120 *Loves yard*: Samuel Love was a wheelwright at Glinton in 1848.

121 *Will Tyers*: The *Stamford Mercury*, 3 June 1825, reports the death by drowning of *John* Tyers of Glinton.

122 *Dwarf Maiden hair*: Grainger failed to identify this fern.

123 *Bradford and Stephenson*: A shared subscription to newspapers was not uncommon. See the Journal for 21 July 1825 when Clare gave up his share.

124 *saw two 'Will o whisps'*: We include Appendix N° 9, see pp.251-2.

125 *Leniuses Botany*: Linnaeus's most important works are the *Systema Naturae* (1735), *Fundementa Botanica* (1736), *Philosophia Botanica* (1751) and *Species Plantarum* (1753) and later revised editions. The 'thorn pointed fern' is the broad buckler fern, *Dryopteris dilitata*.

126 *a beautiful book on insects*: John Curtis, *British Entomology* (16 vols, 1824-39). Clare would have seen the first volume only.

127 *Recievd a letter from Lord Radstock*: This letter has not survived.

128 *Returnd from Milton*: While still at Milton, Clare wrote to C.A. Elton, 18 Dec. (*Letters*, pp.309-11): 'I have got from home a few days to pass away time and try to improve my present miserys by other amusements then reading... I am now amusing myself when I am able at hunting the woods for the Diferrent sorts of Ferns of which I am making a collection for I love wild things almost to foolishness

323

and when I come to Bristol I shall hope to meet with some new Species among your rocks and hills'.

129   *Recievd a letter from M*^{rs} *Emmerson*: 19 Dec., BL Egerton 2246, fol. 411r-12v. Clare's letters to Mrs Emmerson and Sir Francis Freeling have not survived.

130   *Found . . . bottom*: Written through the deleted words 'Returnd from Milton'.

131   *moss missletoe*: Grainger failed to identify.

132   *Recievd an answer from F.Freeling*: 27 Dec., BL Egerton 2246, fol. 413r-v. Clare wrote a letter to H.F. Cary on this date (*Letters*, pp.311-14). The P.S. reads: 'I forget to tell you my present occupation   when my illness alows me to join with any you woud not guess it — I have always had a great fondness for wild flowers — and I am now passionately bent after collecting "English Ferns" and whenever I am able I make journeys about the woods in the neighbourhood   I have discoverd 8 sorts already about us'.

133   *Recieved a letter from Hessey*: This letter has not survived. The letter to H.F. Cary is in fact dated 30 Dec. and is recorded in note 132 above.

134   *Stamford Mercury*: Both items appeared in the *Stamford Mercury*, 31 Dec. 1824. Miss Povey was taking part in a dramatization of *Guy Mannering*.

135   *Recieved a parcel from M*^{rs} *Emmerson*: 28 Dec., BL Egerton 2246, fol. 414r-18v.

136   *sketches*: See MS 15, p.133 for Clare's sketches of snail shells, back fly-leaf for sketch of the hornet moth, and App.IV.

137   *'stamford mercury'*: 7 Jan. 1825. Clare's underlining in the first line of the verse.

138   There is no closing bracket.

139   *Essex herald*: Reprinted in the *Stamford Mercury*, 7 Jan. 1825.

140   *Recieved a letter from C.A.Elton*: 11 Jan., BL Egerton 2246, fol.421r-2v.

141   *'Thus runs the world away'*: Hamlet 3.2.268.

142   *Recieved a letter from M*^{rs} *Emmerson*: 13 Jan., BL Egerton 2246, fol. 423r-5v. Clare's reply has not survived.

143 *corrected the poem...under that character*: See Clare to James Mont-
gomery, 5 Jan. 1825, not recorded in the Journal for that date (*Let-
ters*, pp.314-19) and Montgomery to Clare, 5 May 1826, BL Egerton
2247, fol.171r-2v. James Montgomery (1780-1854), poet and hymn-
writer, editor of the radical *Sheffield Iris*.

144 *Wrote a letter to Hessey*: This letter has not survived.

145 *Stamford Mercury*: All four items appeared in the *Stamford Mercury*,
21 Jan. 1825.

146 *Stamford Mercury*: 21 Jan. 1825; Clare's underlining.

147 *wrote to Mr Sharp*: This letter has not survived. William Sharp
worked in the Dead Letter Office, helped Clare with his finances
and shared his interest in botany.

148 *'two ballads to Mary'*: One, 'The Confession', was published in the
Literary Magnet, June 1826, pp.311-12, which in the MS A31 version
is headed 'Two Ballads — To Mary'; the other is probably 'First
Love's Recollections', pp.50-2 of MS A31 and published in the
M.C., pp.302-3.

149 *three Sonnets to Bloomfield*: Published in the *Scientific Receptacle*
(1825), pp.306-7. See *Letters*, pp.306-8, 321-4.

150 *for the London...at best*: These lines are heavily deleted.

151 *Recieved a letter from Mr Sharp*: 25 Jan., BL Egerton 2246, fol.428r-9v.
The letter from Lord Radstock has not survived. Clare had sent the
'Vanitys of Life' to Montgomery, 5 Jan. (*Letters*, pp.314-19).

152 *cockchaffer*: The cockchafer, *Melolontha melolontha*, is brown; the
dor beetle, *Geotrupes vernalis*, is shining black.

153 *'the beetle winds...sullen horn'*: 'Ode to Evening', ll.11-12.

154 *Recieved a letter from Mrs Emmerson*: 28 Jan., BL Egerton 2246, fol.
430r-1v.

155 *Captain Lyon*: In 1824 George Francis Lyon, commander of HMS
Hecla, published his 'Private Journal' of the 1820-3 voyage under
Capt. Parry to Hudson's Strait, Repulse Bay, and Melville Penin-
sula.

156 *Recieved a letter from Hessey*: 29 Jan., BL Egerton 2246, fol.432r-4v.

157 *'O that ... a book'*: Job 31:35: 'Oh ... that mine adversary had written a book'.

158 *Recieved a joint letter ...*: Lord Radstock 1 and 3 Feb., BL Egerton 2246, fol.435r-9v; Mrs Emmerson, 4 Feb., BL Egerton, fol.440r-1v.

159 *Recieved a letter from Mrs Gilchrist*: 5 Feb., BL Egerton 2246, fol. 442r-3v.

160 *Ned Simpson*: Probably a relative of Frank Simpson, Clare's friend.

161 *Recieved a letter from Van dyke*: 10 Feb., F1, pp.109-12. For 'Peggy Band' see F1 and G. Deacon, *John Clare and the Folk Tradition*.

162 *Recieved a letter from Dr Darling*: 10 Feb., BL Egerton 2246, fol. 444r-5v.

163 *Anna taken very ill*: H.F. Cary to Clare, 19 Feb. 1825: 'I hope the last chapter of your memoirs, if brought up to the present time, will record your children's having got safely over the small-pox, of which you express apprehensions in your last letter' (BL Egerton 2246, fol.452r-3v).

164 *Wrote to Vandyk and Dr Darling*: Neither letter has survived. See Deacon, op. cit., and Clare's tunebooks (Powell, items 12 and 13) for information on the tunes quoted by Clare.

165 *received a Valentine from Mrs Emmerson*: 14 Feb., BL Egerton 2246, fol.446r-7v, which contains her poem 'Valentine'.

166 *this new ... better*: These lines are heavily deleted with the last five words written again.

167 *Cromwells time*: The discovery of relics from Cromwell's time was not uncommon.

168 *'Vanitys of Life'*: See the Journal for 19 Jan. 1825.

169 *Found several pieces of roman pot*: Clare to Artis, 7 March 1825: 'I have found some more fragments of a Roman pot in Harrisons close near Oxey wood and am now convinced my self that there is some more worth the trial   one of the bits had the letter "V" on it a mark of the potters I suppose' (*Letters*, pp.320-1). Tyndale's Field is due east of Oxey Wood. Roman remains were frequently found in the area.

170 *Recieved a Letter from Lord Radstock*: This letter has not survived.

171 *Recieved a letter...John Pooley*: This letter has not survived. John Pooley (b.1800), a native of Kelmarsh in Northamptonshire, author of *Poems, Moral, Rural, Humorous and Satirical* (1825) and *Blackland Farm* (1838). The latter was 'composed for his own amusement during labours of the field'. 'a very dull Fooley' and the doubtful last sentence have been heavily deleted.

172 *black maiden hair*: black spleenwort, *Asplenium adiantum-nigrum*.

173 *curious sort of Iris*: Grainger comments: 'Might be *Iris foetidissima*, stinking iris, rare and an introduction in this area but rampant, for instance, at Casewick; however, this is not a water plant, and *Acorus calamus*, sweet-flag, is more likely'.

174 *Recieved a letter from Lord Radstock and Mrs Emmerson*: The former has not survived, the latter 2 March, BL Egerton 2246 fol.458r-61v. The letter from Joseph Weston, editor of Bloomfield's *Remains* (1824) has not survived.

175 *Miss Kents Sylvan Sketches*: Elizabeth Kent, *Sylvan Sketches* (1825), presented by John Taylor (Powell, item 272).

176 *and tis...birds*: These words have been heavily deleted.

177 *Stamford Mercury*: 4 March 1825.

178 *Wrote to E.T.Artis*: *Letters*, pp.320-1. The other two letters have not survived.

179 *Mrs W. Wright of Clapham*: Taylor to Clare, 18 March 1825: 'Mrs Wright desired me to tell you...She will be very happy to send you the Flowers you mention...' (BL Egerton 2246, fol.470v). They finally came with a letter from Hessey 28 Oct. 1825 (BL Egerton 2247, fol.93r).

180 *Wrote to Hessey and Jos Weston*: The former has not survived. For the latter see *Letters*, pp.321-4 where it is dated a day earlier, 7 March.

181 *the book*: *The Shepherd's Calendar*, eventually published in 1827.

182 *Dr Dodd*: Accounts of his life, which do not include this anecdote, occur in the *Stamford Mercury*, 21 May 1824, and in the *Dictionary of National Biography*. William Dodd (1729-77) was a forger who, according to Horace Walpole, yet.preached 'very eloquently and touchingly'. While under sentence of death he wrote *Thoughts in*

327

Prison (1778). The verses in Micah 7 read: 'Rejoice not against me, O mine enemy: when I fall, I shall arise; when I sit in darkness, the Lord shall be a light unto me. I will bear the indignation of the Lord, because I have sinned against him, until he plead my cause, and execute judgment for me: he will bring me forth to the light, and I shall behold his righteousness. Then she that is mine enemy shall see it, and shame shall cover her which said unto me, Where is the Lord thy God? mine eyes shall behold her: now shall she be trodden down as the mire of the streets'.

183   *letter from Lord Radstock*: This letter has not survived.

184   *Recieved a letter from the Editor of Bloomfields Correspondence*: Joseph Weston, 13 March 1825, BL Egerton 2246, fol.465r-6v.

185   *Mrs Barbaulds Lessons for Childern*: Anna Laetitia Barbauld, *Lessons for Children from Two to Three Years Old* (1779)

186   *sallow trees / Black alder*: Grainger suggests *Salix cinerea*, grey willow and *Alnus glutinosa*, alder.

187   *Recieved a letter*: This letter has not survived. The books are Hannah More, *The Spirit of Prayer* (2nd ed., 1825), Powell, item 312; Thomas Wilson, *Maxims of Piety and of Christianity* (1822), item 404; [Henry Scougal], *The Life of God in the Soul of Man* (1821), item 353; Richard Watson, *An Apology for the Bible* (1819), item 388. The last was written as a series of letters to Thomas Paine.

188   *controvertialists*: Clare has written 'crotrovertialists'.

189   *Had from Drakards*: Presumably MS A40 at Peterborough Museum

190   *Recieved a Letter from Mrs Emmerson*: 18 March, BL Egerton 2246, fol. 471r-4v.

191   *'Every day book' by W.Hone*: William Hone (1780-1842), radical satirist and bookseller, edited *The Every-day Book* in 1826-7 (Powell, item 256). The title page contains Herrick's lines:

> I tell of festivals, and fairs, and plays,
> Of merriment, and mirth, and bonfire blaze;
> I tell of Christmas-mummings, new year's day,
> Of twelfth-night king and queen, and children's play;
> I tell of Valentines, and true-love's-knots,
> Of omens, cunning men, and drawing lots –

I tell of brooks, of blossoms, birds and bowers,
Of April, May, of June, and July-flowers;
I tell of May-poles, hock-carts, wassails, wakes,
Of bridegrooms, brides, and of their bridal cakes;
I tell of groves, of twilights, and I sing
The court of Mab, and of the fairy-king.

192 *Received a parcel from Holbeach*: 20 March, BL Egerton 2246, fol. 475r-6v. *The Scientific Receptacle* (Holbeach, 1825), Powell, item 348, contained five poems by Clare.

193 *'wishing . . . to his memory'*: p.15 of *The Scientific Receptacle*, the end of 'A Memoir' on 'S' of Surfleet's old schoolmaster, Ephraim Prosody: 'A tear fell upon his grave, and I wished it might spring up into a tomb of marble, expressive of my unalterable esteem and gratitude'.

194 *Recievd a letter from Lord Radstock*: 19 March, BL Egerton 2246, fol. 477r-v.

195 *Susan Simpson and her brother*: Frank Simpson, Clare's friend at Stamford.

196 *Recieved a letter from Vandyk*: 29 March, F1, pp.105-8. Clare to Hessey, 17 Apr. 1825: 'and another thing that supprised me very much was the confession that Van Dyk made at my plan for the new book by saying that he had not seen many of the poems mentioned therein' (*Letters*, p.325).

197 *they have . . . hands of*: These words have been heavily deleted and our reading is conjectural.

198 Followed by a heavy 2¼-line deletion, possibly '. . . opinion . . .'.

199 *Recieved from Wilson*: Samuel Wilson, Stamford bookseller, son-in-law of, and successor to, John Drakard. Charles Vyse, *The Tutor's Guide: being a complete system of Arithmetic . . .* (1770).

200 *Lingfield and Crowhurst*: Villages in Surrey.

201 *select*: Clare has written 'selects', a miscopy.

202 *Stamford Mercury*: 1 Apr. 1825.

203 *Recieved a letter from . . .*: Lord Radstock, 6 and 7 Apr., BL Egerton 2247, fol.7r-11v; Mrs Emmerson, 3 Apr., BL Egerton 2247, fol.1r-5v.

204 *first of new May*: May Day is now celebrated eleven days earlier than it was before the calendar was changed in 1752.

205 *My mother is 67 years old this day*: She was in fact 68.

206 *20 years*: Possibly '26'.

207 *Recieved a letter from Lord Radstock*: This letter has not survived.

208 Followed by a heavy two-line deletion, possibly 'I woud...of... before dealing...'.

209 *Sir John Trollop*: Sir John Trollope (1800-74) who lived at Casewick House, near Stamford, but owned Ashton, a hamlet in Ufford. See *Letters*, p.553.

210 *ten times*: These words are heavily deleted.

211 *if I had known...want to*: These lines are heavily deleted and our reading is conjectural.

212 *as every...with them*: These words are heavily deleted and our reading is conjectural.

213 *Recieved a letter from Dr Darling*: 15 Apr., BL Egerton 2247, fol. 14r-15v. See *Letters*, pp.325-6 for Clare's letter to Hessey.

214 *Recieved a letter from Taylor*: See *Letters*, pp.326-7: 'At all Events it is better to terminate the Connection at once than to continue it in Distrust. –'.

215 *red headed brown linnet*: redpoll, *Carduelis flammea*. The bird that made a long continued noise is the grasshopper warbler.

216 *little Willow wren*: chiffchaff, *Phylloscopus collybita*.

217 *Stamford paper*: Stamford Mercury 15 Apr. 1825.

218 *Recieved a Letter from Lord Radstock and Mrs Emmerson*: 23 Apr. in each case, BL Egerton 2247, fol.20r-2v and 18r-19v.

219 *'Break day'*: Herds used to be turned out on the fens through the summer when the ground was not too wet.

220 *Recieved another letter...*: Joseph Weston, 23 Apr., BL Egerton 2247 fol.16r-17v.

221 *Stamford Mercury*: 22 Apr. 1825.

222 *Bradfords Club*: William Bradford, licensee of the Bluebell Inn.

330

He also signed Clare's will (1 Oct.) and shared a subscription to the *Stamford Mercury* with him (10 Dec). See Grainger, p.238: 'After the ailments of winter members of his "Club" apparently celebrated an old May-day with what money might be left; this was kept in the old wall chest, which is still at the Bluebell; its three locks could be opened only when Chairman, Secretary and Treasurer were present'.

223 *Wrote a letter to Taylor and one to Mrs Emmerson*: The former has not survived; the latter is probably the letter dated 5 May (*Letters*, pp.328-9).

224 *Cricket bird / Hawk like bird*: The former is probably the grasshopper warbler as in note 215 above. For the latter Grainger suggests *Falco subbuteo*, hobby.

225 *Recieved a letter last night from Henderson*: 11 May, BL Egerton 2247, fol.25r-6v: 'I have sent you a plant of the double Caltha palustris or Marsh-Marygold. I was almost afraid of medling with my plant, but I have succeeded in geting you a tolerable piece without injuring it.'

226 *letter from Hessey and one from Vandyke*: The former is 10 May, BL Egerton 2247, fol.23r-4v, and the latter 15 March, F1, pp.113-16. The note from Miss Kent has not survived.

227 *Extracts from the Stamford Mercury*: 13 May 1826, not always accurately copied.

228 *'If you will not...when he comes'*: Cf. the parable of the Wicked Husbandman (Mark 12: 1-12; Luke 20: 9-19; Matthew 21:33-46).

229 *Ordoyns / Twineys*: *Stamford Mercury*, 13 May 1825 has 'Ordoyno' and 'Turner's'.

230 *News paper Odditys*: All taken from the *Stamford Mercury*, 20 May 1825. The salt mine at Wieland or Wieliczka, near Krakow, is still magnificent, but overrun with tourists. Lord Radstock's letter is missing, but the one from Sir John Peter Boileau (1794-1869), English archaeologist, is now BL Egerton 2247, fol.27r-9v and dated 21 May.

231 *More Wonders from the Mercury*: Both reports are from the *Stamford Mercury*, 20 May 1825. Christopher Benson (1789-1868), an eloquent preacher of the broader evangelical wing. Edward Irving (1792-1834), founder of the Scottish religious sect, the Irvingites.

232   *The Catholics have lost their bill*: Stamford Mercury, 20 May 1825. The Catholic Emancipation Act was finally achieved in 1829.

233   *Dobberan*: Bad Doberan, near Mecklenburger Bucht, Germany.

234   *Nugents Travels*: Thomas Nugent, *Travels through Germany...in a series of letters to a friend* (2 vols, 1768). Similar lists of relics appear in Hone's *The Every-day Book*, e.g. vol.1, 1826, June 20, cols 813-14.

235   *found a large white Orchis*: Recorded again 29 May.

236   *Recieved a letter...from Mrs Emmerson*: 23 May, BL Egerton 2247, fol. 30r-1v.

237   *Found a very scarce...*: Neither of these orchis plants have been identified with certainty.

238   *Sent a Letter to Mrs Emmerson*: This letter has not survived.

239   *untimlessly*: Possibly for 'untimely'.

240   *note from Hessey and a long letter from Taylor*: The former is 30 May, BL Egerton 2247, fol.32r-3v and the latter 30 May, BL Egerton 2247, fol.34r-5v.

241   *'Iron rail way'*: 'The history of railways in the county begins with an unsolved problem. In John Clare's diary for June 4th 1825 we read... This is an astonishingly early date for a railway scheme in East Anglia — three months before the opening of the Stockton and Darlington, five years before that of the Liverpool and Manchester and twenty years before any railway reached that part of the country — but Grinley in his history of the Great Northern railway mentions a first short epidemic of "railway fever" in the years 1825-27' (Norman Marlowe, 'The Coming of Railways to Northamptonshire', *Northamptonshire Past and Present*, vol.3 no.5, 1964, pp.203-12). Victor Hatley in 'The Poet and the Railway Surveyors, an incident in the life of John Clare' (*Northamptonshire Past and Present*, vol.5 no.2, 1974, pp.101-6) concludes that the men were surveying a route for the 'London Northern Rail Road'. A national financial crisis caused the shelving of this ambitious undertaking in 1825 and it was finally cancelled in 1830. Mr Hatley hazards the guess that one of the 'three fellows' was Josiah Locke (1805-60), railway engineer, who was articled to George Stephenson in 1823.

242   *wrote a note to Hessey*: This note has not survived, nor the note to

Mrs Wright of Clapham. Grainger, p.245, provides some help in identifying the flowers.

243   *'A poor Students struggles thro Cambridge etc'*: 'The Struggles of a Senior Wrangler', *London Magazine*, June 1825, p.161, was the 'continuation' of the article entitled 'Struggles of a poor Student through Cambridge', April 1825, p.491.

244   *'Sorrows of Love'*: See *Cottage Poems* (1993), pp.82-97. There are 564 lines in Clare's version, 330 in Taylor's version.

245   *'Aytons Essays'*: Richard Ayton (1786-1823), *Essays and Sketches of Character* (1825); Powell, item 100. This book came with proofs and a covering letter from James Hessey, 4 June 1825, BL Egerton 2247, fol.32r-3v.

246   *Recieved a letter from Mrs Emmerson*: 6 June, BL Egerton 2247, fol. 36r-7v. 'the Broken Heart' is the sub-title of 'The Sorrows of Love'. Clare's letter to Taylor has not survived.

247   *and I believe it was nothing else*: Grainger comments 'The *Gentleman's Diary* for 1825 forecast an eclipse of the sun on 16 June at 22½ minutes past noon which was invisible from Greenwich. It is, therefore, likely that Clare was not writing all the entry for 13 June actually on that day'.

248   *Recieved a Letter from Taylor*: 15 June, *Letters*, pp.331-2. The letter from Mrs Emmerson may be the undated one at BL Egerton 2250, fol.167r-8v: 'I hope you will like your Waistcoat'.

249   *but*: Clare has written 'by'.

250   *Wrote a letter to Taylor*: Probably the letter dated 19 June in *Letters*, pp.332-5.

251   *Wrote to Mrs Emmerson*: This letter has not survived. For the letter to Hone see *Letters*, pp.335-7. The 'Poem on Death' was published by Hone in June 1825.

252   *recieved a letter from Hessey*: 30 June, BL Egerton 2247, fol.40r-1v.

253   *safe carrige*: Written through another word, possibly 'difficulty'.

254   *The Baloon with Mr Green and Miss Stocks*: Charles Green (1785-1870) made his first ascent as a balloon pilot in 1821 and made at least three ascents in 1825. His companion Miss Stocks survived a ballooning accident in 1824.

255 *Helpstone feast*: Always fell on the first Sunday after 29 June (see *Letters*, p.274).

256 *Wrote an answer to Hesseys letter of the 30ᵗʰ of June*: *Letters*, pp.338-9.

257 *Recieved a letter from Hessey*: 9 July, BL Egerton 2247, fol.42r-3v.

258 *Pennant*: Thomas Pennant, *Genera of Birds* (Edinburgh, 1773). Corn bunting, cirl bunting and reed bunting have all been suggested.

259 *thirty two*: Followed by the deleted words: 'or thirty three I am not certain which'. Clare was indeed thirty-two in 1825.

260 *Mʳˢ P-----r and Mʳˢ B---n*: Mrs Procter and Mrs Byron (see p.307, note 177).

261 Followed by a heavy deletion, possibly: 'a great Statesmen peeped thro the glass of the door to see ?whose ?in The Stewards Robe after dinner there was little ?bemeanings for a son of St ?Stevens'.

262 *Recieved a letter from Lord Radstock*: 11 July, BL Egerton 2247, fol. 44r-6v.

263 *Received a letter from Mʳˢ Emmerson*: 13 July, BL Egerton 2247, fol. 47r-8v. She wrote later, undated, BL Egerton 2250, fol.166r: he 'is not come to London, nor do I think he will'.

264 *Paid Stevenson*: See Journal for 2 July 1825.

265 *a species of Broom*: Dyer's greenweed, *Genista tinctoria*.

266 *Stamford Mercury*: 22 July 1825.

267 *'Poem on Death'*: See Journal for 2 July 1825.

268 *the plan is again altered*: See *Cottage Tales* (1993), pp.xvii-xxxiii and Clare to Taylor, 19 June (*Letters*, pp.332-5).

269 *Recieved a letter from Mʳˢ Emmerson*: 28 July, BL Egerton 2247, fol. 49r-50v.

270 *Wrote a Letter to William Hone*: *Letters*, pp.339-44. where Storey points out that there was a servant at Milton Hall called Frederic Roberts. 'A Farwell and Defiance to Love' was not published in *The Every-day Book*, but in the *European Magazine* for March 1826. Sir John Harington (1561-1612) was noted especially for his letters and miscellaneous writings.

271 *Clay*: The *Scientific Receptacle* was 'conducted by H. Clay, Moulton'.

272 *Recieved a letter from Mrs Gilchrist*: 1 Aug., BL Egerton 2247, fol. 51r-2v.

273 *Baron Field*: Barron Field (1786-1846), lawyer and miscellaneous writer, planned lives of his friend Lamb and Wordsworth. Like his edition of Gilchrist's papers, they never materialized.

274 *Miss Fanny Knowlton*: Grainger records, p.253: 'The will of Charles Knowlton, grazier, of Braunston, Rutland, refers, in 1849, to his daughter Fanny (wife of Charles Morris). In the Land Tax for 1825 Charles Knowlton is listed as an owner and occupier in Helpston, and the 1820 plan of Helpston village shows several cottages, as well as land, owned by him'.

275 *Bloomfields Hazlewood Hall and Remains*: Hazlewood-hall: A Village Drama (1823), Powell, item 120; *The Remains* (1824), item 122. G. Gilleade, *Allworth Abbey; or, Christianity triumphant over tyranny and despotism* (Holbeach, 1825).

276 *a news paper lye*: Stamford Mercury, 12 Aug. 1825, taken from *Bell's Weekly Messenger*, 7 Aug. 1825.

277 *wrote a Letter to Miss Kent*: This letter has not survived. Clare to Taylor, 13 Aug.: 'I am at Milton and have gotten my friend Henderson to read over the proof while I made such alterations as struck me at the time...' (*Letters*, p.345). *The Transactions* of the Horticultural Society were in the Library at Milton.

278 *Wrote a letter to Henderson*: This letter has not survived, nor the one to A.A. Watts. 'First Loves Reccolections' was published in the 1826 *Literary Souvenir*.

279 *Recieved a letter from Mr Emmerson*: 20 Aug., BL Egerton 2247, fol. 55r-6v. Lord Radstock died on 17 Aug.

280 *Recieved a letter from the Editor...*: 20 Aug., BL Egerton 2247, fol. 57r-8v.

281 *Recieved a letter from Mrs Emmerson*: 1st Sept., BL Egerton 2247, fol.59r-60v.

282 *Wrote a letter to Mrs Emmerson*: None of these letters have survived.

283 *Recieved a letter from Hessey...*: 6 Sept., BL Egerton 2247, fol.65r-6v. The letter from 'Messrs Baynes' is 6 Sept., BL Egerton 2247, fol. 63r-4v; from Watts 2 Sept., BL Egerton, fol.61r-2v. Clare wrote to

James Power of the Strand on 24 Sept. (*Letters*, p.348), who responded on 29 Sept. (BL Egerton 2247, fol.77r-8v). Clare's mention of 'October' was clearly an error and indicates that he was writing up the Journal at a later date. No published musical setting of 'Brooms grove' has been found. See *Early Poems*, ii, 438-9.

284   *Dacon the Jew of Cliff*: William Dakin of King's Cliffe in Northamptonshire, who died in 1840 aged eighty-five, was an eccentric who believed himself Jesus Christ returned to earth.

285   *Mʳ and Mʳˢ Emmerson*: Clare to Van Dyk, c.12 Sep. 1825: 'Mr and Mrs E[mmerson] like our Fens very much and I regret that you was not one of the party' (*Letters*, p.346).

286   The entry headed 'Febʸ 6. 1828' (6 through 7) is written in the space intended for Sunday 6 Feb. 1825 and underneath the entry for that day ('Severe frost...'). Feb. 6 actually fell on a Wednesday in 1828. The three 1828 entries are in darker ink than the neighbouring entries for 1825.

Memorandums

1   *Vanity of vanity's*: Ecclesiastes 1:2, 12:8.

Clare's Will

1   *Sophia Kettle*: Clare has written 'Ketwell'. Sophia married William Kettle in 1821.

2   This last paragraph has been deleted and was presumably written before August 1825, when Lord Radstock died.

Business Dealings

1   *Crouch*: See p.313, note 4.
2   *wanted to*: 'to' is repeated.

The Will o Whisp

1   *Mrs Nottingham*: The name Betsey Nottingham occurs in H23 at Peterborough and Northampton 10.

A Remarkable Dream

1   *impercievenly*: For 'imperceptibly' or perhaps 'unperceivingly'.

Journey Out of Essex

1   *an*: Preceded by the deleted words: 'I found'.
2   *'The Labour in vain' Public house*: We have no knowledge of a public house at Enfield Highway called the Labour in Vain. Robson's Directory (1839) lists no less then twelve public houses in Enfield Highway. Nine of these are mentioned by name, but the remaining three are listed under the name of the proprietor. The Labour in Vain may have been one of those three.
3   *my first wife*: Mary Joyce, Clare's childhood sweetheart. When Clare went mad he believed that he had married Mary and had had children by her, but that he had subsequently married Martha (Patty) Turner, his real wife, and had had a family also by her. His

imprisonment at High Beach (actually a voluntary committal) he saw as punishment for his bigamy.

4   [– *when I awoke*]: Supplied from N8, 22-6, a rough draft of part of the journey written *en route*.

5   *the next village*: Baldeck [i.e. Baldock] — Clare's footnote.

6   *the 'Plough'*: This public house has not yet been identified.

7   *the 'Ram'*: Presently an old house, over a mile from Potton on the road to Gamlingay Great Heath. It was a public house within living memory and is still locally known as the Ram. First identified in *The Journal, Essays, The Journey from Essex*, ed. Anne Tibble (Carcanet Press, 1980).

8   *country mans*: The account in N8 ends here.

9   *Tollgate*: There was a turnpike gate at Tempsford.

10   *highland Mary*: See Clare's Journal, 3 June 1825, where Clare says that he got the tune from a gypsy, Wisdom Smith. The words are by Burns but the air is much older and is called 'Katherine Ogie'. It was widely published as a broadside in the nineteenth century and appears in many song books, e.g. *The Garland of New Songs*, Harding Collection, Bodleian Library, A31(9), A51(9) etc.

11   Clare has the following note: 'The man whose daughter is the queen of England is now sitting on a stone heap on the high way to bugden without a farthing in his pocket and without tasting a bit of food ever since yesterday morning — when he was offerd a bit of Bread and cheese at Enfield — he has not had any since but If I put a little fresh speed on hope too may speed to morrow — O Mary mary If you knew how anxious I am to see you and dear Patty with the childern I think you would come and meet me' [N8,25]. This was presumably written late on Wednesday, 21st. Bugden was an accepted variant of Buckden.

12   It was St. Neots [Clare's note].

13   *Shefford Church*: See F.W. Martin's *The Life of John Clare*, ed. by Eric Robinson and Geoffrey Summerfield (London, 1964), p.130: 'Clare's narrative, understandably, is not entirely consistent. For example, when he met the young gypsy woman about a mile and a half West of St Neots it would have been impossible for her to have

pointed to Shefford Church, if by Shefford is intended the town mid-way between Bedford and Hitchin. The confusion may have been due to the fact that Shefford was the home of Thomas Inskip, Clare's friend, and it is symptomatic of Clare's sense of urgency that he did not make the short detour to Shefford where Inskip could have been counted on for help and shelter. Some of Clare's landmarks, however, are tolerably clear and agree with those described in Cary's *New Itinerary*, 1815 edition. His route corresponded for the most part to the recognized Coach Road and Waggon Way.'

14   The Coach did pass me as I sat under some trees by a high wall and the lumps lasshed in my face and wakened me up from a doze when I knocked the gravel out of my shoes and started [Clare's note].

15   *to the right*: i.e. at Norman Cross, 5¾ miles to Peterborough.

16   *the Beehive*: Whellan's Directory, 1849, mentions the Cock, the Blue Bell, the Wheat Sheaf, and the Three Horse Shoes. The nearest 'Beehive' in the area was at Stamford and Clare may have been remembering this one.

17   *Byron*: The quotation is from 'Sonnet on Chillon', ll. 13-14:
          ... May none those marks efface!
       For they appeal from tyranny to God.

Asylum Observations

1   *Jack Randall*: John Randall was born in 1794 in the London slums, but found fame and fortune as undisputed champion of the Prize Ring. He retired in 1819 to keep the 'Hole in the Wall' tavern in Chancery Lane, which became a centre for Prize Ring enthusiasts. Perhaps Clare met him there. Certainly he would have seen him officiating at London prize-fights. 'In consequence of some chaffing at Tom Gibb's benefit at the Fives Court on June 1st, 1824, a match was made between Harry Jones and Brown (the Sprig of

Myrtle)'. See: H.D. Miles, *Pugilistica* (1880), vol.2, pp.516-17. Harry Jones was the 'Sailor Boy', he was seconded by Oliver, and Randall acted as time-keeper. As to the 'Challange To All The World', Miles records that when Randall formally left the ring in 1819 he issued a public challenge to all England at 11 stone, for 500 guineas. Perhaps Clare saw a copy of this challenge, which is no longer extant. See also Tom Bates, 'John Clare and "Boximania"', *The John Clare Society Journal*, no.13, July 1994, pp.5-13.

2   Clare has written below the date, later: 'So let thine enemies perish O Lord'.

3   *Scotch*: Clare has written 'Sctoch'.

4   *C.Redding*: Cyrus Redding (1785-1870), who visited Clare in May 1841, recorded his impressions and published some of Clare's poems in the *English Journal*, 15 and 29 May 1841.

Letter to Matthew Allen

1   *my fancys*: i.e. his wife, Patty.

2   *8 years*: Mary Joyce died on 16 July 1838, three years previously, not eight.

3   *Mrs King*: L.S.H. Young wrote in the John Clare Society *Newsletter*, no.7 — April 1984: 'The licensee [of the Owl Inn] in my boyhood was a Mrs King, a daughter-in-law (or perhaps grand daughter) of the Mrs King in Clare's time'.

4   *'Hours of Idleness'*: N7,55 contains a list, in the margin of the *Morning Chronicle*, 18 June [1841], of 'books lent': 'Byrons Child Harold Mrs Pratt / Barn Houses near Sneston Essex / Don Juan — English Bards and Scotch Reviewers / Mrs Fish's Daughter at the Owl Leopards Hill / Hours of Idleness by Lord Byron — Mrs King Eenfield / Highway — Middlesex' (Barn Houses are so called from some cottages formed out of an old barn in North Shoebury).

5   *I dreamed so*: The Queen Dowager gave 20 guineas to an appeal fund set up in 1840, but which fell well short of Dr Allen's target of £500.

6   York and Co Peterborough or Eaton and Co Stamford [Clare's note].

7   *Campbell*: Thomas Campbell, the son of the poet, was an inmate at High Beach.

8   Clare has written this remarkable draft letter round the edges and even between the columns of print, of the *Lincolnshire Chronicle and General Advertiser* for Friday, 27 Aug. 1841.

Self Identity

1   *The mother . . . yestreen*: Adapted from ll.73-8 of Burns's 'Lament for James, Earl of Glencairn'.

2   *forget*: Clare has written 'forgetting'.

Autumn

1   *'the foggy dew'*: From the folksong, familiar to Clare.

2   *church spire*: Probably Deeping St James.

3   *Bridges*: The 'Nine Bridges' of the 'Viaduct' carrying the main Peterborough-Market Deeping road over the North and South Drains.

4   *Northborough castle*: Northborough Manor, built c.1320, known locally as Northborough castle.

5   *where a couple of flutters*: The addition of 'they make', as Tibble suggests, helps the sense.

6   *Waldram Hall*: North-east of Peakirk.

7   *holts are . . .*: It is possible that Clare has omitted a word here, such as 'covered', 'tinged' or 'withered'.

Letters and Notes of the Northampton Period

1   *Mr and Mrs Sefton*: Samuel Sefton married Clare's first daughter Anna Maria, in 1841, and after her death his second daughter, Eliza Louisa, in 1845.

2   William F. Knight, Steward at the Asylum 1845-50, wrote on the back of this letter: 'Your Father in this letter tells you that you may not see him if you come — I know not why he should say this, for he is allowed to see any one he wishes — and he is at liberty to walk out for his pleasure — when he thinks proper — he has just left my room to walk in the garden — and if any of you think well to come and see him, I am sure he will be pleased to see you — I expect a friend of his from Shefford [Thomas Inskip] to come and see him in a day or two — he is quite well'.

3   Quotation from Bloomfield's *The Farmer's Boy*, 'Spring', l.32.

4   *books on angling*: Piscator, *The Practical Angler* (1842); Henry Phillips, *The True Enjoyment of Angling* (1843); Sir Humphrey Davy, *Salmonia, or Days of Fly Fishing* (1827).

5   *Sally Frisby*: This name occurs in N19, 46.

6   *Mrs Bullimore*: At the age of five Clare attended a local dame-school run by Mrs Bullimore.

7   Cf. Matthew 10:35, Luke 12:53.

8   Revelations 17:5.

9   *the 'Fancy*: The spectators at the Fives Court, the subject of J.H. Reynolds *The Fancy* (1820); Powell, item 342.

10   *Ben Caunt*: A famous prize-fighter who later kept a London public house.

11   *Charles*: Charles Clare, Clare's youngest son and most regular correspondent during these years, died later in 1852, aged nineteen.

12   *James Hipkins*: Hipkins, of 2 Smith Square, Westminster, wrote to Dr Edwin Wing enquiring about Clare. Wing replied: 'I reply to yours of the 6th inst respecting John Clare   I beg to inform you he is still living and in good bodily health though very feeble in mind and still the subject of many mental delusions. I endeavoured to

induce him to write a few lines to you and to make an effort at poetic composition but I could get nothing from him but the few words I enclose.'

13 *conclude*: Clare has amended 'remain' to 'conclude'.

14 Also included is a slip containing some 1826 'Memorandums' by Clare. One reads: 'I intend to send Montgomery a set of my Poems when the Calender is out in acknowlegement of his kindness — A Set also to B. of Peterbro — and Rip: and Cowen'. William Cowen (1797-1861), painter of Irish landscape, made a drawing of Clare's cottage which was engraved in the 1823 reprint of *The Village Minstrel*.

15 This has only recently come to light as Clare's last letter. It is not published in *Letters*, though Storey concludes with a letter from Sophia Clare to her father dated March 15th. After a gap of more than eleven years Clare manages to write three brief letters on successive days (see *Letters*, pp.682-3 for the letter dated March 7th).

GLOSSARY

Abraham (to sham Abraham), to feign illness

ansel, *n.*, handsel, earnest of a bargain

apathised, *a.*, apathetic

armorous, *a.*, amorous

Armours, *n.*, amours

aron, *n.*, arum, lords-and-ladies (*Arum maculatum*)

Avens, *n.*, wood avens (*Geum urbanum*)

awe, *n.*, haw

bark men, *n.*, men who come to strip bark

be, *prep.*, by

Bedlam Cowslip, *n.*, lungwort (*Pulmonaria officinalis*)

bee flye, *n.*, (*Bombylius major*)

black thorn, *n.*, sloe (*Prunus spinosa*)

bluebottles, bluecaps, blue corn bottles, *n.*, cornflowers (*Centaurea cyanthus*)

bogbean hiskhead, *n.*, bogbean huskhead, buckbean (*Menyanthes trifoliata*)

brancing, *a.*, prancing

brasted, *a*, bursting, filled by repletion

brig, *n.*, bridge

brimingham, *n.*, Birmingham

buckbane, *n.*, buckbean (*Menyanthes trifoliata*)

bumbarrel, *n.*, long-tailed tit (*Aegithalos caudatus*)

Burvine, *n.*, probably burweed

(*Xanthium strumarium*)

cade, *a.*, pet

car, *n.*, care

cazons, *n.*, cow pats

century, *n.*, a hundred (miles)

childern, *n.*, children

China rose, *n.*, (*Rosa indica*), a garden rose, one of many species of China roses introduced to this country in the eighteenth century

chusd, *v.*, choosed

cite, *n.*, site

cloths, *n.*, clothes

clowns, *n.*, yokels

collar, *n.*, fork of a tree, where the branches spring out from the trunk

consieting, *part.*, conceiting, an obsolete form of conceiving

Corn tree, *n.*, dogwood (*Swida sanguinea*, formerly *Cornus sanguinea*)

courtois, *a.*, courteous

craunking, *part.*, tapping, croaking

creep, *n.*, hole made in a hedge by an animal to escape danger

crizzling, *part.*, crisping, as of water beginning to freeze

crook horn, *n.*, a game

cross shittles, *n.*, a game played by knocking down skittles with a weighted string hanging from a cross

cubbard, *n.*, cupboard

cuckoos, *n.*, cuckoo flowers
(*Cardamine pratensis*)
cultured, *a.*, cultivated, ploughed
cumberground, *n.*, obstacle

decamp, *v.*, break up camp, leave
descent, *a.*, decent
dilacet, *a.*, delicate
dinging, *part.*, struggling
dotterel, *n.*, a pollarded tree
duck under water, *n.*, a game in
which the players run, two by
two, in rapid succession under a
handkerchief held up by two
others

edding, *n.*, heading, grass at the
end of a ploughed field
eke, *v.*, increase
enew, *a.*, enough
except, *v.*, *obs.*, receive, accept

featherpoke, *n.*, long-tailed tit
(*Aegithalos caudatus*)
feelow, *n.*, fellow
feign, *a.*, fain
flower, *n.*, flour
forced, *a.*, obliged
fresh, *v.*, (to get fresh), to drink
too much
fribble, *n.*, frivolity, nonsense
frumity, *n.*, a dish of steeped
wheat boiled in milk, with sugar
and plums
furzebind, *n.*, tormentil (*Potentilla
erecta*)

gare, *v.*, stare
gighouse, *n.*, coach house

glegging, *part.*, peeping
gog, *v.*, jog
grain, *n.*, branch
grip, *n.*, cart rut, small trench for
draining a field
gropes, *n.*, groups
group, *v.*, grope

hanted, *a.*, haunted
harbour, *n.*, arbour
hedge, *n.*, edge
head aches, *n.*, poppies
heir long, *n.*, heirloom
hernshaw, *n.*, heron (*Ardea
cinerea*)
himny, himyn, *n.*, hymn
hip (to be in a), to be annoyed
hipt, *a.*, annoyed
hollioak, *n.*, hollyhock
holt, *n.*, a small plantation, as of
a bed of osiers
horse bee, *n.*, horse-tick or gad-fly
hugd, *v.*, hugged
hunt the stag, *n.*, children's
catching game similar to fox and
hounds
hurd, *n.*, hoard
huswife, *n.*, housewife

jagonel, *n.*, jargonelle, a kind of
early pear
jeanty, *a.*, jaunty
jiant, *n.*, giant
joal, *n.*, gaol
jobbling, *part.*, moving unevenly
like a choppy sea
joccolate, *a.*, chocolate
Joe Miller, *n.*, joke
Jougler, *n.*, juggler

kidding, *part.*, cutting

knaping, *part.*, stealing, darting

land, *n.*, arable division of a furlong in an open field

learing, *part.*, learning

learn, *v.*, teach

leck, *v.*, bail

leiser, *n.*, leisure

listed, *v.*, enlisted

loath, *a.*, loth

long purples, *n.*, purple loosestrife (*Lythrum salicaria*)

loose, *v.*, lose

lordship, *n.*, the manor

lucifers, *n.*, matches

lunging, *part.*, lounging

maiden earth, *n.*, rich loam

mavis thrush, *n.*, mistle thrush or storm cock (*Turdus viscivorus*)

morts, *n.*, lots

mote, *n.*, moat

mystical, *a.*, mysterious

near, *adv.*, ne'er, never

nimble, *v.*, move quickly, dart

nimbling, *part.*, moving in a nimble fashion

orison, *n.*, horizon

Packman, *n.*, pedlar, hawker

pashd, *v.*, smashed

pawl, *n.*, pall

pested, *v.*, pestered

Pettichap, *n.*, willow warbler or chiffchaff

pewet, *n.*, lapwing

piegon, *n.*, pigeon

pill, *v.*, peel

plashy, *a.*, splashy, wet

poach, *n.*, porch

pooty, *n.*, land snail (*Capaea*), particularly the shell of *C. nemoralis*

Province Rose, *n.*, a beautiful garden rose named after a town in NE France, where it was cultivated

Purse knapper, *n.*, purse stealer, pickpocket

quick, *n.*, (quick lines), quickset hedges, hawthorn

rawky, *a.*, misty, raw and cold

rebus, *n.*, a representation of a word or phrase by pictures, symbols, arrangement of letters etc.

redcap, *n.*, goldfinch (*Carduelis carduelis*)

reddles, *n.*, riddles

rhyme, *n.*, rime

sat, *v.*, set

shanny, *a.*, shame-faced

shield ball, *n.*, cannon ball

shoe knacker, *n.*, traveller in second hand shoes

sholl, *v.*, stroll, saunter

shony, *a.*, shame-faced

showing shony, appearing wary

shoy, *a.*, shy

siled, *v.*, slid

silt, *v.*, choke up with mud, clog

skreekėrs, *n.*, rattles

snubby, *a.*, short, stumpy

346

sock, *n.*, soak, damp of a ditch

sorcer, *n.*, saucer

spaws, *n.*, spas

starnel, *n.*, starling

struttle, *n.*, minnow or stickleback

stunt, *adv.*, abruptly

style, *n.*, stile

suds (in the), in the dumps

swarm, *v.*, climb

swarms, *n.*, throngs or crowds

sweeing, *part.*, swooping, swaying

swinkt, *a.*, wearied with toil, overworked

tamper, *v.*, meddle, gossip

tarbottles, *n.*, tar marks

tent, *v.*, attempt

threbble fares, *n.*, three men in a bed or an insect emitting a high (treble) note

tomorning, *n.*, tomorrow morning

tope, *n.*, top

toto, *a.*, full, entire

tounge, *n.*, tongue

town, *n.*, usually a village

trays, *n.*, hurdles

Tree sparrow, *n.*, reed bunting (*Emberiza schoeniclus*)

two, *adv.*, too

tynes, *n.*, tines, prongs of a fork

waspweed, *n.*, water betony (*Stachys palustris*)

water mouse ear, *n.*, water forget-me-not (*Myosotis scorpioides*)

wauk, *a.*, weak

waukly, *adv.*, weakly

were, *adv.*, where

white thorn, *n.*, hawthorn (*Crataegus monogyna*)

worm stall, *n.*, pig-sty

yestreen, *n.*, yesterday evening

INDEX

Bell's Weekly Messenger   180
Belvoir Castle   127
Bennion, Thomas [John Taylor's
   clerk]   148
Benson, Christopher   229,
   331n.231
Beresford, James, *see Miserys of
   Human Life*
Bible   5-6, 24-5, 40, 75, 89, 108,
   124, 166, 173, 175-6, 178, 193,
   277, 287n.9
Billings brothers, James and John
   viii, xiii, 51-3, 192, 196, 198-9,
   202, 204, 207, 211, 214-15, 225,
   241-3, 280, 290n.43
Billing's Close   212, 216, 218, 251
Billing's Pond   202
Billing's Yard   235
Birmingham   130
Bishop of Peterborough, *see*
   Marsh, Herbert
Blackwood's Magazine   185
Blair, Hugh   120, 188, 191,
   304n.146, 320n.72
Blair, Robert   192, 321n.90
Blake, William   x
Bloodwill, Will [Helpston neigh-
   bour]   280
Bloomfield, George   185
Bloomfield, Hannah   217
Bloomfield, Robert   ix, xv, 61,
   123, 185, 194, 200, 215-17, 225,
   240, 290n.45, 291n.13, 299n.74,
   314n.4, 316n.26, 335n.275, 343n.3
Blue Bell [public house]   2, 8,
   65-7, 72, 288n.16, 330n.222
Blunden, Edmund   ix, xvii-xix
Boilau, Sir John Peter   229,
   331n.231

Bonaparte, Napoleon   89, 93, 96
Bonnycastle, J.   7, 16, 61, 287n.13
Boston   206
Boston Enquirer, see Enquirer, The
Boswell [gypsey family]   83,
   300n.93,94
Botany Bay   94
Bradford, William   180, 201, 226,
   280, 317n.35, 323n.123, 330n.222
Bridge Casterton   21, 79
Bridges, Robert   302n.129
Bristol   138, 207, 299n.73
Bristol Institution   154, 311n.234
Bristol Museum   196, 322n.104
Brown, John, Mary, Lucy [Help-
   ston neighbours]   280
Brown [of Newark]   76
Brown's *Reflections*   131
Buckden   263, 338n.11
Buckhurst Hill   266
Bull, Mr [Helpston neighbour]
   280
Bullimore, John and Mrs   280,
   342n.6
Bullock's Mexico   148, 310n.217
Bunyan, John   ix, 15, 61, 103, 278
Burbidge, Mr and Mrs Jonothan
   280
Burghley House   11-12, 67, 73-5,
   92, 167-8, 288n.20
Burkhardt, J.C.   139, 308n.194
Burnet, Gilbert [preface writer]
   218-19
Burns, Robert   xi-xii, 75, 115, 179,
   341n.1
Burthorp Oak   xv
Bushy Close   227, 238
Byron, Lord   viii, xi-xii, xv, 65,
   108, 122, 124, 141, 145, 156-8,